W9-AQC-793

CHARLEMAGNE AND THE CAROLINGIAN EMPIRE

Europe in the Middle Ages
Selected Studies

Volume 3

General Editor
RICHARD VAUGHAN
University of Hull

NORTH-HOLLAND PUBLISHING COMPANY – AMSTERDAM · NEW YORK · OXFORD

CHARLEMAGNE AND THE CAROLINGIAN EMPIRE

By
LOUIS HALPHEN

Translated by
Giselle de Nie
*University
of Utrecht*

1977

NORTH-HOLLAND PUBLISHING COMPANY – AMSTERDAM · NEW YORK · OXFORD

Library of Congress Catalog Card Number: 76-3514
North-Holland ISBN: 0 7204 9007 3

Published by:
North-Holland Publishing Company – Amsterdam/New York/Oxford

Distributors for the U.S.A. and Canada:
Elsevier North-Holland, Inc.
52 Vanderbilt Avenue, New York, N.Y. 10017

Library of Congress Cataloging in Publication Data
Halphen, Louis, 1880–1950.
    Charlemagne and the Carolingian Empire.

    (Europe in the Middle Ages; 3)
    Translation of Charlemagne et l'empire carolingien.
    1.   France--History--To 987.   2.   Carlovingians.
I.   Title.   II.   Series.
DC70.H313   944'.01   76-3514
ISBN 0-7204-9007-3

This book was originally published in 1947 under the title *Charlemagne et
l'Empire Carolingien*, Editions Albin Michel, Paris

Printed in Singapore by Times Printers Sdn. Bhd.

General Editor's preface

At last the book which represents the crowning masterpiece of Louis Halphen's historical writing has been translated into English, and, believe it or not, apart from his contributions to the *Cambridge medieval history*, this is the first translation into English of any of Halphen's works. Thus, there is now available for the first time in English not only a new subject, but a new author. This is a new subject in the sense that, so far, there exists no detailed account in English of the Carolingian Empire in the ninth century. This book was designed, in Henri Berr's famous 100-volume series *L'évolution de l'humanité*, as a successor to Ferdinand Lot's *The end of the ancient world and the beginning of the Middle Ages* (first published 1931, English translation 1966). It was written partly in wartime Grenoble and partly, after the German occupation of that city in 1944, while its author was in hiding at La Louvesc (Ardèche), having lost, in the turmoil of war, his first draft, his notes and even his library. The first French edition was published in 1947; a new edition came out in 1968.

Louis Halphen, the son of the commandant of artillery at Versailles, was born in 1880 and was Professor in the Faculty of Letters of the University of Bordeaux from 1910 to 1928. From 1928 on he was at Paris, at first in the Ecole Pratique des Hautes Etudes, then, from 1937, in the Faculty of Letters of the University. In 1950 a volume of some eighty essays and papers was planned to commemorate his seventieth birthday, but his sudden death on 7 October of that year meant that the book had to become a memorial.

Halphen's long series of substantial books on early medieval history began, in the first decade of the century, with his studies of the eleventh-century counts of Anjou, Paris under the early Capetians, and

Charles the Bald. He was for many years an editor of the *Revue historique* and he founded two important multi-volume series: the *Classiques de l'histoire de France au Moyen Âge* of texts with parallel translations, later imitated with success in England in the Nelson–Oxford series, and the *Peuples et civilizations : histoire générale*, begun with Phillippe Sagnac in 1926. To this second series Halphen himself contributed two volumes: *Les barbares: des grandes invasions aux conquêtes turques du XI* *siècle* and *L'essor de l'Europe, XI*–*XIII* *siècles*, both admirable syntheses.

The translator of this volume, Ms de Nie, is a lecturer in medieval history at the University of Utrecht. She has specialized in the early history of France and is currently researching on Gregory of Tours. Her version is based on the 1968 edition; the index is her own. While keeping the maps and genealogical table of the original French edition, albeit in altered form, and its illustrations, we have omitted all the notes. Thanks are due to Miss Joan Walton and Mrs Alwyn Thurlow for typing out the greater part of the translator's manuscript.

July 1976   Richard Vaughan
                                                             General Editor

Contents

General Editor's preface   v

List of illustrations   ix

Introduction   1

BOOK ONE   THE FOUNDATIONS OF THE EMPIRE

Chapter 1   The establishment of the Carolingian monarchy   5

Chapter 2   The achievement of Pepin   27

Chapter 3   Charlemagne and the territorial completion of the Frankish kingdom   41

Chapter 4   The annexation of the Lombard kingdom   71

Chapter 5   Charlemagne becomes emperor   85

Chapter 6   The political and administrative organization   99

Chapter 7   The emperor   143

BOOK TWO   THE FATE OF THE EMPIRE UNDER LOUIS THE PIOUS

Chapter 1   The establishment of a unified Empire   157

Chapter 2   The opposition to the new government and the penitence of Attigny   169

Chapter 3   The volte-face of the imperial government,
             822–829   175

Chapter 4   The revolt of Louis' sons and Lothar's coup
             d'état   187

Chapter 5   Louis the Pious' restoration and the last years
             of his reign   203

BOOK THREE   THE DISMEMBERMENT OF THE EMPIRE

Chapter 1   The partition and the policy of concord   215

Chapter 2   The regime of brotherly co-operation   229

Chapter 3   The Church as the guardian of Christian
             unity   249

Chapter 4   The pope's opportunity: Nicholas I   267

Chapter 5   The notion of empire revived: Louis II   281

Chapter 6   The papacy's appeal to Charles the Bald   293

Chapter 7   Charles the Fat   311

Chapter 8   The dissolution of the Carolingian Empire   331

Chapter 9   On the threshold of a new world   339

Conclusion   349

Index   353

List of illustrations

Simplified genealogical table of the Carolingians   x

Plates

1 Carolingian bronze statuette from Metz Cathedral, now in
  the Musée du Louvre, perhaps representing Charlemagne   xiii
2 Ninth-century illumination from the Gospels of the Emperor Lothar in the Bibliothèque nationale, Paris, MS. latin
  266, f.1b, depicting the Emperor Lothar   xiv
3 Ninth-century illumination from the Bible of Charles the
  Bald in the Bibliothèque nationale, MS. latin 1, f.433,
  depicting Count Vivien and the monks of the Marmoutier
  presenting the Bible to the king   xv

Maps

1 The Carolingian Empire at the beginning of the ninth   xvii
  century
2 Central Italy at the time of Pepin the Short and Char-   xviii
  lemagne
3 Saxony at the time of Charlemagne   xix
4 The partition of Verdun in 843   xx

x

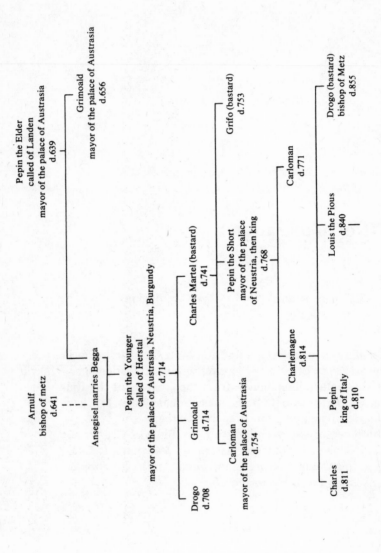

Pepin the Elder
called of Landen
mayor of the palace of Austrasia
d.639

Grimoald
mayor of the palace of Austrasia
d.656

Arnulf
bishop of metz
d.641

Ansegisel marries Begga

Pepin the Younger
called of Herstal
mayor of the palace of Austrasia, Neustria, Burgundy
d.714

Drogo
d.708

Grimoald
d.714

Carloman
mayor of the palace of Austrasia
d.754

Charles Martel (bastard)
d.741

Pepin the Short
mayor of the palace
of Neustria, then king
d.768

Grifo (bastard)
d.753

Carloman
d.771

Charlemagne
d.814

Charles
d.811

Pepin
king of Italy
d.810

Louis the Pious
d.840

Drogo (bastard)
bishop of Metz
d.855

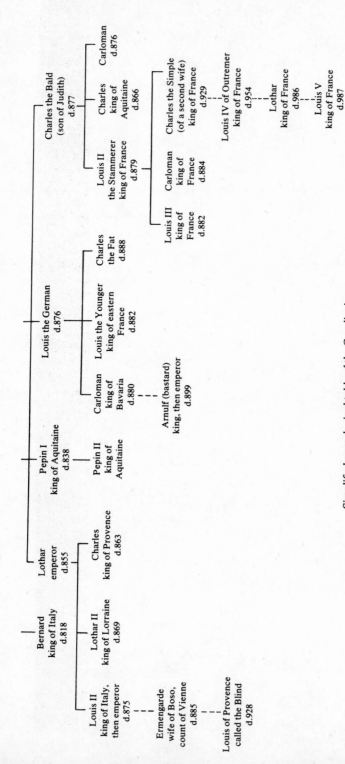

Simplified genealogical table of the Carolingians.

Bernard
king of Italy
d.818

Lothar
emperor
d.855

Louis the German
d.876

Pepin I
king of Aquitaine
d.838

Charles the Bald
(son of Judith)
d.877

Louis II
king of Italy,
then emperor
d.875

Lothar II
king of Lorraine
d.869

Charles
king of Provence
d.863

Charles
the Fat
d.888

Louis the Younger
king of eastern
France
d.882

Carloman
king of
Bavaria
d.880

Pepin II
king of
Aquitaine

Carloman
d.876

Charles
king of Aquitaine
d.866

Louis II
the Stammerer
king of France
d.879

Ermengarde
wife of Boso,
count of Vienne
d.885

Louis of Provence
called the Blind
d.928

Arnulf (bastard)
king, then emperor
d.899

Louis III
king of France
d.882

Carloman
king of
France
d.884

Charles the Simple
(of a second wife)
king of France
d.929

Louis IV of Outremer
king of France
d.954

Lothar
king of France
d.986

Louis V
king of France
d.987

Plate 1. *Carolingian bronze statuette from Metz Cathedral, now in the Musée du Louvre, perhaps representing Charlemagne.*

*Plate 2. Ninth-century illumination from the Gospels of the Emperor Lothar
in the Bibliothèque nationale, Paris, MS. latin 266, f.1b, depicting
the Emperor Lothar.*

Plate 3. Ninth-century illumination from the Bible of Charles the Bald in the Bibliothèque nationale, MS. latin 1, f.433, depicting Count Vivien and the monks of the Marmoutier presenting the Bible to the king.

Map 1. The Carolingian Empire at the beginning of the ninth century.

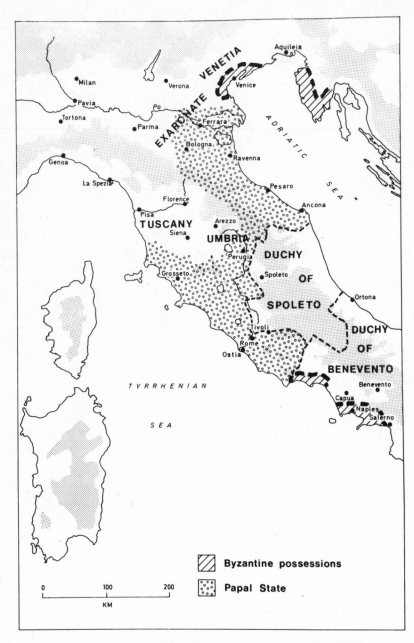

Map 2. Central Italy at the time of Pepin the Short and Charlemagne.

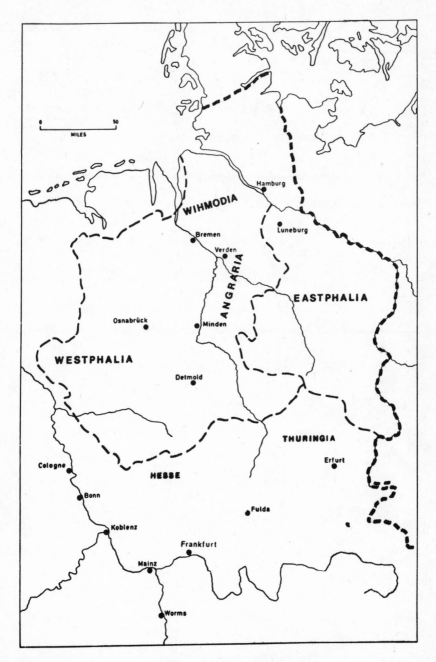

Map 3. Saxony at the time of Charlemagne.

Map 4. The partition of Verdun in 843.

Introduction

The Roman Empire had been a political structure, resting upon the power of Rome, that had gradually expanded to cover the whole Mediterranean basin. After its collapse, order was not restored nor did civilization flourish again in the West until one of the barbarian peoples who had burst upon the ancient world, the Franks, began to build a new empire, one that did not look to the sea, and whose capital was Aachen, no longer Rome. In this empire the 'barbarian' element predominated, but all those whom the conqueror had subjected to his authority, being bound by a common faith, felt themselves to be members of a single great society, constituting as it were a single people: the 'Christian people'. At that moment, Europe was born – a Europe that, although still a rather narrow strip and of precarious existence, would outlive the empire from which it had come forth. Thus, however ephemeral it may have been, the Carolingian Empire in fact appears to us as a step towards the establishment of an order profoundly different from that which the ancient world had known.

The Mediterranean, having become an inland sea, had ensured the cohesion of the Roman Empire. It had made possible first the establishment, and then the maintenance, of an unceasing exchange of commercial articles, ideas and religions among all the countries whose shores it washes. Thanks to this sea the whole Roman world had become dotted with large cities, wealthy and active, where the most diverse civilizations had mingled and blended so that they truly seemed to form one harmonious whole. Yet of this immense activity nothing, in the West at least, remained after the victory of the barbarians. A multiplicity of distinct and usually hostile kingdoms had soon come into existence inside the old Roman frontiers. Other regions, especially in Germany, which had never become part of the Empire and had remained strangers to the Mediterranean world, in the course of time became increasingly important in the political constellation of the West, which was thus in the process of realignment. However, being cut off from the Mediterranean or lacking coastlines of their own, most of the barbarian kingdoms had been forced to rely on their own resources: large-scale commerce had ceased; the cities, where they had existed at all, had withered; everywhere a reversion to an essentially rural economy could be seen, in which the absence of means of transportation reduced the exchange of products to an absolute minimum; particularism and isolation were the rule of the day, and culture had fallen into a dreadful regression.

The fundamental concepts upon which the Roman state had rested had perished with it. That clear consciousness of the collective interest in which Romans had been educated, the awareness of the 'public cause' (*res publica*), of which all citizens, above all the emperor, should regard themselves as servants, had been wiped out entirely. The very notion of public service had vanished, and with it all distinction between public and private affairs (*res publicae, res privatae*). However ambiguous the terms then used may be, there no longer were a public treasury, public functionaries, or a state, but there were coffers from which the princess drew indiscriminately for private and collective purposes; civil servants were charged with domestic work as well as with tasks which concerned the governing of the kingdom; finally, the territories, considered to be the ruler's private properties, were as such liable to be transferred, together with the rest of his estate, through hereditary right and divided among all his direct descendants.

Such was the situation when the Carolingians came to power. They did not attempt to revive the past: on the ruins of the ancient order they tried, taking their inspiration from new principles, to build a new world, and to give back, as it were, a soul to the murdered West. It is from this point of view that we will approach the history of their empire.

BOOK ONE

THE FOUNDATIONS OF
THE EMPIRE

CHAPTER ONE

The establishment of the Carolingian monarchy

From the very beginning of the Middle Ages the Franks of Clovis and his successors had succeeded in establishing their power over great stretches of territory whose geographical contours and ethnic composition already to a very large extent prefigured those of the Carolingian Empire.

At the time of its greatest expansion, during the reign of Dagobert (629–639), their kingdom comprised nearly all of Gaul and a part of the Rhine countries, Alemania and Thuringia; it even began to make its influence felt in Frisia, Saxony, and Bavaria, and to inspire respect in certain of its Slavonic neighbours. The Merovingian monarchy, nevertheless, was but a 'barbarian' monarchy, as were its fellows. Based on conquest, it had no other aim than to increase the territorial bulk that constituted its possessions, the component parts of which had nothing in common other than their belonging to the same masters: the Franks. All were designated indiscriminately as 'the kingdom of the Franks' (*regnum Francorum*).

The descendants of Clovis were qualified to reign by a tradition, henceforth firmly rooted among all the barbarians, which reserved the throne to the family of the chief who had led them to victory. Since the lands conquered by his arms were looked upon as his private property, it seemed normal that the inheritance of these would fall to his legitimate sons and, in turn, to their direct heirs. These distributed it between themselves in portions or 'kingdoms' of what was reckoned to be equal value, and thereafter only the chance occurrence of deaths made it possible to reassemble them now and again into a single kingdom.

But in the second half of the seventh century the vitality of the Merovingian dynasty seemed exhausted, and its degeneration plunged the 'kingdom of the Franks' into steep decline. One by one the formerly subject Germanic territories broke away; Gaul itself fell apart, anarchy prevailed within each of the sub-kingdoms which from then on fought each other regularly on its soil – Austrasia, Neustria, Burgundy – and none of these, moreover, succeeded in holding on to a rebellious Aquitaine. Youthful puppet kings, called to the throne in their tenderest years of childhood through the premature deaths of their parents, did not themselves, because of the degeneracy of their dynasty, usually attain the age of manhood. Around them a crowd of ambitious men plotted, eager to seize power. The ablest of them, those who could muster the largest following or 'faction' of *leudes* or retainers succeeded, in each of the three kingdoms, in taking over the office of 'mayor of the palace' (*major domus*) through which they got the actual exercise of power into their hands. In theory, nevertheless, the unity of Frankish authority survived, notwithstanding its fragmentation in fact, and there was hardly a mayor of the palace who did not wish to restore it to his own advantage by seizing the 'mayoralties' he did not already possess. Through having succeeded in this while their rivals failed, and through having been able to keep the monopoly of this office within their own family as well, the ancestors of the Carolingians laid the foundations for the achievements of their dynasty.

The ancestors of the Carolingians and the achievement of Charles Martel

In the time of Clothar II and his son Dagobert, a member of the family later known as the Carolingians, Pepin the Elder, held the office of mayor of the palace in Austrasia. He seems to have continued in this office for twenty years, excepting a very brief period of disgrace around 634, when the office devolved upon his son-in-law Ansegisel, son of the bishop of Metz, Arnulf. After this Pepin, whom modern historians have become accustomed to calling Pepin of Landen, his son Grimoald, and then his grandson Pepin the Younger – the one whom we call Pepin of Herstal – ruled the palace of Austrasia. The last of these, victor over the Neustrians at Tertry near Péronne in 687, added to it the mayoralties of the palace of Neustria and of Burgundy.

Until 714, the year of his death, Pepin the Younger – even though he had for a time delegated the government of the two palaces of Neustria and Burgundy to his second son Grimoald – remained in fact the sole and all-powerful ruler of the three kingdoms into which the *regnum Francorum* continued to be divided. In this way it had become customary at the beginning of the eighth century to regard the mayor of the palace of Austrasia as the head of the whole kingdom.

In 714, it is true, the new state of affairs was suddenly almost destroyed by the assassination of Grimoald II, the only survivor of the two legitimate sons of Pepin the Younger, who himself passed away a few months later. Pepin's grandsons were children, just as the one Merovingian king still surviving, the king of Neustria, was a child. Was the fiction about to be doubled: was the puppet king to be matched by puppet mayors?

Pepin's window Plectrude unsuccessfully attempted to effect such a combination by ruling in the name of her grandsons. She ran into difficulties when the Neustrians rebelled and elected from amongst themselves a new mayor of the palace, Ragenfred. Thereupon they marched to the Meuse to form an alliance with the duke of the pagan Frisians, Radbod, himself in open revolt, whose troops, more or less in collusion with the Saxons, had marched up the Rhine to Cologne. The Frankish kingdom seemed about to fall back into anarchy when a saviour appeared in the person of a bastard, Charles, born out of Pepin's liaison with the noble Alpaidis. Kept in the background by the ambitious Plectrude and thrown by her into prison or kept under close surveillance, he outwitted the vigilance of his jailers and triumphed over his enemies one after the other. To begin with, he defeated the Neustrians at Amblève near Liège in 716, then at Vincy (or Vinchy) near Cambrai in 717. That same year Plectrude's partisans, who had assembled at Cologne, where she had sought refuge, were forced to hand over to him Pepin's treasure. The Frisians and Saxons were repulsed and pursued into their own countries. A little later (719–720) Charles subdued the Aquitanians and their duke Odo, an ally of Ragenfred. Finally, in 724, he defeated Ragenfred at Angers. The Lord himself, if we are to believe Charles' contemporaries, led him to victory everywhere, and by his prowess rescued the Frankish kingdom from dismemberment and ruin. For nothing now prevented Charles, henceforth without a rival, from ruling as mayor of the palace in the name of the very young Merovingian king, Theoderic IV, son of Dagobert III, and from restoring matters to the condition in which his father had left them. Nevertheless, the Frankish kingdom that emerged from this turmoil was very much reduced in size.

In the south, notwithstanding Charles' victory in 720, Aquitaine remained practically independent under its duke Odo. The Moslems of Spain, after having invaded Roussillon and lower Languedoc in 719 or 720, had advanced simultaneously in the directions of Nîmes and Toulouse; only a rapid and vigorous intervention by Odo of Aquitaine near the latter city kept them out of the Garonne valley. North of Nîmes, however, they were able to dash forward unchecked in 725 through the Rhône and Saône valleys into the heart of Burgundy, sack Autun and carry off their booty without anyone daring to pursue them. East and north of the Rhine the greater part of the Germanic territories had ceased to recognize Frankish hegemony, and at the frontiers it was difficult to hold the Bavarians, Saxons, and Frisians at bay. Never at any moment of its history had the kingdom of which Charles had just taken over the government appeared so weak, so close to destruction.

The new mayor of the palace, however, lacked neither energy nor boldness. He tackled the most dangerous situations with calm courage. In the east, the Bavarians were restored to obedience by force of arms; in 730, the Aleman duchy was reduced to a province; by a series of well-managed offensives (720–738) the Saxons were kept in their place. In the north, in 733–734, the Frisians were subjected to Frankish authority. Meanwhile, the greatest danger that had ever menaced the kingdom, that of the Moslem advance, suddenly materialized: the cavalry of the emir of Spain, Abd ar-Rahman, rushed out from Pamplona and bore down on Gascony and Bordeaux; soon they were at the gates of Poitiers (October 732), heading towards Tours and northern France. The raid of 725 had hit the same region, but this expedition was aimed at the heart of Gaul. Upon the appeal of Odo, who had been defeated, Charles hastened to the scene. On the very outskirts of Poitiers the two armies met. With serried ranks "immobile as a wall", according to a contemporary, but inspired with fierce strength, the Franks resolutely awaited the charge of the enemy, who proceeded to dash themselves to pieces upon the Frankish swords. It turned into a horrifying massacre. Abd ar-Rahman was among the slain, and only the falling dusk saved the remnants of the fleeing

Moslem army from annihilation by the victors.

Gaul, at last, could breathe again. Not that its soil was cleared entirely of Saracens, because these remained in Roussillon and lower Languedoc, whence they made some successful raids, notably in 737 on Avignon and its surroundings. But the retaliation for this was not long in coming: repulsed and defeated that same year by Charles on the Berre, south of Narbonne, the Moslem soldiers were henceforth confined to that region, from where some twenty years later they were to be dislodged without much trouble.

His victories over the Moslems, especially that of Poitiers, gave the mayor of the palace prestige and authority throughout Gaul. Aquitaine, which owed its liberation to him, seemed to have returned to obedience for good. It retained a duke of its own, even after Odo's death in 735; but, immediately after this event, a quick expedition by Charles across the country down to Bordeaux and Blaye was sufficient to impose on all the recognition of Frankish suzerainty. Burgundy and Provence, equally intractable, were also forced to yield. Just as with Aquitaine, several expeditions – in 733, 736 and the following years – quenched their rebellious spirit without much difficulty. But here, instead of simple suzerainty, full and complete sovereignty was imposed: Charles appointed and installed his counts and representatives over the whole extent of the subjected territory.

Wherever the royal authority was thus restored – a royal authority which the mayor of the palace alone exercised, without even trying, after the death of Theoderic IV in 737, to justify it by having a Merovingian at his side – Charles behaved as an absolute ruler, making laws and dispensing justice, disposing as he pleased of episcopal sees and abbacies and distributing church properties to his faithful followers in exchange for their services. In short, he behaved exactly as though he personally possessed the sovereign power. No one at that time even protested against the many usurpations which he perpetrated against the clergy and none of his contemporaries thought of seeing in this the signs of any disfavour toward the Church. On the contrary, he was praised, and with justification, for his devotion to the faith. Pious works and missions found in him a promotor on whom one did not call in vain. In 722 Pope Gregory II "knowing the pious spirit that lives in this glorious duke of the Franks", solicited his support for St Boniface, charged by the Holy See to convert the pagans of Germany to the Christian faith; and Charles responded unhesitatingly to this request by a letter of protection in the official style, drawn up according to the usual model of royal letters of protection, which made the papal missionary his personal protégé.

Such a step, at such a moment, may have seemed reckless, since in 722 the authority of Pepin's son was still not very firmly established. Fifteen years later, however, no one could doubt it any longer: the mayor of the palace had become the outstanding figure, not only in the Merovingian kingdom but in the whole West. Thus it came as no surprise when in 739 and again in 740 a new pope, Gregory III, in his turn approached Charles to ask him, no longer for a simple letter of protection for a missionary, but for aid and support against redoubtable enemies, the Lombards, who threatened at that moment to take possession of Rome.

After Justinian, the See of St Peter had long seemed back for good under the immediate authority of the Roman emperors of Constantinople. But these emperors, who meant to treat the popes as no more than imperial bishops, had ultimately adopted an ecclesiastical policy, and even a dogmatic position, which did not conform to the tradition of orthodoxy of which St. Peter's successors had made themselves the protectors. Since 717 the imperial throne had been occupied by Leo III, whose ambition to rule the Church had precipitated war everywhere in his territories. Being a partisan of the return to a form of worship cleansed of the superstitions and excesses which the veneration of icons had brought about in the East, he had assumed an attitude on this delicate matter so radical that he had not only brought the whole East into turmoil, but had also effected a breach of relations with the pope. For the papacy there could be no question, and there would be no question for a long time, of any understanding whatever with an imperial government determined to dictate its terms to the pope, to use ever harsher reprisals against the properties of the Holy See, and even to attack the authority of this See, whose sphere of competence it diminished by withdrawing from its ecclesiastical jurisdication entire provinces, adding them to the patriarchate of Constantinople: Calabria, Sicily, Dalmatia, the Balkan lands.

Unable to count on the support of an emperor who, anyway, had many other matters on his hands and was himself kept busy defending his Asian and east European possessions, the pope was helpless in the face of the Lombard advance. This is not the place to recount their conquests. Let us recall only that after making their way across

Germany up to the banks of the Danube, they invaded Italy in 568. At that time the whole peninsula had again been for thirty years an integral part of the Roman Empire, and had been governed from Constantinople by the sole surviving successors of the Augusti. The Lombards applied themselves arduously from then on to seizing it from them piece by piece. They occupied a large part of the northerm provinces, and certain provinces in the south, but had not yet been able to take Rome or Ravenna, the ancient capital of the Western emperors, where later the 'exarch' of Italy, the official representative of the emperor for the whole peninsula, resided.

Originally Arians, the Lombards had at the beginning of their rule oppressed Italy with fierce religious persecution, but eventually they were converted to the Roman faith. Their advance, long delayed by their lack of unity and their internal dissensions, was nevertheless a matter of constant anxiety for the papacy. Theoretically an imperial bishop but in practice free in his movements and so far from Constantinople, even from Ravenna, that he was in a position to act as Universal Pontiff, the pope trembled at the idea of becoming a bishop of the Lombard kingdom. The incorporation of the Roman See into this kingdom would have been in every way a catastrophe for the successor of St Peter at a time when his universal authority was still seriously contested by the claims of the patriarch of Constantinople, staunchly supported by the emperor, whose direct associate he was.

How, then, could the danger be averted? There seemed to be only one possible solution: recourse to the Franks. And it was at this moment that, for the first time, the conjunction of Carolingian and papacy, from which thereafter such great and durable consequences would derive, seemed to become indispensable for the welfare of Western Christendom.

In 739 the Lombard king Liutprand camped fifteen leagues from the Eternal City: there was no time for hesitation. Pope Gregory III turned resolutely toward the powerful mayor of the palace of the Merovingians. The letters he addressed at that time to the effective leader of the great barbarian kingdom of the West strike us because of their remarkable tone. The 'viceroy' (*subregulus*) of the Franks is entreated in urgent terms to behave as a "devoted son of the Prince of the Apostles"; to let himself be moved by tears "shed night and day by the eyes" of the pope at the sight of the disasters piling up; to note also that his delay in coming has already provoked jeers from those who enjoy disparaging the Frankish power. The tone of these letters and the brilliancy of the embassy Gregory sent to Charles Martel as early as 739 to explain his request orally indicate how great a value the curia attached to the assistance of the Frankish prince and how great a prestige the latter enjoyed at the time.

His flat refusal to become involved in the affairs of Italy at a moment when he needed the Lombard alliance to keep the Moslems out of Provence, doubtless proves his wisdom. In no case should one interpret this decision as evidence of a weakening of Charles's authority, as Gregory III tried to insinuate in his last letter. For it was very shortly after this incident, in 741 in fact, that we are witness to an unheard-of spectacle: Charles, who since 737 had ruled the whole of the territories subject to the Franks by himself, without even sheltering behind a king, proceeded "after having heard the opinion of his magnates, to divide the kingdom between his sons". Such at least are the terms used by a contemporary who is usually well-informed. He relates that Charles "gave" to the eldest, Carloman, Austrasia, Alemania and Thuringia; to the younger, Pepin, Burgundy, Neustria and Provence. Thereafter, he adds, Charles died at Quierzy on 22 October 741, and – following the example of the great King Dagobert – was buried "in the basilica of St Denis the martyr".

The Carolingian was yet in no way king, but all these events took place as though, already, the Merovingian monarchy had ceased to exist.

The reign of Carloman and Pepin

Ten years were to pass, however, before the Merovingian king disappeared; ten years in the course of which the monarchy, in fact already Carolingian, steadily increased its authority in the West. Carloman and Pepin nonetheless had at once to cope with a whole series of ominous revolts which broke out after their father's death: the rebellion of Grifo, a bastard son of the deceased, jealous of the power that had fallen to his half-brothers; the rebellion of the duke of Aquitaine, Hunald, son of Odo, in 742; revolts of the duke of the Alemans, Theobald, in 742, and of the duke of Bavaria, Odilo, in 743. Everywhere the new rulers' retort was prompt and effective, even though in Bavaria, in the Aleman country and in Aquitaine it was necessary for them to return to the charge several times, and though, to reinforce their power, they judged it prudent as well to put back in 743 on the Merovingian throne – which by a strange paradox had remained vacant since 737 – a puppet king, Childeric III, of whom thereafter only official charters make mention. One of these carries the following superscription which is worth citing: "Childeric, king of the Franks, to the eminent Carloman, mayor of the palace, who has established us on the throne . . ." – which phrase needs no comment. The two mayors of the palace continued, moreover, to issue edicts in their own name and even went so far as to speak of "their kingdom" or to speak of themselves, as did Carloman in 747, as "being entrusted by the Lord with the task of governing".

This task they accomplished in fact as though the kingdom had really been theirs. Undertaking to restore it, they convoked councils and issued capitularies in which their sovereign will was expressed. A capitulary of Carloman dated 21 April 742 – and thus anterior to the re-establishment of a Merovingian king on the throne – begins with these words:

In the name of Our Lord Jesus Christ I, Carloman, duke and prince of the Franks, on the advice of the servants of God and of my magnates have convoked the bishops and priests who are in *my* kingdom . . . so that they might give me advice on the manner of restoring the law of God and of the Church, corrupted in the time of previous princes, so that the Christian people may ensure the salvation of their soul and not lose it through false priests.

Then follow the decisions taken "on the advice of his priests and his magnates" by the "duke and prince" Carloman. These all aim at the restoration of the Frankish church under the aegis of the same Boniface, "sent by St Peter", to whom Charles Martel had already given his support and whom – the apostle of the Germans is himself the witness of this – this eldest son of Charles Martel had on his own initiative "caused to be called to him" to re-establish ecclesiastical discipline in his lands.

Confirmed or amended on 1 March following at Estinnes in Hainault, the measures which were then promulgated and which were intended only for the territories subject to Carloman, were adapted the next year by Pepin for his own lands at a synod held in Soissons on 2 March 744. In the capitulary that lists them the name of Childeric, promoted in the meantime to the monarchy, appears only in the date:

"in 744..., second year of King Childeric". The rest of the document is drawn up according to the model of the capitulary of 742: it is Pepin, "duke and prince of the Franks", who speaks his mind in it, as made up "in agreement with the bishops" and after "having heard the opinion of the clergy and of *his* magnates". It is "Pepin, illustrious lord, mayor of the palace" and not the king who has placed his signature at the foot of the document. In law as well as in fact, this reform of the church of Gaul was the personal achievement of the two sons of Charles Martel, to whom St Boniface lent his assistance.

The abdication of Carloman, who withdrew from secular life in 747 to spend the rest of his days in a monastery, may have hastened the renunciation of the Merovingian fiction. Pepin–whom we call the Short–was now in fact alone at the head of the whole kingdom. Although he had to come to terms with a new revolt of his half-brother Grifo, who had been imprudently released after six years of imprisonment, and with the rebellious support Grifo had found in Saxony and Bavaria, he does not seem to have encountered serious difficulties in making himself obeyed. Grifo and his accomplices were in fact defeated after a few months of hostilities, and contemporary records, even though reflecting only official appearances, show that the role allowed to the Merovingian king was constantly diminishing. One looks in vain in this period for a single piece of authentic legislation emanating from King Childeric; but those demonstrating Pepin's exercise of sovereign power multiplied.

The moment now seemed to have come to take the decisive step. Already in Ausust 750 Pepin appears in a charter as publicly dispensing justice in the Merovingian palace of Attigny, which he calls "*his* palace"; he declares that he sits there "surrounded by *his* magnates" (*proceres nostri*)–bishops, dukes, and counts of the realm–and to exercise there the power "which had been entrusted to him by God". Shortly afterwards he decided at last to discard the shadow-king in whose name he was supposed to be reigning, and to assume the royal title himself.

Pepin the Short's coup d'état

This coup d'état appears to have been carefully planned. During the two preceding years, one of our best informants (a continuator of

Fredegar) notes, "the land remained without wars". Since this was an epoch when the return of good weather was usually the occasion for warlike activity, one suspects strongly that this exceptional peace was above all used for negotiations. It may be assumed that discussions were first taken up with the magnates of the kingdom; and we know from a trustworthy source that they were held with the Church whose support was deemed indispensable. We learn among other things that the bishop of Wurzburg, Burchard, and the abbot of Saint-Denis, Fulrad, were sent to Rome towards the end of 749, or more probably at the beginning of 750, to win the pope over to the idea of a change of government.

For several years the frequency of contacts between the chiefs of the Frankish kingdom and the Holy See had been increasing. The work of religious reform undertaken in their lands by Carloman and Pepin and the patronage all the missionaries, especially Boniface, had enjoyed from them, could not but have predisposed the two powers toward closer co-operation – whatever may sometimes have been said. The pope's political situation, moreover, forced him to adopt such a policy. For, after a short period of calm, relations with the emperor as well as with the Lombards again seemed foreboding. On the side of Byzantium, where in 740 the death of Leo III the Iconoclast, with whom the papacy had lived on a warlike footing, had at first brought hope of a durable reconciliation, new clouds gathered. Once the period of initial friendliness and exchanges of good wishes was past, Pope Zacharias, even though himself a native of Byzantine Italy, had found in Constantine V a bitter opponent of the veneration of images, and therefore a latent enemy of the Holy See. Similarly, on the side of the Lombards, with whom relations had improved during the last months of Liutprand's reign and during that of his successor Ratchis (744–749), peace seemed dangerously threatened by the access to power of Aistulf in June 749. Like his predecessor, Liutprand, the new king had only one objective: to unite Italy under his power, whatever the price. The attack against what remained of the Byzantine province or exarchate of Ravenna was in preparation if not already taking place when Pepin's two envoys arrived in Rome to take up with the pope the negotiations with which the Frankish prince had charged them.

Of these negotiations there is no trace to be found either in the papal chronicles or, more surprisingly, in the *Codex Carolinus*, a copious collection of the letters exchanged between the popes and the first

Carolingians put together in 791 by order of Charlemagne himself. However, according to the semi-official editor of the *Royal Annals* of the Frankish court, whose awkward and incorrect language we have reproduced in our translation of the following excerpts, Bishop Burchard and Abbot Fulrad had been "sent to Pope Zacharias to ask him, concerning the kings in France at that time who did not have the royal power, if it were well or not that it was so"; to which Zacharias is supposed to have replied "that it were better to call the person who has the royal power king rather than he who does not have it". This was the advance approval – we do not know whether with or without conditions being stipulated – of the move the Frankish prince was preparing to carry out.

Fortified by this consent, which, as a source like the one just quoted seems to indicate, was counted on to influence public opinion, Pepin in November 751 decided to relegate the Merovingian Childeric to a monastery, and had himself personally recognized as king in a great assembly held at Soissons. His elevation to the throne, itself in principle contrary to the Frankish tradition restricting the choice of king to members of the Merovingian royal family, took place in a manner that was also new: the customary 'election' by the 'people' required by ancient Frankish usage (*more Francorum*, the annalist says) was at Soissons followed by a ceremony, till then unknown in Gaul, during which the newly elected king received the holy unction from the hands of the bishop of Germany, Boniface. By this the Carolingian doubtless intended to make the pope's consent to the usurpation just effected manifest to all. Was not St Boniface indeed the legate, the personal envoy of the pope, with whom, as his correspondence shows, he was in that period in close and continuous contact? The best-qualified representative of the supreme leader of Christendom thus indicated to those present that the inauguration of the new order took place in full agreement with the person considered to be the most legitimate interpreter of the divine will, namely the pope.

For Boniface's act of pouring the holy unguent on Pepin's head made the Carolingian the elect of God as well as the elect of the people. On this point there is no longer any doubt: reintroduced from biblical examples, the anointing inevitably resumed its ancient meaning in the eyes of contemporaries. Although the significance of this forgotten ceremony might elude most Franks, it would certainly not be lost upon the higher clergy, who had been brought up on the Holy Scriptures.

Like Saul and like David, Pepin was now the anointed of the Lord; after their example he also became His deputy. It was from the Lord that he held the office with which he was now invested, a veritable priesthood, just as, according to the Books of Samuel and Kings, had been the office of those whom divine will and not their birth designated to govern the faithful of the Almighty. The analogy between these situations must have struck the clergy, and for many years the history of Saul and David was constantly in their minds, and constantly referred to as a kind of prototype of Carolingian history itself.

That this revival of the biblical ceremony of anointing may have been facilitated by memories of a more recent past will be readily allowed. The Visigothic monarchy had been acquainted with similar practices before it was itself swept away by the Moslem conquest at the beginning of the eighth century, and there is no reason why one might not suppose that fifty years later some liturgical book or canonical collection containing this information had found its way into Gaul. Perhaps also – but this is very uncertain – anointing had been practised in the Anglo-Saxon lands whence St Boniface had come. But, however transmitted, it is certain that the biblical precedents directly influenced the minds of the eighth-century clergy, and that Pepin drew from this evocation an authority and prestige that caused the revolutionary origin of his power to be forgotten.

The appeal of Pope Stephen II to the Frankish king and the 'promise' of Pepin

We are not given details about the way in which Pepin's coup d'état was received, but we may reasonably conjecture that it did not meet with unanimous adherence, and that new manifestations of the Church's support of "the elect of God" did not seem at all superfluous. The increasing danger to which the Lombard victories exposed the papacy on the other side of the Alps provided an occasion for these at just the right moment. Ravenna had fallen into the hands of Aistulf at the beginning of the summer of 751, and the very next year Rome was threatened with the same fate. Zacharias's successor, Stephen II, elected in March 752, had attempted in vain to negotiate; Aistulf had turned a deaf ear.

Byzantium, at last, had reacted. The loss of Ravenna, with which Constantinople had up to then remained in continuous contact, was bitterly resented, and a high official of the imperial palace, the silentiary John, was dispatched to protest against the Lombard usurpations. In vain! Aistulf, certain of his power, scorned diplomatic protests. And his only reply was to redouble his threats to Rome and its inhabitants.

Emperor Constantine V, son and successor of Leo III the Iconoclast, was obviously unable to enforce his rights in the West. Pope Stephen II knew this so well that while, for the sake of form, he sent an embassy to the emperor to ask him for help, he at the same time despatched a letter in the greatest secrecy to Pepin, by means of a simple pilgrim, in which he informed him of his distress. Stephen furthermore expressed the desire to come and confer with Pepin personally and requested him to send some trusted men to Rome to fetch him. A doubly prudent measure: the roads, being infested with Lombards, were not safe; and on the other hand, before starting on his way the pope doubtless wished to obtain from Pepin an act that unmistakably committed his future ally.

The responses to Pope Stephen's two attempted overtures, the one to Constantinople, the other to Gaul, arrived in Rome within a few weeks of each other toward the end of the summer or the beginning of the autumn of 753. From Constantinople came a request to notify the Lombard king once more, in the name of the emperor, of the order to evacuate the conquered territories: another futile diplomatic protest for which the emperor had recourse to the bishop of Rome as the imperial official that, in his eyes, he still was.

From Gaul came the embassy the pope had hoped for, consisting of two figures of great distinction: the bishop of Metz, Chrodegang, and the duke Autchar. Evidently instructed to set the pope's mind at ease about their ruler's intentions, they were to accompany Stephen II as he had requested into their own country, where a meeting had been planned. Between Byzantium and the Franks the pope could hardly hesitate, and we learn without surprise that he actually started on his way on 14 October 753, in the direction of northern Italy and Gaul, escorted by Pepin's envoys.

Nevertheless, moved by a last scruple and to put his conscience at ease, Stephen stopped on his way at Pavia to see King Aistulf and acquit himself of the task with which the emperor had charged him.

Then, having here – as could easily be foreseen – met with a categorical refusal, and taking no notice of the Lombard king's attempts at intimidation, he started in November, well-escorted, on the way to France.

Realizing the extraordinary importance of the negotiations which were about to be undertaken, Stephen II had taken with him several of the principal figures of the curia: six cardinals, the archdeacon of the Roman Church, the *primicerius* and the *secundicerius* of his palace, who were the highest officials of the Lateran, and a large retinue of Roman priests and deacons. Notwithstanding the cold they crossed the passes without hindrance; but the road was long and it was only on 6 January 754, in the middle of the winter, having stayed a short while at the monastery of Saint-Maurice in the Valais, that the pope could finally be received at the royal estate of Ponthion, not far from present-day Vitry-le-François, by King Pepin, who had come there to meet him. Together they went to the monastery of Saint-Denis, where the pope settled himself for the winter and where the discussions begun at Ponthion were continued.

The details of these discussions are not known to us, but their results are clear. The conclusion of the talks was celebrated by a ceremony in the abbey church of Saint-Denis, in the course of which Stephen II proceeded first to anoint the Frankish prince anew, and then his two sons Charles and Carloman. A contemporary writer adds that on the same day the pope blessed Queen Bertrada, wife of Pepin, and that "he forbade all, on penalty of interdict and excommunication, to dare ever to choose a king from a family other than that of these princes which the Divine Clemency had deigned worthy to elevate and, upon the intercession of the Holy Apostles, to confirm and anoint by the hand of the blessed pontiff, their vicar". This curious text is but a note obscurely placed at the end of a manuscript copied at Saint-Denis itself some years later by a monk of the abbey, perhaps a witness of the events; it has no official value and probably reflects only the personal interpretation of its author. It is permissible to assume, however, that the sentiment it expresses had been shared by others: the new anointing, this time extended to the descendants of Pepin, did not only repeat and reinforce St Boniface's act of a short time before; it conferred upon a family originally no more than a usurper, a solemn consecration; it qualified the entire family permanently for the monarchy. St Boniface had, in the name of the pope, made Pepin the elect of God: the pope

himself, the authorized interpreter of the divine will as the successor of
the Prince of the Apostles, now made the Carolingian family chosen by
God to govern the Frankish people.

Many of the details surrounding this event nevertheless remain
obscure. The very date of the anointing of Saint-Denis is an object of
controversy. Some report it as in the summer of 754, in July or even
after July. But all the evidence points to its having taken place in the
spring, which presupposes several weeks of negotiations before then.
More than the date of the anointing, however, one would like to know
the nature and precise form of the obligations accepted by the Frankish
king in exchange for the support that the papacy brought him. One
would also like to know in what kind of atmosphere these conversations, which were so decisive for the future of both parties concerned,
took place. Unfortunately, the obscurities begin at the very moment
the pope entered Gaul. The honours paid to Stephen II on his arrival at
Ponthion show us the translation into practice of a protocol never
before carried out, and the papal biographer reports this with visible
satisfaction. Pepin rode out three miles from his 'palace' to meet his
august visitor. Upon seeing Stephen II he dismounted and prostrated
himself, along with his wife, children and the magnates of his retinue.
Then, as a token of deference, he walked for a time on foot at the side
of the still-mounted pope and held the bridle, as though he were a
simple squire.

But this is not the last of our surprises. In the royal chapel of
Ponthion, where the king and his guest soon held their first conversation, the pope – still according to his biographer – received from Pepin
the promise, confirmed by an oath, that he would exert himself "to
restore to him by every means the exarchate of Ravenna, as well as the
rights and territories of the republic". The question arises at once:
what did the pope mean by "restore"? For was it not to the emperor
that the territories alluded to belonged?

At this point a remarkable document should be taken out of the file,
a document about whose origins historians have debated for centuries,
but which was probably brought along by Pope Stephen II in his
luggage to impress the Frankish prince: it has come to be called the
False Donation of Constantine. By virtue of this document – which, we
have good reason to believe, had recently been drawn up with the aid
of various legends by a forger in the pay of the Holy See – Emperor
Constantine the Great was supposed to have made very extensive

renunciations of his rights in favour of the Roman pontiff, in the person of Pope Sylvester. Among these, as we shall see shortly, were many that were highly relevant at the moment when, in the chapel at Ponthion and later in the chapel of Saint-Denis, Pepin and the successor of Sylvester, Stephen II, were mutually linking their destinies.

The document is an extensive one: eight to ten large pages. After a long description of the circumstances that led him, after being miraculously cured of leprosy, to renounce paganism and embrace the Christian faith, to which Pope Sylvester himself had introduced him, the Emperor Flavius Constantinus, filled with gratitude, hailing St Peter as "the vicar of the Son of God" and the Roman pontiffs as "the representatives of the Prince of the Apostles", declared that he wished to ensure to these pontiffs, who held their "principate" from above, a greater power than that which he himself held as the emperor of humble men. Desiring, therefore, to increase the "exaltation" of St Peter's See, he decided to "make over to the pope the imperial power, the dignity, the means of government, and the imperial honours, that is to say the primacy over the four principal sees of Antioch, Alexandria, Constantinople, and Jerusalem, as well as over all the churches of the entire world". Here, then, was a solemn charter establishing the primacy of the Roman See and reducing the other patriarchates, including that of Constantinople which played a key role in the empire of the eighth century, to the status of mere subordinates.

To this first concession, Constantine added the gift of the Lateran Palace and the church of St Peter of the Vatican; the right to wear the diadem and the imperial insignia: purple chlamys, scarlet tunic, sceptre and staff; the right to an escort of horsemen "who accompany the imperial glory"; the power to "create patricians and consuls"; in short, and this is the most sensational concession, the full sovereignty over Rome, Italy and indeed the entire West:

In order that the papal dignity shall in no way be degraded but be honoured in glory and power more than the dignity of the earthly empire, we give to the blessed pontiff, our Holy Father Sylvester, universal pope, and thus make over also to his successors not only our above-mentioned palace, the Lateran, but the city of Rome and all the provinces, places, and cities of the whole of Italy as well as of all the Western regions, and by an unalterable decision of our imperial authority, by virtue of this sacred edict and this deed, we assign them in full ownership to the holy Roman Church, that she may enjoy them in perpetuity. We have also found it opportune to transfer our empire and the exercise of our authority to the eastern regions, to build in the province of Byzantium at an especially favorable spot, a city that will bear our name, and to set up our empire

there. Because in the place where the principate of priests and the capital of the Christian
religion have been instituted by the heavenly Emperor, it is not fitting that the earthly
emperor should exercise his power.

This is the essence of the famous text which was to be often alluded
to in the course of the Middle Ages and upon which many resounding
theories were to be based. It contained several other clauses worthy of
note, from which we will select only one: after having alluded to the
passage in which he had renounced his white tiara so that it could crown
the pope, whom he wished to recognize as the Sovereign Pontiff of all
Christendom, Constantine added that "out of esteem for St Peter" he
had performed for Sylvester I "the office of a squire" by holding his
bridle.

The *False Donation of Constantine* is evidently not only the source of
the significant ceremony adopted at Ponthion or at least closely linked
with it; it also explains and purports to justify Stephen II's territorial
claims and seems itself to be the decisive argument intended to
overcome, in case of need, the hesitations of the Frankish king. An
argument all the more necessary since Aistulf had not scrupled to force
Carloman, Pepin's brother, to leave the monastery where he had been
living in seclusion since 747, and to send him off at once to Gaul to
counter the papal propaganda by reminding the Franks of the advantages of their traditional alliance with the Lombards. Doubtless it was
also by virtue of the *False Donation of Constantine* that Stephen II,
after the anointing at Saint-Denis, was able to add another token of
honour to those which he in his turn heaped upon his host in order to
bind him more closely to himself: making use of one of the prerogatives which the false imperial charter granted to the pope, he conferred
upon King Pepin and his sons the title 'patrician of the Romans'; and
the letters sent to them by the curia from this time onward in fact
carried the following superscription: "to the lords our most excellent
sons the King Pepin . . . , Charles and Carloman, all three patricians of
the Romans . . .".

This impressive title of patrician of the Romans, the practical
implications of which remain mysterious, was, like the anointing, the
advance reward for a formal pact which the pope fully intended to
extract from the Frankish prince. At Ponthion nothing definite was
arrived at between them: they restricted themselves to becoming
acquainted. But thereafter negotiations were pursued in a direction
favourable to the papacy. Pepin broke decisively with Aistulf by

having Carloman captured in order to make an end to his intrigues, and had him reinstated by force in the monastic life, where he was to die shortly afterwards. Then the Frankish king committed himself even more firmly by promising to go at the head of his armies to seize from the Lombards the great stretches of territory recently conquered by Aistulf, and to 'restore' them to the pope. Finally, in April 754, at an assembly held at Quierzy on the Oise in the presence of the pope, he pledged solemnly that he would expel the Lombards by resorting to arms if necessary; and he even seems to have specified, in an official charter, the precise extent of his intervention by indicating in advance which 'restitutions' he had in mind. But the – perhaps intentional – disappearance of this document makes it forever impossible to reach definite conclusions on the subject. Strange too is the fact that, on the Frankish side, it was never mentioned, and on the papal side, only its existence was alluded to and its terms never stated. The very idea of 'restitutions' granted to the pope, which presupposes the recognition of a right for which only the *False Donation of Constantine* could have been the justification, doubtless shocked contemporaries less than it does us today, because the pope had long been in fact the master of the 'duchy of Rome' and had already several times in the past been given places evacuated by the Lombards. But this time, if we are to believe the *Liber pontificalis*, this practice was stretched so far as to include among the properties to be 'restored' to the pope territories such as the exarchate of Ravenna, from which the direct representatives of Byzantium had been driven by the Lombards less than three years earlier. The pope evidently tried to draw from the situation advantages which nothing in the past gave him the right to expect.

The monarchy of divine right

The conjunction of interests between the new Frankish monarchy and the papacy was now complete: the future of each of the two parties depended for a large part upon the success of the other. It was more than a question of prestige only: a strong papacy that was nevertheless dependent on the Carolingian was as necessary to Pepin, whose recently acquired power still encountered veiled resistance, as a secure

French monarchy was to the pope, who had no other protection against the Lombards.

For the Frankish monarchy the consequences of such a state of affairs were decisive. The role played by the Church in the dynastic revolution of which the Carolingian house was the beneficiary had as its first effect the imprint of a new character on the royal authority. Certainly, there had already been Merovingian kings who had appealed to God to justify their frequent interventions in church affairs. In 585 the pious King Guntram, in requesting the bishops of his kingdom to preach the return to a stricter observance of the faith and in reminding his subjects of the obligation of the sabbath, supported his decisions by alluding to his duties toward God "from whom", he pointed out, "he held his power to reign" (*facultas regnandi*): a reminiscence of the Book of Proverbs (8:15–16): "It is through me that kings reign and that legislators ordain what is just; through me that princes command and that the powerful dispense justice." This is also the thought of St Paul: "Every soul shall be subject to higher powers, because there is no power that is not derived from God (*non enim potestas nisi a Deo*) and those that exist were instituted by Him. And whosoever resists a power resists the order that God has established". Which is to say – as, since St Augustine, Cassiodorus, Isidore of Seville, Gregory the Great, and the various commentators of St Paul have all explained – that all government, all magistracies, are divinely instituted, because in good as well as in evil, the established order has been willed by God, and a prince, of whatever kind, even though he be a Nero, only has, to use an expression of St Augustine, "the power of command if this power was given him by Providence". It is this very general sense and in this sense only that Guntram considered himself justified in making God the source of his power.

Now it was different. The very person of Pepin and that of his descendants had been the object of a Divine choice. This choice was exercised in the same manner as at the time when, Israel wishing for the first time to have a monarchy, Jehovah personally designated and caused to be anointed for the throne first Saul, then David, then Solomon. To the act of the priest Samuel who, at the command of God, poured holy unguent on Saul and David's head, corresponded the act of Boniface and later that of the pope, in pouring holy unguent on the head of Pepin, then on that of each of his sons. Thus the Carolingian, with Solomon, could say to the Lord: "You have chosen me to be king" (*Tu elegisti me regem*); as with Saul and with David, "the Spirit of God was in him"; he was His deputy. If none of the charters of Pepin that are preserved in the original carry the formula "king by the grace of God" (*Dei gratia rex Francorum*) which his successors regularly used, the idea implied in this phrase is already often expressed: "With the assistance of the Lord, Who has placed us on the throne . . .", may be found at the beginning of a charter of 760; "Divine Providence having anointed us for the royal throne . . .," or "Our elevation to the throne having been accomplished entirely with the assistance of the Lord . . .", we find in charters of 762 and 768; and these are not purely phrases of protocol but conscious and repeated affirmations of a doctrine of which all the capitularies of the first Carolingians would soon be carrying the impression. According to the terms of this doctrine the king of the Franks, since Pepin the Short, actually received from God a personal commission to reign over the Frankish people and to bring about with His aid the triumph of the religion of Christ.

CHAPTER TWO

The achievement of Pepin

Intervention in Italy (755-756) and the 'donation' to the Holy See

Once his monarchy was established on the foundations we have just described, Pepin's first task was to carry out the promises made to Stephen II and on which after all the future of the papacy largely depended, closely linked as it was from then on with the future of the Frankish monarchy itself.

First of all, of course, Pepin had to drive the Lombard king from the territories which he had agreed to give to the pope. He tried, in the beginning, to achieve this by peaceful means: during the summer and autumn of 754 negotiations were pursued in the hope, which was constantly disappointed, that Aistulf might be induced to accept a compromise. The effort was in vain; force alone could decide the contest. In the spring of 755 a Frankish army left the region of Soissons and headed for Lyon and the Maurienne where Pepin, accompanied by Stephen II, joined the main body of his troops. After delivering a final and futile ultimatum to Aistulf, Pepin and his men crossed the Alps over the pass of Mont Cenis. Having overwhelmed the advance guard of the enemy, the Franks pressed on to Pavia, capital of the Lombard kingdom, where Aistulf allowed himself to be besieged. His defense seems to have been rather feeble: it looks as though he quickly resigned himself to surrender, at least in form, in order to get rid of the invader. Pepin in his turn seems to have declared himself satisfied rather too easily. Lacking perspicacity perhaps and also lacking enthusiasm for an undertaking which if prolonged might endanger his position in his own kingdom, and finally, unable to rely on the military aid of his followers – who in any case did not care about papal affairs – beyond

the few weeks that were prescribed by the law, he contented himself
with Aistulf's sworn promise that he would evacuate the exarchate of
Ravenna and several other recently conquered territories, or at least
did not demand more than an illusory guarantee of forty hostages.
After this, his conscience set at ease, Pepin gave the pope an escort
back to Rome and himself returned to the Frankish kingdom, where he
arrived at the beginning of the summer of 755 or somewhat later.

But Pepin's obligation was not yet fully discharged. The promise he
had made to the pope to help him by checking the Lombards and
establishing him in the territories whose possession the pope, rightly or
wrongly, considered to be essential in the absence of an effective
emperor – this promise could not be considered as kept unless Aistulf
carried out this obligations. But, as soon as Pepin had turned his back,
the Lombard king, forgetting his oaths, refused to surrender anything,
and the pope was obliged to acknowledge the failure of the policy his
ally had pursued south of the Alps.

The letters he sent to Pepin only a few months after the capitulation
of Pavia express the bitterest disappointment. What indeed, he asks,
was the worth to Pepin and his sons of the pope's act of anointing in
the ceremony of Saint-Denis now that 'St Peter' had failed to obtain
'justice' after the brilliant victory which the Almighty had nevertheless
granted the Frankish armies? In "anointing them as kings" had not the
pope consecrated them to the service of the Holy Church and had he
not entrusted them with the charge of giving back to the Prince of the
Apostles his due? Had not Pepin pledged to do this in a charter signed
by his own hand? It had been in vain, the pope writes to Pepin, that he
had travelled a long and hard journey from Rome to "put into your
hands, by command of the Lord" this most sacred of all matters: left
alone without supervision, Aistulf "has refused to restore to St Peter
one inch of territory" and his fraud remains unpunished. Soon after
this he even resumed his attacks. At the beginning of January 756 he
camped before Rome. After seizing some villages lying in 'the patrimony of St Peter', that is the private estates of the Roman church, he
completely blockaded the capital of Christianity, and around it,
Stephen II writes, his troops committed innumerable profanations of
churches and monasteries, robberies, rapes and massacres. The Lombards even went so far as to mock the Franks by shouting: "Let them
come now! Let them come now and rescue you from our power!" This
is how the pope's Frankish alliance is being scoffed at, and notwithstanding the gravity of the situation Pepin does not stir!

The pope's plea became more and more urgent, even imploring. In the name of the two young heirs to the Frankish throne whom the anointing of Saint-Denis had made his spiritual sons and who were no less dear to his heart than to that of their natural father, Stephen II – even if only to prevent misfortune one day overwhelming them – adjured Pepin to come at once. Otherwise he would be in for a painful surprise when at the hour of Judgment the Lord, accompanied by St Peter and the other apostles, would ask him to account for his deeds. "I do not know you at all," the Lord would say to him then, if he did not now obtain Pepin's support, "I do not know you at all, because you did not rescue my Church; you did nothing for her defense nor for that of her people when they were in danger". A similar appeal was sent to the Frankish people themselves, and to make a still stronger impression the papal chancery, by recourse to prosopopeia, added to the dossier of these urgent requests a still more urgent letter in which St Peter himself demanded immediate rescue by Pepin and his sons:

You who are my adopted sons, come and rescue from the hands of my enemies my city of Rome and the people who are entrusted to me by God; come and shield the resting place of my body from defilement by these invaders; come and liberate the Church of God which is now exposed to the worst torments and the most severe oppression because of that abominable Lombard people! You whom I hold so dear . . . be assured that among all peoples the Franks are particularly close to my heart. Also I adjure you and warn you, most Christian kings Pepin, Charles and Carloman, and all of you of the priestly order, bishops, abbots, priests and monks, and you, dukes and counts, and you, all of the Frankish people; take my warning to heart as though I were still alive and standing before you, because if I am not there in flesh and bones, I am there in spirit. And with me our Lady, Mother of God, the Virgin Mary, adjures you; she too warns you and commands you, as the whole heavenly host of the martyrs and confessors of Christ command you. Have pity on this city of Rome which God has entrusted to me, on the sheep of the Lord that graze there, and on the Holy Church which I have received in keeping from the Lord. Defend them, without losing a moment; deliver them from the hands of the Lombards who are attacking them, so that my body which has suffered martyrdom for our Lord Jesus Christ and the resting place that God has chosen for it will not be defiled by contact with them, and so that my people will no longer be torn to pieces and massacred by the Lombard tribe, that pack of perjurers and violators of the Holy Scriptures. To my Roman people . . . to your brothers, lend the aid of all your power, so that I Peter, the apostle, may be able to take you into my protection . . . , and provide you as a reward with the eternal felicities and the infinite joys of Paradise.

Come quickly then, come quickly! By the living God, by the God of Truth, I implore you, I beseech you; hasten to help us before . . . our spiritual Mother, the Holy Church of God, through whom you hope to achieve eternal life, is humiliated, trampled upon, and defiled by the ungodly. I adjure you, my dearest adoptive sons, by the grace of the Holy Spirit; I adjure you before God, Creator of all things . . . and with me, Peter, apostle of God, the Holy Catholic and Apostolic Church, which the Lord has entrusted to me, also adjures you: do not let the city of Rome, where the Lord has placed my body, perish; this city that he has entrusted to me as the foundation of the faith . . . .

You are hereby warned. If you obey promptly you will be greatly rewarded for it: not only will my assistance allow you to triumph over all your enemies in this life, but after a long life in which you will have enjoyed the goods of the earth, it will ensure you in the next world the benefit of eternal life. In the case of the contrary – and we cannot believe that this is possible – or if you delay . . . know that in the name of the Holy Trinity and by the grace of the Apostolate which was given to me by our Lord Jesus Christ, your disobedience to my warning will cause you to be excluded from the Kingdom of God and from the eternal life.

Even when some allowance is made for exaggeration, it was obvious that for the defenceless pope the situation was very serious, and that if Pepin really wished to save Rome from Lombard capture he could not delay his return to Italy. He resolved upon it in fact in the first months of 756, and his new expedition at first went off almost in the same way as the preceding one: crossing by Mont Cenis, destruction of the roadblock put up by the enemy troops at the Susa Pass, siege of Aistulf in Pavia, this time with the aid of Bavarian contingents led from the north by Tassilo, duke of Bavaria, and, finally, the surrender of the Lombard king.

Meanwhile at least one event occurred which is worth mentioning: two emissaries of the *basileus*, ordered to get in touch with the Frankish king at the earliest possible moment and to remind him of their master's indefeasible rights to the territories improperly occupied by the Lombards, disembarked in the peninsula. This call to order, probably occasioned by news received at Constantinople about the events of 755, came at the wrong moment. When after some forced detours the emperor's emissaries succeeded at last in reaching Pepin at Pavia, they naively offered him magnificent rewards if he would restore the exarchate of Ravenna, lost in 751, to Byzantine authority. The Frankish king, while he may have lost sight of it for a moment, could thus no longer be unaware of the actual juridical situation in which he found himself. But the papal biographer, from whom we know these details, states that Pepin received the imperial proposal as it deserved to be received: by a flat refusal to "take away from St Peter what he had previously given to him".

Indeed, Aistulf having capitulated, not only was the treaty of 755 again enforced, now with the additional obligation for the Lombard king to pay an indemnity for the cost of the war and to deliver new hostages, but Pepin, if we may continue to believe the papal biographer, at once ordered a charter to be drawn up. This charter contained "the perpetual donation to St Peter, to the holy Roman Church and to all the popes who will occupy the Apostolic See" of all the cities and all the territories that the Lombard king had pledged to evacuate the preceding year and which would now be delivered personally to a representative of the Frankish king: Fulrad, the abbot of Saint-Denis. This was done, and Fulrad was received into Ravenna and Comacchio in the exarchate; also into Forlimpopoli, Cesena, Rimini, Pesaro, Fano, Senigallia, San Marino, Montefeltro (the present San Leo), Urbino, Iesi, and three or four other localities or towns of the Pentapolis; and he had Gubbio in northern Umbria handed over to him, as well as the small town of Narni on the borders of the duchy of Rome and Sabinia, which Aistulf had seized by surprise from the pope not long before. Everywhere the abbot of Saint-Denis exacted hostages. Thereafter he proceeded to place the keys of the ceded cities on the tomb of the Prince of the Apostles, together with the official charter of 'donation', drawn up in Pepin's name.

No more than as regards the initial promise made at Quierzy in 754 are we in a position to know the specific content of this document. Even though the official biographer of Stephen II states that at the time of his writing (between 757 and 759) the original copy is preserved "in the archives of the Holy Roman Church", it must be pointed out that just as with the promise of Quierzy, the Holy See had, while continually referring to it during the eighth and ninth centuries, always kept the text to itself, and that this text has disappeared. Did Pepin promise the pope that the Lombards would evacuate, in favour of the Roman Church, territories other than those which Aistulf had seized after he became king and of which Fulrad accepted the surrender? From the subsequent course of events it may be induced that the official charter, perhaps intentionally, left this matter unclear; the papacy did not fail thereafter to profit from this vagueness. Pepin, however, now left Italy with an easy conscience in about July 756 with the thought that, having through Fulrad's care been effectively invested with the expected territories, the papal government would from now on be in a position to take care of itself.

Pepin's arbitration between King Desiderius and Pope Paul I

This was reckoning without the many sorts of difficulties which the papacy would come up against in making its authority respected in its new possessions over against a Lombard monarchy that, though conquered, was not resigned to its defeat and that in any case could not let itself be confined to the north-west of the peninsula without committing political suicide.

Doubtless, the circumstances appeared favourable for the papacy. Aistulf, who died in a hunting accident in December 756 a few months after Pepin's victory, had been replaced on the throne by a prince whose loyal co-operation was thought, both at Rome and among the entourage of the Frankish king, to have been obtained: the duke of Tuscany, Desiderius, Abbot Fulrad's candidate, whose triumph over his competitors had been achieved through the support of the abbot and the pope. On his side, Desiderius had solemnly sworn to carry out all the commitments made by Aistulf. He had even been obliged to promise the pope that he would surrender to him Imola, Bologna and Ferrara in the region of Faenza in the west of the exarchate, as well as Ancona, Umana, and Osimo in the south-west of the Pentapolis. This was a truly royal gift which made the state of St Peter an impressive territorial unit, seeing that it would from then on comprise – without prejudice to 'the duchy of Rome' which had in fact already been under the direct authority of the pope for a long time – all of the Romagna, the Pentapolis, the march of Ancona and doubtless also the old imperial road that connected these latter provinces to Rome.

But what was this new promise of Desiderius worth? Would he keep his word? Was the Frankish king, for his part, inclined to see to the implementation of this promise? Stephen II requested him to do this at the beginning of 757 in a somewhat embarrassed letter in which, while warmly expressing his gratitude for the concessions achieved and addressing Pepin by flattering titles such as "the new Moses" and "the new David", he explained to him that the promise of Desiderius concerned territories which were in fact inseparable from those mentioned in the donation which Fulrad had placed on St Peter's tomb; that both had up to now always been subject "to the authority of one and same ruler"; and that, consequently, he expected the Frankish king to see to their effective transfer into papal control.

The fact is that Desiderius seemed in no hurry to carry out his

promises. The pope had easily been able to gain possession of the
territories of Faenza and Ferrara, but Desiderius subjected the implementation of his promise to hand over the remaining lands to all
sorts of conditions which were considered unacceptable by Stephen II.
For months and months on end Pepin was to be besieged with
complaints about this matter by Paul I, brother and successor of
Stephen II, who had died on 26 April 757. A deluge of letters then
descended on the Frankish king to press him to undertake a new
intervention in Italy. Not only does Desiderius not keep his word, the
pope writes, but he has taken the liberty of crossing the Pentapolis to
go to the south of Italy and force the Lombard dukes of Spoleto and
Benevento into submission. This he has no right to do, the pope
indignantly complains, since these dukes had made known their
intention of coming over to the papal side. Communications by land
were, furthermore, again cut off between Rome and the Frankish
kingdom, and the pope was forced to use trickery to inform Pepin of
the situation. To mislead the Lombards he dispatched via their lines a
false report in which he praised Desiderius' merits, while by sea at the
same time he sent another, this time sincere, bristling with accusations
against him.

But on this occasion Pepin refused to let himself become involved
and tried to extricate himself by diplomacy. In April 760 two
plenipotentiaries of distinction, his brother Remigius, the bishop of
Rouen, and Duke Autchar, were finally able to extract from Desiderius
the formal pledge to surrender that same month the territories which he
still unlawfully held. They even obtained from him a beginning of
evacuation. Vain promises: under the most mendacious pretexts, or
even without any pretext whatever, Desiderius evaded his commitments. However much Paul I protested, he could not move Pepin, who
at this time had other more urgent cares – notably the affairs of
Aquitaine – north of the Alps.

Pepin probably gave only limited credence to the assertions of the
pope, to whom the whole world seemed to have conspired against the
Church, and who, suspecting Desiderius of collusion with the Byzantine emperor, already visualized the Greek fleet setting armies ashore
in the exarchate, the Pentapolis and the duchy of Rome, ready to aid
the Lombards! For the movements of Byzantium inspired the pope
with no less terror than those of King Desiderius. Around the end of
763 and the beginning of 764 he informed Pepin of a more or less real

plot laid against his government at Ravenna, in complicity with the emissaries of the *basileus*, and he trembled once again at the prospect of a Greek disembarkation on the coast of the Pentapolis. He also implored the Frankish king, as the defender of orthodoxy, to intervene without delay against these heretics or at least to persuade the Lombard king to help him; which seems the height of paradox.

It was nevertheless towards an understanding with Desiderius that Pepin, himself out of patience with so many complaints and so many requests, first urged the pope who, overcoming his repugnance, was indeed obliged to resign himself to drawing up a *modus vivendi* with his recent enemy. The treaty, ratified in 766 or later, even if it left many things uncertain, at least temporarily ended the incessant hostilities that had for a number of years set the pope and the Lombard king against each other. This was, in truth, a very inadequate solution, but it gave the Frankish monarchy time to breathe and the means to pursue under more stable conditions the negotiations with Byzantium which it had taken up several months earlier in order to reach, here too, a provisional agreement regarding the multiple problems raised by Italian affairs.

The restoration of order in Gaul and Germany

Pepin's scant enthusiasm for a direct and decisive intervention south of the Alps was not connected only with the risks involved in an adventure whose immediate advantage for his monarchy was not then very clear. To understand his reserve one must take into account the difficulties the Carolingians still had to overcome in Gaul as well as in Germany in establishing their authority on firm foundations.

In Germany, the originally hostile Alemans seemed at last to have accepted the new rulers of the Frankish kingdom. After successive revolts in 742, 744, 746, and perhaps in 749, they gave up the hope of making their country an independent duchy again. But their submission was of recent date and it was evidently necessary to continue watching them closely.

Bavaria, which for its part had kept its dukes and had always borne the Frankish hegemony impatiently, had only recently – at the time of Pepin's coronation – been reduced to obedience. Their national duke

Odilo, to whom Pepin and Carloman in 743, in the course of their victorious advance to the banks of the Inn, had come to dictate their terms, had been succeeded in 744 by a child of three, his son Tassilo, who was the nephew of the two Frankish princes through his mother Hiltrude. But in 748 or 749 the country was shaken anew by a fierce revolt instigated by Grifo, the bastard brother of Pepin and Carloman, who, since the death of Charles Martel, had been scheming to obtain his share of the power. A Bavarian through his mother Swanahilde, niece of Odilo, Grifo nearly succeeded. But a new and irresistible offensive of Pepin's armies up to the Inn forced him to flee and delivered the duchy to the conqueror.

When he restored Tassilo to the ducal throne Pepin reinstated him on condition that he was to hold the province from him as a benefice (*per suum beneficium*), that is to say, under conditions of subordination and for the services required of a vassal with regard to his lord. In appearance therefore Bavaria's submission was now ensured. The young duke even seemed to have grown docile: in 757, at the moment of his legal coming of age at fifteen, Tassilo went to the palace at Compiègne in the heart of Gaul to take the oath of vassalage in a plenary session of the royal court under exceptionally solemn circumstances which the semi-official editor of the *Royal Annals* describes with evident complacency. Tassilo even obediently rendered to his new lord the military service which he now owed him, and took the field with his troops, notably in the second expedition to Italy in 756. But the fire smouldered in the embers, and in 763 during a campaign in Aquitaine, the duke, having now attained the age of manhood, suddenly deserted the ranks of the royal army under a more or less idle pretext, and thenceforth neglected his duties as a vassal. Pepin's reign drew to an end without Bavaria being brought back to obedience.

Only a few leagues from Cologne and on the southern frontiers of Hesse and Thuringia, the Saxons remained formidable neighbours whose forays into Frankish territory and whose devastations could be avoided only at the price of unceasing vigilance and frequent campaigns into their own country. Chroniclers and annalists report these Frankish retaliations in 744, 747, 753 and 758. The Frankish armies did not hesitate to advance far into Saxon country, while the enemy prudently withdrew and made the invader pay dearly for his 'victory'. The Franks in their turn took revenge by killing, plundering, burning and spreading terror everywhere. After this the Saxons in the devastated areas made their submission, pledged themselves to pay tribute, and sometimes even received baptism–to renew their destructive excursions as soon as the Frankish troops had withdrawn. They were always ready, moreover, to lend their support to any enemies of their conqueror. Thus it happened that in 747 Pepin's half-brother Grifo was defeated while fighting in their ranks.

But it was in Gaul that Pepin encountered the most serious obstacles to the triumph of his authority. He did succeed without too much difficulty in subduing Septimania in the years from 752 till 759, when it was finally seized from the infidels through the complicity of the Visigothic population. But in Aquitaine, Pepin was obliged annually from 760 to 768, except only in the years 764 and 765, to conduct harsh campaigns to achieve the ultimate reduction to the status of a province of the greater part of this vast territorial agglomeration lying between the Loire, the Ocean, the Garonne and the Cévennes. Even then, it was only a very relative assimilation. The Aquitanians remained obstinately recalcitrant towards Frankish penetration as much through their natural pride as heirs of the Roman tradition as through a fierce desire for independence. To defend this their 'national' dukes were able to rely on the permanent aid of the rough mountain Gascons who formed, the chroniclers say, the best part of their armies. Already when he was mayor of the palace Pepin thought he had subdued them in the course of two campaigns conducted in 742 and 745 together with his brother Carloman. Duke Hunald had finally declared himself ready to "carry out Pepin's will on every point". But this submission had been in appearance only. Driven out everywhere, it was at the court of Duke Waifar, Hunald's successor, that Grifo, who was in revolt against the king, had found refuge in 748 or 749, and he had been able to remain there apparently without being troubled until just before he was slain in 753 by an assassin as he fled to the east, trying to reach the Lombard kingdom where he intended to start new intrigues.

Doubtless, Grifo's case was not unique. Pepin reproached Waifar in a general way for opening the frontiers of his duchy with pleasure to outlawed Franks. He reprimanded the duke as well for the nonchalant way he usurped the properties and violated the rights of the Frankish churches in Aquitanian territory. Finally, Pepin accused him of murdering the Visigothic chiefs whom he had taken into his protection when he had annexed Septimania. The campaigns conducted by Pepin south of the Loire from 760 onward aimed at finishing off this irreconcilable adversary. Each year Pepin drove deeper into the interior of the country; in August 767 he held the general assembly of the kingdom at Bourges, where he had placed a garrison since 766, and ventured even to spend the winter in this city with his wife. In 768 he took the queen to Saintes and advanced to the banks of the Garonne where the Gascons living between this river and the Pyrenees came to make their submission; then he dashed to pursue Waifar, of whom he was subsequently relieved by an opportune murder. The conquest of Aquitaine was then at last accomplished: one by one the principal cities were taken by the Frankish king and garrisoned; his counts were everywhere substituted for those of the former duke. Then, suddenly, Pepin fell ill at Saintes of a sickness from which he never recovered. He died on 24 September 768, leaving to his successors the task of achieving, as far as possible, the moral assimilation of an Aquitaine that was physically subdued but not yet won over in spirit to the Carolingian cause.

The religious achievement

In the sphere of religion Pepin's achievement, after his coup d'état, is in more than one way the complement of his political achievement. After having, as mayor of the palace, given his full support to the general reform of the Church undertaken in the Frankish kingdom by St Boniface from 742 onwards, and joining his efforts in this to those of his brother Carloman, he was obliged as king to continue this task. The very character of his kingship, founded as it was upon divine investiture, made it his duty; and Scripture taught him that if he did not "walk with all his heart in the law of God" he would come to ruin, taking his people with him in the catastrophe.

Moreover the restoration of discipline in the Church and the return of the people to a religious life that conformed to the regulations of the divine law were, according to the spirit of the time, essential conditions for the re-establishment of order. Also, it was essential in Pepin's eyes that the attempted restoration should be effected so as to benefit the monarchy. The reform as St Boniface had wished and prepared it, however, would have resulted in the complete subordination of all the Frankish clergy to papal authority: as "legate of St Peter" (*missus*

sancti Petri) St Boniface in fact intended to re-establish a strict
hierarchy in the Frankish church, at the top of which archbishops
would be directly linked to the pope and take their orders from Rome.
A concept that was as simple as it was logical, but not one to entice a
prince careful to preserve his own authority. And we see Pepin, after
having in 744 at the synod of Soissons initially accepted the institution
of archbishops demanded by St Boniface, shortly afterwards hesitating
to carry out the programme of the papal emissary on this point. His
enthusiasm cooled to such a degree that St Boniface noted his
disappointment in his correspondence, and ultimately, after having, at
the command of the pope, administered the holy anointing to the
former mayor of the palace, he departed from the Frankish kingdom
for good and went back to missionary activity in pagan Frisia, where he
found martyrdom on 5 June 754.

In spite of this, Pepin did not abandon the cause of reform; for the
drastic method of St Boniface, however, he meant to substitute one
that was more flexible, in order to allow for certain customs with which
he thought it dangerous to break immediately. This was stated very
clearly in his name by the bishops whom he himself had called together
at the palace of Ver in July 755. After recalling that "if they had been
kept intact" the canonical rules would have sufficed to maintain the
normal church life, but that the evil times had not permitted this, they
declared that the purpose of their meeting was to enforce these rules
anew, as far as this was possible. However, they added, "lacking the
means to re-establish them in their entirety", the king had ordered that
to begin with "those things which he knew to be extremely contrary to
the Church of God should be corrected"; afterwards, "if calm times
and repose should be granted to him by God", he would exert himself
to bring about a complete return to "the sacred canons". For the
moment, "under the pressure of necessity", certain of these were not
observed.

This explains the character of the measures drawn up by the
council. If they all aimed at restoring in their fullness the powers of the
bishops and the episcopal institution itself, which was the foundation
of the ecclesiastical organization of the kingdom, they postponed to a
more propitious time the re-establishment of ecclesiastical provinces
and of metropolitan sees, and restricted themselves to prescribing the
temporary delegation of metropolitan functions to the bishops. About
the archiepiscopal title and the direct linkage of the Frankish church to

Rome by means of these archbishops, of which St. Boniface had dreamed, not a word can be found. On the contrary, for all litigious matters it was to the king and not to the Holy See that one was to turn; because it was he that was looked on to ensure the maintenance of strict discipline, especially in the monasteries, and also to supervise the strict observance of canonical rules in the matter of excommunications. One article even forbade monks to go to Rome without the explicit permission of their abbot. Finally, while the return to the regular holding of synods was decreed, the context chosen for these synods was that of the kingdom: of the two annual meetings that were prescribed, one had to be convoked by and held in the presence of the king, the other was to be held in a city such as Soissons where royal supervision could easily be exercised.

Such are the principal measures which the Frankish episcopate, in agreement with the king, thought feasible in 755. The remaining measures were hardly more than a reiteration of older conciliar decisions. All tended toward the restoration of order in civil as well as in ecclesiastical society under the supreme authority of the king. Did he not through his anointing possess a power that placed him above simple laymen and made him their guide, responsible to God alone? This viewpoint explains the numerous rules relating to marriage which Pepin promulgated at the conclusion of synods held in the course of his reign: nothing that concerned the moral and religious discipline of his people was outside the scope of his concern.

Thus it is not only from a military and political viewpoint that Pepin's reign is an essential phase in the effort of restoration in progress since Charles Martel: at the moment when the first Carolingian king died, in September 768, the Frankish kingdom seemed restored and renewed. The opportunity now presented itself for great achievements that were to assure the young dynasty a commanding position in the Europe of that time.

CHAPTER THREE

Charlemagne and the territorial completion of the Frankish kingdom

However considerable Pepin's achievement, its potentialities were realized only through his eldest son Charles, whose great power and incomparable prestige made him, during the course of a glorious reign of forty-five years, the dominant figure in the West.

The beginning of his reign

Arduous tasks indeed awaited the young prince of twenty-six – it is certain that he was born in 742 – whom posterity was to call Charles the Great (*Carolus Magnus*) or 'Charlemagne'. The first task of all was that of maintaining and if possible reinforcing the cohesion of the kingdom left to him by Pepin. Pepin, however, following ancient Frankish custom, had decreed before his death that his kingdom should be divided between Charles and his other son Carloman, thereby continuing under the new dynasty the difficulties that had caused so many complications and conflicts under the Merovingians. Moreover, he had arranged such a curious partition of territories between his two heirs that contemporaries themselves seemed rather confused by it and even the normally well-informed chroniclers were apparently unable to remember more than a few of its provisions. Only a very close scrutiny of those documents which we have at our disposal for the study of the joint reign of Charles and his brother allows us more or less to reconstitute the facts.

From the study of these texts it becomes evident that instead of following the most recent precedents by giving each of the heirs distinct regions – Austrasia, Neustria, Aquitaine, etc. – so as to form clearly separated portions, Pepin strained his ingenuity in the contrary direction; he tried to juxtapose as much as possible in the same regions the royal governments of his sons, whose capitals – Noyon for Charles and Soissons for Carloman – were both placed in Neustria, close to one another, as had been the case under the first Merovingians. The territories made over to Charles arched in a wide circle around those intended for Carloman. From the easternmost part of Thuringia and from the north of Frisia to Gascony, they included the whole northeast of Austrasia, with the Main valley, the middle Rhine country, Liège, Herstal and the Ardennes, which were the cradle of the Carolingian family. They continued through Neustria, where Charles received the whole territory between the North Sea coast and the Channel up to the Breton borders on one side, and the Oise and the lower course of the Loire, doubtless from the environs of Tours onwards, on the other side, and through Aquitaine, whose whole coast and western half was allotted to him. Carloman received the rest, that is to say, the Massif Central and Languedoc, including the Narbonnaise or Septimania, Provence, Burgundy, Alemania, Alsace and the portions of Austrasia proper and of Neustria that were not included in his brother's kingdom.

It is nevertheless not impossible that this rather confusing partition was intended to oblige Pepin's two successors to cooperate together and so to check the forces of disintegration that had asserted themselves so strongly in the Frankish kingdom from the seventh century until the time of Charles Martel. It is possible too that the share given to Charles aimed at allowing him control of the most important regions, and in fact placed his brother in his power. But experience was to prove that working together with Carloman was difficult. Only a few months after their accession, on the occasion of a revolt in Aquitaine where the brothers, each reigning over half of the province, seemed obliged to unite their efforts, this method of joint government proved to be impracticable. Contempories speak only in veiled phrases about the discord between Charles and Carloman; but one of them – even though he was an ecclesiastic – does not hesitate, once Carloman has disappeared from the scene, to congratulate Charlemagne on his no longer having to reckon with his brother's hostility since, as he says, God willed to call him up to heaven before any bloodshed should occur.

On 4 December 771 Carloman in fact died a premature death which allowed Charles – once the two young sons of the deceased, both still infants, had been set aside – to have himself recognized at once as Carloman's successor and to unite under his rule all the territories left by his father. This happened just in time, because the results achieved under Pepin in Gaul and Germany had not all proved to be equally stable. Even Aquitaine, which had seemed pacified in 768 once Waifar was gone, had again, as we have just seen, revolted in 769 under the leadership of someone whom the annalists call Hunald, who was probably none other than the former duke, father of Waifar, who had been deprived of power fifteen years earlier by Pepin. Having escaped from the monastery into which he had then been forced to retire, Hunald was forced to come to terms in 769 only because of the speed and decision with which Charles retaliated against him. He did not even wait to muster a large army, nor did he allow Carloman's inertia or defection to impede him. Even so, Charles was forced to advance to the borders of Gascony where Hunald had taken refuge with Duke Lupus, who was still practically independent, and to threaten Lupus with an invasion in order to obtain the extradition of the rebel. The whole Aquitanian territory was thus brought back to obedience, and Carloman's death facilitated its pacification, by placing it under a single government again. But it is clear that, even after this swift and decisive campaign of 769, Aquitaine caused Charles such anxiety that he waited until 778, according to a chronicler who is usually well-informed, before gradually substituting Franks for natives in the administrative functions. Shortly afterwards, in 781, he felt obliged to assuage local sensibilities by making the province, although it remained closely subordinated to his authority, into a separate kingdom, in favour of his son Louis, then still an infant.

The annexation of Bavaria

Far more troublesome than that of Aquitaine, however, was the situation of Bavaria, where Tassilo, after having himself recognized as vassal of the Frankish king, had, as we have seen, seized the first favourable opportunity to resume in practice his liberty of action. Supported by his clergy and generally on good terms with the pope, who in 766 intervened in his favour, he was able for a long time to maintain an ambiguous position. About 769, Sturm, abbot of Fulda and a Bavarian by birth, pleaded for him again with Charlemagne, who, preoccupied by other matters, seemed to be content for a number of years with occasional tokens of relative good will, such as Tassilo's dispatch of a military contingent, about whose size we are not informed, to the army mobilized in 778 for a Frankish expedition to Spain.

In 781 Charlemagne seems finally to have decided to make an end to this ambiguous situation. From Rome, where he spent the month of April, be summoned Tassilo to carry out in full all the obligations he had formerly assumed, and Pope Hadrian I was obliged to agree to being associated in this move. Obeying this summons, the duke of Bavaria went to the general assembly at Worms, at the beginning of the summer, to renew his oaths of vassalage there. Under pressure, he even consented to give the twelve hostages which the Frankish king demanded of him as a guarantee of his good faith. But shortly thereafter the defeat in 782 of the Frankish armies in Saxony, in the Süntelgebirge, restored his boldness, and once more the breach seemed complete until Charlemagne, after annihilating the Saxons in 785, finally resolved upon decisive action.

In the first months of 787 the storm clouds gathered. Suddenly apprehensive, Tassilo entreated the good offices of Pope Hadrian, to whom Charlemagne had gone on another visit to Rome for the celebration of Easter. But the Frankish king would not allow himself to be manoeuvred and insisted on the pope himself approving the measures of constraint on which he now declared himself resolved if Tassilo should not submit unconditionally. When, finally, Tassilo refused to appear before a general assembly at Worms at the beginning of the summer of 787, punishment came quickly: Bavaria was subjected to a three-pronged attack. From the west a first army, led by Charlemagne in person, came out of Alemania and marched directly on Augsburg; from the north a second army, consisting of Austrasians, Thuringians and Saxons, reached the Rhine at Pföring, upstream from Regensburg; from the south a third army, commanded by Pepin, a son of Charlemagne, came from Italy via Trent and Bolzano. Realizing that he did not have a chance, Tassilo capitulated. On 3 October, when Charlemagne was camped on the Lechfeld near Augsburg, Tassilo came to him, repented, renewed his oath of vassalage, handed over another twelve hostages of distinction and even agreed to add his own son Theodo, the heir to the ducal throne, to them, as a pledge of his good faith.

Was this submission, with which Charlemagne contented himself for the moment, sincere? It seems not. The Frankish troops had hardly turned their backs when the duke of Bavaria prepared his revenge: a veritable stroke of folly, his contemporaries declared, because Tassilo was no longer supported by his subjects, on whom the deployment of Frankish forces had produced its effect. Indicted on the charge of perjury before the general assembly convoked at Ingelheim in June 788, Tassilo did not deny it. When he was reminded of the hostages he had given the preceding year and the risk of reprisals to which his conduct exposed his own son, he replied cynically that even if he had ten sons he would sooner sacrifice them all than observe the conditions which had been imposed on him. To the accusation of perjury others were added: he was accused of wanting to make an attempt on the king's life, and of contacting the Avars with a view to a joint invasion of Italy; he was even accused of desertion in battle. All these were crimes which among the Franks entailed capital punishment, and this sentence was in fact pronounced by the assembly on Tassilo and his son Theodo, but it was commuted by Charlemagne to life imprisonment in a monastery. Soon after, for the sake of form, the duke and his heir were pardoned by the king and authorized to do permanent penance as monks, Tassilo at Jumièges and Theodo in St Maximin's at Trier, while their principal councillors were sent into exile. What is most surprising in this whole affair is the forbearance which Charlemagne, contrary to his habit, displayed from the start towards Tassilo. Being a country anciently civilized, for a long time Christian, very jealous of its independence, and much attached to its ducal house, Bavaria seemed to him to deserve exceptional consideration. Hence his long-lasting patience, his prudent negotiations with the pope whose agreement he wished to be sure of before embarking on his conquest; hence also his apparent naivety in 787 when he feigned to believe the oaths of a duke who had repeatedly committed perjury. Hence again, at Ingelheim in 788, his recourse to a procedure intended to manifest to everyone both his own indefeasible rights and the accumulation of proofs of guilt against Tassilo; hence, finally, in the accounts of the semi-official annalists, the stress on the generosity of the decisions taken by the Frankish king and on the voluntary character of the duke's retirement.

Once this retirement was a fact, Charlemagne took possession of the duchy of Bavaria. He nevertheless continued to display prudence. The Avar menace alone, rumbling at the borders of the province, would have prompted him to this, if any prompting were necessary. Charlemagne took care not to injure the Bavarians' self-respect and to make the transition as painless as possible. From the spring or beginning of the summer of 791 until the autumn of 793 he stayed almost continuously at Regensburg, convoking general assemblies there and apparently working on the gradual assimilation of the country.

No doubt this careful approach was necessary, but it still did not suffice to enlist the support of the inhabitants, because in 794, Charlemagne, in order to assure an indisputable foundation for his authority in the duchy, felt obliged to take Tassilo from his monastery, produce him in monk's attire before the general assembly at Frankfurt, and have him renounce publicly and unconditionally all his rights and those of his heirs. Drawn up in triplicate, one copy of which was for the ex-duke and his followers, the other two for the royal archive, the written text of this oral renunciation was intended to establish in an indisputable manner the right of Charlemagne and his successors to the duchy and its dependencies.

It should be noted as well that even after its incorporation into the Frankish state, Bavaria was allowed to maintain not only its traditional boundaries but also its individuality. Without appointing a duke there, Charlemagne sent as 'placed over' the government of the country (*Baioariae praefectus*), that is, as governor, one of the most eminent counts in the kingdom, his brother-in-law Gerold, brother of his queen Hildegarde; and the authority of this official extended over the whole complex of the territories thus united to the Frankish Crown. The religious unity of the former duchy was similarly respected; Bavaria was made into a single ecclesiastical province of which Salzburg in 797 became the metropolitan see. Thus everything was done to give Bavaria the illusion that the government of the Frankish king was but the continuation of the former ducal authority.

The conquest of Saxony

The methods Charlemagne used with the Saxons were harsher. This people, it is true, were particularly difficult to keep in check and they had been for centuries a constantly recurring danger to the Franks. Up to this time, the Franks had restricted themselves to making rapid military demonstrations in the Saxon country and, when possible, imposing tribute at sword's point. But, lacking systematic follow-ups, these all-too-short campaigns had never procured more than a temporary lull, and at the slightest slackening of the royal authority the adjacent Frankish provinces – Thuringia, Hesse, the Rhineland – again fell prey to their plundering bands. Inveterate pagans despite the attempts already made to convert them to Christianity, and redoubtable barbarians, the Saxons occupied vast stretches of plain between the Netherlands and the Elbe, between the Harz and the North Sea, reaching even the Baltic Sea along their border with the Danes. As a whole they doubtless lacked unity, consisting of diverse ethnic groups often with divergent tendencies: Westphalians to the west, Eastphalians the east, Angrarians between these two, Nordalbingians and inhabitants of the country of Wihmodia on both sides of the lower Elbe; but, fiercely attached to their independence, they formed a bloc whenever they felt threatened. This had happened during the reign of Pepin the Short and would recur many a time during the reign of his successor.

Although a change of method was obviously called for, Charlemagne's first interventions in Saxony were still of the traditional type: as simple military demonstrations they had no other purpose than to make Frankish power respected and to inflict reprisals. Only the pressure of circumstances forced the king to modify his tactics and to work out a plan of progressive penetration, in order to avoid a perpetual renewal of attacks and retaliations. Thus in 772, the year of his first campaign in Saxony, he pursued the customary Frankish strategy, and the operations were marked by the taking of the Saxon fortress of Eresburg, north of the frontier of Hesse, by the destruction of the idol Irminsul, and finally by a victorious advance up to the Weser. The Saxons submitted at once and gave hostages as pledges of their loyalty. But the following year, taking advantage of the fact that the Frankish king had departed for Italy, they fell upon Hesse and plundered the church of Fritzlar. In 774 a second Frankish campaign in southern Saxony hardly had better results: the valley of the Ruhr was traversed from west to east and the Weser crossed in the middle of its course. But, after advancing a little beyond the Weser, the army returned to its point of departure, taking hostages with it. However, and this was a novelty, permanent garrisons were established at Syburg on the Ruhr and at Eresburg further to the east.

These did not, however, prevent a new Saxon counter-attack in 774 when Charlemagne had left for Italy; but in the summer the Frankish king inflicted a victorious retaliation. The Saxons, who even came to Paderborn to make their submission and to receive baptism, were so numerous that in Charles' entourage there was already talk of a general submission. Nevertheless, for greater security, a large zone of military occupation or 'march', intended to hold the enemy at bay, was established between the border of Hesse and the course of the Lippe: another step toward operations on a larger scale, which perhaps were henceforth under serious consideration.

The Saxons, nevertheless, did not accept defeat. In 778, at the summons of one of their most fiery leaders, Widukind, the Westphalians took the offensive. They broke through the western boundaries of the Frankish kingdom, plundered and sacked the right bank of the Rhine from Deutz to Koblenz, went up the valley of the Lahn and then proceeded, in Hesse, to attack Charlemagne's armies in the rear. It took considerable effort to drive them back. In 779 and 780 two punitive expeditions, one in the valleys of the Lippe and the Weser, the other in Eastphalia, where the River Ocker reaches Ohrum, seemed to suffice to restore the previous situation. But in 782 a large Frankish army, crossing Saxon territory to attack the small Slavonic tribe of the Sorbs in south-east Thuringia, was surprised and cut to pieces at the foot of the Süntelgebirge on the eastern bank of the Weser. Two or three army commanders – the chamberlain Adalgisus and the constable Gailo – and with them four counts "and up to twenty persons belonging to the highest nobility", a semi-official annalist of that period asserts, remained dead on the battlefield; the survivors fled for their lives.

It was a crushing blow; but Charles was fully resolved to answer with a dramatic revenge. He hastened to the scene in person with reinforcements, pushed on towards the enemy, caught up with them and defeated them at Werden, near the confluence of the Weser and the Aller, and proceeded to have 4,500 Saxons who had the misfortune to fall into his hands mercilessly slaughtered. Widukind fled; his companions-in-arms seemed demoralized.

They recovered, nevertheless, and from 783 to 785 fought furiously. Charlemagne, too, was relentless. In 784 he even decided to spend the winter in Saxony in order to be on the spot at the return of good weather. The campaign of 785 started from Paderborn, where the general assembly had been convoked, and destroyed the last strong-holds of resistance. Widukind himself was forced to capitulate and to agree to come shortly afterwards into the heart of Gaul, to Attigny, to take an oath of fidelity there and, with great pomp, to receive baptism with several other Saxon leaders.

In addition to this spectacular conversion, the Frankish king, having learned from his experiences, imposed a series of Draconian measures intended to prevent any possible new defection. An awesome capitulary was promulgated, which aimed at implanting Frankish civilization and the Christian religion in Saxony under the threat of death. The articles of this capitulary are unequalled in harshness:

Whoever enters a church by violence, and by force or by theft takes away any object or sets fire to the building, shall be put to death.

Whoever out of scorn for the Christian religion refuses to respect the holy fast of Lent and at that time eats meat, shall be put to death.

Whoever kills a bishop, priest, or deacon, shall be put to death.

Whoever burns the body of a deceased person and reduces its bones to ashes according to the pagan rite, shall be put to death.

Any unbaptized Saxon who tries to hide among his compatriots and refuses to be baptized, shall be put to death.

Whoever plots with the pagans against the Christians or persists in supporting them in their struggle against the Christians, shall be put to death.

Whoever falls short in the loyalty that he owes to the king, shall be put to death . . . .

Passive obedience to the Frankish king, prohibition of all gatherings and public meetings apart from those which the Frankish counts convoked (Art. 34), baptism and the practice of the Christian religion imposed on the pain of death: never had there been a more brutal method of compelling, at any cost, a country that had been free only a moment ago, to submit to the law of the victor.

Saxony lived for several years under this reign of terror. But its inhabitants were only waiting for an opportunity to shake off the oppression. This opportunity came in the spring of 793. When a detachment of troops coming from Frisia under the command of Count Theoderic crossed Westphalia to catch up with the main body of the royal army in order to undertake an expedition against the Avars, it was cut to pieces by the Saxons on the Weser. This was the signal for the revolt. As a contemporary writes:

> . . . what had already been concealed deep in their hearts for a long time, now burst out into the open. Like the dog who licks up what he has just vomited, the Saxons returned to paganism, betraying God as well as their lord the king, who had nonetheless overwhelmed them with benefits, and they carried along with them the pagan peoples round about . . . . All the churches lying in their territory were destroyed or set on fire; they threw out their bishops and their priests, even laid hands on some of them, killed others, and immersed themselves again in the worship of idols.

Everything had to be begun anew, because the revolt had gained the adherence of the whole of Saxony. Again it was necessary to impose obedience by force of arms and to exact hostages everywhere: more than 7,000 in 795, and a large number again in 796 and 797, when the Frankish army pressed on up to the estuary of the Weser, and from there to Wihmodia. This area, nevertheless, resisted with great tenacity and seems to have remained outside the peace when in 797 most of Saxony could be considered as again subjugated. At this time, realizing the mistake he had made in 785, when he had thought he could subdue the Saxons by using brutal constraint, Charlemagne negotiated an agreement with the Westphalian, Angrarian and Eastphalian leaders which revoked the measures previously enacted. For the punitive regime set up in 785, one based on co-operation was substituted. Saxony was placed under Frankish administration and in principle assimilated to the other territories of the Frankish kingdom; for the constant threat of the death penalty was substituted the normal scale of penalties and fines which in the common law of the Franks sufficed to maintain the public peace; and one article (Art. 9) even declared that no modifications could be made to this scale without the explicit consent of the parties concerned. It was a true edict of pacification, and subsequent events proved that its aim was realized: Westphalians, Angrarians, and Eastphalians henceforth conducted themselves as loyal subjects of the Carolingian king.

The Saxons of the far north, those of Wihmodia and Nordalbingia, still remained to be conquered. That was to be the arduous task of the years 798 to 804. For, during these six years the inhabitants of these regions continued to resist Frankish conquest desperately, massacring royal officials and Christian missionaries, beginning anew the eternal comedy of a feigned submission when the Frankish armies camped in the land, to rise up again in a body and resume the killings as soon as Charlemagne's generals were no longer there. It was no use exacting hostages from these people: this practice did not worry them, nor did it deter them from attacking again.

Charlemagne then decided upon more drastic measures: removing the rebellious populations from their native soil and settling them in small groups in the interior of the Frankish kingdom. He substituted for them everywhere either Franks or other settlers of proven loyalty, and placed among them a number of monks or priests who were to assure Frankish control and the triumph of the Christian religion at one and the same time. Applied in 799 to a first group of inhabitants of Wihmodia, these measures were systematically extended in 804 to a large part, perhaps to the whole, of the native population of that country and Nordalbingia. The instructions were rigorous and Charlemagne supervised their execution in person: Frankish troops traversed the regions that had not submitted and carried off the inhabitants, including the old men, the women and the children; they drove them like herds of cattle to the distant countries that had been assigned to them, where the rebels found themselves scattered among the Frankish population. Then, Franks came from south of the Elbe and Slavs from the other side of that river – the Obodrites, whose aid Charlemagne had been obliged to call on to accomplish this task – arrived to take possession of the vacant territories.

In this way the immense Saxon territory, which for so long had been the source of so much harm to the Frankish kingdom and to Christian civilization, was at last completely subdued. Charlemagne's frontiers were now carried forward to the mouth of the Elbe. On the other side of the river, the Obodrites, up to then obedient to the Frankish king's commands, were given guard-duty against the Danes of Jutland. When, after 808, the Obodrites proved to be too weak to resist the Danes alone, Frankish troops went to reinforce them in the southern part of Nordalbingia, and this military zone temporarily sufficed to protect the Saxon frontiers effectively against surprise attack. The conversion of the country, on the other hand, progressed steadily and with success. This centre of paganism was on the way to extinction and it was with justification that contemporaries praised the brilliant triumph that the Frankish king's tenacity had achieved in these regions.

The subjection of Frisia

North-west of Westphalia, between the estuaries of the Rhine and the Weser, Frisia was inhabited by people very closely related to the Saxons and apparently with the same customs and living conditions. Fiercely independent and inveterate pagans, in spite of efforts made since the seventh century by the Anglo-Saxon missionaries to convert them to the religion of Christ, they had never, except in appearance, been subjected to the Franks before the eighth century. The regions lying to the north-east of the Zuiderzee had proved to be particularly refractory in this respect. Only in 754 St Boniface had died there at Dokkum as a martyr for the faith which he had been preaching with the support of King Pepin; some fifteen years later another missionary from England, Willehad, had resumed the campaign against paganism without any more success.

In the south of the Frisian region, it is true, the conjoined Frankish and Christian causes had made durable progress under Charles Martel and Pepin the Short. The episcopal see established in 695 at Utrecht, in the time of Pepin the Younger, though upset for a moment at the beginning of the eighth century, was restored shortly afterwards, when Charles Martel defeated the Frisian duke, Radbod, and it again became a busy centre of missionary activity into pagan territory and a solid base of operations from where Frankish influence had effectively been able to penetrate as far as the shores of the Zuiderzee.

However, during the first years of Charlemagne's reign, most of Frisia remained for the Franks an uncertain and precarious conquest. In 784 the whole north joined in the revolt of the Saxons; then the plains to the east of the Zuiderzee followed suit. The missionary bishop Liudger, who had established his residence there, was able to flee only just in time in order to avoid the fate of St Boniface.

But this was the Frisians' last attempt to escape Frankish subjugation. In 785, the annihilation of the Saxons forced them to lay down their arms. Bishop Liudger was able to resume his preaching among them and to carry his work of intensive evangelization up to the banks of the Ems and throughout the Frisian archipelago. When it was reduced to a province, Frisia was divided into counties; Frankish officials freely moved about there and, just as in the other parts of the kingdom, its inhabitants were thenceforth obliged to furnish contingents to the royal army each time they were called upon to do so, even for distant expeditions.

It was a long time, certainly, before paganism, which was especially strong in the north and the north-east of the country, could everywhere be rooted out entirely. The so-called *Law of the Frisians*, doubtless no more than a compilation of a private character dating from the beginning of the ninth century, seems to furnish clear proofs of this. We learn from this text, among other things, that in certain regions churches remained very few and far between. Nevertheless, from then on, Christianity was on the whole winning the contest. It was only a question of patience and perseverance: two virtues which Charlemagne's representatives had now learned to practise. As in Saxony, the missionary here proved to be ultimately the surest and most effective auxiliary of Carolingian political power.

The Slavonic peoples of the eastern frontiers

Beyond the frontiers of Saxony, Thuringia, and Bavaria, lay the Slavonic country. Charlemagne's policy does not seem to have aimed at incorporating the various peoples that occupied it into his Empire; he wished only to hold them at a distance, and if possible to place them under his influence.

Wedged between the Baltic Sea and the mountains of Bohemia lived the vanguard of the northern Slavs or Wends. Most important among those who were more or less in contact with the Franks were: the Obodrites, settled in the region lying between the lower Elbe and the Baltic, from the Drava to Warnow; the Wiltzes or Welatabes, more to the east, in the region of Mecklenburg; the Lingones on the right bank of the Elbe between the Havel and the Elbe; and the Sorbs or Sorabes, between the Saale and the Elbe. In the middle, between the Riesengebirge, the Erzgebirge, and the Bohemian Forest, were the Bohemes or Bohemians; south of the Danube, on the right bank of the Enns, the Carinthians who, besides Carinthia, occupied Styria and a part of Austria.

The Carinthians were the most developed, having already entered long ago into the sphere of influence of the duchy of Bavaria, before

that province was incorporated into the Frankish kingdom. From
Salzburg Bishop Virgil – an Irishman by birth who, like all his compatriots was a born missionary – had exerted himself with tireless energy
to make them abjure paganism and had, around 769, succeeded in
winning at least their duke over to the Christian faith. In 772 Tassilo
had by force of arms imposed the recognition of his hegemony on the
Carinthian duke, and the preaching of Christianity continued to spread
throughout the country, not only from Salzburg, thanks to Bishop
Virgil, but also from the monastery founded at Innichen, in Carinthia
itself, in the upper valley of the Drava, in 769 or 770.

By taking possession of the Bavarian duchy Charlemagne at the
same time took over its influence on the country of the Carinthians.
The missions there continued their work. Virgil's successor in the see
of Salzburg, Bishop Arn, a close friend of Alcuin, for whom Charlemagne obtained the pallium and the dignity of archbishop of Bavaria
from Pope Leo III, received from the Frankish king that same year
instructions to go in person to Carinthia to stimulate the preaching of
the Gospel there, to organize the practice of worship, to ordain priests
and to consecrate churches.

This country was henceforth considered as a dependency of Bavaria
and shared its fate, just as though it had in fact been incorporated into
the Frankish kingdom. When, at the beginning of the reign of Louis the
Pious, a partition of the Empire between the emperor's sons was drawn
up, Carinthia was officially assigned to one of them.

For the northern Slavs the situation was different. Those settled to
the east of Saxony came into contact with the Franks only after the
Frankish armies had ventured to advance deep into Saxon territory and
had reached the banks of the Elbe. It was in 780 that the Frankish
annalists alluded to them for the first time and reported the conversion
of several groups of Slavs living on the right bank of the river. But
conversions of this kind remained exceptional: Charlemagne contented
himself with political submission.

Most eager for this and generally most tractable were the Obodrites,
who seem to have been rather a weak people. In 780, having been
exposed to attacks by the Saxons, Danes and Wiltzes, they sought the
aid of the Frankish king. After his first military victory in Saxony in 785
they placed themselves resolutely under his protection. In exchange
for this Charlemagne helped them in 789 to repulse the Wiltzes. After
the revolt of Saxony in 793 they fought dedicatedly on the Frankish

side in the struggle against a common enemy. In 795 their duke was killed on one of these campaigns. In 798 they inflicted a bloody defeat on the Nordalbingians and we learn that on this occasion some of their troops were commanded by a 'legate' of the Frankish king. It was moreover to the Frankish king that, at the conclusion of the campaign, the hostages demanded from the conquered as pledges of their obedience were sent: manifest proof that, on the battlefield, the Obodrites had merely been an instrument of Charlemagne's policy.

Between them and Charlemagne there was complete co-operation. In 804 it was to them that, after the final submission of Nordalbingia, the land, cleared of its inhabitants, was entrusted. Their duke from then on, as though he were no more than a federate, assumed guard duty at the frontier of the Carolingian Empire against the hostile Danes. A harsh task. In 808 he could no longer withstand the pressure and fled, leaving his people behind in confusion; another Obodrite chief, perhaps his rival, was captured by the Danes and hanged; the duke himself, several months later, fell by the dagger of an assassin. To save the situation, Frankish troops were obliged to hasten to Nordalbingia and, as we have seen, settle down to stay, at least at the most seriously threatened points.

In these circumstances the Obodrites ultimately fell under Frankish domination. Charlemagne intervened in their country as though he were their ruler; he arranged the choosing of their next duke; the negotiations with the Danes to re-establish peace were conducted by his representatives, and this peace was concluded and sworn to in 810 and 811 apparently without the Obodrites themselves having any say in the matter. It should be noted, however, that nothing has come down to us about either the conversion of their duke or the evangelization of their country. For the time being, the only aim was make a protectorate of it.

Further to the south the Lingones and their neighbouring Slavonic groups were kept at a distance. In 808, to punish them for their aid to the Danes against the Obodrites, an expedition was sent out against them under the command of Charles, the son of Charlemagne. It was by no means a mere parade. The Frankish annalists confess that there was a brisk engagement and that Charles' army suffered considerable losses. Having learned from experience, however, the Frankish king seized a firm foothold on the right bank of the Elbe, where he built well-fortified bridgeheads and installed permanent garrisons. This did not prevent his having to return in 811 to drive back the Lingones who, although apparently not very numerous, nevertheless for many years continued to oblige the Carolingian government to maintain constant surveillance.

The Wiltzes, although further away, gave the Franks more trouble because they were larger in number and of a restless disposition. Settled behind the Obodrites, they incessantly harassed them. In 789 Charlemagne himself led a great expedition against them. Beside Franks, his army comprised Saxons, Frisians and Obodrites. His progress was irresistible and he was able to advance very far towards the east. The Wiltzes were compelled to submit and to give hostages as pledges of their loyalty. During twenty years they remained quiet, or at least the Franks had nothing in particular with which to reproach them. But in 808 we find them on the side of the Danes, joining in the hostilities against the Obodrites. This brought down an invasion on them in their turn in 809: once more their country was burned and plundered. In 810, by way of revenge, they destroyed one of the small forts established by the Franks on the right bank of the Elbe. Finally in 812 a new campaign put them in their place: following a tactic familiar to Charlemagne which we have already seen applied in Bavaria, three armies were sent from three different points against the Wiltzes and closed in on them like a vice. They could only surrender, make their submission, and, as always, give hostages. But this time the subjection turned out to be permanent. Having thenceforth in their turn entered the sphere of Frankish influence, the Wiltzes proved to be docile allies. We see them appearing at imperial assemblies under Louis the Pious and even in 823 referring to the Frankish emperor the arbitration of a dispute that had arisen among them concerning the attribution of the royal or ducal crown. But for them no more than for the Obodrites or Lingones, was there any question of a conversion to the Christian faith.

The Sorbs or Sorabes were, at the end of the eighth century, much more troublesome for the Franks than the Wiltzes because they were concentrated along the frontiers of Saxony and Thuringia. In 782 their forays into Frankish territory had taken on such proportions that Charlemagne ordered a sizeable expedition to be sent out against them. The command was given to three generals who allowed themselves be surprised in the course of the march by the rebellious Saxons and who were finally crushed in the battle of the Süntelgebirge. For many years thereafter nothing was undertaken against the Sorbs. Only in 806 was there again question of a campaign into their country. It was a short but decisive campaign, apparently entrusted to Charles, Charlemagne's eldest son. The duke of the Sorbs, or one of their dukes, was killed, the country was laid waste, and bridgeheads were established on the right bank of the Saale to hold the enemy at a distance. The Sorbs did try again to free themselves from Frankish domination shortly after Charlemagne's death – in 816 – but they were easily brought to heel, and we see them later coming meekly to receive their orders at the Frankish court.

The Czechs, or Bohemes as they were more usually called (*Behiemi* or *Beeheimi*), had lived for a long time without any contact with the Franks. At the beginning of the ninth century this situation changed. Settled as they now were in Bavaria and encouraged, as we have seen, to develop an interest in the lands of the middle Danube on the occasion of their penetration into Avar territory, this new group of Slavs now forced itself on the attention of the Franks. In 805 a great offensive was directed against them, again under the command of Charles, the eldest son of the emperor. As with the conquest of Bavaria in 787 and of the Wiltzes in 812, three invading armies converged upon the country simultaneously: one coming from the west, through the Bohemian Forest, under the direct command of the young Charles; another coming from the south-west, and composed mostly of Bavarians; the last coming from the north via the Erzgebirge, and consisting of Saxon and perhaps Slavonic contingents. The three armies advanced up to the banks of the Eger, where they united; then, in concert, they laid waste the plain of the Elbe. The duke of the Bohemes was killed in battle and to escape annihilation his troops were forced to withdraw into the mountains.

What happened next is not clear. There is mention of a new Frankish army arriving from Saxony via the Elbe to reinforce the first one. We may deduce from this that the subjugation of the country had turned out to be more difficult than had initially been expected. It was evidently necessary to return the following year, in 806, with fresh troops; about this we hear only that "after devastating a very large part of the country, they returned without suffering serious losses", an implicit confession of a discouraging result. Bohemia had, nonetheless, come under Frankish influence to some degree, because in 817 Louis the Pious mentioned it among the territories reserved to his son Louis, the future Louis the German, in the partition to be made after his death; and in 822 the Bohemes performed an act of deference toward the Carolingian emperor by sending him envoys and gifts at the time of a general assembly held at Frankfurt. This was far from real submission, however; and no one had yet thought of converting them.

In sum, except for the Carinthians, who had already been half-gained for Christian civilization by the Bavarians, Charlemagne was content to make those Slavonic peoples with whom the Franks were henceforth called upon to live in contact into neighbours respectful of the Carolingian military power, but to reserve their conversion for later. Doubtless it was possible at the end of the eighth century to think for a moment of extending without delay the evangelization undertaken with so much zeal and success in the Germanic countries to all the Slavonic peoples: Alcuin's correspondence shows traces of this concern; but, having learned from the formidable experience of Saxony, Charlemagne wisely limited himself to furthering the task undertaken among the Carinthians at the time of Tassilo and postponed the rest until more propitious times.

The submission of the Avars

Far bolder was the strategy used with the Avar people. The Avars had come from central Asia and, after many tribulations, had settled in the middle of the Danube valley, from the Tisza to the borders of Carinthia. Their frontiers were uncertain, however, because they continued to carry out their pillaging forays in all directions at the expense of the Balkan, as well as of the western European countries. Their chief, who continued to bear the Asiatic title 'khaghan', was in the first place the military leader, under whose command they set out to plunder far-away places. The treasures accumulated in this way were hoarded in a fortified enclosure which, following the example of their ancestors, they had built in an inaccessible place and which constituted as it were the nucleus of their defense. Westerners spoke of this with a Germanic term, as their *ring* or 'circle'. The evidence seems to indicate that this *ring*, at the end of the eighth century, was established between the Tisza and the Danube, in the same area where formerly Attila had ruled his Huns, with whom the Franks often confused the Avars, calling them without distinction Avars or Huns.

At the end of the eighth century they still constituted a serious danger. From 787 onward their diplomacy was behind the treachery of Duke Tassilo of Bavaria, who is explicitly accused of having an understanding with them. In 788, at the time of the trial at Ingelheim, their attacks multiplied, doubtless with the aim of loosening Charlemagne's hold on Bavaria. The frontiers of this province and that of Friuli were aimed at in turn, but on both Charlemagne retaliated vigorously. On the borders of Friuli the Avars were put to flight in 788; in the same year, further north, on the Bavarian frontier, they were twice driven back towards the east, within a few weeks, by the Frankish troops, who crossed the Enns and drove them out of the region of the Ips on the Danube.

These engagements, however, still aimed at nothing more than the protection of the frontiers. In October Charlemagne came to Regensburg to make the appropriate arrangements to assure its defense. In 790 he negotiated with the enemy for a *modus vivendi*; but the negotiations miscarried, and the barbarian incursions were resumed so extensively that the Frankish king was finally obliged in the summer of 791 to carry the war onto Avar soil. The total strength of the army that was assembled was very great and, following the precedent of the campaign conducted in Bavaria four years earlier, it was divided into three invading bodies marching from three different directions to converge at one point: one, composed of Franks, Saxons, Frisians and Thuringians, passed through Bohemia in the direction of the left bank of the Danube; another, composed of Franks, Alemans and Bavarians, advanced from Bavaria along the right bank of the Danube under the personal command of Charlemagne, and was supplied with provisions by river; the third army marched up from Italy. Pressing on east, the first two armies succeeded in defeating the Avars in the very heart of Pannonia. At the beginning of September the results obtained were such that, just as he had hoped, Charlemagne sent "to his precious and beloved wife, the queen Fastrada" a letter that was full of joy and confidence. The rest of the campaign went as expected: Charlemagne reached the Raab, then crossed the river, and marched along its right bank as far as its confluence with the Danube. The country passed through was burned and looted, and the Frankish king acquired numerous prisoners and a great deal of booty.

From Bavaria, where he had taken up position, Charlemagne at once made preparations for a second campaign into enemy territory. But he was twice obliged to postpone the execution of his plan: in 792 because he was tied to the spot by the discovery of a large-scale conspiracy which he had to repress; and in 793 because at the last moment, when the troops were being mustered for the invasion, he was faced with the great revolt of Saxony which we mentioned above and which was to keep him busy for a long time. Nevertheless, while waiting for an opportunity to strike the decisive blow, he availed himself of diplomatic means and, in 795, having succeeded in allying himself with one of the Avar chiefs, he sent a small army from northern Italy as an advance guard into Pannonia. Its success surpassed all expectations: the famous *ring* fell into the hands of the attackers, who were too few, however, to take full advantage of their victory, but came back loaded with a booty that dazzled the entourage of the Frankish king. At the command of Charles, a chorus of thanksgiving to Heaven rose up throughout the kingdom; he did not forget to set aside for the churches, for St Peter's at Rome first of all, and for the Sovereign Pontiff himself, part of these riches seized at sword's point.

Meanwhile, the Frankish king decided in 796 to complete the conquest of the treasures amassed in the *ring* with appropriate means, while at the same time continuing to negotiate with those of the Avar chiefs whose loyalty to the khaghan seemed loosest. One of them even came to Aachen with a large following to receive baptism, Charles standing as his godfather. Finally, in the course of the summer of 796, a powerful army was sent towards the Danube under the command of the king of Italy, Pepin. Crossing the river, this army threw the Avars into confusion on the other side of the Tisza and proceeded, in its turn, to camp in the *ring*, which was then emptied of all it contained, a feat that caused contemporaries to marvel greatly and to extol in prose and in verse the brilliance of such a victory.

The Avars were never to recover from this blow. Undermined by discord, these people, who had so long caused the world to tremble, were now an easy prey for their powerful neighbour to the West. The first conversions had even raised expectations that they would allow themselves to be won over easily to Christian civilization if it could be introduced to them without the drastic methods used with the Saxons. Alcuin, who was then an adviser much listened to in religious matters, continued on the whole to encourage the hopes of those in Charlemagne's entourage who believed in the success of a rapid evangelization, and, tirelessly, to advise prudence. First preach, he repeated, then baptize; don't drive the pagans to the baptismal font at sword's point; proceed by steps: be flexible at first about details and above all postpone till later material obligations such as the payment of the tithe, which had very unnecessarily driven the Saxons to exasperation and contributed to making Christianity unbearable for them.

This was wise counsel, henceforth carefully followed. In the summer of 796 we even see the leader of the expeditionary force, King Pepin of Italy, holding in his camp in the conquered country a kind of war council composed of the bishops who had accompanied the armies or had come to join them there, and drawing up with them rules to follow in the evangelization of the Avars. Putting forward Alcuin's observations as though they were his own, the patriarch of Aquileia, Paulinus, pleaded in his written advice for prudence, more than ever necessary according to him, when one has to do with a "barbarian people, inaccessible to reason; ignorant, illiterate, narrow-minded, slow to accept the holy mysteries" (*gens bruta et inrationabilis vel certe idiota et sine literis, tardior atque laboriosa ad cognoscenda sacra mysteria*). "For a people like this, not familiar with the language of the Holy Scriptures," he adds,

... it is not advisable to confer the sacrament of baptism as quickly as is the normal custom; it is necessary first to implant faith in them, by arranging a certain time of respite, for the Lord has said to his disciples: 'Go and preach to all peoples, baptizing them in the name of the Father, the Son and the Holy Ghost, and teaching them to observe all that I have commanded you' . . . . He did not say to them: 'Go and baptize all peoples'–but first: 'Preach,' and only thereafter: 'Baptize'.

The technique of religious conquest, if one may call it that, was then adjusted to fit the situation; and it was successful, since from this time onward large numbers of Avars were converted. The assimilation of the country, nevertheless, met with some resistance. In 799 a revolt broke out against the Frankish overlordship, and two of Charlemagne's best officials, Eric, the duke of Friuli, and Count Gerold, prefect of Bavaria, were killed; in 802 two counts of Bavaria perished in similar circumstances. But a few military demonstrations, particularly in 803, sufficed to restore order. And imperceptibly the Avars, while preserving an autonomous government, sank to the status of a vassal people. In 805 the power of their khaghan was apparently reduced to such a point that he asked Charlemagne to give him, as a favour, territories less exposed to Slav attacks than his own, and he was only too happy

when the Frankish king granted him 'Upper Pannonia', which seems to
have been the region immediately bordering on Bavaria. That same
year, as a token of gratitude, he embraced the Christian faith and did
homage to the emperor, who from then on became his official protector. Charlemagne was even obliged to send him some relief troops in
811 to rescue him from a new menace of the Slavs – and the khaghan
went to the palace of Aachen to thank him. The supreme chief of the
Avars coming to Aachen as a deferential vassal to pay his court to the
Carolingian emperor! Times had certainly changed.

The Moslems of Spain

At the other end of the Frankish kingdom, the safety of Gaul itself
required the overcoming of other 'pagans' whom the Christian West
held to be just as barbarous and as dangerous as the Slavs and Avars:
the Moslems of Spain, with whom under the name of Moors or
Saracens Gaul had become all too well acquainted in the time of
Charles Martel.

Since the middle of the eighth century, Spain had in fact been
detached from the caliphate, which the Abbasids had transferred to
Baghdad. Having escaped almost by a miracle from the systematic
massacre of the members of his family, an Umayyad prince had taken
over the government at Cordoba in 756; but his authority was contested even in the peninsula itself. An excellent opportunity, it may
have appeared, for the Franks to cross the Pyrenees and make an end
to the rule of the infidel in Europe.

In 778 Charlemagne allowed himself to be tempted by the more or
less sincere promises of the governor of Barcelona, Suleiman ibn
al-Arabi, who was in rebellion against the emir Abd ar-Rahman, and
thought he would be able to seize the whole northern region down to
the Ebro in one campaign. Two armies, one of which was under his
direct command, crossed the Pyrenees by two different routes, then
marched across Pamplona heading for Saragossa; but they failed to
accomplish anything and the expedition ended in disaster. Called to the
north by a revolt of the Saxons, Charles was suddenly forced to beat a
retreat without even having been able to take Saragossa. He avenged
himself by destroying Pamplona on his return march; but, as he passed

through the Pyrenees at the gorge of Roncevaux, his rearguard was surprised and cut to pieces by the Basques on 15 August 778.

This was a distressing incident, originally concealed by the annalists, who at first never mentioned it and later confessed to it in discreet terms. We know what use legend was to make of it later. Several of the army's best generals, among whom the king's seneschal, the count palatine, and Count Roland, prefect of the guard on the Breton border, fell under the enemy's blows. At the beginning of the ninth century the author of the later section of the *Royal Annals* no longer concealed the fact that it had caused Charlemagne profound "grief" which, he observes "obscured in his heart a large part of the successes obtained in Spain".

These successes, if one may call them so, had in fact been only temporary ones. The painful retreat at Roncevaux was perhaps even followed by a counter-offensive of Abd ar-Rahman into Gascony and Cerdagne. But Charlemagne was not one to accept defeat. Renouncing only the large-scale plans which in 778 had seemed feasible, he limited himself henceforth to a slow and methodical advance towards Catalonia and the lower Ebro, with the evident intention of setting up a defensive 'march' in enemy territory in this area, which was most exposed to Moslem incursions. In 785 his troops took Gerona in the northernmost part of Catalonia; in 790 they advanced along the coast. The enemy retaliated in 793 and crossed the Pyrenees. Without warning they went on to set the suburbs of Narbonne on fire and even sent an advance guard into Rouergue. A bloody battle took place on the River Orbieu, between Narbonne and Carcassonne; after which the Moslems finally retired south of the Pyrenees.

To prevent further surprises, the Frankish troops were reinforced in 795 around Gerona, at Cardona, Vich, and Casseres, from where they in their turn established a few outposts to the south. At the same time negotiations were actively pursued with the Christian king of Galicia and with Moslem rulers or officials ready to intrigue against the emir of Cordoba. In this way the Franks allowed themselves to be invited to the Balearic Islands in 799. In the same year Huesca, which Charlemagne's son Louis the Pious, king of Aquitaine, had tried in vain to seize with a large army in 797, sent the keys of its gates to Charlemagne as a token of deference. In 801, after two years of siege, Barcelona capitulated and Louis the Pious, hastily sent for, went there to make a solemn entry. In 806 Pamplona also surrendered, and with it all of Navarre. In

811, finally, Tortosa, near the mouth of the Ebro, which had resisted two successive sieges in 809 and 810, opened its gates after a siege of forty days.

The zone lying between the Pyrenees and the Ebro thus ultimately fell piece by piece under the power of the Franks, even though neither Huesca nor Saragossa, notwithstanding repeated offers of submission, could be actually occupied, and even though the Basques, who were obviously unreliable, had attempted in 813 – without success, however – to repeat the assault of Roncevaux against an army returning to Gaul, perhaps by the same route as Roland had taken. But if, to the west, Navarre and the Basque country proved beyond their grasp, Frankish power was more firmly established in the east. Septimania was now freed from the constant menace of Saracen incursions. South of the Pyrenees a broad strip of territories comprising all of Catalonia, with Barcelona as capital, held by military force and forming what was called a 'march' – the 'march of Spain' (*Marca Hispaniae or marca Hispanica*) – protected the Frankish kingdom on the south.

Barcelona, a large city, was henceforth the chief town of a Frankish county, the *pagus* or *comitatus Barcinoniensis*. There resided the principal count of the March, which apparently comprised seven other subordinate counties as well, notably those of Gerona, Ampurias and Urgel. Most of the Moslems had moved away, but in these regions there seem still to have existed many small enclaves of people either Visigoths themselves or bearing the stamp of the Visigothic culture, and the Frankish ruler did not neglect to recruit from them at least a few of his officials. The first count of Barcelona, a certain Bera, was a Goth, and the city's garrison was partly composed of Goths. In this way the transition was skilfully managed and the inhabitants, who had long been Christians, were quickly inclined to rally to their new masters. On the lands deserted by the fleeing Moslems, tenant farmers were induced to settle by the concession of fiscal privileges which, it was hoped, would enlist their firm support for the Carolingian government.

Brittany

At the beginning of the ninth century the Armorican Peninsula, in western Gaul, still remained beyond the reach of Frankish authority.

Its population, a large part of which had come from the other side of
the Channel at the time of the Anglo-Saxon occupation of Roman
'Britain', was in every way very different from its neighbours: the
customs, language and social forms were all different, nor did they have
the same civil and religious institutions.

The Merovingians had never succeeded in subjecting the Bretons,
although several expeditions had attempted to do so in the course of the
sixth century. Beyond the line of the Rivers Vilaine, Ille and Couesnon,
one was outside the Frankish kingdom. On several occasions the
Bretons had been forced to pay tribute; but such an obligation had
never been fulfilled for any length of time, and the Bretons did not
recognize Frankish hegemony except when they could not avoid it. To
keep this very restless people in check it had been necessary to set up a
march or military zone between the Frankish kingdom and their
territory. The administration of this march was entrusted, as in all
cases of this kind, to one of the counts of the region, specially
'appointed' (*praefectus*) to this charge. The famous Count Roland, the
unfortunate hero of Roncevaux, had been one of these. Since his death
in 778 new revolts had occurred along the border. In 786 Charlemagne
was obliged to send an army against the Bretons under the command of
his seneschal Audulf. Pursued across moors and marshes, hunted into
their fortresses, they were forced to admit defeat and to hand over
some of their notables as hostages. Charlemagne had them taken to
Worms, on the Rhine, where he held his general assembly that year.

Could the Breton problem henceforth be considered solved? In no
wise. At the very most this could be seen as a temporary *modus
vivendi*, which assumed that the Bretons would from then on abstain
from harassing the Frankish borders. But the Breton frontier was more
firmly organized than ever. At the end of 789 or at the beginning of 790,
Charles the Younger, eldest son of Charlemagne, received, together
with the royal crown, the government of the western territories
between the Loire and the Seine. The 'march of Brittany' (*marca
Brittaniae* or *marca Brittannica*, or even, in classical Latin, *limes
Britannicus*) was part of it, just as shortly afterwards the 'march of
Spain' belonged to the kingdom of Aquitaine, which constituted the
share of Louis the Pious, another son of Charlemagne.

In the last years of the eighth century this 'march of Brittany' was
ruled by a count named Guy, an eminent member of one of the greatest
families of the Moselle region, for whom Alcuin, who dedicated one of

his works to him, cherished feelings of particular respect and intense affection. This was the trusted agent who, along with the other counties placed under his command, was charged in 799 with the task of finally forcing the Bretons to acknowledge Frankish hegemony. The campaign took place in the customary manner, that is to say the country was invaded and pillaged; but its purpose was extended, for not only was respect for the Frankish frontiers demanded, but total submission was required. The Breton chiefs or *machtiern* were deprived of their arms, the complete list of their names, carefully recorded in writing, was sent to Charlemagne, and they were henceforth held responsible for the obedience of their 'province'. This, "all of it", added the contemporary semi-official annalist, "was subjected to the authority of the Franks – something that had never before been witnessed".

We have no further information about this event, of which the annalist is obviously proud. Brittany at last conquered and subdued! A brilliant success, on the face of it, but the annalist does not say a word about any measures drawn up at the Frankish court to consolidate the situation. Were the tribal chiefs, just as in the other conquered countries, to be replaced by Frankish counts? Were the Bretons to be subjected to the type of ecclesiastical discipline and church life current in the other provinces of the kingdom, while up to then they had lived under the in every respect very different kind of regime customary in the Celtic lands such as Ireland? There was hardly time for any decisions about this because it was necessary at once to abandon any such plans. Several years later, a reviser who had taken over the role of semi-official annalist, altered the sentence we have just cited, substituting the following passage: "It seemed as though the province was entirely subjected; and it would have been thus if the fickleness of this treacherous people had not led them, as is their habit, to a prompt repudiation." The Bretons had in fact submitted only in appearance. In 811 Charlemagne's government, tired of being flouted by these 'rebels', was forced to send a new army against them which achieved, so the annalist assures us, some new 'successes'. But the successes of 811 were no more decisive than the preceding ones; during the reign of Louis the Pious, it was found necessary to conduct several other campaigns against the Bretons, without there being any question of the incorporation of their country into the Frankish kingdom, nor even of a durable subjugation.

The only positive result in this area was indeed the organization or re-organization – perhaps the consolidation – of a 'march'; placed under the authority of one of the most eminent counts of the kingdom, which seemed at least to eliminate the possibility of another surprise attack, and which constituted a first step towards systematic penetration into the interior of the Breton country.

The defence of the maritime frontiers

In addition to the reinforcement of his land frontiers, Charlemagne had to make arrangements for the defense of the maritime frontiers. It was not only the privateering of the Moslems on the Mediterranean coasts which caused him anxiety; other pirates began to be heard of in the north and even along the Atlantic shores: the Danes, whose aggressive spirit we have already seen on the continent along the borders of Saxony.

There, from the beginning of his reign onward, Charlemagne came into conflict with them. In 782 it was in their country that Widukind found refuge. Later, the Danes were constantly found to be in collusion with the Frankish king's enemies in the region of the Elbe, and they attacked the Obodrites, his allies. At the end of 799 or the beginning of 800 they were sighted for the first time off the coast of Gaul. This however, was not their first attempt on the West; for some time before then the English coasts had been visited by them or their Norwegian rivals. The two were at first not distinguished by contemporaries, who called them without distinction 'Northmen', *Northmanni*. In Aquitaine a band of these Nordic pirates suddenly disembarked and pillaged the country. The alert was given and 150 of them were slaughtered on the shore. Informed at once, Charlemagne went in March 800 to inspect the Atlantic and Channel coast defenses and organized coastguard squadrons for the defense of the seaboard. The king of Denmark, Godfrey, proved to be aggressive: while negotiating with Charlemagne he simultaneously sent ships to cruise along the coast in the neighbourhood of the Elbe, so that from 808 onwards the king of the Franks was led to set up gradually, north of the river, a system of advance defenses that constituted a new march, the 'march of the Northmen' (*marca Northmannica* or *limes Northmannicus*) on the borders of Scandinavia (*Northmannia*).

In the spring of 810 Charlemagne was occupied in preparing an invasion of Denmark when, at the beginning of June, it was learned at the court of Aachen that a fleet of some two hundred ships from Scandinavia had laid waste the Frisian archipelago, set troops ashore in Frisia, and thrice defeated the hastily mobilized inhabitants. After this, Godfrey had imposed a heavy tribute upon the conquered, of which a hundred pounds of silver had to be paid at once; the Danish king had then put to sea and had been able to get back to his country unobstructed, perhaps with the intention of soon repeating an excursion as profitable as it was easy.

Charlemagne, after this warning, at once gave the order to strengthen the coastal defenses. Ships were brought together at Boulogne-sur-mer and at Ghent on the Scheldt; a capitulary of 810, in an article of which unfortunately only the summary is preserved, orders the requisition or at least the collection of all the materials necessary for the construction of ships. The emperor's son, Louis the Pious, perhaps also received the order to take similar measures in Aquitaine, and on the Mediterranean side of Languedoc, where Moslem piracy presented the Carolingian government with similar problems. In 811 the emperor went in person to visit the port at Boulogne, to inspect the fleet and cause the lighthouse, which had been built in Roman times, to be restored and then put back in service. A new capitulary promulgated in October of that year on the occasion of his visit to the town, reminded everyone of the military duties which they were expected to perform, particularly the services of watch and ward (*wacta* and *warda*) and added, in a final article, that all lords with bodies of men should hold themselves in readiness to embark at once if the emperor should decide upon a naval expedition.

At this time it was still possible to cherish the vain hope that quiet would return in the North Sea region. King Godfrey of Denmark died in 810; his successor, with whom a first agreement had been concluded, had disappeared the following year, and the Danes, torn apart by a murderous war of succession, wished for peace abroad, or so it seemed. At the end of the summer of 813, an understanding with the Frankish emperor had been drawn up in a pact solemnly sworn to by both parties at the frontier between the two states. But the events of that same year 813 were to convince the Carolingian government that negotiating with the Danish kings would not suffice to make an end to the pirate attacks, if at least we are to believe the statements of an annalist who reports, precisely in that year, a new plundering of Frisia, in which the pirates carried off a great deal of booty and numerous prisoners.

However this may be, it was clear from then on that the means of defense improvised by Charlemagne at the beginning to ensure the protection of the coasts forming the northern, western and southern frontiers of his Empire were insufficient. In the Mediteranean the Carolingian government had Italian or Provençal ships at its disposal, and although the Moors of Spain and Africa, after starting pirate wars in Italy, Corsica and Sardinia, grew so bold as to attack Nice in 813, the Franks were capable of retaliation; in 799, as we have seen, they even ventured to establish themselves in the Balearic Islands. But in the Atlantic, the Channel and the North Sea, their fleet was still in a rudimentary state.

It is impossible to conjecture what programme Charlemagne, if he had lived longer, would have devised to meet these problems, but the few facts which we have noted lead us to think that, no more at sea than on land, would he have remained passive in the face of the growing menace of the Viking and Saracen pirates to his kingdom.

The Frankish kingdom at the end of Charlemagne's reign

Considering only the positive results, Charlemagne's achievement in terms of the territorial completion of the Frankish kingdom and the protection of his frontiers seems to have been substantial. To Gaul – which was itself brought back entirely under his hegemony, except for the Armorican peninsula whose Celtic population remained irreducible and even obdurate – Charlemagne had succeeded in joining the Germanic territories on the far side of the Rhine. One after the other they were integrated into the Frankish unity and henceforth participated in the same political organization and in the same religious faith. As a Christian soldier, Charles had subjected all of them at whatever price to the rules of the life from which he expected salvation; he had caused the culture of which he was proud to be diffused among them; he had accustomed them gradually to a feeling of solidarity against barbarians from without, now kept at a distance, and several of whom had already begun to allow themselves to be won over to the Christian faith.

Along the land frontiers of his kingdom, thus extended, were established a series of outlying 'marches' which protected these frontiers wherever necessary against the danger of the devastating raids from which they formerly had suffered so much, when the Saxons, Frisians and Saracens had penetrated there unobstructed at the least slackening of royal authority. Thus the Frankish kingdom formed a whole, solidly protected on the landward side, whose vulnerability in case of attack from the sea the future alone was to reveal.

This danger, which occupied Charlemagne's attention during the last years of his life, was unfortunately neglected by his successors. Notwithstanding its immense maritime front, the Frankish kingdom remained as it were an inland kingdom. Never did it have at its disposal a fleet capable of resisting the small mobile ships of the Scandinavians; and they, who had already had the opportunity of noticing this extraordinary omission, were not slow to take advantage of it when, after Charlemagne, the Carolingian Empire sank into discord and anarchy.

CHAPTER FOUR

The annexation of the Lombard kingdom

Whether or not he wished to do so, Charlemagne could not limit his activities to the territories that constituted the Frankish monarchy's natural zone of expansion. Italy, where its fortunes since Pepin the Short had been bound up with those of the papacy, inevitably demanded attention, and whether he liked it or not it occupied a principal place in his policies.

Desiderius' ventures and the pope's new appeal to the Franks

The Lombard throne had been occupied since 756, as the reader will remember, by Desiderius the ex-duke of Tuscany, whom Pepin had intended to make into an ally of the Frankish monarchy and the Holy See. But it was a precarious alliance at best and its value in practice was demonstrated by an incident that occurred even before Pepin died. In July 768 Desiderius was very unwisely invited by two high officials of the curia, the *primicerius* of the notaries, Christopher and his son the *secundicerius*, Sergius, to help expel a usurper pope, Constantine II, who by a surprise manoeuvre had been irregularly installed the previous year as Paul I's successor. Desiderius had taken advantage of the occasion to attempt the installation of one of his candidates on the throne of St Peter, the priest Philip who, notwithstanding the intervention of a group of Lombard soldiers, had been able to maintain himself for only one day. But this missed opportunity would not be forgotten and Pope Stephen III, elected on 1 August 768 in place of Philip, had good reason to distrust such a treacherous 'ally'. The rumour even

circulated in the Lateran that a certain priest by the name of Waldipert, who in the affair of Pope Philip had been the Lombard king's
instrument, had conceived the plan of assassinating the *primicerius*
Christopher and several other persons of distinction and then handing
Rome over to his master's army.

No doubt this was but one of the many false rumours that frequently
circulated in Rome at that time; perhaps it was even pure invention,
intended to justify the odious revenge which, a few days after his
anointing, Stephen III and his partisans inflicted on Waldipert, having
him tortured horribly and then murdered by an employee of the papal
palace. We can understand, however, the new pope's discomfiture at
the news that, on the suggestion of their mother Bertrada, the two
young successors of Pepin the Short – who had died in the meanwhile
on 24 September 768 – were since their accession exerting themselves
to strengthen their alliance with the Lombard king by means of
marriages that seemed to entail considerable obligations in the future.
Their sister Gisela, when of marriageable age, was to marry a son of
King Desiderius, and Charles himself was to take to wife in 770,
without waiting any longer, one of the daughters of this same king. On
the Frankish side, doubtless, the hope was cherished that Desiderius
could be induced to settle down, and Queen Bertrada had the naivety
to negotiate with him as well about the last 'restitutions' to which he
had pledged himself when Pepin was still alive. But the Sovereign
Pontiff became indignant, called it treachery, and denounced the work
of "the devil" himself in these marriages, because, as he wrote, the
descendants of "the illustrious race of the Franks" could not, without
repudiating themselves, unite themselves to these sons "of pagans", to
this "fetid race of Lombards", fit at best to "beget lepers"!

As for Desiderius, he did not lose courage at the miscarriage of his
first attempt to seize control of the papacy. In 771 under the pretence
of coming to pray at the tomb of the Prince of the Apostles and to
discuss some 'restitutions' with Stephen III, he entered St Peter's
Church with a detachment of soldiers, seized the *primicerius* Christopher and his son the *secundicerius* Sergius and had their eyes put out.
Henceforth he held the pope in his power, all the more easily since the
primicerius Christopher, actual ruler of the Lateran, soon died of his
wounds. This time Desiderius seemed at last assured of success, when
Stephen III, who had died at the end of January 772, was immediately

succeeded by an energetic pontiff, a scion of an old Roman family, the deacon Hadrian. This event caused great discomfiture to the Lombard party, represented by the *cubicularius* Paul Afiarta in the very bosom of the curia.

Without leaving Desiderius and his adherents time to strike again, the new pope, who assumed the name Hadrian I, in his first act recalled from exile and extracted from their prisons the still surviving victims of the conspiracy of 771 and then prepared himself to fight. Desiderius' treachery was obvious to everyone: at the very moment it was learned that he had just captured, by surprise, Faenza, Ferrara, and Comacchio, and besieged Ravenna (March–April 772), he pretended that he wanted to take up the discussions again about the pending 'restitutions' and cynically avowed his unalterable desire for an agreement.

For the Franks the moment had come to take sides. Charlemagne seems to have made his decision at the beginning of 772 or somewhat later, because everything points to his having repudiated the daughter of the Lombard king at the end of April of this year and having also broken with him. In his turn Desiderius, hoping to make an intervention beyond the Alps impossible for Charlemagne, prepared a coup-d'état in the Frankish kingdom in favour of the young sons of Carloman, who had fled to his court with their mother. He tried to have them anointed by the Sovereign Pontiff, while at the same time he prepared to place the pope under his protection, having calmed his suspicions by sham negotiations. But how could Hadrian allow himself to be fooled by this manoeuvre when, to the unceasing requests for evacuation of the territories stipulated by the curia, the Lombard king responded by unceasing seizures of provinces or localities that had formerly been evacuated? After the exarchate of Ravenna, Urbino, Montefeltro, Senigallia, in the Pentapolis; it was the turn of Gubbio in Umbria; and finally Otricoli and Viterbo in the northeast and northwest of the 'duchy' of Rome. The danger became so acute that, at St Peter's, Hadrian commanded the bolts of the doors to be reinforced as a precaution, and he warned the Frankish king by sending him via the sea route – the communications by land having been cut off by the Lombards – an especially urgent appeal: was Charles going to leave "the holy Church of God" exposed any longer to the attacks of its enemies? Was he going to delay any longer imitating his father's deed of coming to the rescue of the imperilled papacy? Was he going to allow the Lombard king to keep for himself, unpunished, the cities and provinces he had stolen from St Peter? Notwithstanding the denials of Desiderius, who claimed to have already carried out all the prescribed restitutions, a swift inquiry soon convinced Charlemagne that the complaints formulated by Hadrian were entirely justified and that the Lombard king's growing audacity would become a risk in the near future if he were not checked very quickly; and, having consulted his magnates, he finally decided to act.

The conquest of the Lombard kingdom

The Frankish troops were assembled at Geneva towards the end of the spring of 773; then, after three ultimatums had been sent to Desiderius to evacuate the territories he had conquered and to proceed without further delay to the 'restitutions' that had still to be carried out, Charlemagne gave the order to attack. He had divided his army into two bodies, one of which made its way over the pass of Mont Cenis, while the other came via that of the Great Saint-Bernard, obliging the enemy to retreat hastily to Pavia where, as at the time of Pepin's campaigns, the Lombard king made the mistake of letting himself be surrounded. He did put up a fierce resistance, while his son Adalgisus hastily went to seek refuge at Verona with Carloman's widow and children, where the Frankish king could hardly go to apprehend them. In the Po plain there was everywhere confusion at the approach of the Frankish army which, instead of disbanding as usual at the end of the autumn, waited patiently during eight or nine months alongside the walls of Pavia, letting famine, epidemics and weariness do their work in the city. Finally, at the beginning of June 774, Desiderius was forced to surrender unconditionally.

But the situation now was very different from that after Pepin's campaigns. Instead of the Frankish king having no other care but to fulfil his obligations at the least possible cost as had formerly been the case, Charles' campaign had been conducted with the intention of actually destroying Lombard power. This is the reason why, by an unusual measure, of which, however, Charlemagne's history contains other examples – during the Saxon wars for instance – the king and his army remained for a whole year in enemy country, this being the only effective means of obtaining a decisive result. From Pavia to beyond Verona the Lombard provinces had submitted to the conqueror; and in the provinces where his armies had not yet penetrated, Desiderius' officials had for the most part hastened to offer their submission so that after the fall of Pavia, Charles found himself in fact ruler of every part of the kingdom over which the Lombard king's authority had been directly exercised. As for Adalgisus, he had given up and gone to seek refuge in the Byzantine Empire.

The conclusion was inescapable: Desiderius and his wife were placed in custody and, rather than begin another experience of deception with a new Lombard prince, the Frankish king kept the crown he had seized from Desiderius for himself. In official documents from 5 June 774 on he bore the double title of 'king of the Franks' and 'king of the Lombards' (*rex Francorum et Langobardorum*).

The new 'promise of donation' to the Holy See in 774

To these two titles Charlemagne almost immediately added a third, of which up to then neither he nor his father had thought it prudent to avail himself: that of 'patrician of the Romans' (*patricius Romanorum*), which had been conferred by Pope Stephen II on Pepin and his sons at the time of his journey to France, and this addition is possibly significant, especially when placed alongside certain details of the protocol carried out in Rome during a visit the Frankish king had made there several weeks earlier.

During the siege of Pavia Charles had as a matter of fact expressed the desire to go to the tombs of the Apostles for the feast of Easter, and the reception that the Sovereign Pontiff had given him had been of the same kind, notes the official biographer of Hadrian I, as that formerly reserved "for an exarch or a patrician". It consisted of sending to meet the king at a place called *Ad Novas*, thirty leagues from Rome, a delegation consisting of all the officials of the capital, preceded by banners; the despatch as far as the first milestone of various sections (*scholae*) of the city militia and of the youth of the schools, all carrying palms and olive branches, and singing praises; and finally the placing of crosses at the entrance to the city to greet the distinguished visitor. By the revival of this ceremonial, doubtless arranged in agreement with the person who was its object, the 'patriciate' of the Frankish king, which had up to then remained purely honorary, seemed to have taken on effective value.

Charles was permitted to go into Rome twice to pray there. Having arrived on Holy Saturday (2 April 774) at St Peter's, on the right bank of the Tiber, he had gone the same day, with his retinue and in the company of Hadrian I, to hear mass inside the city, at the church of St John Lateran. The following day, Easter Sunday, a delegation of city officials and soldiers had come with great pomp to find him in his camp, close to St Peter's, and escort him again into the city to the church of Santa Maria Maggiore from where, after the mass, the pope had taken him for lunch in the Lateran Palace. All these marks of honour were nevertheless accompanied by numerous precautions. Before letting him enter the capital the pope had exacted from his guest the formal pledge that he would not abuse this token of trust, and per contra Charlemagne had exacted from Hadrian the pledge to provide for his safety. But why, if there was so much mutual distrust, all the ceremonies and the spectacular gestures?

It was because in reality, as they both saw it, the time had come to clarify a situation that threatened to become extremely complicated. Although Pavia had not yet fallen at the time of their meeting, its impending fall was beyond doubt. But this fall itself would not settle anything if, as in the time of Pepin, no more than half-hearted measures were taken. A preliminary understanding thus seemed necessary between the Frankish king and the Sovereign Pontiff if painful discussions after the event were to be avoided; and, on the other hand, Pavia's long-lasting defence inclined Charlemagne to prudence. He had too many matters on his hands, in any case, to be able to neglect the support that papal diplomacy might bring him in Italy – a diplomacy that was more active than ever since Hadrian occupied the throne of St Peter. Because of its incessant activity in Lombard circles, especially in the provinces around Rome, the papacy was a force that had to be reckoned with.

Its most recent successes especially gave cause for reflection. In the course of the summer of 773 Spoleto had betrayed the Lombard cause and gone over to the pope. Before the end of that year the whole Spoletan duchy recognized papal supremacy and Hadrian I installed the new duke whom the inhabitants had more or less freely chosen. In fact it could henceforth be expected that, without communications with north Italy, the duchy of Benevento, also under great pressure from papal emissaries, would follow this example. These were facts which a realist like Charlemagne had to take into account. Once more political necessity induced the papacy and the Frankish monarchy to clarify their respective positions, and the reception given to 'the patrician of the Romans' was but the prelude to important conversations concerning the future status of Italy. Indeed, after having met Charles again on Easter Monday at St Peter's – where in the course of divine service prayers of thanks were intoned in honour of "the most excellent king of the Franks, patrician of the Romans" – and after having again celebrated mass in his presence the next day in St Paul's 'outside the walls', we see Hadrian seeking out Charlemagne on Wednesday 6 April, in the sacristy of St Peter, and concluding with him a general agreement, of whose terms we unfortunately know very little. Indeed the only clauses preserved – in the form of an abstract of dubious authenticity – are those which were to the advantage of the papacy. The king, writes the official biographer of Pope Hadrian, "having had read to him again the promise which had been made in France, at Quierzy" by his father, King Pepin, confirmed its provisions; then "of his own accord and quite voluntarily he commanded Ithier, his chaplain and notary, to draw up another promise of donation on the model of the preceding one". It was thus the 'promise' of 754, not the actual donation of 756, which, if the account of the papal biographer may be believed, the document of 774 was supposed to confirm and replace.

The Frankish king, the papal biographer continues, "ceded, in it, to St Peter the same cities and territories and promised to hand them over to the pope up to the boundary line indicated" in Pepin's charter. This boundary line, according to the biographer, was the following: starting from Luna (near La Spezia), at the mouth of the Magra, whose course it then followed, it crossed the Apennines at the pass of the Cisa, and included Parma, Reggio, Mantua, Monselice, the whole exarchate of Ravenna "according to its ancient boundaries" (that is to say, before the conquests of Liutprand), and finally Venice and Istria. Corsica, and the duchies of Spoleto and Benevento, were likewise included in the list of provinces that the new promise reserved to the Holy See, but the southern boundary was not specified.

The above list, assuming that it did indeed appear in the original text of the *Liber pontificalis*, suffices in any case to prove that the aim envisaged was not to draw a map of the territories that were to be directly accessible to the agents of the Holy See, but only to trace a clear line of demarcation between the zone of papal expansion and that of the Frankish king, in case of a decisive victory of the Franks over the Lombard king; and it is characteristic that, among the provinces reserved to the papacy there are some, like Venice and Istria, which in 774 were still actually under Byzantine hegemony. But the question may be raised whether on this point the text of the biographer of Hadrian has not undergone alterations in the interest of the papacy, and it is to say the least a striking fact that the document of 774, by a disturbing coincidence, is no better preserved than those of 754 and 756.

Whatever the case may be it is possible that our informant, consciously or not, has somewhat modified the terms because, for many a detail, subsequent events, in so far as they can be indisputably verified, do not seem to fit in very well with the precise stipulations he gives us. But it is undoubtedly true that on the papal as well as on the Frankish side, a keen desire existed to delineate well in advance in an official document what would be assigned to each in the division of the Lombard spoils, and in this way to avoid possible complications.

The application of the pact of 774

It was nevertheless inevitable that, once Desiderius had been defeated and his kingdom taken over directly by Charlemagne, the interests of the papacy and those of the Frankish monarchy would find themselves in opposition. To Charles the conquest of the Lombard kingdom doubtless marked the end of a phase: freed of all anxiety about northern Italy he now believed himself to be in a position to concentrate entirely on the affairs of Saxony, which in that period required prompt intervention. For Hadrian, on the contrary, it was the beginning of an era of fulfilment. Through the promise made by the Frankish king he would be able, he thought, to achieve immediate advantages, thereby completing the undertaking begun in the time of Pepin; and for this he indeed counted upon the aid which, according to the statement of his biographer, the Frankish king had led him to expect.

Consequently, Charlemagne had only just taken possession of the Lombard throne when the Sovereign Pontiff requested him to intervene on his behalf. The pope's correspondence again displays an impatience that would make one smile if it did not portend very troublesome misunderstandings in the near future. What now, the pope writes, made the new ruler of Pavia put off seeing to the evacuation of the territories to whose return the Holy See had looked forward for so many years? When he had come to Rome had Charlemagne not declared solemnly that he would not yield to the lure "of gold, precious stones or silver", nor to a vain thirst for glory or conquests, and that his only ambition was, as his father's had been, "to fight to have justice done to St Peter, to complete the glorification of the Holy Church of God, and to increase the safety" of its ruler? But, as soon as the conquest of the northern provinces was complete, Charlemagne had gone back over the Alps: Hadrian almost reproached him with it as a desertion. The archbishop of Ravenna, moreover, tempted by the example, also wished to create a temporal lordship for himself at the expense of the territories of St Peter, and had seized the exarchate and the Pentapolis. The pope complained bitterly of this to Charles:

To what humiliation, contrary to all expectations, is the Roman Church reduced! What a downfall, what a dishonour is it for us when today, while you are alive, we see wretches, impious persons, who are no less your enemies than ours, stealing from us territories which in the time of Lombard power, we ruled ourselves! And look how our enemies begin to humiliate us with words like this: What use has the destruction of the Lombard nation and its submission to the Frankish king been to you? Look! Not only have none of the promises made to you been kept, but even the territories ceded to St Peter by King Pepin of blessed memory are now stolen from you!

The archbishop of Ravenna, however, was not the only one involved. One year after his visit to Rome, Charles himself appeared to some degree to have lost sight of the agreements that bound him to the Sovereign Pontiff. At Spoleto Charlemagne's emissaries did something that justifiably worried the pope: the duke whom Hadrian had invested in 773 seemed to let himself be invited, or at least encouraged, by them to change his obedience and to recognize Carolingian overlordship instead. He was soon, however, to betray the Frankish king, in his turn, in favour of Desiderius' son, Adalgisus, who was secretly operating in Italy. In vain did Hadrian remind Charles in 775 of his solemn promise; Charles did not scruple the next year to enter Venice, camp at Treviso and then take possession of Friuli, whose duke had likewise been involved in the plot in favour of Adalgisus. In the same period the Frankish king also intervened in Istria. Thus, far from helping the

Sovereign Pontiff to realize his hopes, Charles was gradually caught up again in the imbroglio of Italian affairs, and seemed now to be working against papal interests.

But, while taking alarm at these interventions, Hadrian continued to demand others in his own favour. At the beginning of 778 he urged Charles to come and confer with him at Rome. He was surprised, he wrote, to see him so careless about the interests of the Holy See, and would wish him to be less forgetful of the example given by "the pious Constantine of blessed memory", this "great emperor by whose generosity the Holy Roman Church, catholic and apostolic, was elevated and glorified, and who deigned to grant it power in the countries of Hesperia", that is to say, Italy. Vehemently, he denounced the intrigues of the duke of Benevento who, in connivance with the Byzantine patrician of Sicily and several other rather shady persons, was preparing to strike a blow of which the Frankish king would be no less the victim than he himself.

Held up for a long time by other cares, Charles finally came back to Italy. In 780 he went to spend Christmas at Pavia, remained there the whole winter and then in the spring of 781 moved to Rome for Easter. There his second son Pepin was baptised by Hadrian, who also conferred the royal anointing on the child and on his younger brother Louis; while Pepin also received the title 'king of Italy'. We have no details about this sojourn of Charles in the papal city; in particular, we do not know to what degree he displayed the same discretion as in 774, but the attribution of the Lombard crown to Pepin, the setting up, around this child, of a court and of administrative personnel for the purpose of applying Frankish legislation in the peninsula, are proof enough of his having begun to interest himself seriously in Italy.

But, while papal affairs engaged the Frankish king's attention less and less, Hadrian, in the years that followed, continually demanded justice for the Holy See. His complaints aimed not only at the implementation of the promises made in 774, which had already been forgotten; he insisted upon the restitution of simple 'patrimonies' of the Church of Rome, that is to say of landed estates scattered over the whole peninsula by the chance of gifts made by the faithful in the course of centuries. The Carolingian government, which had inherited the results of the Lombard spoliations, displayed a visible lack of eagerness to give these up, so that for each domain it was necessary to engage in endless negotiations, and to collect proofs and witnesses.

The pope finally lost patience and, without for the most part departing from the unctious language that was customary in his chancery, often let his bad temper show through. He even went so far as to castigate the spirit of chicanery in which the agents of the Frankish monarchy executed their charge.

There could no longer be any question of a full application of the programme of 774. Charles, who after he had awarded the throne of Pavia to his son Pepin, continued nevertheless to preside over the fortunes of the Lombard kingdom, intended in any case to reconstitute it in its fullest extent. In 786 he travelled for the third time to Italy, went to celebrate Christmas at Florence, reached Rome, where he stayed for several days, and then invaded the duchy of Benevento where, from Capua at the beginning of 787, he dictated his terms to Duke Arichis, who had fled to ensconce himself in Salerno. The duke was forced, as were his subjects, to take an oath of allegiance to the conqueror and to deliver hostages to him, among whom was his own son Grimoald.

Doubtless the pope gained various territorial advantages from the new Frankish victories. Among these was the cession of Capua, even though Charlemagne had at first had the oath of allegiance sworn to him personally, and though the occupation of the city and its environs, if it was ever effective, had been but temporary. Hadrian obtained at the same time – and this time in fact – a correction of the frontiers north of Roman Tuscia where the Frankish king detached from the Lombard territories, and gave to the pope, the towns of Viterbo, Bagnorea, Toscanella and Soana. To these were added in principle – and in principle only – the already more distant localities of Russellae near Grosseto and Populonia near Piombino. But, whether effectuated or not, these gifts implied the renunciation of the rest. Not a word was said about Tuscany proper, all of which had been included, nonetheless, in the papal zone specified in 774; no more was said either about the territories that were then to round off the exarchate in Emilia as well as north of the Po: neither Modena, Reggio, Mantua, Vicenza, nor Verona, to list only a few, were ever to become part of the Papal State, and one need only glance at the series of official documents produced by Charlemagne's chancery to be convinced that Desiderius' successor had never at any moment even considered relinquishing them.

The Frankish king also kept for himself the sovereignty over Sabinia, notwithstanding the attempts made by the pope to create

confusion in this matter by using the ambiguous term 'territory' for an
old domain or 'patrimony' of his church there, the restitution of which
he ultimately obtained in about 782. And when Hadrian was so bold as
to recall that the whole duchy of Benevento should be handed over to
him, Charles turned a deaf ear. At best the Sovereign Pontiff and his
agents might serve as his informants in these regions, but Charlemagne
did not consider himself in the least bound to follow their advice. Even
when in the summer of 787 there was question of designating a
successor to Duke Arichis, who had just died, Charles set aside the
advice of the pope, who opposed with all his might the choice of
Grimoald, son of the deceased, who had been kept in France for
several months as a hostage. Grimoald's designation by Charles was
accompanied by measures intended to strengthen the Frankish king's
authority in the duchy, but they proved valueless. Grimoald, as
Hadrian had foreseen, at once repudiated his allegiance and conducted
himself as an independent prince. But the papacy gained nothing from
this, since it furnished a pretext for the Frankish armies to intervene on
numerous occasions in this part of Italy, where there was no longer any
question of papal rights.

Charlemagne as ruler of Italy

The transfer of the crown of Pavia to the Frankish king thus had the
consequence of making him the heir of Lombard ambitions. Highly
respectful of the papacy and without initially having wished to retract
in principle any of the gifts granted by his father, and later by himself,
when generosity could easily be practised with another's possessions,
Charlemagne saw things in a different light when he personally guided
the affairs of Italy. Following the example of his Lombard predecessors, he was now inclined to consider the political unity of the
peninsula as an absolute necessity, so much so that it became increasingly difficult for him to satisfy papal demands which were, moreover,
very imprudent, considering the absence of the means to satisfy them.
This was shown by Hadrian's incessant appeals to his ally for aid.

   To maintain a clear demarcation between the territories reserved for
the Sovereign Pontiff and those which Charles had decided to keep
under his direct rule was, moreover, very difficult if not impossible.

The multiplicity and the dispersion of the 'patrimonies' of the Roman Church, the confusion that could so easily arise – as has just been seen in the case of the patrimony in Sabinia – between the most extensive of these and the provinces ceded in full sovereignty to the ruler of the Church, as well as their overlapping, and the obligation which the pope had – seeing the configuration of his states, which cut the peninsula into two almost equal parts – to leave a right of passage over his soil to the agents and even to the armies of the Frankish king – all this created problems which could not be solved unless one of the two powers was in actual practice subordinate to the other in temporal affairs. All the charters in the world – authentic or not – were powerless to resolve the difficulty.

Hadrian soon realized his disadvantage. It is extraordinarily significant to note how this proud pontiff, whose haughty spirit now and then emerges from under the formal humility of the papal style, was reduced after a few years to the role of docile auxiliary to the policy pursued by the Frankish prince. Now and then there were spasms of independence; he protested several times against the encroachments of the king and his agents. Thus in 790 or 791 in a long letter to Charles abounding with ambiguous phrases about his correspondent's devotion to the interests of the Holy See, he ventured to protest against the nonchalant manner in which his judicial prerogatives were being violated, and even dared to write sentences such as the following:

Your royal Excellency has informed me that you yourself do not see any objection to a bishop or count, or any other subject of your territories coming to us, be it upon our summons, be it of his own will; similarly it would not displease our Fatherhood if one or another of our people went to you, be it to greet you, be it to request justice from you. No doubt this is true. But do not be offended if, when your subjects are not allowed to come *ad limina apostolorum* to see us without an authorization from you, our people, when they desire to see you, are similarly constrained to ask us for permission and a letter of authorization. And just as we shall not fail to exhort those of your subjects whom we receive to use all their power to serve you in all purity of heart and with absolute allegiance, we pray your royal wisdom to request those of our subjects who come into your presence to do the same with regard to us.

But what effect could such protestations have in the face of harsh reality? The inevitable occurred. The papacy had given itself, on the soil of Italy in the person of the Frankish king, an encroaching protector, so that the pope's temporal rule though only just established, was threatened by the very person who had created it. In contrast to the Lombard king, who had presented himself to Rome as an enemy, Charles presented himself to Rome as a sincere friend, even as a loyal friend; but Rome and the Papal State as a whole were already in certain regards no more than an extension of the Italy that the new king of Pavia strove to reconstitute. His interventions there became more and more numerous and indiscreet: not only did his agents as we have seen cross through there constantly; not only – witness the letter of 790 or 791 which we have just cited – could the pope's subjects find themselves summoned before Charlemagne or his representatives; but he interfered in many other affairs which were in principle outside his competence. Thus it happened that Hadrian was twice obliged to remind Charlemagne firmly that he had no business intervening in Ravenna in the choice of the archbishop, nor even to have the elections supervised by one of his emissaries. The time was approaching when, once Hadrian had disappeared from the scene, Charles, whose power had continued to grow, would allow himself far more serious usurpations, even up to the banks of the Tiber.

CHAPTER FIVE

Charlemagne becomes emperor

At the end of the eighth century, before all the conquests that he had undertaken had been successfully concluded, Charlemagne emerged as master of the West. Saxony had been conquered; at least, only the far north still remained to be pacified. The *ring* of the Avars with its fabulous treasures had fallen into Frankish hands. Charlemagne's power now extended as far as Pannonia and penetrated effectively into the Slavonic lands. Italy had been placed under his rule and we have just seen that a pope as proud as Hadrian was often obliged to yield precedence to Charlemagne within his own state. Under circumstances such as these, was it not normal that to the accumulation of titles of 'king of the Franks', 'king of the Lombards' and 'patrician of the Romans', which he then bore, a general title, better adapted to the predominating position that he had acquired, should be added or substituted, which would at last indicate clearly to everyone the role that he had actually come to occupy in the West?

Charlemagne as arbiter of the West

One fact of cardinal importance dominates the whole issue: in the course of the events that occurred in Italy since Charlemagne's intervention in Lombard affairs the West had, around him and through him, achieved full consciousness of its unity over against the 'Roman Empire' which, while pursuing its secular career in the Eastern

Mediterranean, continued to embody the tradition of ancient Rome. Withdrawn to the 'New Rome' on the Bosporus, this empire preserved no more of its ancient territories west of the Adriatic and Ionian Seas than a few stray pieces whose potential for the future was negligible. The papacy itself had given up looking to the successor of Constantine and Theodosius for protection, and had turned resolutely towards the Carolingians with whom it henceforth felt united through common interests; and with the papacy all of the West, or at least all of the continental West, had at last realized that if it rallied around the conqueror of Saxony, it would gain in strength and opportunities for the future.

At the very end of the eighth century, after the death of Pope Hadrian I on 25 December 795, this situation became still more evident. Having originally been employed in the ranks of the small clerks in the offices of the Lateran and having risen step by step from the lowliest to the highest posts in the papal palace, to be promoted finally to the Sovereign Pontificate on 26 December 795, Hadrian's successor, Leo III had felt, more than any other pope, the need to ensure the Frankish king's complete support of his rule. The reservations which Hadrian had still believed himself in a position to make, the resistance he had thought necessary to put up against his colleague's encroachments, were no longer opportune: from the moment of his succession, Leo, accepting facts as they were, treated Charlemagne with the regard due to a ruler and resigned himself to being no more than a docile subordinate beside him. He let pass without protest the letter in which the Frankish king, congratulating him on his elevation to the throne of St Peter, doubtless in Alcuin's phrasing, thought fit to remind him that he counted on him to work "for the consolidation of his own patriciate" that is to say, of his rule over Rome as patrician of the Romans, and then added these pregnant sentences:

I desire to establish with your Beatitude an inviolable pact of faith and charity, through which . . . the apostolic benediction will be able to follow me everywhere and the most Holy See of the Roman Church will be constantly protected by my devotion. It is my duty, with the aid of the Divine Mercy, to defend the holy Church of Christ by arms everywhere: without, against the incursions of the pagans and the devastations of the infidels; within, by being her patron in the dissemination of the catholic faith. Your duty, most Holy Father, is to raise your hands towards God as did Moses and through your prayers to hasten the success of our arms . . . . Let your Prudence hold fast to the canonical regulations in all matters and follow constantly the rules established by the holy fathers so that your life will provide the example of holiness to all, and let only pious exhortations leave your lips so that your light may shine before all men.

Thus restricting the pope to prayer, Charlemagne reserved the whole domain of action for himself. The bearer of the letter, his trusted counsellor Angilbert, had even been charged to see carefully to the proper distribution of these tasks. His instructions were:

Be sure to warn the pope that he is expected to live honourably and above all to observe the sacred canons; tell him that he should govern the holy Church of God piously according to the agreements you make between you and according to his own conscience. Repeat to him often that the honour to which he has just acceded is a transitory thing, whereas the reward for good deeds is eternal. Persuade him to exert himself with the greatest diligence to root out the heresy of simony that is defiling the holy body of the Church in many places. Tell him what you remember about the problems discussed between us.... May the Lord guide and direct his heart in all goodness, so that he will be able to serve the holy Church of God effectively and to intercede with the Almighty in our favour.

This is equivalent to saying that even the spiritual guidance of the Western World was henceforth claimed by the Frankish king.

Leo III apparently resigned himself more easily to this situation since his personal position was more uncertain. His election, carried out by surprise the day after Hadrian's death, had encountered in Rome an opposition that, in the summer of 798, had degenerated into riots. The following spring a sensational event occurred. On 25 April 799, as he went in procession from the Lateran to the church of San Lorenzo in Lucina, Leo III was attacked by a group of conspirators. This happened with the complicity of two high officials of the papal palace, one of whom was his predecessor's own nephew. He was thrown on the ground, beaten black and blue, and was subjected to odious and cruel violence; they attempted to tear out his tongue and put out his eyes, and finally they set him on his feet again, covered in blood, only to throw him into a cell of the monastery of St Erasmus, from where only the timely intervention of two *missi* of the Frankish king succeeded in rescuing him. But the conspirators had not disbanded and they overwhelmed the pope with their accusations, calling him, among other things, an adulterer and a perjurer. Who, other than Charles himself, was capable of delivering the papacy from this impasse? In the heart of Saxony, where he was still grappling with the pagans, the pope's desperate appeal reached him.

At the very moment the pope decided to go to Paderborn, where Charles had invited him to come and inform him of his situation, the writings of contemporaries and especially the correspondence of Alcuin, sounded a note that was in part new. In a letter of June 799 Alcuin wrote to the Frankish king:

Up to now, there have been three persons at the summit of the hierarchy in this world. First, the representative of the Apostolic Sublimity, vicar of the blessed Peter, Prince of the Apostles, whose See he occupies. What has befallen the present occupant of this See, your Excellence has taken care to inform me. Next, the holder of the imperial dignity, who exercises secular power in the second Rome. In what impious manner the ruler of this Empire has been deposed, not by strangers but by his own people and by his fellow citizens, has become known everywhere. In the third place comes the royal dignity which our Lord Jesus Christ has reserved for you because you rule over the Christian people. This dignity prevails over the other two, eclipses them in wisdom and surpasses them. It is now upon you alone that all the churches of Christ depend, from you alone that they expect well-being: from you, avenger of crimes, guide to those who have lost their way, counsellor of the afflicted, supporter of the good.

It is impossible to say more plainly than this that the Frankish monarchy remained the only hope of the Christian world now that the papacy itself had collapsed; and it could not be more sharply emphasized that the power of the Frankish king had now been substituted for the ancient imperial power – ruined, as it was thought, by the deposition of Constantine VI in 797.

Furthermore a new expression to describe the state of affairs thus created began to slip from Alcuin's pen: that of 'Christian empire'. It was the frontiers of this 'Christian empire' that the Frankish dukes guarded; it was of this 'empire' that Charlemagne was 'the protector'; it was with its expansion by arms that he was constantly occupied. This term 'Christian empire', which had been up to then strange to Alcuin but had suddenly become familiar to him, corresponded with that of 'Christian people', which had been used already for some time, even in official documents, to designate Western Christianity. It was this 'Christian empire' which was, more than ever, united behind the Frankish king, and over which his rule extended. But this expression, which Alcuin then readily contrasted with that of 'Roman Empire', did not yet have in his writing a comparable meaning. The use he made of it, however, acted as an additional factor that, consciously or not, prepared his contemporaries for the events which were soon to take place at Rome.

Meanwhile during the summer of 799 everything combined to strengthen Charlemagne's position and to cause the notion to prevail that he was the supreme arbiter of the West. The arrival of the pope who, having scarcely recovered from his wounds, had come to the heart of Saxony to ask Charlemagne for help, had made a great impression. In an epic composition, written shortly after the encounter, a poet believed to be Angilbert took it as his text to glorify, in sonorous verse and with many hyperbolic epithets, "the king Charles, head of the world and pinnacle of Europe" alone capable of "subjecting [the pope's] conduct to a fair judgment" and to "avenge the cruel blows" that he had been dealt. Among the flood of classical allusions in his writings, the poet twice uses, in reference to Charlemagne, the epithet 'august'. Three times he even calls him "the Augustus", "the great Augustus", implying by this that in his eyes the Frankish king actually occupied in the Europe of that time – and the name 'Europe' was familiar to him – the position of an Augustus.

In the same period and under the impression of the same events Theodulf, the bishop of Orleans, addressed a complimentary poem to the king in which, after having recalled that Charlemagne was "the honour and the glory of the Christian people", he did not scruple to write that it was St Peter himself who, "desiring to find a substitute for himself in him", "had sent him to rescue" the pope. "He who has the keys of heaven" he continues, "has ordained that you will have them" and he concludes: "You rule the Church.... the clergy and the people".

Finally, at the moment when Charles, after having in the autumn of 799 caused Leo III to be escorted back into his capital, made himself ready to join him there to investigate on the spot the guilt incurred by the conspirators as well as by the pope himself, Alcuin, completely opposed as he had from the first been to any kind of procedure against the Sovereign Pontiff, could not refrain from addressing to his "precious David" – that was the Frankish king's nickname – a small poem in which his hopes and wishes are expressed in elegant verse. Might he dress the wounds from which Rome suffered, re-establish harmony between the pope and the people, restore order and bring well-being to all. "Rome, capital of the world, sees in you its protector", he writes; cause "peace and piety" to reign there anew; "guide the ruler of the Church, the Lord guiding you yourself with His mighty hand". A conclusion which, as we can see, agrees with that of Theodulf; Charlemagne, placed at the top of the earthly hierarchy, becomes the immediate deputy of God for all the Christians of the West including the Sovereign Pontiff himself.

The coronation

It was certainly with this in mind that Charlemagne started on his way to Rome in the autumn of 800; and his journey turned into a triumph. The pope, not yet cleared of the grave accusations with which the Romans continued to attack him, came to meet Charlemagne at Mentana, twenty kilometres from the city, whence he returned hastily to prepare a reception worthy of his illustrious visitor. The following day, 24 November 800, he received the Frankish king with great pomp, at the top of the steps of St Peter's, surrounded by all his clergy and amidst a chorus of thanksgiving.

Two weeks later, on 1 December, Charlemagne presided, at St Peter's itself, over an assembly composed at one and the same time of prelates, humble clerks and lay dignitaries, to whose scrutiny he referred the complaints made against the pope. Leo III was requested to prove his innocence by an oath – the supreme humiliation that Alcuin would fain have spared him and which was, it seems, without precedent. In vain had Alcuin, in a letter several months before, recalled the already anciently formulated rule according to which "the Apostolic See cannot be judged by anyone"; in face of the will of Charlemagne, who had personally taken the matter into his hands and who conducted the investigation, Leo III was obliged to yield and, after three weeks, to submit in the church of St Peter on 23 December to the harsh obligation that the ruler of the West imposed on him. Before an assembly of the same composition as that of 1 December and in the presence of the king he submitted, but not without expressing the most explicit reservations about the legitimacy of the procedure: "To hear this case", he began by declaring "the most clement and most serene lord King Charles, here present, has come to this city with his clergy and his magnates"; then he added, without dwelling on the contradictory character of his statements:

Wherefore I Leo, Pontiff of the holy Roman Church, without being judged or constrained by anyone, but by a voluntary and spontaneous act, do purify and cleanse myself in your presence, before God who knows my conscience, before the angels, before the blessed Peter, Prince of the Apostles, in the basilica wherein we find ourselves, and I declare not to have perpetrated nor commanded to have perpetrated the criminal and villainous things I am accused of . . . .

This meant, whatever he might have said, an acceptance as valid of the intervention of the Frankish king in this painful affair, in which the dignity of the pope's private life was placed in doubt, and to recognize, in fact, Charlemagne's right to act as though he were sovereign ruler in Rome.

By a coincidence which was perhaps not entirely due to chance, on the very day that Leo III thus submitted himself to this purgative ceremony demanded of him in the presence of the Frankish king, a delegation arrived at Rome from Jerusalem to present to Charles, in the name of its patriarch, a banner and the keys of the Holy Sepulchre of Calvary and of the holy city itself. This was a simple token of honour, like the pope's despatch to him five years earlier of the keys of the 'confession' of St Peter and a standard of Rome. But the mention we find of these two gestures in the semi-official *Royal Annals*, and the satisfaction that Alcuin expressed about the second one when he was informed of it, seem to indicate the importance attached to them in Frankish circles. After the homage of Roman Christianity, that of the Eastern Christians as well seemed to be brought to Charles.

Other matters as well had meanwhile engaged Charlemagne's attention. The author of the *Royal Annals* speaks of them in enigmatic terms. Charles, he says, having on 1 December one week after his arrival at Rome, "called together an assembly, explained to everyone the reasons for his journey and henceforth occupied himself daily with settling the matters for which he had come. Among these the most important and arduous was the one which was taken up first – the investigation of the crimes of which the pope had been accused". What were the other matters? The annalist does not say. But once the pope's rehabilitation had been achieved on 23 December the field was clear for the implementation of projects of a different nature, which had been carefully worked out by the Frankish king in the secrecy of deliberations continued for almost a month.

Two days later, on 25 December, when Charles had returned to St Peter's for the feast of Christmas and had kneeled, prior to the celebration of divine service, to pray before the 'confession' of the Prince of the Apostles, Pope Leo approached him, and at the moment Charlemagne rose placed on his head a crown while the 'Roman people' thrice shouted the acclamation: "To Charles Augustus, crowned by God, great and pacific emperor of the Romans, life and victory!" After which the Pontiff, prostrating himself before the new Augustus "adored him", as the ancient imperial protocollary formula inaugurated under Diocletian has it. Thus, by a sensational turn of

events, quietly prepared during the preceding weeks and perhaps
months, Charles suddenly found himself raised to the dignity of Roman
emperor.

The principal object of this ceremonial, copied as it was from the
one enacted since the fifth century by the patriarch of Constantinople
at the coronation of the Byzantine emperor, was without any doubt the
clarification of the existing situation. The title 'patrician of the Romans'
was up to then the only one that Charlemagne had made use of in his
relations with the Sovereign Pontiff and with the Romans themselves;
but none of the prerogatives he had gradually arrogated to himself
under cover of this title, which had originally been purely honorary,
were legally justified. When, for example, he required from the new
popes immediate notification of their election, he usurped a prerogative
which, up to the middle of the eighth century, the 'Roman emperors' of
Byzantium had continuously exercised. But since then, the situation
had imperceptibly changed, so that by Christmas of the year 800 the
Frankish king had, with regard to the papacy, already appropriated
almost all the prerogatives formerly acknowledged to belong to the
emperor. The disputes that had arisen in the relations between the two
powers during Hadrian's pontificate had in any case made the incon-
venience of a state of affairs so legally ill-defined quite evident. To
replace the ambiguous title of 'patrician of the Romans' by the decisive
and clear 'emperor of the Romans' was the primary object of the
ceremony in St Peter's on 25 December 800, and this was what
impressed its contemporaries. The author of the *Royal Annals*, after
telling the story of the coronation in almost the same terms as those we
have used ourselves, restricts himself to the laconic conclusion
"... and, discarding his title of patrician, he was called emperor and
Augustus."

After the ceremony, from which time Charles in fact replaced the
title of 'patrician of the Romans', at the beginning of all his documents,
by that of 'emperor Augustus governing the Roman Empire', there
were no songs of triumph, no poems, to celebrate the event, although
there had never before been so many court poets. Even Alcuin in his
correspondence scarcely allowed himself the briefest allusions, and
when he did so it was to express in measured terms the satisfaction he
experienced at the 'elevation' in dignity (*exaltatio*) of his lord the king,
and friend, to whom he addressed a letter of affectionate congratulations: "Blessed is the Lord and blessed is His mercy towards His

servants, for the prosperity and welfare to which, my most precious David, He has happily led you and peacefully taken you, honoured you and raised you (*honoravit et exaltavit*)...", and this time again the only allusion to the imperial coronation contains everything in these simple words: the Lord "has raised you". However important the political transformation effected at Christmas 800 may have been in the eyes of contemporaries, they display as it were a purposeful discretion about it which may perhaps be explained by reasons of diplomacy.

The reader will remember, indeed, Alcuin's famous letter intended for a larger audience, in which he set the primacy of the Frankish monarchy over against the ruin of the imperial power. The information that the West had at its disposal at that moment – in June 799 – about events in the East led men to think that Irene's deed, in dethroning her son Constantine VI and having him blinded, had in effect created a vacancy on the imperial throne. This is why in 803 or soon after an annalist who wrote under the influence of the Carolingian court could present the facts as follows:

When, in the land of Greeks, there was no longer an emperor, and when the imperial power was being exercised by a woman, it seemed to Pope Leo himself and to all the holy fathers who were then assembled in the council, and thus to the whole Christian people, that it would be fitting to give the title of emperor to the king of the Franks, Charles, who had the city of Rome, the normal residence of the Caesars, in his power as well as the other cities of Italy, Gaul and Germany. The Almighty God having consented to place them all under his suzerainty it seemed to them fitting that, according to the desire of the Christian people, he should also bear the imperial title. This request Charles in no way wished to refuse but, submitting himself humbly to God at the same time as to the desire expressed by the priests and the Christian people, he received the title of emperor and the consecration from Pope Leo.

This amounts to saying: first, that the absence of an emperor had made the conferment of the title on Charlemagne indispensable to meet the needs of the moment; second, that being the *de facto* emperor, it had seemed legitimate to award him the title that corresponded to his real power in the same way as fifty years earlier the royal title had been granted to his father Pepin, *de facto* king alongside a king without power; third, that the initiative for this change lay with the clergy, especially the pope, and with the people whose requests Charlemagne did not wish to turn down. It was not the first time in history and it was not to be the last, that an emperor had himself proclaimed by plebiscite – and to support this hypothesis one could point to the actual meeting of a large preliminary council of which the annalist speaks and whose mysterious deliberations about the fate of Christianity excited Alcuin's curiosity at the beginning of 801.

It would be rather naive, in our view, to accept as correct the whole of the explanation just offered. It obviously meets a need for justification, which is doubtless explained by the desire to spare the feelings of the Byzantine government whose reaction to these events seems, as might have been expected, to have been exceedingly hostile. But on one essential point it agrees with our earlier explanation and underscores still more clearly the undeniable need, in 800, to bring reality and legality into agreement by conferring on Charlemagne the imperial title, which the circumstances at that moment seemed to allow to be transferred without the risk of serious opposition.

The consequences of Charlemagne's imperial coronation

Once recognized as emperor, Charlemagne exercised power at Rome with a freer hand, and henceforth it was possible to invoke definite precedents to support this. In principle, all ambiguity had now disappeared: traditionally, the emperor was the sovereign of Rome; he spoke there as its lord, judged there as its lord. As regards the pope, he enjoyed the prestige there and the authority attached to the See of St Peter, but was obliged in the exercise of his authority to conform to the rules that for centuries had regulated relations between the two powers: not only should he notify the emperor of his election, but custom decreed that his consecration should be subject to the emperor's consent, and this rule was explicitly recalled at the death of Leo III in 816.

If one compares Charlemagne's position in Rome at the time of his first visit in 774 with that which he occupied the day after the imperial coronation, the contrast is significant. In 774 Charles entered upon the formal pledge not to abuse the pope's signal favour of an exceptional permission to be in the city for several hours to pray. After the coronation he was at home there and felt he could behave accordingly. He certainly had not waited until the coronation to conduct himself in such a free manner on the banks of the Tiber; but from then on he could claim that the law was on his side, and poor Leo III was not in a position to contradict him.

However, although clarified in one sense, the situation resulting from the ceremony in St Peter's at Christmas 800 created, when one looks at it more closely, complicated problems, of an external as well as an internal kind.

From without, a sharp reaction on the part of Byzantium, the sole legitimate repository of the imperial power, could be expected. By placing at the head of his documents the title 'emperor and Augustus ... governing the Roman Empire' the Frankish king – who continued at the same time to style himself 'king of the Franks and the Lombards' – committed a usurpation of style which no Byzantine ruler could let pass without protest: there was only one Roman Empire, that of the authentic successors of Augustus and Constantine, long since residing on the shores of the Bosporus, and they alone were entitled to carry on the Roman tradition. They did, in fact, protest, and one of the most serious difficulties confronting the Carolingian government after 800 was precisely the one created by this inevitable conflict.

On the Frankish side it was believed or pretended that Charles' election to the dignity of emperor had been perfectly legitimate. Had he not been proclaimed emperor on Roman territory in the legally correct forms according to the ancient protocol still in use and at a moment when the throne of the Augusti was vacant? Because at the end of the year 800, as Alcuin had stressed before the coronation, and as the annalists of the West had recalled afterwards, Constantine VI, overthrown by his mother the Empress Irene, had not been replaced on the throne. Irene, it is true, claimed to exercise the imperial power herself; but that was a scandalous novelty against which Constantinople itself rose up in revolt. And, moreover, since Irene claimed to rule, was it not possible to settle everything by recourse to the convenient solution of a marriage between the two rivals? By this means the ancient Roman Empire would have been reconstituted from one end of the Mediterranean to the other, for the benefit of the imperial couple. A solitary Byzantine chronicler maintains that such a plan was actually conceived, but his statements are suspect in more than one instance and we hesitate to accept his words. In any event this romantic solution of the 'eastern question', if it was actually considered, proved not to be feasible; because, before it could have been put into effect, a new usurper appeared at Byzantium in the person of the logothete Nicephorus, and he was soon firmly settled upon the imperial throne. Thus it became necessary to negotiate an accord upon other grounds, and this turned out to be a longlasting and sensitive affair which was settled only with considerable difficulty. The tension was so great between the two governments of Aachen and Constantinople that the rumour circulated that soon Frankish armies would come down to Sicily – then still Byzantine territory. The negotiations continued in a sabre-rattling atmosphere to end only in 812 under the successor of Nicephorus, Michael I Rangabe, in a lame compromise, in terms of which the emperor of the 'New Rome' – that of the Bosporus – finally agreed to treat his colleague of ancient Rome in his correspondence, no longer simply as a barbarian king $ρήξ$) but to address him as 'brother'. This reduced everything to a question of protocol only, and left the real problem unsolved: that of the co-existence of two emperors and their mutual relations within the boundaries of the ancient Roman Empire.

In its internal affairs, the Empire suffered a similar ambiguity. Was there a new authority inherent in the new title that Charlemagne had received? The question seems not to have been asked. Again only the protocollary aspect was considered: a new oath of fidelity to the sovereign as emperor was required of everyone, because the oaths sworn before had been to him only in the quality of king. For the rest, nothing was changed. It is possible, however, that Charles considered instituting some reforms after his accession to the imperial dignity. Abstaining for some time from all military operations, he studied, with his lay and ecclesiastical magnates, the possibilities for the revision and restatement of the 'laws' in use, as well as the codification of canonical and disciplinary texts concerning the religious life; but the result of this activity seems to have been mediocre, and nothing in the capitularies issued at that time or in the course of the following year reveals a new orientation in these matters. As emperor Charles continued, and nothing more, the policies begun before 800.

Did he at least envisage a special kind of future for his 'Roman Empire'? It must be confessed that once again there is no certainty about this. More precisely, there is nothing to indicate that Charles viewed the Empire as more than a temporary creation, destined to disappear with his person. At the beginning of 806 he in fact issued a decree regulating the succession in case of his death, and the document proves that at that time, in accordance with the ancient Frankish custom, he held the partition of the territorial aggregate which had been assembled under his authority to be inevitable. After expressing gratefulness to the Almighty, who had given him three legitimate sons, Charles, Pepin and Louis, he expressed the double wish to see them jointly associated in his power during his lifetime and thereafter to transfer the whole of his kingdom to them after his death. Wishing, however, to avoid all confusion and all disorder, he declared that he would specify beforehand the portion that would be allotted to each of them at that time. He thus divided his "empire or kingdom" into three parts, the first comprising Aquitaine, Gascony, Septimania, Provence and western 'Burgundy'; the second consisting of Italy, Bavaria and eastern Alemania; and the third, finally, containing all the rest. This last share, which was the most important because the ancient Frankish homeland – *Francia*, as it was then called – was in its entirety included in it, was reserved for the eldest son, Charles, whereas the first share was granted to Louis and the second to Pepin. The emperor stipulated that each of his three sons was expected to "be content with his share" and should ensure its defence without undertaking anything against the territories of his brothers, with whom the emperor expected him to maintain relations of "peace and charity", implying duties of mutual assistance in case of serious danger to the safety of one of them. Moreover, in Art. 6 the three brothers pledged themselves explicitly to lend assistance to one another against enemies from within or from without, and arrangements for crossing the Alps were made for each of them, in Art. 3, to ward off dangers that might in particular threaten Pepin. But Art. 6 also stipulated that each of the three brothers was to refrain from all interference in the affairs of his neighbour, and several articles (Arts. 10, 11 and 12) aimed at establishing and maintaining a strict separation between the three future kingdoms in matters regarding private properties as well as those concerning the personal bonds of commendation and fidelity.

On one point only the emperor expected his sons to follow a common policy after his death: by Art. 15, alluding to his own example and that of his father and grandfather, he enjoined them to "ensure all of them together the defence of the Church of St Peter [that is to say, the papacy] . . . and to cause justice to be rendered to it". For the rest, all the measures drawn up by the emperor presuppose the permanent break-up of the Empire's unity after his death. The Frankish custom of partitioning was maintained intact not only for the immediate future, but even in the provisions for new possibilities: the death of one or other of his sons, the birth of grandsons capable or not of succeeding the deceased (Arts. 4 and 5). Thus, although Charles was categorical about the necessity of keeping his absolute power over the whole of the Empire unimpaired during his lifetime (Art. 20), on his death his Empire was destined to disappear, and the unity of his heirs would amount to no more than what their reciprocal goodwill would allow (Arts. 14 and 16).

Of the new perspectives opened up by the coronation of 800 not much, as we have just seen, remained. Less than six years after the event the 'Empire' seemed indeed to be no more than a kind of personal apotheosis of Charlemagne, an apotheosis whose duration was limited to his own lifetime. And yet the premature deaths, at short intervals from each other, of his two eldest sons before he himself was in his grave, was to have the unforeseen consequence that this Empire, founded in 800 in uncertainty and ambiguity, not only survived the circumstances which brought it into being, but, without retaining any of those aspects which for a moment gave the illusion of a resurrection of ancient Rome, gradually took the form of a new organism – the organism that we call the Carolingian Empire, which was to dominate western Europe for almost a century.

CHAPTER SIX

The political and administrative organization

The territories

Was Western Europe, now that it had come under Frankish rule, a cohesive unit? At first glance one might doubt it. The Frankish kingdom had steadily grown by conquest, but the peoples annexed in this manner had preserved their own character, customs, legal codes, and in more than one case, some of their political individuality. In many regions, even in Gaul itself, ethnic particularisms stoutly resisted every attempt at assimilation.

Brittany, of course, was a case apart. With its Celtic population, its clergy organized in a manner without parallel on the continent, and its numerous counts or national dukes, it had never yet been integrated into the Frankish kingdom. All that Charlemagne had been able to obtain, at the price of two harsh campaigns in 786 and 799, were promises of fidelity, whose value in practice we have already observed.

But there was, on another periphery of Gaul, a province whose theoretical incorporation into the Frankish kingdom had nevertheless scarcely diminished its liberty: Gascony. In contrast to the Armorican Peninsula, Gascony was considered an integral part of the Empire and in 806 it was one of the territories that Charlemagne decided to award to his sons after his death. It comprised our Gascony as well as the present day Basque country, the words Basque and Gascony being, as is well known, two versions of the same name (*Vasco* in Latin). Inhabited by an ancient people of Iberian descent whose language, customs and even dress – a wide-sleeved shirt, baggy trousers, a small cape – were different from those of the more southern regions, it had required long and bloody struggles to compel them, first to pay tribute to, and finally under Charlemagne, to recognize the hegemony of, the Frankish king. The country had nevertheless retained a national duke, whose loyalty to the Frankish ruler could not be counted upon, and under whose rule the country was always ready to revolt at any moment. In this regard the incident at Roncevaux had been only one among many. In 813 again, a few weeks before Charlemagne's death, the Gascons, just as in 778, attempted a surprise attack on a Frankish army while it was crossing the Pyrenees.

From the Garonne to the Loire and from the Atlantic Ocean to the Cévennes, the cluster of territories that at that time constituted Aquitaine carried the imprint of a past that made its complete assimilation to the other Frankish provinces difficult. For a long time Aquitaine had remained a kind of zone of exploitation which the Frankish kings partitioned between them as though it were booty. Proud of the culture they had received from the Romans, the inhabitants detested the coarseness of the barbarian conquerors and fiercely defended themselves against their undertakings. King Dagobert had tried to humour them in 629 by making their country a separate kingdom which, although it remained under his supreme authority, was given to his brother Caribert. But when Caribert died in 632, the kingdom of Aquitaine disappeared with him. Since then Aquitaine had gradually regained its more or less independent status. At the end of the seventh century it possessed a duke from among its own people and the Merovingians had only barely succeeded in compelling him to recognize their suzerainty. Charles Martel and Pepin the Short had been obliged to impose their suzerainty on them by force of arms until 768, when Duke Waifar yielded after eight years of merciless fighting and Frankish officials could finally be installed in the interior of the country.

Aquitanian particularism had remained so deeply entrenched, notwithstanding this, that in 781 or somewhat later Charlemagne, possibly inspired by Dagobert's example, had judged it prudent to make a sub-kingdom of it once more, entrusted, under his suzerainty, to his son Louis. Since by chance the child had been born shortly before in Poitou, in the course of his father's travels, could he not be considered an Aquitanian? Charlemagne seems to have taken trouble in any case to gratify the self respect of the southerly peoples by ordering that the child be dressed in the Gascon manner which was then doubtless prevalent in part of Aquitaine, by gracing him with the title 'king of the Aquitanians' (*rex Aquitanorum*), and by setting up a royal court for him after the fashion of his own court, with a similar hierarchy of high officials, a chancery producing documents styled in the same solemn manner as his own, and with workshops minting money in the young prince's name. Everything was calculated to give the Aquitanians the illusion of a semi-autonomous status. And in fact this arrangement proved viable, because it was to last not only until Charlemagne's death but even to survive him.

In the Germanic regions, Bavaria possessed a government which somewhat resembled that of Aquitaine. Even though they had belonged to the Frankish kingdom since the sixth century, the Bavarians too had proven unamenable to all attempts at assimilation, they had retained their legal code (the 'Law of the Bavarians') and their national dukes of the ancient family of the Agilolfings. In the seventh century these had succeeded in almost entirely throwing off Frankish hegemony. Two campaigns by Charles Martel in 725 and 728 had not been able to crush their independent spirit permanently, since, as we have seen, thirty-five years later their duke Tassilo was again in a state of rebellion; he refused all military assistance to the Frankish king and, behaving as an independent prince, began to date his documents only by the years of his own 'reign' in Bavaria. We know the consequences! Compelled to take the oath of fidelity to Charlemagne in 781, and having thereafter again revolted, he was obliged in 794, after various vicissitudes, to renounce his rights, in his own name as well as in the name of his heirs, in favour of the Carolingians.

However, although there no longer was a Bavarian duke, Bavaria endured. Judging it prudent not to break up the country's unity, Charlemagne restricted himself to substituting for the Agilolfing duke a governor of high rank, his brother-in-law Gerold, who with the title of duke or 'prefect of Bavaria' (*praefectus Baioariae*) had received a commission to govern the entire duchy, whose boundaries remained intact. This system of government was continued after Gerold's death in 799, the only change being that the 'prefect' had then been replaced by a directorship of two *praefecti Baioariae* acting jointly. Bavaria was to preserve its individuality for a long time: one of Louis the Pious' first cares was to entrust its government to one of his sons, granting him, with the title of 'king of the Bavarians' the same prerogatives and the same

apparent autonomy as the 'king of the Aquitanians'. This is sufficient to
indicate that Bavaria was no more subject to the normal structure of
government than Aquitaine or Gascony.

Italy was even more clearly outside it. Those parts of the peninsula
which had formerly been subject to Aistulf's and Desiderius' rule had
never lost their character as a separate kingdom. In the list of his titles
Charlemagne did not fail to include that of 'king of the Lombards', and
not only did the Lombard legal code remain in force but it was
generally acknowledged that the capitularies promulgated for the
whole of the Empire might require modification to suit the special
customs of 'Lombardy'. As in the case of Aquitaine, the government of
the kingdom had been entrusted since 781 to a prince of the Carolingian
family reigning under the suzerainty of the head of the royal house:
Pepin, the second son of Charlemagne and first occupant of the office,
was succeeded in 813, according to the wishes of the emperor, by
Pepin's own son, Bernard. It need hardly be said that this kingship was
more apparent than real; but appearances were maintained: the king of
the Lombards had his own court, his administrative personnel, his
diplomacy, and he carried on direct negotiations with Byzantium, even
though he did no more than carry out orders received from Aachen. He
even went so far as to issue capitularies.

The Lombard duchies of the south continued, just as before the
Frankish conquest, to elude the grasp of the king of Pavia. The duke of
Benevento had ultimately succeeded in preserving his independence,
although recognizing Carolingian suzerainty and submitting to the
payment of tribute. The duke of Spoleto was in a situation analogous to
that of Tassilo of Bavaria after his last revolt: his duchy was in theory
made part of the Carolingian Empire, but continued to be governed in
the Lombard manner and by Lombards.

Blocking the peninsula, from the mouth of the Tiber to the Adriatic
Sea, the Papal State or, as it was called in the then current expression,
the 'republic of St Peter' likewise maintained a distinct political and
administrative organization, with a population for the greatest part
subject to Roman law and ruled in the name of the pope by papal
officials. Charlemagne did not scruple to intervene in it unceasingly.
But could one be said to be within the Empire there? It seems that this
point was purposely left obscure.

Finally, on the verges of the Carolingian Empire, there were regions
that had been recently or relatively recently acquired, such as Frisia

and Saxony, in which for a long time and in spite of all efforts, violent or peaceful, there remained the nostalgic memory of an independence that had yielded only to force of arms, and strong national traditions against which every contrary move came to nought. Moreover, the fact that the Franks had never up to then aimed at subjecting the conquered regions to a uniform legislation, and that each people, even each of its constituent individuals, always and everywhere kept his original juridical status, contributed much to the maintenance of a certain particularism, even in the regions which had been added to the kingdom long before. The Salian Frank lived under the rules of the Salian Law, the Ripuarian under those of the Ripuarian Law; the Frisian was answerable to the Frisian Law, the Saxon, Bavarian, Lombard, Burgundian and Roman each had his own law. Certainly, one's legal status was a personal thing, independent of where one lived: but in all the recently annexed regions and in all those where the substratum of the population remained homogeneous, the ethnic boundaries delimited, more or less, the principal field of application of each code. This code in practice regulated the everyday life of most of the inhabitants in such questions as the age of majority, the regulation of marriage, hereditary rights, and penalties, which differed from one code to another and consequently between one ethnic group and another. The appearance of diversity that Charlemagne's Empire at first glance seems to have is reinforced by these differences.

Local administration

This diversity, however, did not prevent the Empire from actually forming a unit. Although the laws might vary, although concessions had to be made to the particularist aspirations of several of the conquered territories, everywhere, even where national dukes had been temporarily maintained, officials trained in Frankish methods and appointed by the Carolingians saw to the business of government.

The most important of these officials was the count, *comes* in classical Latin and *graf* (Latinized into *grafio*) in the Germanic language. He contributed as it were the essential gear-wheel of the administrative machine; consequently the emperor selected him very carefully. Preferably, he was the son of a great Frankish or at least

Austrasian family, educated and trained at court. The emperor appointed one only when he was well-acquainted with the person in question. The count's field of action was the 'county' (*comitatus*) which was also called *pagus* and *gau* in the Germanic language. Counts could be found from one end of the Empire to the other, having been introduced all the more easily since the office already existed in quite a few Germanic regions before the Frankish conquest, notably among the Lombards. The total number of counties into which the imperial administration was divided came to several hundred. Their size was variable and depended on the density of the population. There were counties which were larger than the largest French *départements*; there were also some whose area did not exceed that of a single *arrondissement*.

The count represented the emperor in the fullness of his administrative powers: he promulgated the capitularies and all the imperial edicts, saw to it that they were carried out, levied the taxes, directed public works (maintenance and construction of roads and bridges and all other construction works), supervised the preservation of the public peace, dispensed justice, raised and commanded the military contingents, and finally – to mention only the essential things – received the oaths of allegiance of the subjects. Removable *ad nutum*, he could also be transferred according to the emperor's wish; but dismissals and transfers were rare: the same count remained fifteen, twenty, even thirty years in the same district. It was possible for him to acquire properties there, and contrary to what has sometimes been said, it occurred that from this time onward members of his family, particularly his son or his son-in-law, succeeded him in his office. By way of exception some counts held more than one county, but it was usual to administer only one at a time.

In any case, the count remained closely dependent on the sovereign, from whom he held his office and the estates that were attached to it. Because he was not paid a salary he received as remuneration, besides incidental emoluments consisting of a fixed percentage of the profits of justice and of the taxes levied by him, only revenues from the estates and monasteries which, despite the latter's religious character, were normally awarded to him within the county in return for his services. If a count took some liberty adjudged to be reprehensible it was not only his office but all that was connected with it, perhaps even his own properties, that he risked losing: this was to occur several times during the reign of Louis the Pious.

The emperor furthermore took care to limit the initiatives left to his lieutenants by frequently sending them written or oral instructions, by the obligation he imposed upon them to consult him on difficult matters, and above all by the obligation to come to court to report and account for their actions at least once a year, during the 'general assembly'. He was careful, too, to inform himself about their administration: the complaints referred to his tribunal, the inspection circuits of his *missi*, the more or less direct supervision which the bishop owing to force of circumstances exercised on the activities of the civil officials alongside whom he found himself – all these were precious sources of information for the sovereign which he was careful not to neglect.

The count had a lieutenant: the viscount (*vicecomes*), whom he himself nominated and presented to the emperor for approval. Furthermore, there were various minor officials under his command, the most important of which were the 'vicars' (*vicarii*), each charged with the administration of part of the county, the 'vicary' (*vicaria*). The vicary was also called 'hundred' (*centena*) and the vicar 'hundredman' (*centenarius*). This double terminology may, as certain historians believe, have arisen from two institutions that were originally distinct and ultimately merged, or it may be that the double terms simply correspond to diverse regional customs, which is what a good many of the sources seem to indicate. Whatever the case may be, the vicars, as well as the viscounts and the other subordinate officials of the county, appear to have been nominated by the count and to have been under his direct control. Their sphere of competence comprised, just like the count's, all the sectors of government administration, but in a smaller territorial unit and to a different degree. Their competence in judicial affairs, particularly, was limited to so-called 'minor' cases (*minores*), and several capitularies of the first years of the ninth century, which will be discussed later, indicate exactly what this meant.

Having looked at the agents of the civil administration we must next consider those of the ecclesiastical government, which should not be left out in the description of a state in which the civil and religious elements, as we shall presently see, were indissolubly linked. The bishop, whose diocese often had the same boundaries as the county because both usually corresponded to the territory of an old Roman *civitas*, was on the whole no more than an imperial official. Indeed he was one of the most useful instruments in the unifying and centralizing policy pursued by the sovereign. Because in general the Christian religion was instituted wherever Frankish power penetrated, there was no region in the Empire where the bishops could not play an active role in promoting the Frankish cause. The way in which they were nominated, as we shall see later, made them creatures of the emperor, who had to be able to count on their loyalty and who used them as true agents of public authority; he supervised their activities, sent them instructions, just as he did his counts; he also ordered them to publish his capitularies and to see to their implementation in so far as they concerned ecclesiastical matters; he summoned the bishops to his presence and insisted upon their attendance at the great assemblies; through them, finally, he brought his influence to bear on the lower clergy, whose activities could thus be directed according to his views.

Simple as it was, this administrative machinery would have been in danger of derangement and liable to execute inadequately the directives of the central authority if this had not had at its disposal devoted inspectors capable of making the commands of the sovereign respected from one end of the Empire to the other. These inspectors were the *missi dominici* or 'ruler's envoys' who each year travelled through every part of the Empire.

The Merovingians had already made occasional use of this type of envoy. At the end of Charlemagne's reign the practice became general but this did not mean that the *missi* constituted, properly speaking, a class of officials separate from those we have listed. Chosen only exceptionally from among the abbots and usually from the counts and bishops in office, their duties as inspectors were additional to those with which they were already invested and continued to perform. Their 'missions' were, moreover, only temporary and, even towards the end of Charlemagne's reign, when their journeys became more frequent, did not occupy more than a few weeks each year. They travelled in pairs – a count and a bishop, or a count and an abbot – provided with instructions from the emperor, to visit the group of six or more counties that constituted the zone of inspection or *missaticum* which had been assigned to them. It sometimes happened that there were more than two persons for a single *missaticum*; but both counts and bishops or abbots always participated in the task, which indeed demanded in turn the competence of a layman and that of an ecclesiastic.

For their inspection extended to very diverse spheres: the administrative conduct of officials of every rank and category, the implementation of capitularies and conciliar decisions, the verdicts rendered by local tribunals, the hearing of complaints lodged against the counts or their subordinates, the publication of measures drawn up by the central government, the receiving of oaths of allegiance if a change of sovereign necessitated the general renewal of these, and so on. One can get some idea of the scope of their duties by looking at a memorandum which at the beginning of the ninth century four of these *missi* sent to each count in the district they were about to inspect:

We send you this letter to direct you on behalf of the emperor and to request you earnestly on our own behalf to make every effort to fulfil carefully all the duties of your office, both those that concern the worship of God as well as those that have to do with serving our lord the emperor and the welfare and the protection of the Christian people. For our lord has charged us, as he has charged all his other *missi*, to present him with a true report in the middle of April about the manner in which, in his kingdom, the instructions are carried out which he has had delivered by his *missi* in the last few years, wishing to provide those who have observed them with a worthy recompense and to rebuke those who have evaded them as they deserve.... We urge you to reread your capitularies, to recall the oral instructions which have been given to you, and to display such zeal in carrying them out that you may be rewarded by God and by your lord, the great emperor. We charge you then first of all and enjoin you to obey punctually and to demand of your subordinates and subjects a strict obedience to the commands of your bishop in all things that pertain to his office. Exert yourself to maintain all the emperor's rights, as he has specified them to you in writing or orally, for you will be held accountable for them. Render full, correct and fair justice to the churches, widows, orphans and to all others, without fraud, without corruption, without tardiness or unwarranted delays, and see to it that your subordinates do the same, so that you may be rewarded by God and by our lord. If you come up against acts of insubordination, or disobedience, or if anyone refuses to accept the decisions that you have made according to the law and justice, make a note of it and inform us, be it at once, in an urgent matter, be it at the time of our journey, so that we may deal with it according to the instructions that we have received from our lord. Do not hesitate, if you are not sure about the meaning of a passage in these instructions ... to send us immediately one of your representatives capable of understanding our explanation, so that you may yourself understand everything and, with the aid of God, carry out everything. Above all, take care that you are not overheard, you or your subordinates, saying to people with the intention of thwarting or delaying the execution of justice: 'Say nothing until the *missi* have departed; thereafter we will settle the matter between us!' On the contrary, expedite the judgment of pending cases before our arrival, for if you play some evil trick of this kind or if you by negligence or malice delay the cause of justice until our coming, you may be sure that we shall make a severe report against you. Read and reread this letter and preserve it carefully, so that it may serve as a memorandum between you and us.

Such a letter shows how much care the emperor took to keep his lieutenants in suspense and how he hoped to achieve administrative unity through his *missi.* In the course of their travels the *missi* were presented with the difficult cases, which they either settled themselves or sent on at once for examination by the sovereign: questions concerning procedure, the ownership of properties, the personal status of free and unfree persons, the validity of documents, etc. In any case, the problems raised, complicated as they were by the diversity of the legal codes, required a broad competence and extensive experience in administrative affairs. The task that confronted the *missi* appeared even heavier as the number of annual circuits they were expected to make constantly increased. From a capitulary of Charlemagne's last years it appears that a total of four journeys a year had become the rule: in January, April, July and October. One wonders how these inspectors were able at the same time to fulfil their normal tasks adequately as counts, bishops or abbots, especially if one considers the length of the journeys demanded of many of them, the military expeditions in which they were obliged to participate, and the general assemblies at which their presence was required. How, under these conditions, could these high officials simultaneously see in person to the orderly execution of the public services of which they had the direct supervision?

To make matters even more difficult their zones of inspection were, naturally, never supposed to coincide with their own administrative districts. The whole expanse of the territories incorporated into the empire, Aquitaine as well as Lombardy, was in principle subject to their circuits of inspection. They even had access to the Papal State, though their interference there was considered questionable. The *missi* seem to have accomplished their task zealously over the whole of this immense field of action and to have simultaneously acted as permanent liaison officers between the emperor and all the officials scattered about in the provinces.

There is no doubt at all that Charlemagne in this way succeeded in keeping the supervision of the whole government firmly in hand, even in the regions which he had left semi-autonomous. The 'kings' of Aquitaine or Lombardy, just like the counts, were required to execute the emperor's orders, to see to the implementation of the capitularies, to refer difficult cases to him, to be present in person at the general assemblies, and to render account for their management. The slightest inclination toward independence on their part was immediately checked: Bernard, 'king of the Lombards', experienced this to his regret at the beginning of Louis the Pious' reign. The same happened in Gascony, where the national duke risked being treated as a rebel if he did not keep to the role that was assigned to him.

Nevertheless, the provinces adjoining the land frontiers all remained outside the normal administrative organization. Being permanently exposed to contact with the enemy, they constituted military territories called 'marches'. In the sources we find mention of the following 'marches': the 'march of Brittany' on the border of independent Brittany, and comprising Nantes, Vannes and Rennes; a 'march of Spain', along the boundary with Moslem Spain and including Gerona, Urgel and Barcelona; a 'march of Friuli', on the frontier with the southern Slavonic countries; an 'Avar march', a 'Wendish march', a 'Danish march'. In each march (*marca* or *marcha* or even, in classical Latin, *limes*) all power was vested in the commander of the garrison, who had the rank of count and bore the title 'count of the march', being in Latin *comes marcae*, and in the Germanic language *markgraf*, of which we have made 'margrave'. The term *marchio* was also used, and later *marchisus*, from which we have made 'marquis' or 'marquess'. This personage, however designated, was commander-in-chief of the troops that it had been adjudged wise to leave at his disposal in order to withstand unforeseen attacks, and this is why he was sometimes also called 'duke' (*dux*), that is to say, 'general'. But his powers were greater than those of an ordinary general, since he, like the counts, administered, judged, levied taxes, published imperial decisions, and in short worked as they did, for the unity of the Frankish lands in the administrative sphere.

The central administration

In the Carolingian state all things converged on the emperor. Yet, remarkably enough, he had no more than a very rudimentary central administration to support him in his task.

The basic reason for this was the very simplicity of contemporary concepts about the nature of government. Since the representatives of the sovereign in the provinces lived from the emoluments of their office and the prebends attached to them, and the expenses in the collective interest, such as those for public works, were directly collected from their users, as we shall see, in the form of payments in kind, the imperial government found itself relieved of the load that, more than anything else, encumbers the administrative machine of a modern state. The portion of the public income that went into the emperor's treasury, after the counts had taken the percentage that was allotted to them in remuneration for their services, was added to the sums deriving from the exploitation of their domains, insofar as these products had not been consumed on the spot, and this combined amount the emperor could dispose of as he pleased.

Moreover, there was nothing that resembled a ministry of finance. The very words 'public treasure' (*aerarium publicum* or *fiscus*) were, when they happened to be used at all, no more than a learned archaism borrowed from the administrative language of ancient Rome. More properly it was called the 'chamber' (*camera*) of the emperor, where in fact were stored the coins, ingots of precious metal, and jewels which were considered to be his private property, about which he owed no one an explanation, and of which consequently he could dispose freely, rewarding living persons as well as making bequests to his heirs.

In the same way as the public treasury coincided with his private treasure chest, his court or, as it was then called, 'palace' (*palatium*), merged with what in other times would have been called his 'household'. The service of his person was not distinguished from that of the state, and the confusion that existed in this respect in Merovingian times continued into the period of Charlemagne. The tasks continued to be distributed in almost the same manner. Only, and this is self-evident, the office of mayor of the palace went out of existence when Pepin the Short, who had held it, became king. It seems, however, that the 'chamberlain' (*camerarius*), the keeper of the 'imperial chamber' where the treasure was stored, thenceforward had the supervision of all the household services proper and in this way took over part of the role that had formerly belonged to the mayor of the palace. The chamberlain was a personage of great distinction, whom Alcuin advised to provide the king with considered opinions, to acquit himself wisely of the charges entrusted to him, to judge fairly, and to display generosity in the giving of alms. Under Louis the Pious the threat to the monarchy from this influential post became evident once the power of the sovereign began to weaken.

Beside the chamberlain were the following officials: the highest in rank was the 'seneschal' (*senescalcus*) who was charged with the provision of food for the palace and for this reason was apt to be called in classical Latin *regiae mensae praepositus*, that is to say 'the prefect of the royal table'; the 'butler' (*buticularius*) or 'master of the cup-bearers' (*magister pincernarum*); and finally the 'count of the stable', that is to say the *écurie*, or constable (*comes stabuli*). These three had various subordinates under their control: grooms of the chamber or *cubicularii*, attached to the *cubiculum* or private apartment of the emperor, ushers (*ostiarii*), cooks, cupbearers, 'marshals' *mariscalci*) or palfreys, etc. But, no more than the chamberlain, did the three heads of the services which we have just mentioned view their role as limited to the emperor's private affairs: one need only look at the contemporary documents to see that they also held military commands and performed missions of every kind, according to the imperial wishes.

Just as there was no ministry of finance, there were also, generally speaking, no separate departments at the palace for the various categories of affairs to be dealt with. The need for them was not even felt, since in the counties all matters of whatever sort were also without distinction within the count's competence. There were nevertheless, through force of circumstances, a few departments which were specialized because they demanded a staff having a special competence, and in particular there were two departments reserved to clergy, the one exclusively, the other by preference: the chapel and the chancery.

Chapel (*cappella* or *capella*) was the name given to the royal oratory. For a long time this name was applied exclusively to this oratory, the word *cappella* being the diminutive of *cappa*, designating one of the most precious relics kept there – a cape of St Martin, on which from the seventh century onward the Frankish kings had caused oaths to be sworn in their own oratory. Charlemagne's ancestors seem to have appropriated it for their own use at the beginning of the eighth century, and later on the clergy of their personal oratory themselves took the name of chaplains (*cappellani* or *capellani*). After that time the terms chapel and chaplains were extended to all categories of oratories, without, however, it being forgotten that they had at first applied only to the oratory of the Carolingian prince. More than one writer of the ninth century recalled this fact and praised the miraculous powers of the venerable cloak entrusted to the keeping of the imperial chaplains.

The chief of these, who did not yet carry a special name – only
during the next reign was he to be called 'arch-chaplain' (*archicapellanus* or *summus capellanus*) – was, for all that, not a chaplain of the
same rank as the others. To succeed the abbot of Saint-Denis, Fulrad,
who died in 784, and who had occupied the post at the beginning of his
reign, Charlemagne named two great prelates: first the bishop of Metz,
Angilram (d. 791), then the bishop of Cologne, Hildebald, who lived
until 818. In order to attach these two men to his oratory, Charlemagne
was obliged to request the pope for a dispensation, since the fact of
their nomination made residence in their respective dioceses impossible. He even obtained for them the archiepiscopal dignity, which had
not been attached to their sees. It is worth noting that in both cases his
request for a dispensation was based on the need to have the prelate in
question at his side "constantly" for the affairs of the Church.
Charlemagne had even submitted the case of Hildebald to a council
held in 794 at Frankfurt, in the presence of a legate of the Holy See, to
examine the adoptionist heresy. This bespeaks the importance of some
of the questions on which he needed the advice of a qualified prelate.
As head of his chapel, the arch-chaplain was at the same time
Charlemagne's permanent councillor in ecclesiastical or religious matters, and the sources seem to indicate that his role must have been an
influential one. The record of a council held at Mainz in 813 attributed
to the arch-chaplain Hildebald the significant title of 'archbishop of the
sacred palace' and gave him a place of honour at the head of the list of
the bishops in attendance. From this fact his position in the state may
be inferred.

Between the chapel and the chancery there were close connections.
The drawing up and despatch of official documents at a time when in
the West the only official language was Latin, presupposed a degree of
education more often found in clergy than in laymen. Consequently
more than one chaplain worked in the offices of the chancery as a
'notary' (*notarius*). Nevertheless, the chancery constituted a separate
department, the direction of which was entrusted to one of these
notaries, to whom the title 'chancellor' (*cancellarius*) was then usually
given. This chancellor himself was always chosen from among the
clergy.

Beside the chaplain and the chancellor a third high official existed at
the Carolingian court: the 'count of the palace' (*comes palatii*), who
assisted the sovereign in the dispensing of justice and more and more

often presided in his place over the imperial tribunal. The number of cases was in fact increasing constantly, as Charles' power and prestige grew greater. Therefore, however modest this task may have been at the end of the Merovingian epoch, it increased in importance daily. A special chancery, occupying itself exclusively with the drawing up of its judicial verdicts, established itself on the periphery of the official one run by the chancellor. Their staffs were separate. Being as it seems composed exclusively of laymen (while the notaries placed under the direction of the chancellor were clerics) it was through force of circumstances that it became accustomed to receive its orders from the count of the palace. From the beginning of the ninth century onward, the documents that this chancery despatched were sealed with a special seal and they had their own formal style, indicating the unity of its direction; they bear witness to the important positions acquired by the head of the administration in which they originated.

But once we have mentioned the few administrative departments just surveyed, the picture of Charlemagne's central administration may be considered complete. Although there are, nevertheless, a small number of other services sometimes mentioned in the sources – such as those of *mansionarii*, doubtless charged with arranging the lodgings of the emperor and his train in the course of their travels, or those of huntsmen (*venatores*) and falconers (*falconarii*), in charge of the hunts – these cannot be considered as having any connection with the government of the state. The emperor, indeed, counted for the task of government directly on the officials representing him in the provinces, whom he attempted to keep constantly under his supervision, as his capitularies show.

The general assembly

It was not only with his representatives in the provinces but with all his subjects that the emperor meant to remain in contact. The general assembly (*conventus generalis*) which was also called 'general tribunal' (*placitum generale*) gave him the opportunity to do this.

Every year, according to an already very old tradition, the emperor summoned his subjects to his presence just before departing on the year's campaign; for, in the case of a warlike nation such as the Franks, military operations were naturally resumed every year with the return of spring. Since this assembly coincided with the mustering of the troops, the date of convocation was chosen in accordance with military necessity. At the beginning of the eighth century it still took place in March–whence its ancient name 'field of March' (*campus martis*)– but later it seems to have been held in May, thereby becoming the 'field of May' (*campus maii* or *campus madius*). This name, which was sometimes extended to indicate the general assembly itself, remained in use even though gradually its convocation date was delayed until June, July or even until August.

Every imperial subject was supposed to be summoned to and to be present at this assembly. In this way decisions were drawn up in it with the consent of "all the people" (*omnis populus*). The emperor never neglected to mention in his acts that he issued them by decision of the assembly. Naturally, however, in actual practice only the 'magnates' (*optimates* or *proceres*) that is to say mainly, officials and persons of note, as well as (representing the mass of the subjects) the troops that had come to the meetingplace in response to the order of mobilization, were present. The place of the meeting was decided upon every year by the emperor, who chose the surroundings of one of his palaces or country residences selected for its relative proximity to the scene of the next military operations. The assembly proper was held in the residential buildings and consequently comprised only an elite; the mass of soldiers, camped in the vicinity, could do no more than give their approval as a pure formality to the measures decided on.

Restricted as it was, the elite that was thus gathered around the sovereign nevertheless comprised several hundred persons: high palace officials, dukes and counts, bishops, abbots, and royal vassals. For anyone holding any office in the Empire attendance was absolutely required. Even Alcuin, when old age and infirmities had begun to wear him down, experienced considerable trouble in having his excuses on account of his poor health accepted as valid. This kind of excuse seems to have been the only one that had any chance of being accepted, because, when he summoned them, the emperor expected from his 'magnates' not only advice but also an obligation: their participation in enacting the measures, whether this was actual or in appearance only, bound them to see to their implementation. It was therefore important that no one should evade attendance. After Charlemagne this evasion occurred so often, at critical moments for the monarchy, that one cannot fail to appreciate the profound reasons for the obligation the sovereign imposed on his subjects in this respect.

When the assembly began, the agenda of questions that were to be discussed had been carefully studied in advance by the emperor together with those of the high dignitaries of the palace or those of his intimate friends whom he had made into his habitual advisers. One may assume, for instance, that the arch-chaplain was always consulted in every matter that pertained to religion or the Church, and Alcuin's correspondence shows that for a long time this celebrated abbot of the monastery of St Martin of Tours was also one of those whose advice Charlemagne sought in these matters.

The prepared agenda set the assembly its task and gave direction to the discussion, as we can see in the following specimen believed to date from the year 811:

We desire at the very start to have our bishops and abbots on one side, our counts on the other, and to discuss separately with each of these groups the following matters:

(1) To what causes must be attributed the fact that people refuse to help one another, not only on the frontiers but also in the army, when it is necessary to act in defense of the country?

(2) Whence come those perpetual litigations caused by people laying claim to what they see possessed by one of their equals?

(3) Concerning another's man (that is to say, the vassal) who, deserting his lord, finds a welcome elsewhere.

(4) They will be asked in what respect and in which places laymen are hindered by churchmen, and the churchmen by laymen, in the performance of their duties, and in this connection should be discussed and decided the question of how far a bishop or abbot should intervene in secular affairs and a count or other layman in church affairs, which leads to the scrutiny of the meaning of this saying of the Apostle: *Nemo militans Deo implicat se negotiis secularibus* ('let no member of the militia of God involve himself in secular affairs') and also to deciding to whom this saying applies.

After various questions concerning problems of a religious nature, the agenda – which is not devoid of a certain irony – calls for the study of several other matters which are worth noting:

(9) Concerning the life and morals of our pastors, to wit the bishops, who should give a good example to God's people not only by their preaching but also by their conduct; because it is to them, we believe, that the Apostle addressed himself when he said: *Imitatores mei estote et observate eos qui ita ambulant sicut habetis formam nostram.* ('By my imitators and look at those who conduct themselves according to the example that you have in us').

(10) Concerning the life of those called canons; what it ought to be like.

(11) Concerning the monastic life; can anyone be a monk without observing the *Rule of St Benedict*? It will be necessary to look into the question whether there were monks in Gaul before this rule arrived there.

The division of the assembly into the two groups, that of the clerics and that of the laymen, such as was prescribed in this text, was customary. The clergy constituted a veritable national synod charged with studying all matters of ecclesiastical discipline and organization, whereas politics and administration were left to the competence of the laymen. The answers of these two groups, sometimes brought together in plenary sessions thereafter, helped the emperor to make his decisions with the relevant information.

These decisions were then formulated in a series of articles called 'chapters' (*capitula*) the collection of which constituted the ordinance or 'capitulary' (*capitulare*) which the emperor customarily issued at the end of the meeting. It was read to the whole of the 'people' gathered around the buildings and doubtless their approval was given by acclamation. The assembly then broke up and the army moved off towards the nearby frontier.

Sometimes the assembly had to deal with other matters. If a plot had been discovered or a revolt had taken place in the course of the preceding weeks or months, the emperor let "his people" decide the fate of the guilty parties. In this way in 786 when a plot had been organized in Thuringia, the suspects, of whom several were counts, were referred to the general assembly of Worms, which passed sentences ranging from dismissal from office and confiscation of property to exile and even the putting-out of eyes. Two years later, the duke of Bavaria was referred to an assembly held in that year at Ingelheim, and, being adjudged guilty of high treason, was condemned to death by it.

Recourse to the general assembly was moreover the rule each time the general interests of state were at stake; for instance when, as in 806, the imperial territories were partitioned, or indeed as in 813 on the projected occasion of the designation and coronation of an emperor to be associated in the exercise of power. Let us add that the assembly gave the emperor the opportunity to inform himself about affairs in the most distant regions, to make his views and his instructions known to all, to receive from his representatives his share of the taxes and penalties collected in the counties, as well as the 'annual gifts', which a considerable number of his subjects seem to have been compelled to make. Finally, through direct contact with persons of influence coming from all quarters, he had the opportunity to work directly at the great task of conciliation and unification on which the future of the Empire depended.

The oath of allegiance

From the political point of view, the unity that was sought was ensured by the strongest of all bonds: the oath of allegiance which individually attached to the emperor all the male inhabitants of the Empire from their twelfth year onward.

The obligation assumed was simple but absolute. The following is an example, from the beginning of the ninth century:

I promise to be loyal, from this day on, to the lord Charles, most pious emperor, son of King Pepin and Queen Bertha, sincerely, without fraud or guile and for the honour of his kingdom, as by law a man owes it to his lord and master. May God and all his saints, whose relics are here, protect me; for all the days of my life, with all my will and all the intelligence that God gives me, I shall exert myself for this and consecrate my energies to it.

Such a pledge, in a society imbued with religious belief, was held to be indissoluble. To infringe it was to commit perjury, and this would entail the loss, thenceforward, of the right of recourse to an oath to justify oneself before accusers, and seeing oneself disqualified as a witness before tribunals; it might even lead to the cutting-off of the right hand, the penalty for a false oath; it meant placing oneself in the category of the disloyal, outside the law, whose property and even whose life itself were not protected; even more, it meant the certainty of eternal damnation.

The pledge excluded every restriction and every loophole. This becomes evident when one reads the instructions given in 802 to the *missi* charged with demanding of all the subjects without exception the new oath which incorporated the imperial title that Charlemagne had received shortly before. They were actually directed to point out in their preliminary comments on this occasion "how great and numerous" were the obligations assumed by those pledging their fealty in this way. They were called upon to explain that the oath included not only, "as many up to now had believed", a promise of "allegiance to the living emperor", but that it implied beyond that many and varied obligations beyond the person of the sovereign himself, such as: "to keep oneself with all one's intelligence and all one's energy in the service of God"; to undertake nothing, "neither by perjury, nor by evil trickery, nor by deceit nor by bribery, nor by sums of silver", against the properties of the fisc; to perpetrate "neither fraud, nor rapine, nor any injury whatever against the holy churches of God or against widows, orphans and travellers, because our master the emperor had set himself up to be, after the lord and his saints, their protector and patron"; "not to make worthless the land held in benefice from the emperor nor to seize it for oneself"; "not to evade the mustering for service in the army" nor to use one's influence to help any one to evade it; to obey promptly and without cheating "the orders and instructions of the emperor"; to pay rents and all sums due punctually; and finally to do nothing that might warp or impede the course of justice.

The oath of allegiance thus implied an unconditional submission to the wishes of the emperor. Every disobedience, every deceit, even every attempt at deceit, was equivalent to a violation of this oath. It would be difficult to demand a more absolute docility.

Military duties

Of all the duties imposed on subjects of the Empire, which they were obliged through their oath to perform scrupulously, the military ones were the most onerous. For the Franks, war was a national institution. We have already noted that spring led them almost invariably to the frontiers of the Empire accompanied by one or other, and often by several, of the peoples living along them. The annalists noted those years in which no wars were fought as exceptional ones. Each year, consequently, every subject of the Empire could be required to take arms at the first summons. Four years after Charlemagne's death, for a campaign aimed at repressing a sudden revolt in Italy, the men to be mobilized were warned that they were to hold themselves ready to leave the very same afternoon of the day they received the order if they received it in the morning, and on the morning of the next day if the summons reached them in the afternoon.

Everyone was obliged to equip himself at his own cost and to take along three months' provisions. He was also supposed to carry with him clothing, arms and utensils for six months, providing the very carts himself. These periods of time started, not at the point of departure, but from a line which was sometimes very far away from it. For example, from either the Loire or the Rhine, whichever was relevant, for men who lived on the far side of one of these rivers; from the Elbe for those who went on a campaign in Slavonic country from Germany; and from the Pyrenees for Aquitanians sent into Spain.

The equipment was subject to detailed regulation. The man who was called up was supposed to present himself at the point of mustering equipped, under constraint of penalty, with a lance, a shield, a bow with a spare string, and twelve arrows. The leaders of the detachments were moreover required to wear a helmet and a cuirass or a coat of mail, that is to say, a jerkin of leather covered with pieces of metal. The utensils to be taken were also prescribed in detail, as is shown by this memorandum, which is believed to date approximately from the year 806, and of which the copy sent by the emperor to the abbot of Saint-Quentin has been found:

Know that our general tribunal is to be held this year in eastern Saxony, at Strassfurt, on the Bode. We enjoin you to be there by the fifteenth of the calends of July [17 June], that is seven days before the feast of St John the Baptist, with all your men well-armed and well-equipped. You should present yourself there with them ready to go on campaign, in the direction which I shall indicate, with arms, baggage and all the soldiers' equipment in victuals and clothing. Each horseman is to have a shield, a lance, a long sword and a short sword, a bow and a quiver full of arrows. In your waggons you are to have tools of all kinds – axes, adzes, augers, hatchets, matlocks, iron shovels – as well as the rest of the equipment necessary on the campaign. You must also have in your waggons rations for three months, counting from the departure from Strassfurt, and arms and clothing for half a year. You must be careful that during your journey, and in the place just mentioned, you cause no disturbance whatever, through whichever part of our kingdom your journey takes you. Nothing should be touched except grass, wood and water . . . .

Each military expedition thus entailed considerable sacrifices for all the mobilized men without any recompense other than an uncertain booty. There were no privileged regions: Neustria as well as Austrasia, Frisia as well as Burgundy, Saxony as well as Aquitaine, Bavaria as well as Lombardy, furnished in turn, when not simultaneously, their contingents, even when the scene of military operations was not in any direct way connected with them. In 778, when the war in Spain ended so unfortunately at Roncevaux, Charlemagne's army comprised, beside troops mustered in southern Gaul, Austrasians,

Burgundians, Bavarians and Lombards. However, gradually, as the military expeditions lost some of their strength in numbers, the method seems to have been changed and the musterings limited as much as possible to the inhabitants of the provinces closest to the projected scene of battle. However, when there was war simultaneously or successively on all the frontiers, no region could in the end have considered itself much more spared than the others.

Except in cases of incapacity duly verified, all freeborn men – the only people liable to this duty – were affected by the call to arms and, to borrow the language of the times, were required to respond to the 'ban of the host'. The only persons excused were the few employees whom the counts, bishops and abbots were permitted to leave at home to ensure the normal course of administration, old men and the infirm who had individually obtained from the emperor a permanent exemption from military service, and finally priests and monks, kept for the needs of worship and prayer. Even their exemption was not valid for bishops or abbots, both of whom were required to lead their contingents to the armies in person.

In practice, however, it would have been impossible to remove every time in each region all the free men at once from their normal activities, notwithstanding the enormous contribution servile labour made to work in the fields and in the workshop. Accordingly, such a total levy was rare. Usually, the emperor called up only a part of the contingent, taking into account the needs of manpower, the distance to be traversed, the economic situation, and possibilities of all kinds. For example, a capitulary which is believed to date from the beginning of the ninth century distinguishes three cases when the Saxons would have to turn out: a campaign in Avar country or in the direction of Istria; a campaign in Bohemia; war against the Sorbs. In the first case the mobilization affected one man in six, in the second one in three, and in the third case the whole male population, because the Sorbs were immediate neighbours of Saxony, and the "defense of the home country" was then at stake. Another capitulary, which is dated by its most recent editor to 807, prescribes, on the occasion of a general levy between the Seine and Loire, the following degrees of application, which were less rigorous than was customary. In consideration of the famine there, this document explains, only those possessing three manses or more – besides the holders of royal 'benefices' who were bound to the emperor by a special bond, about which we will say more later – owed individual service (the manse being at that time the current land unit). Over and above this number came the landowners who combined together to equip and send one man at their shared expense: this single man to be sent either by two men possessing three or four manses together; by three men who each held only one manse; or by six men who each possessed only half a manse each or the equivalent in cash or movable goods. In 808 these measures were again mitigated: military service was to be owed individually only by owners of at least four manses, the others being required to join together to pay collectively for one man per four manses.

In a few cases the emperor himself seems to have left to the local authorities the task of organizing a rota among the men liable to mobilization, for some of them complained about being called up more often than they should have been, for lack of having ingratiated themselves with the count or his subordinates, or even with the bishop or abbot. However, it seems that in general military service was distributed equally among the inhabitants of all the territories composing the Empire and that this burden was heavy.

It is true that the campaigns were usually not very long. Normally, the departure took place in July or in the course of August, and the return at the latest in September or October. But the emperor had the right to keep the army in being for longer, if he judged this useful, without making himself responsible for provisions until the three months were past during which everyone was to live from his own means. Leaving the army, for however short a time, without a formal command to do so by the sovereign was considered as desertion pure and simple: a crime designated by the old Germanic word of *herisliz* (which meant precisely 'leaving the army') which entailed capital punishment with confiscation of property.

Every tardiness at the assembly place of the troops was penalized; any evasion was considered as an infraction of the 'ban' (*bannus*) or command of the sovereign, and as such liable to a penalty of sixty shillings, which was made harsher by the fact that, since it concerned the 'ban of the host'–commonly called 'heriban' (*heribannus* or *haribannus*) from the Germanic word *heri*, army, it could be exacted on the spot. If the delinquent could not pay, he was condemned to servitude until his debt was fully paid.

When one appreciates that, in addition to the above obligations, others were expected, such as taking care of the defense of the frontiers, the watch, the patrols, the permanent defense of the coast, in which everyone was supposed to be ready to assist at any moment, it will be seen that military service risked overburdening the inhabitants and causing serious impairment to the normal life of the country.

Requisitions and corvées

In addition to military duties there were various other charges in kind which applied to every part of the Empire. First of all, there were requisitions of lodging and food, horses and carts, for the agents or representatives of the government. The Roman Empire had known an efficient service of postal couriers, with lodging stations (*mansiones*) and relays of horses (*veredi* and *paraveredi*). Each lodging station consisted of a sort of caravansary in which every governmental official, even every civil or ecclesiastical person accredited by the emperor, could find, on showing his letter of instructions, food and lodging for himself and his suite, as well as the means necessary for continuing his journey. It is possible that some elements of this organization still persisted at least in Italy, in the Carolingian period: but in any case they cannot have been very significant. Nevertheless, the principle survived that every representative of the government, bearing an order drawn up in the correct style, ought to be able to procure for himself for the duration of his journey, food, lodgings and transport by means of requisition.

The model of a 'travelling letter' (*epistola tractoria* or simply *tractoria*) issued for this purpose to *missi dominici* has been preserved. It is addressed not only to all the agents of the administration, but "to all faithful subjects" of the emperor, and requires them to furnish its bearer with the necessary means of transport (*evectio*) and supplies (*humanitas*). Details are given: so many horses for the relays, so much bread, wine, barley beer, lard, pigs or piglets, sheep and lambs or other meats, chickens, geese, pheasants, eggs, honey, oil, vinegar, cumin, pepper, cloves and other spices; so much salt, vegetables, cheeses, wax, so much fodder for the horses, wood for the fire, etc. According to a capitulary of this period, the supplies prescribed varied according to the rank of the beneficiary (which would indicate, evidently, the presumed size of his suite). For example, the number of loaves of bread to be furnished was forty for a bishop, thirty for an abbot or a count, and seventeen for a simple vassal of the emperor.

It is difficult to say whether all the inhabitants, without distinction, were subject to this requirement. We may assume, on the contrary, that, leaving aside the general privileges of 'immunity', which will be described later, there were many individual and collective dispensations. It appears also that the right of requisition was limited to certain clearly specified cases, such as the circuits of the *missi dominici*, for there are capitularies which aimed, among other things, at calling to order the counts, bishops, abbots or royal vassals who during their personal travels took the liberty of demanding hospitality from the people within their zone of administration and abusing their property. The obligation must have been oppressive nonetheless, because the missions which, like those of the *missi dominici*, gave the right to food and transport, appear to have been very numerous, not to speak of the accommodation and firewood which, in the winter at least, had to be furnished to every traveller without a place to sleep, whether or not he carried a *tractoria*; and these supplies were, apparently, never paid for. This was a heavy burden, and we know that churches and monasteries unceasingly attempted for free themselves from it.

To it must be added the corvées for the maintenance and, ultimately, the construction of roads, bridges and public buildings. The sources, however, mention these rarely, which makes it likely that works of this kind had but a modest place in the preoccupations of the imperial government.

Taxation

Carolingian fiscal administration was, for the most part, no more than a relic of Roman practice. Taxation not being absolutely necessary for the functioning of the public services, such as they were then conceived – since the agents of the central government, living from the emoluments deriving from their offices and from the products of the lands that were assigned to them, did not need any salary, and since the subjects contributed in person to meet almost all the needs of the state, military as well as civil – the emperor generally contented himself with the little that had been salvaged by his predecessors from the ancient fiscal system instituted by Rome.

As for direct taxation, what remained was so minimal that it has sometimes been held to have disappeared completely. There is nevertheless from time to time question of a poll tax or a land tax in the capitularies promulgated by Charlemagne or his first successor. In 805, for instance, the emperor ordered the levy of a royal tax (*census*) either on the persons of those liable to contribute or upon their property, wherever it had been up to now legally payable, and shortly afterwards in another act he mentioned the necessity of drawing up a list of the lands obliged to pay this tax: "Let our *missi* begin a diligent inquiry concerning our tax in all places in which from ancient times the custom existed of paying it to the king, and let them make a report for us, so that we may be able to prescribe the conduct henceforth to be followed in this matter". It need hardly be doubted that these dues were those which other sources usually call 'tributes' and which we commonly call taxes; it is also evident when one reads the other sources of the period that the two categories of tax mentioned in the capitulary of 805 were a capitation (poll) tax and a land tax. But in many places these taxes had ceased to be collected, either because on many of the large estates Charlemagne's predecessors and Charlemagne himself had voluntarily renounced them in favour of the churches, monasteries and beneficiaries of immunities, or even by simple negligence or as a consequence of evasion by the taxpayers, so that it was necessary in 802 to remind all the subjects of the Empire that "to defraud the king of his due or of the tax" (*debitum suum vel censum marrire*) was, except in the case of lawful exemption, to renege on one's oath of allegiance. Useless remonstrances: the tax, no longer being necessary for the maintenance of public services, was everywhere held to be "unwarranted" and about to disappear.

The only public contribution comparable to a direct tax that was actually current was the tithe. Although collected by the Church and in principle for its exclusive benefit, it was exacted of everyone from one end of the Empire to the other, by command of the sovereign himself, for, since Pepin, the Frankish monarchy no longer separated its cause from that of the Christian religion, and it left to no other authority the task of legislating in these matters.

The payment of the ecclesiastical tithe was thus henceforth rendered obligatory by the government and many of Charlemagne's capitularies mention the matter, be it to remind his subjects that it was a duty which no-one under any pretext whatever could escape, be it to regulate the collection and use of the tax, be it finally to deal severely with those who attempted to evade it. It was the agents of the emperor who were supposed to see that "the law" – the word is mentioned several times – was obeyed in this matter and to search out defaulters, who suffered a civil fine as well as ecclesiastical censure. This then, was really a tax the proceeds of which, amounting to a tenth of the land revenues of every subject (*fidelis*), were intended to make possible the public service of divine worship and the works of charity that accompanied it.

However, the imperial treasury did not itself take any of the tithe, unless it were by usurpation, and more than one capitulary reminds even the representatives of the government that the lands of the sovereign, just like all the others, were liable to this tax for the benefit of the clergy.

Direct taxes for the benefit of the state would thus have been no more than a memory, if to the land tax and the poll tax there had not been added a special type of tribute, which was gradually introduced into administrative practice: the 'gift' or rather the 'annual gifts' (*annua dona* or *dona annualia*). This was the name for a contribution in kind given each year, in principle voluntarily, but in fact under constraint, by all the great lay and ecclesiastical proprietors of the Empire, at the time of the general assembly.

The income from these contributions was anticipated by the imperial administration in the same way as that of a true tax: "You should send to the place where I will be in the middle of May", Charlemagne ordered the abbot of Saint-Quentin, Fulrad, "the gifts you are required (*debes*) to give me at the next assembly". Obviously the obligation was absolute, and the sources mentioning it straightforwardly are numerous; but, without exception, the amount of the payment was left to the discretion of the contributors themselves, which made this tax in principle more tolerable to the self-respect of those subjected to it.

Under the general denomination of 'tolls' (*telonea*), a word derived from the Greek which had gradually replaced the Latin *portorium*, were included the various customs duties, urban tolls, and passage tolls that had been levied on the transport of merchandize in the Roman Empire. The collection offices had usually remained in the traditional places, had sometimes even multiplied, either abusively or by the conscious wish of certain kings or their officials, only too happy to be able to fill their coffers at little cost. These tolls were in principle applicable, as in the Roman Empire, only on goods intended for sale; but the instructions sent on this matter in the capitularies by the king to his representatives, point to the fact that the toll collectors were inclined to tax even goods intended for the personal use of the carriers or their employers. The rule, nevertheless, remained that the toll was supposed to be required only for goods intended for sale, and the toll exemptions often granted by the royal power usually stipulate this explicitly.

The tolls most often mentioned in the sources are taxes on the transit of goods collected at bridges or locks, along the course of roads or rivers; and special names came into use denoting the precise nature of these: *rotaticum* for the transport by vehicles on wheels (*rotae*); *portaticum* for the transports on men's backs; *saumaticum* for transports by beasts of burden; *barganaticum* for transports by barges; *pontaticum* for crossing a bridge, *exclusaticum* for a lock, etc. But it is certainly incorrect to distinguish, as some scholars have tried to do, these taxes from tolls proper, for it is clear that the sources of the period do not make any such distinction.

Charlemagne's contemporaries also counted among tolls the dues collected on commercial transactions in the markets and fairs, the holding of which was itself subject to royal authorization. A legacy, like the above-mentioned taxes, from the Roman Empire, these various categories of tolls probably formed "a non inconsiderable supplement to the receipts of the treasury, although certainly insufficient – if we remember the slowing down of large-scale commerce in the West – to furnish the royal budget with more than a small contribution".

The royal domains, the monetary monopoly, and the chancery fees

The monarchy, it is true, could count on some other sources of revenue: those which it drew either from the exploitation of its estates or from the exercise of governmental power.

The number of domains (*villae*) which Charlemagne possessed was considerable and they were scattered over the whole extent of the Empire, though in the northern regions of Gaul and the Meuse and Rhine country they constituted a more compact bloc, because it was here that the properties of the Carolingian family had joined the mass of those which Pepin, upon usurping the royal power, had inherited from the Merovingians, themselves perhaps heirs of the Roman fisc. These estates comprised, as was usual, plough-land, meadows, vineyards, vegetable gardens and orchards, woods and wastelands, of which part remained under the direct administration of the king, whereas the rest was assigned to tenants. Stewards (*villici*) were appointed to supervise operations and to maintain the residential buildings, which consisted, as in all the large domains, of stables, cattlesheds, a poultry-yard, an apiary, a wine-press, a mill, workshops for the repair of the implements, workshops for weaving, and, if possible, fisheries and fishing ponds.

There are several capitularies that attest the emperor's interest in the good administration of his estates. The best known is the capitulary called *de villis* – though it is difficult to ascertain whether it was issued by Charlemagne himself or by his son Louis (the future Louis the Pious), then delegated by his father to the government of Aquitaine – which displays very well, from the first article onward, the sovereign's primary care: to let none of the income he ought personally to receive from his estate be turned to the advantage of someone else. To this point more than one article returns, for the small receipts from the few taxes that still existed obliged the king to ensure that no one encroached on his rights over a category of revenues that constituted an important part of his upkeep. Another point to note is the use of the two words *villae* and *fisci* to designate the royal domains: even though they originally belonged to the family, these estates had been assimilated to those which at Rome were held to be territories of the fisc (treasury) which, however, should not surprise us because, since then, every distinction between the private and the public aspect of the royal person seems to have vanished.

Of the various monopolies held by the Roman emperors, the only one that the Carolingian king had been able to preserve was that of the minting of money. After the anarchy of the later Merovingian period the administration of the mints had been firmly recovered by Pepin the Short. His efforts and those of his successor made possible a systematic reorganization of the minting workshops and even of the monetary system. The number of workshops, having become too large, was reduced so as to make their supervision easier. In 805 and 808 Charlemagne even went so far as to reserve the minting of money in principle to the single mint of Aachen. An exceptional measure, doubtless of a temporary nature (since it does not seem to have been in force under Louis the Pious), it resulted in a reorganization of the currency.

The costs of minting were covered by the deductions which the overseers – the 'moneyers' (*monetarii*) – were permitted to take from the metal or the old coins delivered to be melted. A capitulary from the reign of Pepin the Short had fixed this deduction at one shilling per pound of silver, at a time when 22 shillings were counted to the pound. As no other deduction was prescribed for the work it is probable either that each workshop had been rented from the sovereign, or that part of the profits were reserved for him.

This monopoly had the advantage, besides, of allowing the unification of the monetary system; a tangible sign of the unity of the Empire. Charlemagne made every effort to obtain this result. Thus he withdrew from circulation the old coins, among which the greatest diversity existed, and replaced them by new coins of a uniform type, weight, and content. This measure seems to have been the more easily applied since the only currency that officially remained in circulation was that of the silver penny, of which twelve were counted to the shilling, and 240 to the pound, without the need being felt to mint coins corresponding to either of these higher values. The sources indicate, however, that the reform did not succeed easily, and the various types of coin that have come down to us reveal that Charlemagne's government was indeed not powerful enough to bring about the uniform currency it had hoped for. It is undeniable nevertheless that the pennies of Charlemagne's time – which in practice could not have been used without half-pennies or obols – display a relatively uniform character that compares favourably to those of the Merovingian period.

If it is not easy to assess the revenues which the Carolingian monarchy was able to draw from the minting of money, it is still more difficult to calculate those which it received from the collection of chancery fees. All that one can say is that the authority and prestige which his military successes and the successful exercise of power brought to Charlemagne, lent a daily increasing authority to the documents he issued to grant or confirm property rights and privileges. Hence a rush of requests came to his court, as the documents of the period attest. The continuous growth of the territories that constituted the Empire also increased the number of those who were led to solicit favours from the ruler, and provided the chancery with opportunities for income which, without the slightest doubt, would be underestimated if we measured it by the 160 documents of which the original text has survived. It is in fact impossible, in the present state of research, to risk the slightest evaluation or even to say whether the profits made by the chancery were notably greater than the expenses necessary for its proper functioning.

To be sure, the Carolingian monarchy could no longer expect, as in the time of the great invasions, to obtain the booty from war which, together with the tributes imposed on the vanquished, were its most obvious resources; and it was supplemented only feebly by the taxes and the normal proceeds from the rights it exercised. The cries of joy uttered by the Frankish troops in 796, at the news that the 'treasures' hoarded by the Avars had just fallen into Frankish hands, help to put things in proportion: such a booty seemed to everyone a windfall that would instantly open an era of exceptional abundance.

However, the exercise of judicial power, which remains to be discussed, brought the monarchy a not inconsiderable income in a more regular manner, and at the same time allowed the sovereign to assert his governing authority in a useful way throughout the Empire, in the service of peace and public order.

Justice

Notwithstanding the diversity of the legal codes – the Salic, Ripuarian, Burgundian and other laws – to which the Empire's inhabitants remained subject, even within the Frankish kingdom alone – nothing, we may recall, having changed their individual judicial status, which derived from their ethnic origin – the judicial organization was, at least in its general characteristics, uniform throughout the territories placed under Charlemagne's authority.

One principle ruled all action in this sector: among the duties incumbent on the sovereign ruler there was none more absolute than that of ensuring to each the full respect for his rights – of 'his law', the sources say – and a scrupulous justice. This principle, stated many times in the capitularies, was valid not only for the emperor himself but for all those, laymen or ecclesiastics, who exercised authority in his name. For it must be noted that the duty of justice imposed itself in such an absolute way upon the sovereign that he considered himself responsible for the proper execution of the sentences pronounced in his lands, whether by bishops or abbots or by the counts and other agents of the civil order. Hence we often find directions about the exercise of justice in the capitularies.

They are most frequently addressed to the counts, whose role here appears to be of primary importance, just as it was in the other administrative sectors. Because it was in principle to their judicial assembly that, except in special cases, every case concerning two subjects of the emperor, was referred, excluding only matters that were of a purely ecclesiastical nature, which were reserved to the tribunals of the Church. In his county, every count thus held regular sessions, the so-called 'mall' (*mallus*) or 'plea' (*placitum*) – the former held in the town where he had his residence, the latter in other towns or villages within his jurisdiction. The count presided, assisted by assessors who through most of the eighth century had been chosen from among the notables of the county, as our present day jurors are; they were then called 'rachimburgs' (*rachineburgi, rachinburgi, racineburgi, racinburgi*) or 'good men' (*boni homines*). Since the last quarter of the century, at least within the Frankish kingdom proper, they had become a body of professional magistrates – the 'echevins' (*scabini*) – whose duty it was to say what the law was, leaving to the count who presided over the tribunal the task of formulating the verdicts and pronouncing them. Recruited within each county by the count himself in agreement with the *missi dominici*, the body of echevins was limited to a dozen members, at the very most, per county. But it was usually enough for seven of them to be present for the judicial assembly to be able to function lawfully. They followed the count in his judicial circuits and were subjected just as he was to inspection by the *missi*.

The number of judicial assemblies or 'pleas' which the count was expected to hold in the course of the year was limited to three by Charlemagne in order to end all sorts of abuses which too frequent summonses to appear entailed, and the discomfort which often resulted from this for the interested parties. Several capitularies recall moreover that only the parties concerned in the case were required to attend the sessions.

The competence of the count's tribunal extended to all categories of affairs, civil and criminal, which the litigants referred to it. It does not seem that the count was entitled to initiate prosecutions himself, except when the interests or commands of the sovereign, whom the count represented, were directly concerned. But his zeal was sustained by the lure of the profits brought in by the application of the penalties he pronounced.

The general principle was, in fact, that whatever the judicial status of the person to be judged, every injury to the right of another entailed, in case of conviction, the payment of a 'composition', the amount of which was proportionate to the seriousness of the wrong caused, but of which a part was always reserved as a fine (*fredum*) to the royal authority, the guardian of the public peace throughout the Empire. This fraction consisted, at least in Frankish law, of a third; and of the sum thus collected the count kept, in his turn, a third, in remuneration for his services.

To this should be added a third of the product of the fines collected for the benefit of the treasurer for the infraction of the command, or as it was then called of the 'ban', of the sovereign (*bannus dominicus*): a frequent occurrence because of the many civil, religious and military measures through which every subject risked coming into conflict with what was called the 'ban of the sovereign'. A large number of sources prove that under this heading not only capitularies, ordinances or official acts duly published were meant, but everything which in whatever form and whatever degree expressed or even implied a decision on his part. This included, for example, his desire to take into his protection the churches, widows, orphans, and all those disinherited of their fortunes, wherever in the Empire they lived, as well as his wish to prosecute incendiaries, rapists, burglars, deserters . . . . This is a list that has no natural end and which the emperor and his agents were in fact inclined to extend almost indefinitely, seeing that Charlemagne included in it: poaching in the royal forests, the refusing of legal currency, the repeated refusal to pay tithes, the sale of objects of worship, the violation by clergy of the conciliar measures concerning the presence of women in their homes, the excessive collection of tolls or passage-fees, the concealment of fugitives, the stealing of grain or fodder by the armies at the expense of the inhabitants of the regions traversed, the theft of beasts of burden, the sale of taxable products without paying the tax, the sale of slaves or serfs outside the boundaries of the kingdom, the murder of pilgrims, etc. The possibilities for measures against violators of the royal or imperial 'ban' were obviously unlimited, since every injury to another's right, every infringement of the laws of the Church which had been endorsed by the emperor, every disturbance of the public peace, could be construed as violating the wishes of the king. The fine imposed upon the delinquent was, in this case, sixty shillings, a considerable sum for the period, which could sometimes be doubled, even tripled, if the crime committed seemed especially serious, while on the other hand it was seldom reduced to less than sixty shillings. How productive this source of revenue could be for a vigilant and active count can easily be imagined.

But this was not all. Certain kinds of prosecution could, by their very nature, bring the count extra profits, if the crimes in question were ones such as incest, murder of one's own parents, the renunciation of sworn fidelity, which entailed, in case of conviction, the penalty of the confiscation of property. The beneficiary of this was, it is true, the king himself; but some sources seem to indicate that the counts too could profit here, because they were sometimes accused of allowing themselves to be driven by an "insatiable cupidity" into multiplying this kind of conviction.

Besides, the count was not alone in the handling of cases brought to trial in the provinces. Distinction was made in fact between so-called 'major' cases which, except in special circumstances, must be dealt with by his tribunal, and the cases of lesser importance, so-called 'minor cases', which could be referred to the judgement of his subordinates, the vicars or hundredmen. According to the capitularies promulgated at the beginning of the ninth century, all criminal cases and proceedings concerning the free status were reserved to the count's tribunal. From the ninth century on, disputes concerning property rights – at least landed property – were no longer to be judged by vicars except temporarily and doubtless if the object of contention was not very great; when "less serious cases" (*leviores causae*) were concerned, as one capitulary formulates it. The range of the vicar's competence was thus a much reduced one. Their exercise of justice followed a procedure similar to that of the counts. The vicar or hundredman presided over a tribunal called a 'plea' or *mall*, likewise composed of seven judges – at first rachinburgs, then echevins once the institution of echevinage had come into being. But probably because of the increasingly restricted competence of this tribunal, sources attesting to its functioning in this period are extremely rare.

If the count's tribunal was qualified to settle the cases with which his vicar's courts could only deal provisionally, the sentences of the count were themselves subject to revision by the *missi*, who moreover were required to handle the cases which, for one reason or another, were still pending. They were enjoined to hold, in the month they spent on each circuit, four sessions in four different localities throughout the counties subject to their inspection. Each time they sat they were assisted, not only by the seven echevins henceforth prescribed for all ordinary judicial assemblies, but by the count within whose competence had originated the case that was submitted to their inspection. In all the cases in which referral to the *missi* was motivated by a complaint against a verdict rendered, or by a dispute concerning the cogency of a judgement passed by this or that count, the sentence given in the name of the king by his representatives on circuit brought in profits, like those of the count's trials, divided according to the rules described above. It should be noted also that suits concerning the inheritance of landed properties, the handling of which seems to have been reserved to the *missi*, provided special rights for the benefit of the treasury, which claimed for its good offices one-tenth of the lands and of the servile labour.

The king's own tribunal was the court of highest instance, to which were referred cases which the ordinary tribunals, especially the ecclesiastical ones, and even the tribunals of the *missi*, found themselves powerless to settle or which they refused to judge, as well as those which were the subject of an appeal as "badly judged". The king's tribunal judged cases concerning royal officials in the first instance, especially those concerning counts against whom some complaint had been brought by their subjects, certain serious cases of disobedience to royal orders, such as desertion (*herisliz*) which the king reserved to his own judgement, and finally the cases concerning 'powerful men' (*potentiores*): high officials, bishops, abbots, great proprietors.

The king, naturally, did not usually preside in person except in cases where the seriousness of the matters submitted to his tribunal made his intervention advisable. He was then assisted by the count palatine, whose role we have described earlier and who normally presided in his place. Whoever presided, the tribunal held its sessions in the palace where the king was at that moment residing and the role of judges was here assumed not by echevins but by several of the 'magnates' who constituted the king's entourage.

Immunities

Neither the administrative nor the judicial regime which we have just described applied as such to all ecclesiastical domains. An increasingly large number of these acquired a privileged status, that of the 'immunity', which made of them territories in which the proprietor to a very large extent took over the functions of the count and his agents. This arrangement was not born in the Carolingian period; it was indeed, in its most important elements, a legacy of Merovingian times, though it was developed, generalized and transformed under Charlemagne, until it became in his hands a regular means of government applicable to the lands of the Church.

'Immunity' (*immunitas* or *emunitas*) was a privilege in terms of which an estate was withdrawn from the competence of the ordinary officials of the king; to speak the language of the time, these estates were declared 'exempt' (*immunis*) from the intervention of royal officials and linked directly with the central government, before which the proprietor was thenceforth personally responsible for most of the administrative and judicial services with which the count and his subordinates were otherwise usually charged. No 'public official' (*judex publicus*), according to most of the charters granting or confirming the privilege, "is henceforth allowed to penetrate" the domains of the beneficiary, neither "to dispense justice there, nor to take fines, nor to demand witnesses, nor to take lodging or demand services, nor to collect taxes or dues, nor to exercise there any constraint upon the free or unfree inhabitants", which implied – the charters prove it – that the task of mustering troops was also taken out of the hands of the count. The count and his subordinates were thus replaced by the immunist lord, who by special favour and for the whole extent of his estates, present and future, saw himself delegated with the necessary powers to act in the name of the king.

From the judicial viewpoint, the practical consequences of this measure were the following: for 'minor' cases the inhabitants of the 'immunity' were referred exclusively to the tribunal of the immunist lord; for the 'major' cases and notably for criminal cases, it was the immunist's duty, if he was requested to do so, to personally produce the accused before the public tribunal whether they regularly lived in the immunity or whether they had sought refuge there. It was only if the immunist lord refused to do this and in so doing voluntarily impeded justice, that after three summonses the count was authorized to enter his territory to arrest the accused there. There were, moreover, sanctions against a recalcitrant immunist lord, in the form of a fine of from fifteen to thirty or sixty shillings, even up to 600 shillings in the case of armed resistance, and furthermore, if occasion arose, the confiscation of the royal 'benefices' held and the revocation of the governmental powers exercised. But armed resistance was obviously only a rare case: a true act of rebellion against the royal authority of which, by virtue of his very privilege, the immunist lord had become the auxiliary and even the direct representative in the whole extent of his domains.

Military affairs were handled in the same way. It was to the immunist lord that in case of mobilization the duty fell to raise the contingent and provide for its leadership; it was his task to have the necessary services of watch and ward performed; to him was left the task of compelling the refractory to pay the 'heriban'.

Finally, from the point of view of taxation, it was again the immunist lord who was the king's direct representative in all that concerned the taxes proper as well as requisitions, corvées, and the collection of fines.

In short, in the whole extent of the immunity governmental responsibility was, in essence, transferred to the immunist lord, on condition that he saw to the carrying out of the king's orders concerning the collection of taxes, the appearance of the inhabitants before public tribunals in all cases that were beyond the limits of his own jurisdiction, as well as in the levy of taxes and the payment of fines.

In this state of affairs, the immunist lord, while benefiting from an arrangement that left him a greater liberty of movement within his estates, which were henceforth protected against the too frequent harassments of the counts and their subordinates, became in fact a cog in the administrative machinery in the same way as the counts. Just as they were, so was he personally responsible to the king, and we have seen the sanctions he risked incurring if he did his job badly. The threat of finding himself deprived of his office and his 'benefices' was not an empty one, since most of these immunist lords were bishops or abbots, all of whom were subject to the nomination or approval of the king. Indeed the privileges of immunity granted or confirmed in this period concerned, without exception, churches or monasteries, for whom the arrangements we have just described increasingly tended to become the normal ones.

The immunist lords' situation, which itself permanently ensured direct royal supervision, prompted the king to display generosity to them. Thus he was frequently induced to make over to them the sums collected in principle for the benefit of the fisc, and an increasing number of privileges of immunity granted by Charlemagne contained a new clause stating that, in the lands of the immunity, receipts from taxes and fines were granted to the immunist in order to meet the cost of public worship. At the end of the reign the king may have renounced to the benefit of certain immunists the exaction of military service from the inhabitants of the immunity; in 817, in any case, several sources seem to show that such an alleviation of the burden was already rather widespread. Finally, because the status of the immunist lords could hardly, whatever its terms, fail to excite jealousy, and because it was necessary to effectively prevent unwarranted intervention by the counts and their subordinates, we see Charlemagne already very early decreeing the most severe sanctions against the violators of the immunity: to the fine of 600 shillings which could be exacted from a rebellious immunist lord, corresponded, in the case of violation of the privilege of immunity, a 'composition' of equal value, of which one third went in the form of *fredum* to the king, and two thirds to the immunist lord.

For the immunist, even though he received all the proceeds of the collections made for the royal treasury on his lands, this was not all straight profit. In order to fulfil the needs that constituted the price of the privileges he enjoyed, he needed administrative machinery analogous in all respects to that of the count from whom he was liberated. On the other hand, his ecclesiastical office forbade him to exercise, in person at least, any of the civil functions with which the privilege of immunity charged him. The king thus obliged him to take as his associate a special agent or deputy, whose official title was 'advocate' (*advocatus*) – or sometimes vice-lord (*vice-dominus*) when a bishop was concerned – whose nomination and administration was closely supervised by the king. It was the advocate who discharged in his place most of the obligations which, in virtue of the privilege of immunity, weighed on the immunist. However, in the present state of research, it seems impossible to know exactly how the advocate carried out his task. We know nothing, in particular, about the composition of his tribunal, though it may be assumed that it was modeled on the public tribunals; and we should doubtless not be too far amiss if we assumed that the administrative organization of the immunity was modeled fairly closely on that of the other territories of the Empire. As for the extent of this privilege, we may be sure it was considerable. The number of domains that benefited from the privilege of immunity increased with the growing number of ecclesiastical estates themselves, and in the time of Charlemagne eventually constituted an important proportion of the territorial aggregate subject to the suzerainty of the Frankish emperor.

Vassalage

The immunist lords were not the only intermediaries to whom the emperor could turn, besides his normal representatives, to communicate with his subjects and to have them carry out his orders. The rapid spread of vassalage gave him other auxiliaries who, by relieving the counts and their associates of some of their duties at least in appearance strengthened the administrative machine and increased its efficiency.

In contrast to the immunity, vassalage was not, in principle, an institution of public law. The contract of vassalage was a contract of private law between two persons of free status who had drawn up between them an agreement in terms of which one of them, the 'vassal' (*vassus, vassalus*) pledged himself or–to use the language of the times–'commended himself' (*se commendat*) to the service (*servitium*) and 'in the obedience of' (*in obsequio*) the other whom he recognized as 'master' (*dominus*) or 'lord' (*senior*) in exchange for the protection the lord guaranteed him.

At first glance, these very words of service, obedience, master and lord indicate that, although he did not renounce his free status, one of the contracting parties agreed to let himself be assimilated in some degree to the status of a humble servant. The use of the term 'vassal' which was ultimately to evoke very different ideas, is far from contradicting this since originally, and sometimes well into the eighth century, even exceptionally in the ninth, it was a prevalent designation for people of servile condition. This was because the very insecurity of life during the seventh and a large part of the eighth century, and the social upheavals that resulted from this, had compelled numerous free men to look for protectors among those who had been spared by ill-fortune, and often to place themselves at their mercy.

A formula that probably dates from the middle of the eighth century has preserved the model of a contract drawn up between one of these destitute persons and the protector of his choice. The charter begins by recalling the request addressed to the desired "magnificent lord" (*domino magnifico*) by the one whom misfortune – as indicated by the title placed above it by the compiler of the formulary (*Qui se in alterius potestate commendat*) – has placed in the harsh necessity of "commending himself into the power of another":

Whereas it is well known to all that I have nothing to eat or to clothe myself with, I have requested your mercy and you have granted me permission to surrender and commend myself into your patronage [in other words: to place myself in your protection] which I have done on the following conditions. 1. You shall be obliged to assist and support me in food as well as in clothing, to the degree to which I shall be able to deserve this by serving you; 2. As long as I am personally alive I am bound to give you the service and obedience which may be expected from a free man, and I may not, during your lifetime, withdraw from your power and patronage; 3. It is agreed that if one of us should try to act counter to this agreement, he shall be compelled to pay to his peer [his partner] a fine of so many shillings, and the agreement will nonetheless remain in force; 4. It is agreed finally that, concerning this matter, two letters of the same content shall be exchanged and confirmed by the parties, which has been done.

This case was probably an extreme one. The person who declared himself ready to enter the service of another recognized that he did this because he was at the end of his resources and did not have any other means of existence. But this confession which perhaps was, on the whole, no more than an additional proof of humility, tainted with some exaggeration, did not prevent the poor man from preserving his dignity as a free man treating his protector as his equal, the formula itself purposely emphasizing that he is his 'peer' (*par*). The terms of the agreement concluded balanced each other, as was fitting for a contract voluntarily entered into between equals; and the violation of this contract by the one or the other of the two parties was punishable by an equal penalty. It is to a 'master' (*dominus*) that the vassal addresses himself, but a master chosen voluntarily, and what he has asked from him is in principle not something to live from, but his protection. In a society in which the idea of public order had slowly been lost, the custom had arisen for those who did not themselves have sufficient power to make their rights respected, to place themselves in this way under the protection (*mundeburdium* or *mundium*) of someone more powerful than they. The king himself had given the example by agreeing to take into his protection or guardianship (*tuitio*) many of the churches and monasteries of his kingdom. It was a sought-after favour through which the beneficiaries and their property themselves fell under the same guarantee as the persons and property of the 'family' of the protector or even as his own property.

In principle the agreement bound both parties indissolubly for the duration of their lives. Sources half a century later state, at any rate, that the 'commended' person – for whom increasingly from then on the designation 'vassal' is reserved – could consider himself discharged from all obligations if his lord failed seriously in his duties as a protector; for instance by threatening him with death, or using violence towards him, or by making attempts on the virtue of his wife or daughter, or even by trying to rob him of his personal property. Except in cases of this kind, the vassal was bound in an irrevocable manner and in principle without any limitations on his services other than that they be of such a kind as free men might suitably perform. Literally and within these limits, that is to say with the exclusion of manual labour with which at that time serfs were burdened, the vassal was no longer his own master: he was placed at the discretion of the lord when, to use the language of the time, he "surrendered and recommended himself". A capitulary of Pepin the Short which is thought to date from around 760 even considers it normal for the vassal to be obliged to leave his homeland with his lord, if the lord himself is compelled to do so. Because not to do so, the legislator observes, would be "to violate his sworn fidelity" (*fidem mentiri*).

About that time, the contract of vassalage in fact began to be supplemented and reinforced, if possible, by the taking of an oath of fidelity, which from the end of the eighth century was to become the compulsory accompaniment of all feudal contracts. This oath matched the one which the king demanded of his subjects, and it may be significant that the oldest source in which it appears concerns a royal vassal; because the king had had vassals from a very early period, just as ordinary private individuals had had them. It was in 757, on the occasion of the entering into vassalage of the duke of Bavaria, Tassilo, that for the first time such an oath of fidelity is mentioned. Tassilo "commending himself into vassalage" (*in vassatico se commendans*), took an oath on the relics of the saints "promising fidelity (*fidelitatem*) to Pepin, as a vassal (*vassus*), by law and by justice, with all the devotion he can owe to his lord". By the beginning of the ninth century this practice had become so usual that, in a capitulary of 805, Charlemagne did not hesitate to place the vassal's oath of fidelity on the same plane as the subject's oath of allegiance to his king, in noting that these were the only two types of oath of fidelity that were valid. It may even be imagined that the formula of the oath required in 802 of the emperor's subjects (*fideles*), the text of which we have translated above, was modelled to some extent on the oath which was required of vassals, since Charles' subject (*fidelis*) bound himself to behave "as by law a man should do toward his lord".

It was also on the occasion of Tassilo's entering into vassalage in 757 that the formal act may be seen taking shape that would later be called homage. To emphasize the full significance of his deed, notes the author of the *Royal Annals*, Tassilo commended himself to the king "with (his) hands" (*per manus*): in other words, he put his hands between those of his lord according to a rite whose meaning is clear and which, as the sources show, experienced a rapid diffusion shortly afterward. They show us this rite, moreover, becoming fixed and fully developed, thereby relegating the original written contract to the background, so that every trace of it had apparently disappeared before the end of the eighth century.

In fact, there no longer was any need of a written charter; it was enough that the entering into vassalage according to the forms we have just described had publicly taken place, for the vassal's obligation to be indisputable. On the other hand, nothing concrete would any longer have indicated the lord's obligation if a new practice had not at a timely moment come into being to witness to it: instead of restricting himself, as in the original contract, to a general and vague promise of material assistance, the lord was now increasingly induced to reward his vassal with some land or some other property which the vassal was to hold of him as a 'benefice' (*beneficium*) that is to say – if one leaves the word *beneficium* in its original meaning – as a witness to his generosity.

Although this practice became general only gradually, a capitulary of Charlemagne of the first years of the ninth century already specifies that, except in unusual circumstances, no vassal should leave his lord "from the moment he has received from him the value of one shilling". The possession of any benefice whatever, however mediocre it be, thus created presumptive evidence for the bond of vassalage or confirmed it, and inversely, from the same period onward, vassalage generally seemed to entail the awarding of a 'benefice'.

Even though, let us repeat, this awarding was not yet held to be necessary, at least not immediately, in this period the 'benefice' – which in the tenth century came to be called 'fief' – became the complement and counterpart of vassalage. It followed its vicissitudes: the vassal's violation of his sworn fidelity entailed the taking back of the benefice, just as would the dissolution of the vassal's bond by death or any other cause. The contract of vassalage thus tended in every way to pass, as the lawyers say, from a 'personal' plane to a 'material' one, and this process continued unchecked after Charlemagne's death.

This evolution, however, is less important for our discussion than vassalage itself and the direct personal bond it implied between protected and protector. For the lord, the vassals constituted a group of loyal men (*fideles*) always ready to carry out his orders and to assist him in accomplishing his task. The king himself had his own vassals – which were distinguished from the others by the designation *vassi dominici* – who, already considerable in number at the time of Charlemagne, constituted for him a numerous team of devoted auxiliaries, whom he controlled more closely than the mass of his ordinary subjects through the benefices which he had given them and of which he could deprive them at their slightest inclination towards disobedience.

Royal vassalage above all provided the backbone of the army. It is indeed obvious that this consideration was dominant around the middle of the eighth century. In 743 Carloman recognized that "because of the wars" he had been forced to create a large number of benefices by taking them out of the properties of monasteries and churches in order to reward in a sufficient manner the vassals he needed for his armies. The method was in principle exceptional, but he had already been obliged to turn to it for a considerable time, in order to supplement his military resources.

It was on this occasion that was conceived the singular procedure of the "leases in the name of the king" (*precaria verbo regis*), which will not be studied here. By means of them the king could draw from the properties of the Church, in return for certain at least apparent compensations, in order to distribute adequate benefices to numerous vassals, without alienating his own properties. The sources seem to show that at the end of the eighth and during the ninth century the royal vassals occupied, beside the counts, commanding positions in Charlemagne's armies, and that at the time of mobilization they were summoned directly to lead their own vassals and other troops called up within their jurisdiction to the host without going via the counts.

In itself vassalage provided the monarchy with a convenient means of simplifying and accelerating the mobilization of all the royal contingents, for in the words of several capitularies of the beginning of the ninth century, and notably of the years 808 and 811, the rule was that for all those who were responsible to a lord, mobilization was carried out under the command of the lord, except when, for a valid reason, this lord was excused from coming to the army in person.

It is easy to understand that, in these circumstances, Charlemagne's government, far from impeding vassalage, on the contrary did all in its power to stimulate its development. It not only accepted but regulated vassalage, the distribution of 'benefices' and the oath of vassalage appearing to be a convenient means of extending its field of action. That in this way the government exposed itself to certain dangers whose seriousness was to appear later, is not to be doubted; but above all in the beginning vassalage was seen as, and found to be, a useful and sure means to reinforce and supplement governmental authority.

From whatever angle it is seen, the whole political and administrative organization of the Empire eventually converged in the emperor himself. He was the central motor of the state; his commands, his capitularies, had to be carried out in the whole extent of the territories subject to his overlordship, where the counts and the *missi* carried out his decisions; the immunist lords and the vassals escaped the supervision normal for his agents only to attach themselves to his person by a bond of more direct dependence. The emperor remained in every case the master of all, the person whose will was law. The moment has now come to examine the principles on which his government was founded and the guiding ideas to which his acts conformed.

CHAPTER SEVEN

The emperor

The principles of government

A first point must be made: Charlemagne, who at the head of his edicts, since 800, declared himself to be "governing the Roman Empire" (*Romanum gubernans imperium*) was, nevertheless, not a Roman Emperor. If his biographer Einhard tried hard to liken him to the rulers of ancient Rome, it was because he had taken as his model the biographer of the twelve 'Caesars', the Latin historian Suetonius, but in fact the power which Charles wielded only remotely resembled that of the ancient Caesars. The idea of a *respublica*, as Fustel de Coulanges has amply demonstrated, which at Rome stood above the emperor and made him the interpreter and executor of the collective will of the whole people, had in the West long ago vanished from the minds of men. In the course of the centuries of anarchy which followed the triumphs of the barbarian conquerors, the habit set in of seeing in the kings no more than all-powerful lords by right of conquest, having power over the soil, with its inhabitants, as over a piece of property, arduously acquired at sword's point.

This summary manner of viewing the role of the royal power was now, however, transcended. Under the influence of the Church, the Carolingian ruler had become conscious of the duties resting on him as the head of the community of peoples subject to his government. By virtue of the sacring, the Carolingian prince held his authority from God; as a new David he was the ruler designated by the Almighty to guide, to their salvation, the new chosen people, Christ's people. Because, as happened with ancient Israel, the limits of the ruler's activity tended to become identical to the territories occupied by the believers of the true faith, seeing that even those who were at first strangers to it were generally obliged to be converted as soon as they were incorporated into his kingdom. Also, by a simplification which in the end the facts clearly justified, people were persuaded that he reigned over "the whole Christian people" (*omnis populus christianus*) – wishing to consider worthy of this name only those who had constantly remained obedient to the successor of St Peter.

Consequently, for the king of the Franks, there was no more imperious obligation than that of a life conforming to the teachings of the catholic religion. Charlemagne was imbued with this necessity of which the churchmen did not fail to remind him, and which, at the beginning of his reign, a priest by the name of Cathulf in a frequently cited letter formulated in these instructions: refer everything to God, who has drawn us from the least to the greatest, out of nothingness to make of us what we are; to God, to whom the king owes his victories and his domination over "Europe"; to God, whose "place he occupies here below" and by whom he has been commissioned to govern and to "exalt the law". A programme identical with that of the biblical king, whose example was constantly invoked in the documents of the time and on whom Charles was invited to model himself. This is why Cathulf advised him to have a copy of the law always at his fingertips, according to the command of Moses, in *Deuteronomy* (17: 18–19): "As soon as he is seated on the throne, the king shall have a copy of the law transcribed for him . . .; he shall have it in his possession and shall read it every day of his life, in order to learn to fear the Lord his God and to observe His precepts . . .".

The edicts promulgated by Charlemagne witness to his persistent desire to carry out this programme. No one realized more clearly than he how heavy were the responsibilities, spiritual as well as material, that weighed upon his shoulders. One of the most famous capitularies, which has come to be called the 'General admonition' (*Admonitio generalis*), gives us, in the year 789 or thereabouts, a general statement of the principles he had decided on. Recalling the precedent of King Josiah who, according to the Book of Kings (2: 22–23), made bitter war on 'superstitions' and exerted himself untiringly to re-establish the worship of the true God everywhere in Israel, Charles considered himself too as having no more urgent a task than that of leading the 'people of God' back to the way of the Lord, and to aid them with all his might in their search for salvation. Therefore, his first care was to reproduce (Arts. 1–60), for the benefit of the bishops and their clergy, the essential prescriptions of the great councils which, since those of Nicaea, Laodicea and Antioch, had formulated the rules for the religious life. Through these alone could be ensured that purity of faith which the churchmen were to preach to the people without fail (Art. 61) and which was to consolidate the unity of all believers around the king, who was its official guardian. "May peace, harmony and unanimity reign amongst the whole Christian people and among the bishops, abbots, counts and our other representatives; amongst all, great and small; because without peace, one cannot please God", Art. 62 explains, referring to passages in the scriptures in which neighbourly love and concord are cited as the necessary conditions for the well-being of all. It is by virtue of this concord and 'unanimity' that, united as brothers among themselves and to the king, all men will form one body in Christ and, beyond the tomb, will attain the kingdom of heaven (Art. 82).

The same ideas and often the same words, particularly the expressive one of 'unanimity' (*unanimitas* or *unianimitas*), were repeated, with fresh elaborations, in the instructions which Emperor Charlemagne gave in 802 to the *missi* sent to receive the new oaths of allegiance which he considered it wise to demand from his subjects now he had become emperor. No government is possible, he repeats, without the support of all men's good will: all are obliged "to remain unanimous when they discharge their obligations and their offices" and to observe amongst themselves "relations of charity and peace". This presupposed first of all, as we have seen, that each "keeps himself fully in God's service", in order to protect the faith, without which everyone would perish, because it would be impossible for the Emperor "himself to impart to each privately all the necessary attention and teachings" (Art. 3). This also assumes that each subject, not only would obey his orders strictly, but would exert himself to facilitate their execution (Art. 8); that he would not only not obstruct justice, but would place all his resources at the service of equity (Art. 9); that he would not only undertake nothing against the properties of the sovereign, but would aid the ruler in his task as defender of the property of others and protector of churches, widows and orphans and strangers by abstaining from injuring them (Arts. 2, 4, 5). Of the holders of public authority, "bishops, abbots, abbesses, counts", Charles expected that they "show themselves unanimous . . . in all charity and in full concord" in the execution of their mandates (Art. 14). It is by supporting one another and carrying on in full union of heads and minds – which the term 'unanimity' signifies – that, from high to low on the social ladder, all those who were part of the 'Christian people' would help the emperor not to succumb under the weight of the responsibilities with which God had invested him.

To live always in perfect agreement with one another, never to depart from the principles of solidarity and charity (*caritas*), in the true sense of this word, which recurs constantly in his capitularies, such were the virtues which Charles untiringly preached or caused to be preached by his *missi* to all the subjects of the Empire as indispensable for the accomplishment of his task; and some of the measures he took derived from this generous thought. This was the case, for example, when on the occasion of the famines which several times devastated his lands, he ordered anyone who disposed of sufficient supplies to feed at his own cost one or several needy persons, according to a scale set up in terms of the means of each; or when he recalled the obligation imposed on all to receive under their roof travellers, rich or poor, and pilgrims in the course of their journeys.

It was only by putting into practice this grand law of mutual aid and human solidarity, and by the constant harmony between all those of good will, that the emperor could hope to maintain interior peace, without which no state can survive. He was convinced, regarding this, that only the harmony of all men – which he expressed with the word 'concord' (*concordia*) – could establish peace, and in his capitularies these two terms were constantly paired to the point of resulting, in some cases, in an expression difficult to translate into our language: *concordia pacis* ('the harmony of peace'). This was inspired perhaps by those pages in which St Augustine, in his *City of God* – which Einhard states Charles made one of his favourite readings – after having exalted (19: 11 and 12) "the sweetness of peace, clear to all" and shown it to be the sovereign good on this earth, defined it as the fruit of perfect harmony (*concordia*) among all the parts of the social organism, guaranteed by the good ordering of all the elements comprising it, which he summed up by saying that "human peace is harmony with the order of things": *pax hominum est ordinata concordia.*

Faithful to the teachings from scripture, Charlemagne knew equally well, as again St Augustine had said – whose arresting formulation has nevertheless left no trace in the capitularies – that "kingdoms without justice are no more than the enterprises of brigands"; he also knew that good kings were those who "governed justly". Accordingly he applied himself untiringly to ensure justice in his reign, and the highest, most imperative task he gave his representatives was to render fair justice to all: "Let those to whom the power of judging is given", we read in Art. 63 of the *Admonitio generalis* cited above, "judge justly, because it is written: 'Judge justly', and 'Judge according to justice', because 'the judgement is God's'." Everyone, the emperor repeats to his *missi* in his instructions of 802, should always be able to count on a just application of the law; he should feel himself protected against arbitrariness; he has the right to a strict justice, excluding all trickery and all fraud. From one capitulary to the other, with an unflagging perseverance, Charles repeated these instructions, which appealed at one and the same time to the Old Testament and to Christ's words: "With what judgement ye judge, ye shall be judged" (Matthew 7: 2).

The emperor multiplied his prescriptions, which were intended not only to guarantee the proper functioning of the courts and the sincerity of the debates taking place in them, but to prevent litigation by avoiding illegalities, usurpations, frauds and particularly by watching closely over the honesty of commercial transactions. He spared nothing in order to be considered among those rulers who, again according to St Augustine, the faithful interpreter of biblical passages, by their care to give to each his due bring about the happiness of their peoples.

Charlemagne's policy in the sphere of religion

Let us listen further to the teaching of St Augustine. "If we describe as happy the reigns of certain Christian emperors", he writes in the *City of God* (5: 24), . . .

it is not at all because they ruled for a long time, nor because they died in peace and transmitted their power to their sons, nor because they triumphed over the enemies of their lands, nor because they were able to avoid the revolt of their subjects or contrived to subdue them . . .. We call them happy because they ruled justly; when among the praises that flatterers bestowed upon them and the compliments of those who lavished tokens of humility on them, they knew how not to become vain, by remembering that they were men; when they made their power serve to propagate the worship of God; when they feared

God, loved Him and worshipped Him . . .; when they let themselves be guided, not by the pursuit of a vain glory, but by the love of eternal felicity.

Charlemagne's ambition was to translate this doctrine into action. He did not feel the need to search for its formulation in St Augustine's works, (here again none of his capitularies seem to echo any of them directly), since it was vigorously expressed in the Holy Scriptures themselves, which he and his associates had evidently consulted often, as Cathulf had advised at the beginning of the reign. Charles thus considered himself to be invested with a veritable priesthood. After the model of the biblical kings, his primary preoccupation, let us repeat, was to guide his subjects in the way of the good; it is around this idea that a large part of his activity was organized. Because he knew that he could expect divine aid only insofar as he had kept firm, even strengthened, the Christian sensibilities of his people, he served the cause of religion and arranged everything in view of the eternal felicity promised to rulers and peoples who had carried out the Lord's will on earth.

It cannot be claimed that this doctrine implies, as has often been said, the subordination of the spiritual to the temporal, by reason of Charlemagne being a layman. What is true, however, is that there was a systematic confusion of the two spheres, and that the role of spiritual leader was perhaps the one that came most naturally to Charlemagne. His capitularies, that deal with everything and in which, sometimes, all things occur together, treat more often of religion and the life of the clergy than of administration and political affairs. They go into details that are explained only by the concepts of the period and the aims which the king had set himself. Whether it was a question of ecclesiastical discipline, life within the monasteries, the education and recruitment of the clergy, the religious instruction of the faithful, their zeal in attending the Divine Services and communion, the observance of the sabbath rest and religious feasts, the liturgy, sacraments, and particularly baptism, or whether it was a question of dogma, nothing escaped the emperor's attention; nothing seemed to be alien to his normal range of competence.

When there was a famine or a public calamity, he ordered expiatory prayers, fasts and penances; on the occasion of great victories, gestures of thanksgiving. His thoughts turned naturally toward God, and every catastrophe that befell the Empire could in his eyes only be the chastisement for impiety. It was the same kind of religious atmosphere as that found in the Old Testament.

Charlemagne wrote to the bishop of Liège and the archbishop of Milan to outline to them their pastoral duties; and they, far from being surprised by this and protesting, expressed their gratitude to him and praised his pious zeal. He took the problem of the education of the clergy in hand; called the priests to the fulfillment of their duties; scolded those who fell short in this, and, according to need, spoke ironically about them, as in the capitulary of 811 in which he asked the bishops and other clerics assembled upon his summons to answer the question whether the words "renouncing the world" had no other meaning than "renouncing the bearing of arms and the *public* state of marriage"!

He presided over councils in which were discussed affairs of a purely ecclesiastical nature and sometimes also problems concerning dogmas. At the Council of Frankfurt in 794, where the discussion turned among other things to the 'adoptionist' heresy of the bishops of Urgel and Toledo, he pronounced the opening statement, drew up the programme of the debates, and thereafter participated in the deliberations; the official records make explicit mention of this. In the affair of the veneration of images, discussed at the same council, it was due to his impetus that the famous 'Caroline books' were written, which purported to formulate the official doctrine of the West, opposing it to that of the Byzantines, without even a preliminary agreement having been attempted with the Sovereign Pontiff; and the pope was compelled, ultimately, to leave the decision in so delicate a matter to the Frankish king and his theologians. It was again before a council presided over by Charlemagne in person that at the palace of Aachen in 800 the bishop of Urgel was summoned to come and explain himself; and the question of adoptionism preoccupied the emperor to such a degree that he personally saw to it that it was refuted by the churchmen of his realm, notably by Alcuin.

In another council, held at the palace of Aachen in 802, he may be seen intervening to call the secular clergy back to the respect of the canons of the Church and causing to be distributed to them a collection of texts, carefully edited on the lines of a copy received from Pope Hadrian. Likewise, in the course of the same council, he ordered the *Rule of St Benedict* to be read in the presence of the monks and called on those concerned to conform themselves to it.

Finally in 813, returning once more to the question of the reform of the Church already broached by him many a time, he arranged to have drawn up by the Frankish clergy, who were divided into five conciliary assemblies held simultaneously at Mainz, Reims, Chalon, Tours, and Arles, an enormous number of propositions, from which he reserved for himself the right to draw such practical conclusions as he deemed wise. This method of five assemblies deliberating separately even had the advantage of leaving him a larger freedom of decision. In any case it is difficult to imagine a clergy more pliant or deferential. In the letter of advice which they sent with the text of their resolutions, the Fathers of the Council of Mainz declared that they thanked the Lord for having "given the Church a head"–they meant Charlemagne–

... so pious, so devoted to the service of God, who made the spring of sacred wisdom gush forth, and dispensed holy nourishment with such constancy to the sheep of Christ, to form them according to the divine teachings; a ruler who exerted himself by untiring labour to increase the Christian flock; who joyfully honoured the churches of Christ and occupied himself in extracting as many souls as possible from the mouth of the hideous dragon, to lead them into the bosom of our holy mother the Church and to direct them all together towards the joys of Paradise and the Kingdom of Heaven; a ruler, finally, who surpassed all other kings of the earth in his holy wisdom and pious zeal".

The signatories of this letter even thought it necessary to add that they would not be able to decide anything without him; that "they needed his assistance and knowledge", the support of which they demanded, in order to avoid the mistakes which "his imperial Magnificence" would set right, for the greater benefit of "all of them, of the Christian people, and of their posterity".

For their part, the churchmen assembled at Chalon stated in their letter of advice that they submitted their resolutions confidently "to the sacred judgement" of the king (*ad ejus sacratissimum judicium*), who would correct their insufficience; and, stating among other things that the ancient rules of penitence, excommunication and reconciliation had been forgotten, they "solicited the aid of their lord the emperor" for the return to the canonical tradition, adding that they "awaited his decision" (*sententia*) concerning the priests and deacons who believed themselves to be absolved from all sins if they went to pray at Rome or even simply at the tomb of St Martin at Tours.

The Fathers of the Council of Arles made similar declarations: they relied on the 'wisdom' and 'judgement' of the emperor, who would be

able to complete and correct their resolutions. Those of the Council of
Tours, although a little less inclined to flatter, also concluded by
retreating before the ruler of the Empire. "All the measures which our
most pious king wishes to draw up we, his faithful servants, are ready
to accept, bowing graciously in advance before his will." Finally the
bishops charged after the five councils to co-ordinate the resolutions
made at them emphasized that one particularly difficult question, that
of priests tonsured before they were legally of age, had by common
accord been reserved to the emperor's judgement (*ad arbitrium domni
imperatoris*) who was once again requested to settle this point "as he
pleased". And Charles, who had already sovereignly drawn up the
working agenda followed by the five councils, in fact had the last word
in everything.

The supreme head of the clergy

Thus, the emperor's authority had eventually extended itself to the
point where there no longer was any sphere of activity that was alien to
him. To priests, bishops, even the pope he dictated the law, with the
conviction that he never went beyond his rights but, on the contrary,
was strictly fulfilling his duty. He dealt very freely with the clergy of
his realm. The bishops, among others, were treated as ordinary
officials, whose essential task was indeed to work for the salvation of
souls, but to work in accordance with the views of the emperor, who
expected of them unlimited co-operation in the functioning of his
government.

We have already seen that he employed them in all kinds of tasks for
which they were not especially suited, and under the weight of which
some of them eventually felt themselves over-burdened. The time that
many of them could devote to their pastoral ministry was more and
more reduced, torn as they were between the multiple obligations
heaped on them by the imperial will: summons to court, to the general
assemblies of the Frankish king, circuits of inspection as *missi
dominici*, participation in military campaigns, diplomatic or other
missions. There were even a few who had to be released from the
obligatory residence in their dioceses because it pleased the emperor to
entrust them with permanent functions at his court. This was the case

with the bishop of Metz, Angilram, and later with the bishop of
Cologne, Hildebald, whom Charlemagne kept with him as arch-
chaplains, not without the permission of superior ecclesiastical authorities who had been obliged to accede to his wishes. It occurred that
some prelate or other discreetly complained about the impossibility in
which he found himself of fulfilling his pastoral duties as he would
have wished, distracted as he was at every moment by some demand or
other of the emperor; but these complaints were useless: whether he
wished it or not, the bishop was, above all, required to be the king's
docile auxiliary. Whoever dared to protest against Charles' will would
be dismissed immediately, just as any other representative of the
public authority.

Notwithstanding the canonical rules, the bishops were, in practice,
nominated by the emperor. Election by 'the faithful' had for long been
no more than a semblance. Each time there was a vacancy in an
episcopal see, the emperor suggested to the clergy of the church
concerned, which thenceforth alone constituted the electoral body, the
name of the man whom he desired to be the new bishop, and this desire
expressed by the sovereign was equivalent to a command. From
Charlemagne's point of view, nothing could be more normal, considering the role of the bishop in the conduct of the affairs of the realm. It
was necessary for the emperor to have men upon whom he could count
on every occasion; and for additional surety he usually chose them
from among his palace clergy. Well-trained, as it were under his direct
supervision, they would be assistants imprinted with the same spirit as
their lord and accustomed to his methods, and it must be admitted that
Charlemagne's choices were generally good ones, even with regard to
the Church: sincerely religious, his preference went to those whom he
judged worthy in all respects, and the composition of the Frankish
episcopate during his reign did, on the whole, honour to his discern-
ment.

Towards the Sovereign Pontiff Charles showed himself full of
respect; but the sphere of action which he ultimately left to him was
extremely reduced. Invited at his accession to confine himself to
prayer, Leo III was, since Charlemagne's accession as emperor, no
more than a faithful assistant whose least inclination towards independence would be effectively checked. Because, beside the emperor who
considered himself the supreme head of Western christendom, there
was room only for subordinate authorities, and we have just recalled

that even in the matter of dogma, Charlemagne intended to remain the pope's superior. Nothing shows this better than the attitude of independence he adopted in the burning question of the *filioque*, by persisting, despite Leo III's veto, in having chanted even in his chapel, in the recitation of the Nicene Creed, the formula according to which the Holy Spirit proceeds from God the Son as well as God the Father.

The favours he lavished on monasteries, in which he saw sanctuaries of payer indispensable to the welfare of his realm, nevertheless did not prevent him from keeping them under close surveillance. His correspondence and his capitularies indicate the constant care he took to make them conform to the requirements of the Benedictine Rule, to which his taste for order demanded that they should be uniformly subject. This, however, did not prevent him from treating abbatial offices just as his predecessors had, as rich prebends intended as much to reward the zeal of his vassals as to ensure, in part, the upkeep of his counts. Again, 'lay abbots', whose abbacy consisted solely in the enjoyment of part of the monastic revenues, were not only tolerated, but multiplied at will, and the liberty of abbatial election stipulated by the *Rule of St Benedict* (Chapter 64) was largely neglected. This was not the least of the contradictions of a regime where everything converged on the person of the emperor and his will was the supreme law of the realm.

But, in reality, this contradiction partly eluded contemporaries; or if they happened to notice it, they could only sincerely praise the lofty thought that, on the whole, inspired Charlemagne's conduct. Doubtless the praises which they bestowed on him in public tasted of flattery; the Fathers of the five councils held in the Frankish kingdom in 813 had even gone a bit further in this, as we have been able to judge for ourselves. But how can we impugn the evidence of fervent admiration in a spirit as independent as that of Alcuin, when around 794 or 795, just after the Council of Frankfurt, he exclaimed in a burst of feeling:

'Blessed', the Psalmist has said, 'is the nation whose God is the Lord'; blessed are the people exalted by a ruler and supported by a preacher of the faith whose right hand brandishes the sword of triumph and whose mouth makes the trumpet of the catholic faith ring. It was thus that David, chosen by God to be king of the people, who were then His chosen people . . ., subjected the neighbouring nations to Israel with his victorious sword, and preached the divine law to his subjects. From the noble lineage of Israel came forth, for the salvation of the world, the 'flower of the fields and valleys', the Christ, from whom in our time the [new] people, whom He has made His, has received another

King David. Bearing the same name, inspired by the same virtue and the same faith, this king is presently our ruler and guide: a ruler 'in whose shadow' the Christian people remains in peace and who everywhere inspires fear in the pagan nations; a guide whose devotion, by its evangelical steadfastness, constantly strengthens the catholic faith against the followers of heresy, seeing to it that nothing contrary to the doctrine of the Apostles slips in anywhere and exerting himself to make this catholic faith shine everywhere with the light of heavenly grace.

This was a magnificent panegyric, from such a pen, and one that more than any other answered the profoundest aspirations of the ruler who was its subject.

BOOK TWO

THE FATE OF THE EMPIRE UNDER
LOUIS THE PIOUS

CHAPTER ONE

The establishment of a unified Empire

Charlemagne's reign ended in ambiguity, for in 806 the emperor had proceeded to divide his realm among his sons without even making the least mention of the supreme dignity with which he had been invested six years earlier. Death alone, which had made two of the three legitimate sons he still had disappear one after the other, had ultimately rescued the unity of the Empire, whose crown had been given to the surviving youngest son, Louis, by the old emperor, in an assembly held at the palace of Aachen in September 813. Would the task of deciding the political future of Western Christianity thus continue to be left to chance? Or indeed to consolidate the achievement that had been realized and to set the new Empire on solid foundations, would the new situation, at last, be resolutely confirmed? It is worth noting that from the very day of his accession Louis the Pious tried without pause to resolve this problem, and the lucidity no less than the trenchancy of the solutions adopted seem to indicate that his advisers had not waited for the death of his father before reflecting upon it and working out their plans.

In search of unity

In fact, from the beginning, the policy of the new ruler found expression in the very protocol of the documents despatched by the imperial chancery. While Charlemagne, in his diplomas, had maintained until the last days of his life, his three titles of king of the Franks, king of the Lombards, and emperor, and, in the dating, had kept the indication of the number of years he had exercised his power in this triple quality, Louis the Pious at once set aside everything that recalled from what laborious juxtaposition of territories and dignities the Empire had come forth, to retain only the fact of its existence and the unity it incarnated. Instead of the complicated formula by which his father's acts began: "Charles, most serene Augustus, crowned by God, great and pacific emperor, governing the Roman Empire, and at the same time, by the mercy of God, king of the Franks and of the Lombards", the brief and clear formula: "Louis by command of divine providence emperor Augustus" was soon substituted; for the date, in 814, this simple notation: "the year I of our being emperor", instead of the one which Charlemagne had still been using a few days earlier: "the fourteenth year of our being emperor, the fortyfifth of our reign in Francia and the thirtieth of our reign in Italy". The change seems minimal, but it was a whole programme. It signified, doubtless, that only one reality counted in the eyes of the new king: one Empire; or at least that this henceforth eclipsed the notion of separate kingdoms.

Kingdoms could survive or could be established within the imperial boundaries. This was the case with the kingdom of Italy, at the head of which was maintained Bernard, the son of Pepin, whom Charlemagne had sent there with the royal title in 813; and in the course of the summer of 814, Louis the Pious himself did not hesitate to delegate to his two eldest sons Lothar and Pepin the governments respectively of Bavaria and Aquitaine. But this satisfaction granted to the particularism of certain provinces did not diminish their subordination to imperial authority: being kingdoms of a lower order, such as there had always been within the Frankish kingdom, their kings owed the emperor strict obedience, so that the unity of the Empire was not in any way affected.

This first and discreet reform in the imperial chancery indicated the sovereign's wish to go beyond the ethnic diversities and the traditions belonging to each of the parts composing the Empire to what was the common denominator which would, in its spirit, ensure unity: namely, the Christian religion, whose triumph had been made possible by the success of Frankish arms even in the territories most recently subdued. To the kings ruling over the various ethnic groups an emperor super-imposed himself, reigning over 'the Christian people', and this expression, already used in Charlemagne's time, thenceforth constantly returned in the writings of those who best represented the thought of Louis the Pious and his advisers. It expressed perfectly, in every respect, their essential preoccupation, which was to ensure by every means in their power the flowering of the Christian life in the context of the Empire whose boundaries more or less coincided, excepting England and Ireland, with those of Western Christendom itself.

The religious programme of the new government

Thus, from the beginning of the reign, everything was done to reinforce the religious character of this Empire. In contrast to his father, Louis, who was already thirty-six, had received a thorough education, modeled on the training which was given, since the end of the eighth century, to future clerics: contemporaries agree on this point, and one of them adds that the monastic life exercised such an attraction for the emperor that he would have entered a monastery if he had not felt himself called upon by God to rule. When, before Charlemagne's death, he had been initiated in Aquitaine to his work as king, he had applied himself to the reform of the monasteries with all the enthusiasm of his faith, inspired by a holy man whom he had made his closest adviser: the abbot of Aniane, Benedict, restorer of the strict Benedictine Rule in the monasteries of Languedoc. At the same time, as one of his biographers tells us, Louis had worked on the moral reform of the provinces subject to this authority, deserving already by this constant care for morality and religion the appellation of 'Pious' (*Pius*), which he was to be given constantly after his death, and also to some extent that of 'Monk', which some attributed to him, to tease him mildly with his tendency to wish to subject the whole world, including his court, to a kind of monastic discipline.

His accession to the imperial throne brought with it an immediate change of atmosphere. However obsessed he had been with religious principles, Charlemagne had lived in this world; he lived in it fully, and no more than his entourage did he himself always present a very edifying spectacle. The adventures of his legitimate daughters – to mention them only, for the others were very numerous – had caused some stir in the world, especially those of Bertha, who had several children, born out of wedlock, by the well-known poet Angilbert–

the 'Homer' of Aachen–which, however, had not kept Charlemagne from gratifying the happy lover by granting him the abbacy of St Riquier.

Hardly had the old emperor heaved his last sigh before this life of complaisance and laxity was banned from the court. From the moment of his arrival at Aachen, Louis the Pious requested his sisters to withdraw to monasteries, restricted the female personnel permitted to reside in the palace to a minimum, and unmercifully expelled all women of loose morals. A capitulary on the policy of the court which doubtless dates from this period, forbids them not only to stay at the palace itself, but also in the houses around it; it organizes the inspection of all the places of habitation in and around Aachen and orders all individuals, men and women, of doubtful morality to be expelled from them at once. One article states that "every man who is found with ladies of pleasure is to carry them on his shoulders to the market, where they are to be whipped, and in case he refuses, he is to be whipped in the market with them". At the same time as he purged Aachen of these undesirable elements, the emperor installed Benedict of Aniane there; or rather, the pious abbot, not wishing to find himself mixed up in the life of the palace even after the purification measures which we have just described, was settled in a monastery which the emperor founded for him at the gates of Aachen, at Inda (present-day Kornelimünster), where it was possible to consult him on every occasion.

It was, however, not only the life of the court that was transformed: the trusted personnel of Charlemagne was sent away and replaced by men in touch with the ideas of the new emperor. At their head stood the person who had been his chancellor in Aquitaine, the priest Helisachar, well known for his theological learning. It was a true government of priests. As much by the general climate of austerity that he created around the palace, as by the selection of the men with whom he surrounded himself and the convictions that dominated his first acts, Louis the Pious indicated at once the orientation which he intended to give to his policy: while under Charlemagne the Church appeared to be incorporated into the state, the new regime manifestly purposed from the beginning to let the spirit of the Church predominate over reasons of state.

The reader may judge this for himself from the veritable profession of faith that occurs in the preamble of a charter issued around this time in the emperor's name:

> The piety which our most holy emperor Louis feels towards God is unceasing in its search for anything that might correspond more closely to the will of the Lord, so as to increase the prestige of the faith, promote day by day a greater development of devotion, further the celebration of divine worship, and ensure greater honour and dignity to the holy office . . . . The emperor constantly has in mind this saying of God: 'I have found in David a man according to my heart who will carry out all my wishes'.

This programme of Christian action sums up the essential views of Louis the Pious concerning the government of the Empire; and this is why the first measures he drew up were measures of moral and religious reform.

The reform of ecclesiastical society

In these conditions it is hardly surprising that we find, foremost among these measures, those concerning the reform of ecclesiastical society itself. The idea was not new. A few months before his death, in May 813, Charlemagne, as the reader will remember, had already taken the initiative of assembling the clergy of the Frankish kingdom in five regional synods, at Mainz, Reims, Tours, Chalon-sur-Saône and Arles, to "remedy the condition of the churches"; but these deliberations, contrary to what was usual in cases of this kind, resulted only in some measures of detailed reform. In August 816, Louis the Pious, at a general assembly held at Aachen, adopted a totally different method. He had himself, with his advisers, prepared the fundamental texts that aimed as a body at effecting what he himself called a "reform of the holy Church of God". Presented for comment to the scrutiny of the members of the clergy assembled in a single great council which discussed them thoroughly until September, these texts were thereafter emended and issued by the emperor, to whose piety and wisdom their publication was officially attributed.

There were two of them. The first, directed at the canons of cathedral churches, was a statute uniformly applicable in the whole Empire, which constrained them to live in common and in confinement, subjecting them to a rule copied from that of the Benedictine monks. The influence of Benedict of Aniane is easily recognizable here. The second text, issued in September 816, was a statue for nuns. Inspired

by the same spirit, it likewise aimed at introducing a perfect regularity
and a perfect uniformity in the type of life imposed on nuns, adapting
the *Rule of St Benedict* to their needs. These first two statutes were
despatched to all dioceses, where the emperor prescribed their full
application within at most one year, under pain of sanctions, and the
bishops were informed that the *missi* on their next circuit were to make
sure the necessary measures had indeed been taken from one end of the
realm to the other, in order to make the imperial will obeyed.

The reform of monasteries of men, which could not be drawn up at
the general assembly of 816, was attended to a year later at the general
assembly of July 817, also held at Aachen. A committee of monks and
abbots, among whom Benedict of Aniane was one of the most
influential, dealt with the means of combating the laxity of the
monastic life and the clearing up of any doubts which the
interpretation of the Benedictine Rule might engender, by drawing up
once again a definitive text, uniformly applicable in the whole Empire,
which Louis the Pious issued in the same way as the preceding ones,
again charging his *missi* to see to its strict execution. The reform was
completed by an accurate list of the charges of all kinds imposed on
monasteries, under the burden of which some of them had been
relaxing their discipline, so that a better allocation of these might allow
them to consecrate themselves in full liberty of spirit to mediation and
prayer.

Finally, in the course of a third general assembly, in 818 or 819,
another series of texts was issued on the reform of the episcopate and,
in general, of the secular clergy, by recalling the canonical rules too
often forgotten, which the emperor in his turn pledged to respect
thenceforth. One of the best informed chroniclers of the period adds
that the measures taken on this occasion were designed to lead the
parties concerned to change a way of life which was the very negation
of the evangelical spirit: bishops and priests, he wrote "saw themselves
putting down their sword-belts and their gilded shoulder-belts, their
heavy poniards decorated with gems, their luxurious clothes, the spurs
that encumbered their heels". It was, in short, a return to a way of life
that better conformed to the ideals of the Church, and which it was
hoped might serve as an example for the whole of society.

A capitulary also issued in 818 or 819 commanded the insertion in all
laws, Frankish and otherwise, which were recognized in the Empire, of
a series of articles of which several aimed at repressing crimes or
offences against religion, such as murders, blows or wounds inside or

at the doors of churches, or the murder of penitents. Thus the Church and the faith were cornerstones of the new edifice that was about to be built: it was through her that the Carolingian Empire would, it was thought, accomplish the task which was assigned to it.

The restoration of papal power

But how was this goal to be achieved without first restoring the prestige of the papacy? What a decline had there been since the accession of Leo III! That unfortunate pope, rehabilitated at the end of the year 800 by Charlemagne, but treated by him in the off-hand manner we have seen, proved to the end to be powerless to triumph over the opposition which at Rome itself impeded the exercise of his authority. At the beginning of the summer of 815, he narrowly escaped assassination there for the second time; then, having ordered the guilty persons to be put to death, he found himself resisting a veritable revolt which had only just begun to be quieted when, in May 816, he departed from this life.

It was not possible to improve such a situation except by changing methods. The new pope, Stephen IV, imitating at sixty years of age the deed of his namesake, Stephen II, did not hesitate to make the journey to Gaul, a few months after his consecration, to meet the successor of Charlemagne there. He hoped, trusting in the sentiments with which he knew Louis the Pious to be animated, to induce him to lend the papacy assistance.

The interview took place at Reims, in October 816, according to a protocol modeled closely upon that of Ponthion. Like his grandfather Pepin, Louis the Pious went out a mile to meet the Sovereign Pontiff, dismounted, went respectfully to take the bridle of his guest's horse and to assist him, like an ordinary squire, in descending from the saddle, then after three genuflexions and several embraces, led him to the cathedral to hear mass. The conversations which began immediately afterwards led, after four days, to an agreement in principle, including notably a confirmation of the promises formerly made to the papacy by Louis the Pious' predecessors. Then – still according to the precedent of Stephen II – the Sovereign Pontiff proceeded to a new coronation and to the sacring of the emperor, as well as of his wife, Irmengarde.

Thus was restored the same situation that existed in the period when papacy and Frankish monarchy, having need of one another, dealt tactfully with each other. Consequently, we are not surprised when we learn that, Stephen IV having died on 24 January 817 shortly after his return to Italy, the chancery of Louis the Pious despatched to his successor Paschal I, elected almost immediately, a charter which, following up the conversations at Reims, marks a clear change of orientation in the emperor's policy to the advantage of the Holy See.

After a list summing up all the territories constituting the state of St Peter as a consequence of gifts granted progressively since the time of Pepin the Short, this document specifies that the emperor pledges for himself, his sons and all their successors:

(1) never, "by whatever dispute or intrigue", to injure the papal interests in the least way, to cause the papal authority to be respected in all its plenitude, and to ensure the protection of the papacy by every means within his power;

(2) henceforth not to intervene in papal affairs, neither in political, administrative, nor judicial matters, unless by explicit request of the pope;

(3) to surrender to the papal representatives any accused persons who came to seek asylum in the territory of the Empire, except in a small number of clearly specified cases;

(4) not to interfere personally on the occasion of the deaths of Sovereign Pontiffs, nor to allow any of his subjects to intervene in arranging the succession to the throne of St Peter, so that the election of the pope should always remain free; its result to be announced to the emperor at once but only after the consecration has taken place, this in view of the renewal of the pact "of friendship, charity and peace" that bound the two powers.

In this way the papacy, kept in leading-strings by Charlemagne, recovered the political independence necessary for its restoration as well as for that of the whole of the Church.

The charter of 817

But did not Christendom itself incur a mortal risk if the Empire was not definitively secured against the dislocation which had been avoided at Charlemagne's death only by an exceptional concurrence of circumstances? Justifiably preoccupied by this situation, Louis the Pious in July 817 turned to tackle the most inveterate Frankish traditions in a new charter of still greater import.

When, in the course of the general assembly – the same one in which the reform of the monasteries for men was decided on – his subjects (*fideles*) had requested their lord, as we read in the preamable of this document, "to take advantage of the fact that he was then in good health and that peace, thanks to God, reigned everywhere" to arrange in advance, in full tranquillity of spirit, the future fate of his realm and its ultimate partition among his sons "according to the custom of our ancestors" (*more parentum nostrorum*), Louis suddenly unveiled his plans.

Although this request, the emperor himself observes at the beginning of the charter, was presented with "devotion and fidelity" (*devote ac fideliter*),

... it does not seem to us, nor to people of sound judgement (*qui sanum sapiunt*), that it is possible, out of love for our sons, to allow, in setting about a partition, the breaking of the unity of an Empire which God has maintained to our advantage. We do not wish to run the risk of unleashing, in this way, a scandal in the holy Church and of offending Him in whose power the titles to all the kingdoms rest.

This is why three days of fasts and prayers were decreed in order to implore divine inspiration. The result was the adoption "in full agreement with the Almighty" of the following measures, which Louis promulgated at once:

(1) The eldest of his three sons, Lothar, then aged about twenty-two, was proclaimed emperor, solemnly girded with the imperial diadem, associated from that moment in the exercise of power alongside his father, and finally declared the sole ultimate heir to the whole Empire.

(2) Of the two younger sons, Pepin and Louis, the first kept the royal crown of Aquitaine, which his father had transferred to him in 814, and the second was to become king of Bavaria, both on condition of governing under the supervision of the emperor.

(3) On the death of their father, Pepin and Louis would have their respective kingdoms expanded, the one by the annexation of Gascony, the march of Toulouse, the county of Carcassonne and the three counties of Autun, Avallon and Nevers; the other by those of Carinthia, Bohemia and the Slav and Avar marches; nevertheless both kings would remain subordinate to the imperial authority.

(4) The same was to apply to the kingdom of Italy, which was reserved for Bernard, to whom Charlemagne had awarded it in 813.

(5) Once having become sole emperor, Lothar was to allow his two brothers, as soon as they attained the age of majority of fifteen years required by the Ripuarian Law in force in the Carolingian family (Art. 16), the free disposal within their respective kingdoms of the "honours" (Art. 3), and the receipts of the taxes, tolls, fines and fiscal revenues (Art. 2); but for the rest, he was to keep his ascendancy over them. They were obliged, as a consequence, once a year "at an opportune moment", that is to say at the time of the general assembly, to bring to him in person their "annual gifts", and to come to an understanding with him "in a spirit of fraternal love", for the settlement of affairs of common concern (Art. 4). Save in the case of unexpected attack, they could not take up arms without the emperor's consent (Art. 7). They were not to conclude treaties or even to receive ambassadors without previously notifying him and consulting him about the answers to be given (Art. 8). They were obliged, on the contrary, to facilitate the access to him of all embassies which were intended for him and to keep him precisely informed about what happened on their frontiers, so that he would always be able to intervene wherever the interests of the Empire made it necessary (Art. 8). They were not to contract a marriage without his consent (Art. 13). They were even, for every abuse of power and every act of "tyranny", subject to a reprimand at one and the same time "paternal and fraternal" by their elder brother, who in case of obstinacy on their part was to consult the general assembly about the penalty to be inflicted on them (Art. 10).

(6) Lothar was obliged, for his part, to give them a fraternal welcome when they brought him their "annual gifts" and, recalling that "with the agreement of God" he disposed of an authority superior to theirs, to bestow on them in return gifts of greater value (Art. 5); moreover he owed them military aid and protection against attacks by "alien nations" (Art. 6).

(7) Finally, to prevent the basis of these arrangements being one day questioned, it was stipulated that in case of the death of one of Lothar's brothers, the people of the affected kingdom were to choose one of the sons of the deceased to whom the vacant succession should devolve, without any possibility of the kingdom being split up or held upon other conditions than those specified above (Art. 14). It was also

laid down that if the deceased did not leave legitimate sons, his kingdom would be placed under the direct rule of the emperor (Art. 15); that if Lothar himself should die, his subjects, "to assure the welfare of all, the tranquillity of the church and the unity of the Empire", were to meditate and implore divine inspiration with their prayers, in order to proceed, with the aid of the Almighty, to the designation of one of the other two brothers to whom the imperial authority would then be entrusted (Art. 18).

As one can see, these measures form together a coherent whole which, by a bold initiative, did not retain more than the minimum of the traditional customs of the Frankish kingdom necessary to assuage to some extent the appetites of those whom the new regime put at the greatest disadvantage. While arranging some satisfactions of prestige for them, it proclaimed and consolidated the unity of the Empire, of which Louis the Pious and his son Lothar were constituted the guardians.

The ideal of Christian unity

Would it have been possible to go still further? Some appear to have thought so. Dreaming of a complete fusion of peoples and territories subject to the ruler of the Frankish kingdom, the impetuous archbishop of Lyon, Agobard, in a letter which he sent to Louis at that time, expressed a desire for the unification of the law in force in the Empire by the uniform application to all of one single code, that of the Salian Franks. Emphasizing the shocking disagreements in the procedures followed in one and the same place, according to whether, because of the principle of personal law, an accused person belonged by his personal status to one code or to another, and above all the extreme inequality of punishments to which one was liable, Agobard, who lived in a region of very mixed populations, was indignant about the confusion that had come about through such a state of affairs. How can one accept, he exclaimed, the maintenance of such differences in treatment between the subjects of the emperor who are all equally the faithful of Christ? And yet one single truth had been

... proclaimed to all the nations of the world, one and the same faith had been given them by God, one and the same hope ..., one and the same charity, one and the same will, one and the same wish, one and the same prayer; whatever the diversity of their condition, sex, or birth, nobles and serfs, all without exception, say with one heart to the single God, who is Father to all of them: 'Our Father who art in heaven, hallowed be Thy name'; they call on a single Father . . . , ask only for a single Kingdom, His heavenly Kingdom, wish for the carrying out of one will, all pray to have granted to them the same daily bread and to have, all of them, their sins forgiven . . . .

"There is no longer", he says again – taking up and reinterpreting a famous passage of St Paul – "there is no longer Gentile or Jew . . . , nor barbarian or Scythian, nor Aquitanian or Lombard, Burgundian or Aleman, serf or free; all are one in Christ". Because "if the Lord has suffered the Passion, it was so that in his blood all those who are separated should be brought together and the separations should disappear". Can one accept, the archbishop asks Louis, that

. . . to this unity, the work of God, such a diversity of laws should constitute an obstacle, so that in one and the same region, in one and the same city, even in one and the same house, it happens constantly [he exaggerates!] that with five men walking side by side, sitting side by side, none on the level of human affairs belongs to the same law, while in their hearts, on the level of eternal things, they fall under the same law of Christ?

And does not the conclusion impose itself that "the Frankish law should be transferred" to those who invoke other codes?

Without going so far, it is a fact that at least in the first years of his reign, Louis the Pious applied himself to some extent to the task of the desired judicial unification, by the promulgation of several capitularies whose aim was to insert some of his own measures into the various codes in force in order to reduce their differences. It is also a fact that from 817 onward the word "unity" (*unitas*) began to return again and again in the writings of the emperor's partisans and of his adversaries. People fought for or against the "unity" of the Empire, and always people evoked, in this connection, the grand idea of Christian unity, of the unity of faith, which constituted, it was then thought, the firmest foundation of the Empire.

CHAPTER TWO

The opposition to the new government and the penitence of Attigny

The revolt of Bernard of Italy

It is not surprising, however, to find that a political revolution such as the one whose programme was formulated in the act of 817 could not take place without eliciting, beside outbursts of enthusiasm such as Agobard's, other outbursts in the contrary direction on the part of those whose interests were to be directly injured.

Louis the Pious' two younger sons, although worst hit, were still too young to react: Louis was at the very most eleven or twelve years of age; Pepin, although his elder, was himself still also a child. But the king of Italy, Bernard, the emperor's nephew, who was then probably twenty years old, allowed himself to be induced to revolt by his entourage, even though nothing had been changed in the status of his kingdom in the Empire. It looks very much as though he was primarily an instrument in the hands of a crowd of malcontents, among whom one is surprised to meet some persons of distinction: not only several occupants of high offices at the court, but even prelates such as the bishops of Milan, Cremona, and in Gaul itself the bishop of Orléans, the illustrious poet Theodulf.

Notwithstanding the extreme discretion observed by the contemporary annalists and chroniclers, all devoted to the cause of the emperor, it seems that there was a very serious attempt at general revolt, which was meant to spread from Italy to Gaul. Only the decisive manner in which Louis the Pious and his advisers coped with the situation allowed them to crush it before it had taken on dangerous forms: the army was called up with the greatest urgency in the autumn, and the commanders of the detachments were requested to hold themselves in readiness to depart without delay for the Alpine frontier. Louis the Pious assumed the command of his troops in person and made his way to Italy. The promptitude of the reaction was enough to crush the revolt; Bernard, abandoned by some of the rebels, and with only the lukewarm support of the others, dared not resist. Taken to Chalon-sur-Saône, which the emperor had reached on his way to Italy, he surrendered unconditionally.

The punishment of the rebels was an example to others. Referred to a general assembly convoked in advance for April 818, Bernard and those of his accomplices who were not members of the clergy were condemned to death for the crime of high treason; the bishops, abbots and other ecclesiastical personages implicated in the plot were referred to a council which pronounced their deposition. They were, moreover, on the orders of Louis the Pious and according to their degree of guilt, either sent into exile or relegated to a monastery to do perpetual penance there. As for Bernard and his lay accomplices, the sovereign exercised a measure of clemency towards them: instead of having them executed, he contented himself with having their eyes put out – which came to the same thing for Bernard and one of his principal advisers, the chamberlain Reginhard, since neither survived this punishment. Finally, as a precaution, Louis had all his bastard brothers, whom he distrusted, tonsured and interned in monasteries.

In this way the emperor had the last word and his will imposed the constitution of 817. For the time being the only visible result of the revolt for which Bernard had given the signal was the abolition of the separate Italian kingdom; the ancient Lombard kingdom was simply attached to the territories which Lothar was to govern directly after his father's death. Thus the revolt resulted in a reinforcement, not an attenuation, of the principles stated in 817.

The strengthening of governmental unity

At the same time as the great reforms of church organization carried out in 818–819, it seems that the very structure of the imperial government underwent profound alterations. The system of general assemblies had continued up to then to function as it did under

Charlemagne. Sooner or later in the summer, at the moment of departure for the summer campaign, the *conventus generalis* was held close to the future scene of military operations in which the emperor himself usually participated, and in the course of the meeting he took advice about any measures that needed to be taken. The rhythm of governmental activity was thus regulated by military affairs. But now, gradually, new practices arose. The emperor participated less and less frequently in the battles of his armies. The wars took place in more and more distant areas, and the armies that were engaged in them were those of the neighbouring regions only, except in major crises, such as in 817 when the revolt of Bernard of Italy had to be coped with, and in 818 when a revolt of Brittany compelled Louis to convoke the assembly at Vannes and to take command of the expedition himself. Apart from cases of this sort, the normal assembly, the one in which the 'annual gifts' were to be brought to the ruler, was from that time on usually held in the very heart of the Frankish kingdom, for example at Quierzy, Attigny, Compiègne, as well as Aachen, Ingelheim, or Frankfurt. Moreover – and it is here that the most important novelty is to be found – while the normal assembly continued to be convoked in the summer, although at much more variable dates than previously, Louis formed the habit of convoking others, large or small, at other times of the year, sometimes in January or February, sometimes in October or November, to prepare reforms, work out campaign plans, or exchange views about the general situation. Lacking sources that throw light on this, it is difficult to say what purpose exactly the emperor had in mind by this multiplication of assemblies; but it is obvious that it resulted in strengthening the ties between all parts of the Empire and consequently in strengthening the unity that constituted the fundamental article of his political program. At one of these extra assemblies, in May 821 at Nijmegen, the emperor considered it necessary to stress this forcefully anew by having the charter of 817 read again before the gathering of magnates and demanding an oath from everyone that they would respect its provisions. This same oath was, at the time of the general assembly held in October at Thionville, required of all those who had not been present at Nijmegen. Were these perhaps precautionary measures against those who had not yet resigned themselves to the 817 constitution? In any case this charter was, in 821 no less than before, the cornerstone of the political edifice erected by Louis the Pious.

But this charter by itself could not suffice to guarantee the durable unity of the Christian world if the spirit of unity did not inspire the conduct of all those who were part of it. As in the time of Charlemagne, the words peace and concord constantly flowed from the pens of the clerics who at that time expressed the thought of the emperor and his advisers; without this peace between all the subjects of the emperor, alike brothers in Christ, it would be vain, they emphasized, to hope for stability in the realm which had just been constituted, and this realm itself would have been meaningless. It is therefore not surprising to find that, immediately after causing new oaths to be taken to the new constitution, Louis concerned himself with erasing all traces of former discord by proceeding to a general reconciliation between his subjects. Thus, at the assembly of Thionville, he decided to grant substantial measures of amnesty towards those who had been involved in the revolt of Bernard of Italy. Not only did he pardon them but he returned to them all their confiscated property. Furthermore, he recalled from exile the abbot of Corbie Adalard, a former adviser of Charlemagne whom he had relegated to Noirmoutier in 814, and let him resume the direction of the monastery. Finally in August 822, at the general assembly held that year at Attigny on the Aisne, he resolved "on the advice of this bishops and his magnates", writes the semi-official annalist, to extend these measures of clemency and reconciliation to the two of his bastard brothers who were still alive. Taken out of the monasteries in which they had been interned in 817, they were recalled to active life and were soon provided with important ecclesiastical offices: the eldest, Drogo, with the bishopric of Metz in June 823, at the age of scarcely twenty-two; the other, Hugh, shortly afterwards, with various abbacies.

The general penitence of Attigny (822)

These measures of reparation still did not suffice to quench the thirst for appeasement that tormented the emperor; and even though his pious adviser Benedict of Aniane died on 11 February 821, he was more than ever obsessed by the idea that only an unconditional submission of all to the commands of religion and to the requirements of Christian humility would ensure the welfare of the Empire. Thus, at this same assembly of Attigny, he decided on a general penitence, with himself leading the way. He publicly confessed his past deplorable conduct towards King Bernard of Italy, as well as that towards the abbot of Corbie, Adalard, and his brother the monk Wala, both exiled after the revolt of 817, and asked for absolution. After him, the bishops in their turn made an act of contrition. "Inspired by God Almighty and following the advice of your pious zeal, as well as stirred by your salutary example", they declared, addressing Louis who presided, "we confess ourselves to have been on several points, which at present it is neither useful nor possible to enumerate, proved negligent, in our conduct as well as in our doctrine and in the exercise of our ministry". The effect of this confession was somewhat attenuated by the remark the bishops added immediately afterwards, that they would be able at last to act as they should if the emperor, as he had pledged to do, would give them the freedom of action necessary for the accomplishment of their duties. But in the end they recognized themselves to have, up to then, lacking a proper religious instruction, very imperfectly discharged their task, and they accused themselves of having shown insufficient zeal in the organization of the schools in their dioceses, to which they should have, they confessed, devoted more care, in order to permit the formation of a well trained clergy. These were rather limited confessions of faults for which, in the end, the authors once again threw the responsibility on those who had not, they claimed, furnished them with the financial means of action; but they were confessions all the same, which balanced those made by Louis in person. After the bishops, did the great laymen also come to make their confession? We do not know; but their case was presented – and not very gracefully – by the prelates convoked in a special session. The archbishop of Lyon, Agobard, in answer to the desire of the emperor to ascertain the evils which most urgently needed attention, prided himself on having suggested that the appropriation of church properties by laymen should be attacked first; furthermore, a summary of several resolutions has been preserved at the end of the bishops' confession, among which there is one aimed at laymen who excused themselves from going to church.

As we can see, it was a general examination of conscience that occurred at Attigny. Each person there either made or had been ordered to make the confessions and sacrifices necessary for the common good. By his personal act of contrition the emperor certainly did not believe, as has been said, that he was degrading the imperial dignity, and no contemporary ever addressed this reproach to him; one of them even congratulated him on this renewed deed of Theodosius. With this act, Louis wished only to give a striking indication of his ardent desire for a reconciliation of all in view of the peace so much hoped for, without which imperial unity would have been no more than an empty word. It cannot be denied, however, that at Attigny the religious character of the imperial government was accentuated. Not only was the unity of the Empire founded on the unity of faith; not only did people consequently speak of this unity of the Empire and the Church as equivalents, but everything was subordinated to the cause of religion and the Church came to occupy a preponderant place in the life of the state. The churchmen were consulted before all others; since the death of Benedict of Aniane, the abbot of Corbie, Adalard, and his brother, the monk Wala, exercised pressure on the emperor on every occasion. Ultimately he saw things only through their eyes and acted entirely according to their wishes. What a contrast with the reign of Charlemagne! Instead of the clergy being entirely at the disposal of the ruler, we now see the clergy as masters of the situation and the emperor always ready to listen to and follow their advice. Instead of the government of the Church by the emperor, was there now to be a government of the state by the Church?

CHAPTER THREE

The volte-face of the imperial government, 822–829

The emperor's second marriage

However, in this same period a change of attitude began to become evident in Louis the Pious; one that is bound up with events in his personal life. This pious emperor was at the same time a weak man, who was easily dominated by his entourage. Under the influence of Benedict of Aniane and other clerics who had inspired him up to then, he had, notwithstanding all obstacles, proceeded without deviation in the direction we have just seen; because, however feeble and susceptible to influence he was, he was nonetheless authoritarian, as many weak men are, and perfectly capable at certain moments of stiffening himself into an attitude of intransigence. But his personal life had undergone a decisive modification: widower since the death on 3 October 818 of his first wife, Irmengarde, he remarried in the following February with the beautiful Judith of Bavaria, who soon gained a considerable ascendancy over this man of forty.

The writers of the time boasted of the dazzling beauty of the new empress. Several years later one of the most cultivated spirits of the Empire, the bishop of Lisieux, Freculf, dedicating to her the second volume of his great universal history, wrote to her, perfect courtier as he was: "In truth and without flattery you surpass in beauty all the queens whom I have been able to see and of whom I have heard tell". And he knew what he was talking about, having had to evoke in his work the memory of so many queens and empresses! Moreover all Freculf's contemporaries agree on this point, and the historiography of the period is abundantly filled with talk of the adventures in which she was implicated. Most of the chroniclers furthermore – with a complaisance that arouses our suspicion and with an excessive tendency to simplify – make Judith the evil genius of the reign.

However this may be, her influence came to be felt only gradually in the affairs of the Empire. For we should not forget that in 821 her husband caused the oath to the constitution of 817 to be retaken and that the penitence of Attigny occurred in August 822. But in the course of this same year, just after the assembly of Attigny in which he had given his subjects such a striking proof of his desire for concord in order to maintain Christian unity, Louis sent his son Lothar, up to then associated in the exercise of imperial government, to Italy, and had him accompanied in this mission, which looked like an exile, by the monk of Corbie, Wala, brother of Abbot Adalard, and by the chief usher of the palace at Aachen, Gerung, both charged to guide him with their advice. Doubtless in appearance nothing so far was changed in the rules drawn up in 817. Lothar continued to bear the title of emperor: "Lothar Augustus, son of my lord the unconquered emperor Louis", could be read at the beginning of his charters; but his activity was henceforth limited to Italy, where he convoked general assemblies, published capitularies, and issued charters benefiting the churches and monasteries of the peninsula. He acted, except in title, as an ordinary king of Italy, where he resided, following the ancient Lombard kings by usually holding his court in the north, either at Pavia, or more frequently near this city in his domain of Corteolona.

It was from there that, on the invitation of the Sovereign Pontiff, he went to Rome at the beginning of April 823. He was solemnly anointed emperor by Paschal I at St Peter's on Easter Sunday, without however this ceremony being more than purely protocollary or resulting in the least alteration in the powers attributed to him. His stay in Italy lasted until the summer of 825, except for a short interlude, from the middle of 823 to the beginning of 824, during which we see him take up contact again with the Frankish kingdom. Everything took place indeed, during the rest of the time, as if since 822 Lothar's presence at the imperial court had been judged undesirable or at least useless and as if, without altering anything whatever in the provisions drawn up in 817 for the future, Louis preferred for the present to confine his eldest son, like his younger sons, within the boundaries of a particular kingdom.

The subjection of the papacy

Lothar's presence in Italy had as a further consequence the gradual reversal, again in favour of the imperial power, of the nature of the relations between the Frankish court and the Holy See. Soon after the imperial anointing at St Peter's in April 823, Lothar intervened in the affairs of the Papal State by presiding at Rome over a tribunal to which was submitted some litigation pending for a long time between the Roman curia and the abbot of a large monastery of Sabinia, that of Farfa, on the subject of the abbey's temporal goods and its juridical rights. The matter itself was not very important, but it is a characteristic instance of the meddling of the imperial power in the internal affairs of the State of St Peter. It should, furthermore, be added that the tribunal, presided over by Lothar, pronounced against the claims of the papal administrator, represented by a high official, the librarian of the Holy See.

Soon, however, the situation became more serious. While Lothar was temporarily absent from Italy, news spread that a drama had occurred at the Lateran Palace, the residence of the Sovereign Pontiff, in which two heads of service of the curia, the *primicerius* of the notaries, Theodore and the *nomenclator* Leo, accused of being too obliging toward the Franks and of collusion with the government of Lothar, had been put to death by men of the papal entourage; and the initiative for this summary execution was imputed by public report to the pope in person. There was great agitation at the Frankish court, where Louis the Pious decided on the immediate despatch of two *missi*, a count and an abbot, to make inquiries on the spot. Indignant protestations of innocence were made by Paschal I, a personage without great authority and of mediocre prestige. He immediately sent two cardinals to Louis, who arrived at the imperial palace even before the departure of the *missi*, and who hastened to request justice for their master, unworthily calumniated. The pope's attitude was nonetheless judged severely by Louis the Pious' entourage. The semi-official author of the *Royal Annals*, from whom we learn these details, gives one a glimpse of it when he notes with scepticism:

The two *missi* were unable to bring matters into the open in any definite manner, because Pope Paschal, together with a large number of bishops, exculpated themselves by oath from any involvement in the affair, and taking on the defense of the murderers, since they belonged to the family of St Peter (that is to say, to his own household), they affirmed that the victims had been put to death justly, as being guilty of lèse-majesté.

The emperor did not venture to inquire still further, but no doubt reserved the right to take any necessary precautions.

Meanwhile, Paschal I died on 11 February 824 and his successor Eugenius II was elected, in the absence of Lothar, but under the watchful eye of a representative of the imperial government, who seems to have been Wala. Eugenius II was compelled to take an oath in Wala's presence which can only have been an oath of allegiance to the Empire and its ruler. In any case the new pope, obliged like so many of his predecessors to reckon with a strong party of opposition trying to put a rival in his place, found himself at the mercy of his Frankish protectors, and Louis the Pious took advantage of this by sending Lothar to Rome immediately to take, as the semi-official source says, "measures required by the situation".

For this situation, after an inquiry conducted on the spot, the Frankish authorities held the papacy and its staff to be largely responsible: Lothar ordered certain restitutions of properties usurped with the complicity of the Holy See, and a charter was published in the course of Nobember 824 to regulate in an unambiguous manner the relations of the two powers: that of the emperor and that of the pope. This document is of capital importance. Of its nine articles, some had as their sole object the re-establishment of order in the State of St Peter, the proclamation of an amnesty for the past deeds of violence, and the stipulation of reparations for the victims and the damages caused. These provisions of a temporary character, it must be noted, all proceeded from imperial initiative, and the implementation of some of them was explicitly entrusted to the representatives of the emperor alone. This was true of those in Art. 6, which ran in part as follows: "For the properties of churches unduly occupied, be it under cover of an alleged papal confirmation, be it ... by the papal government itself, we desire that reparation be exacted by our *missi*". In this way the emperor reserved for himself the exclusive right to correct past excesses.

The provisions of permanent character and general bearing which occupied the principal place in the charter were more significant. The essential ones are:

(1) The papal administration shall from now on be placed under the

supervision of a mixed delegation residing at Rome and composed of a representative of the pope and a representative of the emperor. These are to present a report annually to the emperor; they will receive complaints brought against papal officials and will refer them to the pope, who is to dispense justice without delay. In cases where this does not occur, the imperial delegate shall inform the emperor, who will despatch *missi dominici* to settle the matter on the spot (Art. 4).

(2) The papal officials of Rome shall present themselves before the emperor (or, very probably, before his representative), who will have the list of nominations and "will admonish them individually on the exercise of their offices", that is to say, will communicate to them his instructions (Art. 8).

(3) Art. 5 extended the Frankish rule of personal law to the Papal State and even to Rome by stating the principle that each 'Roman' would be requested to declare under which law he intended to live and be judged; the imperial authorities would make all the necessary arrangements for this, together with the papal authorities – which, once more opened the door to Frankish interventions in the internal affairs of the State of St Peter.

(4) By another article (1) all persons under the special protection either of the emperor or of the pope were exempted from the common law, the violator exposing himself to the death penalty.

(5) The election of the pope was left to the Romans alone, who would proceed with it according to the most ancient rules (Art. 3), that is to say, it seems, without excluding laymen, contrary to the new rule drawn up in 769 just after the accession of Stephen III. This would allow the imperial government to exercise strong pressure on the electoral body. In any case, the elect could no longer be consecrated before having taken publicly, and in the presence of the permanent delegate of the emperor at Rome, an oath similar to the one that had been required of Eugenius II in 824, that is to say, an oath of allegiance to the emperor.

(6) Finally – to crown the whole construction – an oath of allegiance to the emperor was required of all the pope's subjects: "In the name of God Almighty, upon the holy Gospels and this cross of our lord Jesus Christ, as well as upon the body of the blessed Peter, Prince of the Apostles, I promise that from this day till my death I shall be loyal to our lords the emperors Louis and Lothar, with all my strength and all my mind without fraud or deceit, excepting the loyalty promised to my

lord the pope . . .". The subjects of the pope thus found themselves becoming at the same time subjects of the emperor; and, as a final detail, they were required to add: "I oppose with all my strength and all my mind any election for the See of Rome taking place otherwise than in accordance with canon law and justice, and I shall not consent to the consecration of the elect until he has taken the required oath publicly and in the presence of the delegate of my lord the emperor" – a bold formula that transformed the Romans into guarantors of the statute to which the papacy and the papal state were henceforth subjected. In sum, the Papal State became a sort of Frankish protectorate, and in temporal affairs the pope found himself clearly subordinated to the imperial authority. This was, as one can see, a complete reversal of the previous situation as defined in 817. For the papacy it was even worse than the system practiced under Charlemagne, all the more so since this time it was a system legalized and defined in an official statute and constitutionally promulgated. Thus the whole policy toward the Holy See, as it had been at the beginning of Louis' reign, was reversed.

The intrigues around Lothar

In the same period, a change of attitude also occurred in the internal affairs of the realm. On 13 June 823 the second wife of Louis the Pious, Judith, gave birth to a son, Charles – who would later be called Charles the Bald – and this birth created a problem which could hinder the application of the succession statute published in 817. It had been thought that every possibility was thoroughly taken care of in this charter: premature decease of one of Louis' three sons, the marriage of any of them, the birth of children to them. The possibility of their having no direct heirs had been foreseen, as also the possibility that they would fail in their duties, and many hypothetical situations had been foreseen, except the birth of one or more further sons to Louis himself, as though this emperor of scarcely forty (he was born in 778) had made a vow of chastity until the end of his days. The birth of this fourth legitimate son, without upsetting the principles proclaimed in 817, thus required the reconsideration, in order to adapt them to new data, of certain of the provisions drawn up concerning the kingdoms awarded to the younger sons.

In order to gain the confidence of Lothar, his designated successor, for this purpose, the emperor summoned him to his court in the summer of 823. Louis was skilful enough to make him the godfather of the newborn child and to entrust it to his protection. Lothar was also persuaded to accept the principle of awarding to the new heir a kingdom analogous to what had been provided for Pepin and Louis. But at this point things became more complicated. Lothar, who felt himself to be indispensable, began to play the situation to his advantage, or rather he became the instrument of a group which tried to profit from it and which soon became more and more indiscreet. This group included men of all origins and consequently of very diverse propensities. Among them, some were simply ambitious, and sought only to rise, to obtain office, to fill their pockets and to round out their domains; there were others, particularly clerics, who thought they would be able, through Lothar, to realize their dreams of the purification of society; some even, still more naive, hoped to realize through him the imperial unity, which was threatened – so they believed at least – by the ambitions of Judith, in whom they saw an instrument of Satan.

In the forefront of this last category stood the monk Wala, brother of Abbot Adalard of Corbie. Charged, after his return to favour, with accompanying Lothar to Italy, he had come to have an influence on him which, although it was unjustifiably exaggerated by his apologist Paschasius Radbert, was nevertheless great, and would become even greater in the course of the events that followed. Others who thought to profit from the situation were men such as Hugh, count of Tours, father-in-law of Lothar, Matfrid, count of Orleans, and several other personages of doubtful repute, whose role quickly became disturbing.

At first, it is true, nothing seemed changed in the relations between Lothar and his father. Immediately after the arrangements he had made concerning the young Charles, Lothar was sent back to Italy where he finished the work he had begun, displaying in the ancient Lombard kingdom an activity to which the numerous charters published in his name bear witness, and he was much absorbed, as we have seen, by the affairs of the Papal State. But in the course of the summer of 825 he returned to the Frankish kingdom and seemed resolved to make good the support he had promised Empress Judith in the promotion of the last-born imperial child.

A first gratification to Lothar's self-esteem was given to him: his name was placed beside that of his father in the protocols of official charters, and the members of his personal entourage, the Walas, Hughs, and Matfrids, began to be the subject of a great deal of talk at the imperial court. At the time of the celebrations held at the palace of Ingelheim in June 826 on the occasion of the baptism of Harald king of Denmark, Empress Judith, if one may believe the poet Ermold the Black, appeared in a procession led by the counts Hugh and Matfrid, and a letter of the archbishop of Lyon, Agobard, to the "most illustrious Matfrid, the most eminent of men" to ask him to use his influence with the emperor "to whom God has assigned him as minister since the origin of the world", in his favour, informs us, in addition to many other documents, about the importance gained by this time by this singular personage. As for Wala, abbot of Corbie after the death of his brother Adalard at the beginning of 826, it was probably from this time onward that, if we may believe his biographer Paschasius Radbert, he began to besiege Louis the Pious with what Paschasius himself calls jeremiads demanding new reforms in the Church, and especially among the clerics of the imperial chapel. In this way the palace of Louis was gradually monopolized by Lothar's circle.

The affair of the counts Hugh and Matfrid (826)

While intrigues thus took their course at the Frankish court, serious troubles arose on the frontiers of the Empire. Up to 826 these had not only been kept intact but sometimes even, at various points, slightly extended, and imperial prestige was still considerable outside the imperial borders. But in the Iberian Peninsula clouds began to gather. The 'march' set up in the time of Charlemagne along the border of Moslem Spain had become, for a number of years, a source of constant trouble. In 826 a revolt against Frankish authority broke out there under the leadership of a Goth named Aizo, who was supported by the Umayyad emir of Cordoba, Abd ar-Rahman II. At the beginning of 827 the situation became alarming: the rebels gained ground rapidly; defections multiplied; Moslem troops, called to their aid, traversed the country up to Cerdagne and Gerona; they laid siege to Barcelona. The first reinforcements sent in haste by the emperor proved to be insufficient; but a large army placed officially under the command of

Pepin, king of Aquitaine, was mobilized immediately and sent to the theatre of war. The effective command was entrusted to Counts Hugh and Matfrid, the two instruments of Lothar. But their advance was so slow that Count Bernard, governor of the march of Spain, surrounded in his capital Barcelona, was reduced to resisting the invasion almost alone. He succeeded in repulsing the enemy only with the greatest difficulty.

Rumour soon had it at the palace of Louis the Pious that Hugh and Matfrid had moved slowly on purpose. They had systematically retarded their army's march in the hope that Bernard, tackling alone an enemy superior in number, would succumb under the onslaught. A son of William, count of Toulouse, who had distinguished himself in the time of Charlemagne by his bravery in the struggle against the Basques and the Moslems before ending his days piously at the monastery of Gellona, Bernard was the godchild of Emperor Louis, to whom he was furthermore related by blood, and in whose presence his marriage had been celebrated in the course of the summer of 824. By entrusting to him at that time the county of Barcelona and the march of Spain, sometimes also called the march of Septimania, the emperor had given him a brilliant mark of confidence, and events had just proved that the choice had been a wise one. As for the attitude taken by Counts Hugh and Matfrid: it can probably be explained by jealousy. Their punishment was not long in coming. An assembly convoked in February 828 at Aachen was informed both of their conduct and of that of the duke of Friuli, who at almost the same moment had displayed a considerable laxity in the defense of the march of Istria against the Bulgars. The three culprits were dismissed from their offices and deprived of their 'benefices'. But in the case of Hugh and Matfrid, it is easy to see whence the blow came, for their disgrace was to be accompanied by the rapid rise of Count Bernard himself, and it was to one of his cousins, Odo, that the county of Orleans, which had been taken away from Matfrid, was given.

The bishops' warning (829)

Lothar's circle, however, did not submit without protest. Though Hugh and Matfrid had been disgraced, Wala and his friends were still there to speak loud and strong, especially Wala. He redoubled his remonstrances addressed to the emperor, accused him of encroaching on the rights and properties of the Church, and clamoured for reforms; so much so and so well that in December 828 the emperor finally decided to accede to his demands and ordered the holding of four great synods charged with proposing reforms to him, the plans for which he would submit to the next general assembly.

In the letter of convocation sent to the bishops and drawn up, according to the previously established protocol, in the name of his son Lothar as well as in his own name, the emperor did not hesitate to justify these synods by the necessity of an overall reform (*communis correctio*) capable of remedying the vices of a society whose attitude was a perpetual offence to God; and the order given at the same time to proceed throughout the Empire with preliminary investigations into these matters was based on analogous reasons. The prelates, assembled in May and June 829 at Paris, Lyon, Mainz and Toulouse, according to the seat of their bishopric, took this to heart, and the deliberations resulted in an ample dossier, composed partly of general remarks about society – the religious society above all, but also civil society, without excepting the monarchy itself – partly of concrete proposals which the emperor was earnestly bidden to make his own.

The synod of Paris is the only one whose resolutions have been preserved. They reveal the state of mind in which the Frankish episcopate took up the problems submitted to it. After reviewing the reasons which, in the presence of the misfortunes besetting the Empire, required its subjects to proceed to carry out a serious examination of their consciences and a general reform, the bishops pointed out with satisfaction that in order to cope with the situation and to appease the anger of the Almighty, the two emperors had decided, as was normal, to have recourse in the first place to those to whom God had given the power to bind and loose upon this earth, namely the "vicars of the Apostle and lights of the world", according to the saying of the prophet Haggai (2:11): "Ask now the priests concerning the law."

Strengthened by these preliminary remarks, the reverend Fathers of the synod of Paris insisted on the primacy of the spiritual authority and on the superiority which should be accorded to clerics throughout the Empire; they even recalled, rather boldly, at the beginning of their declaration, the famous opinion of Pope Gelasius, who set the 'authority' (*auctoritas*) with which the body of priests is invested by God well above the simple 'power' of command (*potestas*) which temporal princes have, whether they be kings or emperors. Expected to render account to God for the conduct of princes, the clergy, they declared, is charged with the heaviest responsibilities; this is why the bishops devoted many long pages to describing the reforms to which the clergy ought to subject themselves.

For all that, they did not forget to point out the responsibilities that weigh on the shoulders of kings; and seeking to define the special duties that were theirs, they pointed out, recalling Isidore of Seville and the unknown author of a much-quoted treatise on the *Abuses of the age*, that a prince who does not govern according to equity and the law of God is no more than a 'tyrant' of unsteady power. They added that he is accountable for his acts to God, from whom alone he holds his kingdom, without his ancestors counting at all in this respect; that he places himself in a state of sin when he delegates his power to wicked judges and ministers; that he should not permit the "men invested with palatine dignities to tear each other apart out of envy" and sate themselves with their mutual hatreds to the great profit of the "enemies of Christ"–and it is not difficult to see in this insistence a direct allusion to the intrigues then taking place at court and to the changes which had occurred in the confidential personnel of the palace since the disgrace of Counts Hugh and Matfrid.

The resolutions which, by way of conclusion, the bishops very respectfully submitted to the emperor, were also rather bold. They requested above all, as Wala had demanded, that the emperor remind his sons and his 'magnates' of the respect due to the clergy (Arts. 8 and 9); they went further: the emperor was asked to request his subjects not to suspect the purity of their intentions when, according to the duties of their ministry, they suggested measures which they judged necessary for the salvation of all (Art. 10); they asked that the clerics and monks on the loose who congested the palace and abused the hospitality of the ruler be driven out (Art. 14); they furthermore asked the emperor to put an end to the activities in the Empire of men who made Christian blood flow in carrying out their vengeances (Art. 17), to remind his chaplains and the clerics of his palace to respect the canonical rules, to request the magnates and the officials of the court to attend mass on holy days and himself to give an example of assiduity at the divine services (Art. 19); they advised him to take communion often (Art. 20), to make sure that good bishops and abbots were elected, worthy of the offices that were entrusted to them (Arts. 22–23); finally and above all, "for his salvation, for the welfare of the whole people, for the honour and stability of the kingdom", to see to the choice of advisers and holders of offices who would be respectful in their mutual relations, of the precepts of "charity, peace and concord", enemies of "dissimulation and deceit", "guardians of his soul at the same time as of his body", "giving the example of honourable character and goodness of heart" and making, in sum, of his "sacred palace" a house worthy of respect (Art. 24).

This brief survey of the resolutions made by the synod of Paris in 829 shows the evolution that had taken place and reveals the contentious atmosphere of the day. Louis the Pious let them talk away but, as Abbot Wala's biographer noted with vexation a dozen years later, no positive results emerged from all this. And this disillusioned remark echoed the one which, in 836, the Fathers of a synod held at Aachen presented to the emperor in the following terms: "We remember that in previous meetings several articles were, at your request, discussed and worked out in view of the common good and welfare of the two orders, ecclesiastical and lay; but we do not know why these articles were relegated to oblivion."

CHAPTER FOUR

The revolt of Louis' sons and Lothar's coup d'état

Lothar's disgrace and Count Bernard's appointment to the office of chamberlain

If, to take up the euphemism of the Fathers of the synod of Aachen, the texts they submitted to the approval of the emperor were "relegated to oblivion" it was because, a few weeks afterwards, tired of being kept in leading-strings by Lothar's circle, troubled about the "intrigues being surreptitiously prepared", as one of his biographers writes, and probably urged on by Judith, who felt herself to be the first target of these secret schemings, Louis the Pious decided on energetic measures.

At the conclusion of the general assembly held at Worms in August 829, it was learnt that, successively, Lothar had been sent back to Italy, Bernard, count of Barcelona, had been summoned to court to become chamberlain, and finally – apparently without the grant being submitted for approval to the assembly – a territory comprising the Aleman country (cradle of the Welf family, to which Judith belonged), Rhaetia, Alsace and part of Burgundy had been awarded to Charles, the last-born of the emperor's children. This last measure in itself was not at all revolutionary: it did not contradict the principles regulating the imperial succession drawn up in 817; the share awarded to Charles was even, in appearance, considerably inferior to those of his brothers, which were left intact, and to the kingdom of Italy which Louis, after having stationed his nephew Bernard there in 817, had judged it prudent to place under the special supervision of Lothar. It is not even

known – no source mentions anything about it – whether Charles was
given the title of king. But the awarding of territories to the young
prince, be it upon the initiative of the emperor alone, be it due to the
pressure of his entourage, would in any case make a supplement to the
charter of 817 necessary, since nothing of this sort had been foreseen.
However, at no time was there any question of this.

What made the decision that had been taken seem especially suspect
was that it was accompanied by the two others which we have
mentioned and about whose significance there can be no doubt at all:
the sending back of Lothar into Italy with as its corollary the omission
of his name from the protocol of official charters, where he had been
placed alongside his father since his return to the imperial palace, and
the nomination of Count Bernard to the office of chamberlain, one of
the most important of the court. To these two measures was added,
moreover, the fall from favour of all those who had up to then had a
voice in the counsels of the government, and in the first place of the
abbot of Corbie, Wala, sent back to his monastery shortly afterwards
with the order not to leave it.

Anger now broke out among the formerly powerful, as one after
another they were dismissed from the palace and replaced by the
empress's or the new chamberlain's creatures. Holding both the
empress and the chamberlain responsible for their misfortune, these
men did not forgive the pair the loss of the offices which they had up to
then occupied and which, twenty years later, Wala's biographer did not
hesitate to describe as their "due". Having protested against the
spoliation, they proceeded to attack. Judith's and Bernard's reputa-
tions were dragged through the mud: the most distasteful calumnies
were disseminated against them. It was only too clear, they said, what
this 'scoundrel' Bernard was after when he arrived from his distant
Spain! "Wallowing in the mire", digging "like a furious wild boar", he
had begun by "turning the palace upside down, reducing the council to
nothing, driving away and treading under foot the high officials, clerics
as well as laymen . . ., upsetting everything, changing in turn day into
night and then night into day". Dead set against all those who at the
palace or elsewhere had acquired a justified renown, he became so bold
as to capture the heart of the empress, and she became his mistress; he
had made a 'house of prostitution' of the palace; young and flighty,
Judith had let herself be drawn into the worst excesses, and had from
then on seen only through the eyes of her lover, soon to become so

powerful, due to his charms, that the life of the emperor himself was feared for – the emperor, who had himself been blindfolded!

It is impossible to distinguish whatever there may be of truth in this gossip, the essence of which was repeated soon afterwards in the accusations officially pronounced against the emperor and his wife. But the violence of the campaign waged from then on indicates sufficiently that the dispossessed people did not intend to let things be. Furthermore, Wala's biographer confessed that, from his monastery of Corbie, his hero had been "begged in the name of Christ together with certain great men and holy bishops to find means to prevent such deeds from resulting in the subversion of the entire Empire". Abbot Wala's friends thus exerted themselves, it was claimed, "to rescue religion, the Empire, the peace of the Church," and to protect "the king and kingdom" against the traitors who had conspired to destroy them: a significant confession, and a harbinger of the tumultuous events that were to take place shortly afterwards.

The revolt of 830

Prepared in secrecy, the revolt suddenly broke out in April 830 and rapidly became widespread. It was occasioned by the discontent caused among the people by the mobilization of the army at an unusual date, during Lent, under the pretext of having to quell troubles in Brittany. The meeting-place of the host and of the general assembly had been fixed at Rennes, but people complained that this place was far off and "difficult to reach". The usefulness or at least the urgency of the projected campaign was challenged; people saw it as a manoeuvre by the chamberlain Bernard. The conspirators forthwith posed as liberators of "the emperor and his sons". The moment had come, they said, to prevent the Empire succumbing to "traps laid by the enemy", to get rid of the traitor and "his accomplices", to draw Louis the Pious from his state of "abjectness" in which Bernard's insolence had kept him. Some of the assembled troops allowed themselves to be drawn into the movement of revolt and concentrated near Paris. Louis' second son, Pepin of Aquitaine, also won over to the rebels' cause, soon joined them, having on the way, at Orléans, re-established Matfrid in his function of count. Lothar was expected to come from Italy; his brother Louis, from Bavaria.

Panic broke out at the emperor's palace. Louis the Pious left for Rennes at the beginning of March, making a long detour via Saint-Omer and the Channel coast. The empress Judith remained alone at Aachen with the chamberlain Bernard and a few high officials. Threatened with death, Bernard fled in haste to Barcelona, and Judith hurried to hide herself in a convent at Laon. The rebels extracted her thence and took her to Compiègne where, bravely, Louis had come to meet them; they persuaded her to try to obtain from her husband a voluntary renunciation of the throne and a pious retreat to a monastery. The emperor was not inclined to surrender: he requested time to consider. But Judith was not given time to consider. Pepin had her taken to the abbey of St Radegund at Poitiers, where she was compelled to take the veil, at the same time as he sent her two brothers, the Counts Conrad and Rodulf, to other Aquitanian monasteries.

In the presence of Lothar, who had meanwhile arrived at Compiègne, Louis was obliged to promise to rely henceforth on the advice of his former counsellors and to see to the maintenance of the provisions previously drawn up for the Empire's well-being. Reprisals were carried out against the family of the ex-chamberlain Bernard: his brother Herbert was blinded and sent securely guarded to Italy; his cousin Odo, a short time previously count of Orléans, was deported. Other suspects were arrested and imprisoned. Lothar was re-established in the fullness of his powers as associate emperor, and his name again followed that of his father in the protocol of official charters.

The reaction of 831

Was this simply a return to the previous situation? For that, trust would have had to be restored between the two parties, which was far from being the case. Each side distrusted the other, and took its precautions. Louis the Pious, separated from Judith, who was kept in the cloister of St Radegund at Poitiers where she was supposed, in principle, to do penance until her death, was himself watched by Lothar, who left him no more than the appearance of power. One of his partisans, his nephew Nithard, wrote that the emperor, just like his son Charles, was "in supervised freedom" (*sub libera custodia*), a gracious euphemism which speaks volumes. Lothar himself, it is true, like his partisans, did not feel very sure of his father's feelings toward him. Louis the Pious had yielded to force, but he prepared his revenge by seeking, through the mediation of a monk named Gombald, to come to an understanding with his other two sons, Pepin and Louis, behind their elder brother's back.

In October 830 a general assembly held at Nijmegen took place in an atmosphere of contention. An anonymous witness – the chronicler called 'The Astronomer' because of the interest he displays in astronomical phenomena – has sketched its vicissitudes in an astonishingly lively manner. It is worth the trouble to follow them with him. The meeting-place had been fixed by Louis in a region where he believed he could count on more loyalty than in Neustria and, out of prudence, the order had been given for everyone to go there without arms or escort. To the general surprise, the emperor suddenly dared speak again as though he were the ruler and began to demand vengeance on those who had betrayed him several months earlier. Hilduin, abbot of Saint-Denis and arch-chaplain of the imperial Palace, since he had come armed, notwithstanding his sacred status, and in violation of the instructions that had been given, was the first to be requested to explain himself, and he was ultimately exiled to Paderborn, in Saxony. Wala, in his turn, was curtly dismissed and requested to return to his monastery of Corbie. These two moves threw Lothar's partisans into confusion. They passed the following night with him in secret meetings, pressing him to carry out a new revolution. Lothar hesitated. Taking advantage of this, Louis summoned him as well, without warning. Lothar's partisans felt that they were lost and Lothar, feeling put out, did not dare disobey. Contrary to his expectations, he was received calmly by a father ready to forgive him. Outside, however, dissatisfaction grew. Louis showed himself to the crowd with his son. The tumult redoubled. Louis faced up to it and harangued his people. Calm returned. Louis went so far as to arrest the instigators and decided to refer them to a new general assembly convoked at Aachen; one of the most conspicuous figures beside Wala and Hilduin, Bishop Jesse of Amiens, was even deposed without waiting for that; finally, it was agreed that Empress Judith would be permitted to come and justify herself at Aachen.

The projected assembly opened in Aachen on 2 February 831. Never had Louis the Pious seemed more sure of himself. His sons were all at his side; Empress Judith made a triumphal re-entry accompanied by her brothers Conrad and Rodulf. The emperor had hastly sent her son Charles and his own half-brother Bishop Drogo of Metz to receive her honourably. Her head high, Judith declared her wish to cleanse herself of the insulting accusations brought against her. When no one replied to the question: who wishes to uphold the accusation? she swore her innocence according to the Frankish custom and was immediately re-established in her former dignity. Upon the agitators and rebels of the months just past, punishment descended, inexorably. The penalty of death, which the assembly awarded for those guilty of high treason, was commuted by the emperor into imprisonment for laymen, relegation to monasteries for clerics, and in certain cases confiscation of property and exile. Wala was deported to the region of the Lake of Geneva. Lothar, eventually recognized as having been involved, was once again excluded from power, and his name was again removed from official charters. The order was given to him to return to the kingdom of Italy and not to leave it without special permission.

A state of affairs had now been created which was the opposite of what had been stipulated in 817; and it was not without reason that Wala's biographer denounced this abrogation of all the established conventions and all the oaths of allegiance that had been taken. Of Lothar, as associate emperor, an essential element of the edifice then so arduously constructed, not a word was now said; the provisions of the charter by which in 817 the imperial succession had been regulated in advance were, without any ambiguity at all, considered null and void. Lothar's two brothers, whose support or at least neutrality had had to be obtained, were rewarded for their good will by a considerable enlargement of their future kingdoms, and an undated charter, which however cannot, it seems, be placed at any other moment, determined how the territories were now to be divided.

Its content is significant. Indeed it is immediately obvious that the charter is copied, almost from beginning to end, from the one by which in 806 Charlemagne, at the time when he still had three legitimate sons, had arranged the partition of his entire Empire into three equal portions according to Frankish custom. In the same way, twenty-five years later, Louis the Pious ordered the partition of his Empire into three equal portions among the only three sons whom he still recognized, Pepin, Louis and Charles, excepting only Italy, which was left to Lothar – just as in 813, Charlemagne had left it to his grandson Bernard – without the need even being felt this time to make explicit mention of it, or to pronounce the name of the person to whom it was granted.

To Pepin, the eldest of the three sons allowed to benefit from this division of Frankish lands, were reserved, besides Aquitaine and the additions provided for in 817, the whole area between the Loire and the Seine and a large part of Neustria proper. To Louis, besides Bavaria and the neighbouring provinces, as they had been defined in 817, the charter awarded almost all of Austrasia, Thuringia, Saxony, Frisia, Flanders, Brabant and Hainault, as well as the extreme north of Neustria. Besides Alemania, Alsace and Rhaetia, Charles received the Moselle region, the counties of Reims and Laon, the whole of the ancient Burgundian kingdom down to the Mediteranean, excepting the three counties reserved in 817 to Pepin (those of Autun, Avallon and Nevers), and finally all of Gothia (Septimania and the Spanish march).

The three kingdoms, which would be created after the death of the reigning emperor, were declared independent under the same conditions and with the same reservations as in 806, namely on condition that the three brothers joined in the common defense of their frontiers and of the Roman Church when their father was no longer there. For it was taken for granted that there would be no question of anyone being emperor once Louis the Pious had departed from the scene, and that the three kings would act in their own individual best interests, without concerning themselves with their eldest brother. While Louis the Pious was still alive, however, submission and absolute obedience was expected of them, and a threatening article (Article 13) even declared that the emperor reserves the right to take away territories from anyone who misbehaves and to add them to the portion of those who show themselves worthy of "additional honours and power", so that each may be rewarded "according to his merits". Against whom was this threat directed? Obviously, not against Charles, the son of Judith, a child of seven, completely unable, for some time still, to act on his own; but having learnt from experience, Louis the Pious distrusted Pepin and Louis – especially Pepin, who in 830 had been the instrument of the rebels until the arrival of his eldest brother from Italy.

The revolt of 833

This distrust was justified, for at the end of 831 Pepin again rebelled. But at the very moment that Louis the Pious prepared to march against him, in the first weeks of 832, it was learned that Louis of Bavaria, aware of this, was about to invade Alemania which, as the reader will remember, had been awarded to his brother Charles.

Revolt was now indeed endemic in the Empire. Louis the Pious made desperate efforts to break up this ever-recurring conspiracy, by using in turn force and persuasion. He thwarted Louis of Bavaria's manoeuvre by anticipating him with a rapid march; entering Bavaria himself in May at the head of a large army, he reached Augsburg, on the Lech, where his rebellious son considered himself fortunate to be able to obtain his father's pardon. Thereafter he turned upon Pepin, had him arrested, sent him to prison in Trier in September 832 and placed Charles, the son of Judith, on the throne of Aquitaine in his place. At the same time he speculated on the distrust between his three eldest sons by trying to negotiate with Lothar a new agreement, for which Pepin and perhaps Louis would be obliged to pay the costs. But obviously any durable agreement between the emperor and any of his three older sons was thenceforth impossible; not one of them believed any longer in the good faith of any other, and each sought to prepare himself against new surprises.

Pepin, who had succeeded in escaping from Trier, was soon conniving with his brothers Louis and Lothar to make another joint attempt at seizing power. This time the revolt was carefully prepared and the three brothers drew up their plan of operations in detail. Having left Pavia, probably in April 833, Lothar made his way over the Alps and hastened to join Pepin and Louis in Alsace. More than ever the three brothers brandished the constitution of 817, already completely forgotten, and posed as defenders of the established order. A clamorous propaganda tried to present them, not as sedition-mongers but as saviours. Archbishop Agobard of Lyon, always ready to stick his neck out, published the rebels' demands in the form of an open letter to the emperor. His writing to the emperor, Agobard declared, was to ease his conscience. Instead of leading, as he could have done, with his sons, "a tranquil life like his father and his grandfather", Louis after having at first made wise provisions for the future of his kingdom and the maintenance of imperial unity, had suddenly "changed his mind and torn up his obligations"; "without reasons and without taking counsel he had repudiated without God the measures he had drawn up with God". He should come to himself and let God bring him back to the right path; he should fear lest "the wrath of God would come upon him". Let him take care: the crowd "grumbles loudly because of the various and contradictory oaths" required of it; and, moreover, "they are not content to grumble, they grieve about and they censure it". And Agobard concluded by recalling St Jerome's words about the forgetting of an oath which leads to perjury.... As one can see, the accusation was not even veiled. The emperor knew what he could expect, because to a perjurer no one any longer owed allegiance.

With him, furthermore, by a masterstroke, Lothar brought the Sovereign Pontiff, Gregory IV, who had let himself be drawn into the affair in the conviction that he could thus protect the peace of Christendom and that "he alone would be in a position to reconcile the father and his sons". The presence of such an authority in the camp of the rebels threw Louis the Pious' entourage into confusion, the rumour circulating that the pope had come to excommunicate the emperor and all those who resisted Lothar's orders.

This papal intervention was skilfully orchestrated. In a first letter, which has not come down to us, the pope invited all the Frankish bishops to appear before him, which was an indirect way of driving them into the arms of Lothar. A good many apologized for not being able to accede to the invitation since they were not authorized to do so by the emperor. A second letter of Gregory, whose text we do have, protested against such an attitude: the command given by the pope took precedence over the one given by the emperor, Gregory pointed out, and the pope's command moreover came earlier. The bishops, furthermore, "should not be ignorant of the fact that the rule of souls, which belongs to the pope, is more important than the government of temporal things, which belongs to the emperor". Had not St Gregory of Nazianzus, in a full church, said to the emperors: "The law of Christ has subjected you to our priestly power. It has given us a principate much more perfect than yours'." "Why have you not answered as true priests?" the pope added, addressing the recalcitrant bishops.

Why did you not reply to the emperor whose commands, you say, forestalled you, by using for yourself this answer of the same St Gregory to an emperor: 'Remember that you differ neither by nature nor in substance from all those who are subject to you. Be in spirit with God and exult not so much in commanding the world as in being commanded by Christ!' Instead of remaining with the emperor, why do you not stop your stupid flatteries and tell him, with St Augustine: 'Blessed are emperors if they command righteously and do not become proud through the flattering praises bestowed on them or the tokens of excessive humility lavished on them...; let them put off the hour of vengeance and be forgiving; let them not have recourse to vengeance except for the welfare and the defense of the state, and not to satisfy their hates'... You who have not wished to be good labourers of the truth, you are no better than liars....

Do you hesitate? But he who hesitates is like the wave of the sea that the wind drives; and in your hesitations you stupidly go so far as to declare that it is we who are forgetful of our pastoral office!... You shamelessly go on to accuse us of coming to pronounce some presumptuous and unreasonable excommunication...; of wishing to insult and dishonour the imperial power, as well as to weaken and degrade our authority! What do you mean by such words? And what is it that dishonours the imperial power most: acts worthy of excommunication or excommunication itself?... Such matters arouse disgust.... You remind me to respect the oath of allegiance I have taken to the emperor! But I wish specifically to avoid neglecting it by denouncing every wrong that he commits against the unity and peace, of the Church as much as of the kingdom. Not to do this would be to fall short of my oath, as you yourself are falling short of yours, you who have sworn always to be faithful toward him, and now, seeing him act against all good faith and rushing headlong to his downfall, do not dissuade him from it.... Finally you promise me a respectful reception on condition that I go to meet him, as he wishes. But you have not read this answer in the divine Scriptures! Doing nothing except for temporal rewards, you are like reeds blown by the wind and you bend with the slightest breeze. Judge, judge my brothers, how far your spirit is from that prayer which in the celebration of mass you are accustomed to address to God – with your mouth but not with your heart: 'give us, for your sake, the power to scorn the vanities of the world and to fear no adversity'. If your prayer had come from the heart, He would already have granted it Who said: 'ask and it shall be given to you'....

Possibly drawn up by Agobard, this proclamation of the Sovereign Pontiff skilfully shifted the problem. The fact of the rebellion of three power-hungry sons against the legitimate emperor was forgotten and no more than a scruple remained; the unity of the Empire and the Church having been broken, the supreme ruler of Christendom had come, in the name of the authority he held from God, to re-establish peace among Christians; how could one dare not to acknowledge his supreme power?

A second letter of Agobard reminds the emperor of this, in reply to an invitation he had received to come to a general assembly hastily convoked at Worms for the beginning of June. Had not St Augustine, the archbishop of Lyon asked Louis the Pious, already noted that whoever separated himself from the Apostolic See was a schismatic?

And had not St Leo, the pope, said in his turn, that whoever excluded himself from the See of St Peter "ceased to participate in the divine mystery"? How then can you suspect Pope Gregory's intentions, having come to re-establish peace, to put things back into the state in which "by your wish in the name of your power and with the consent of the whole Empire, you had placed them yourself and had them confirmed by the Holy See"? Agobard concluded in these terms:

Let your sublime prudence condescend to weigh these words of the Apostle: 'In the last days perilous times will come.' These perils, the blessed Pope Gregory had already deplored at a time when the situation was incomparably better than now, when he said: 'I am so much tossed about by the waves of this world that I am unable to guide to port the old half-rotten ship whose protection the hidden plans of God have charged me with. Sometimes the waves beat on the bow; sometimes the foaming billows of the sea swell along the sides; sometimes the tempest blows against the stern; and in this anguish I see myself compelled sometimes to charge right down upon an obstacle, sometimes to tack and present the side of the ship to the menace of the waves. I sigh when I realize that as soon as my vigilance slackens, the sink of iniquity will grow, and that in face of the storm that is raging, the rotten planks will sound the impending shipwreck.' Alas! if the ship of the Church and the planks from which it is made were already rotten then, what must we say now?

This skilful propaganda made men troubled. How could it be doubted that the Sovereign Pontiff had taken the side of Louis the Pious' sons in all good conscience? When they heard it said that he had undertaken such a journey only to re-establish peace, to prevent the rupture of Christian unity, and to ensure the safety of the churches, the people and the Empire, even those most devoted to the emperor were perturbed.

Louis the Pious kept his head; he handled the tempest with energy and dignity. To the threat of war he replied with a very resolute statement whose approximate content we know, even if not the exact terms. In it he reminded Lothar and his younger brothers Pepin and Louis:

(1) that they were all three his sons and should remember this in their conduct towards him;

(2) that they were 'his vassals' and had taken oaths of fealty as such;

(3) that he himself was the official defender of the Apostolic See and would not allow them to usurp this role;

(4) he accused them of preventing the pope from coming to him.

(5) Lothar, especially, he reproached for isolating Pepin and Louis and inducing them to rebel;

(6) he accused them, finally, of the seduction of his vassals.

Point by point, Lothar answered:

(1) that he and his brothers were full of respect toward their father; that they were in no way rebelling against him, as was claimed, but that they would come to him as devoted sons to request his indulgence;

(2) that, having been associated in the Empire by wish of the emperor himself, and having been sent by him to the Holy See, he was obliged to help the emperor defend the Sovereign Pontiff;

(3) that far from preventing the pope from meeting the emperor, he had helped him to leave Italy, whose passes Louis the Pious, on the contrary, had kept blocked;

(4) that, far from separating the emperor from his two sons Pepin and Louis, he had brought them to him, while their father had driven them away;

(5) that he had done the same regarding the vassals whom the emperor had driven away, exiled or imprisoned; that "having heard him say that worthy men who deserve well from the ruler should be honoured and rewarded", he brought them to him also so that he might treat them with mercy.

Plausible arguments, but ones that aimed to shift the responsibility, by imputing all the wrongs to the emperor.

The 'Field of Lies' and Lothar's usurpation

Meanwhile, the armies had met close to Colmar, Louis the Pious camping at Rothfeld, his sons near Sigolsheim. On 24 June, when battle seemed about to begin, the Sovereign Pontiff's arrival was unexpectedly announced to the emperor: a supreme manoeuvre intended to keep up appearances and to cause desertions in the imperial entourage. Perhaps it was hoped that a last-minute gesture of contrition on Louis the Pious' part would settle everything.

The reception was cautious, even decidedly cool. The emperor drew his guest's attention to the fact that if the ceremonial was not at all what a pope might legitimately expect, it was because the visit itself did not take place under normal conditions. After which they had a talk.

The conversation even extended over several days, and one cannot help thinking that beside the two principal interlocutors, there were others in the wings. Because, hardly had the pope withdrawn on the day of SS Peter and Paul (29 June) with proposals for an agreement, when during the following night Louis the Pious' camp suddenly became empty, as though by enchantment. The gifts, the promises, and the threats had produced their effect, a witness notes, and, he says, from the camp of Louis the Pious to that of his sons, "a torrent of deserters ran", so much so that, according to another observer, the following morning in the rebels' camp, when people saw all the new tents set up around those of Lothar and the Sovereign Pontiff, they cried that it was a miracle; the hand of God seemed to have been at work. Because, by God's will, there was suddenly only "one single people", which found itself entirely collected around the person whom Louis the Pious himself had designated for this position by making him his associate in government.

Thus the 'Rothfeld' or 'Red Field' had become, by Divine Will, the 'Field of denial' or to speak with contemporaries, the 'Field of Lies', the *Lügenfeld*; and Louis the Pious, Wala's biographer observes ironically, found himself alone "with his Judith" and his son Charles.

"Alone" is an oversimplification. But the emperor could now count on only a handful of loyal men, and among the troops still stationed around him, anger mounted; his life was in danger. He resigned himself to asking for protection from his sons. And then came the supreme humiliation: accompanied by the empress and the young Charles, Louis the Pious went towards his sons' camp. They came to meet him. Only a few words were necessary to ask for mercy. They dismounted, embraced him, and led him to their camp. But after having thus shown him their deference, they separated him from Judith, who was entrusted to the supervision of Louis of Bavaria, while waiting to be sent as a prisoner to Tortona in Italy; they even confined her with her young son in another part of the camp. From the events which had just taken place people drew the inevitable conclusion. Since "by a righteous judgement of God" Louis had lost his power; and since, on the other hand, Lothar had already for a long time been designated as his legal heir and had even become associate emperor in advance; and, finally, because the subjects as a whole had voluntarily transferred their allegiance to Lothar, he was proclaimed to be henceforth the sole legitimate possessor of imperial authority.

Thenceforth, indeed, official charters were promulgated in the name of the sole Emperor Lothar and dated from the year I of his imperial reign "in France". At the same time Agobard was entrusted with the task of drawing up a new declaration to justify the coup d'état to the public. This declaration was expressed in blunt terms. Louis the Pious was no more spared then Empress Judith, that monster of impudence and moral perversion: "Hear ye peoples" the author exclaimed at the beginning:

> Hear, peoples of the whole earth, from the East to the West, from the North to the sea, and acknowledge how justified the indignation felt by the sons of Emperor Louis was and is. Salute the soundness of their views when they mean to cleanse the paternal palace of the crimes that defiled it and the factions that made iniquity rule there, and when they propose to free the kingdom from the miserable and tumultuous intrigues that throw it into confusion, in order to unassailably re-establish and to ensure there the brotherly trust and loyalty which, alone, are worthy of God.

This grandiloquent preamble was followed by a highly coloured picture of the gradual downfall of the emperor, betrayed by the person he had made his wife, and of the degeneration of this young woman, sensual and flighty, increasingly neglected by her husband, toward a life of debauchery, at first concealed, later shamelessly displayed. At first, the author says, it was spoken of cryptically in a small circle, but soon it was "the laughing stock of the palace, then of the kingdom, then of the whole world", until "the magnates grieved and considered this an intolerable scandal". The emperor's sons could no longer endure such an affront being inflicted on their father, or the kingdom, or the Franks themselves, whose reputation up to then had remained unblemished. United in a common desire to make an end to the crime, they had driven from the palace the person who was the source of the evil. Having placed her in well-guarded isolation and forced her to exchange her royal garments for the monastic robe, they had restored peace and honour to their father.

Not for very long, alas! Because, taking advantage of "the excessive indulgence of his sons" and incapable of resisting the "temptations of the flesh", yielding moreover to "criminous and indecent flatteries," the emperor had allowed himself be induced to "recall this woman to the palace" and to "place her above the councils and counsellors". Since then, "being of a changed mind", and pursuing his sons with hatred, the emperor had sown confusion among the people, from whom unceasingly "contradictory oaths were required".

Has such a thing ever been seen? Everyone first swore allegiance to the emperor, the father; then upon his command to the emperor, his son; then, again on his command, certain men swore allegience to the brother (King Louis); then almost all were compelled to swear allegiance to the child (Charles). After which, as if nothing had happened, still more oaths have become necessary!

Was it to be tolerated that God's name should thus be profaned with impunity and that the armies, which should be used to combat barbarian peoples and to subject them to the Christian faith, should thus be divided against themselves?

O Lord of Heaven and Earth, why hast Thou allowed thy faithful and most Christian servant, our emperor, to be reduced to no longer discerning the evils that threaten him from all sides? To cherishing those who hate him and to hating those who cherish him? And what should be expected of him if it were true, as many of those who seem to see things clearly affirm, that there are at his side people who avidly hope for the death of his sons and have planned amongst themselves to despatch the emperor as well, and then to divide up his kingdom? . . . . . It is obvious that if God does not provide otherwise the Empire will fall into the hands of foreign peoples or will crumble under a crowd of tyrants, because the emperor, who should be leading just wars against barbarian kings, prepares to lead unjust ones against sons who love him.

In the presence of the growing evils which the "scandalous and indecent" return of Judith has precipitated, "what should now be done? Dissimulate? Keep quiet? Remain idle?" God, who watches over His people, did not will this. He brought the sons of the emperor to a new unity, in order to protect their father from the same fate as that of King Ahab. Driven by his wife Jezebel, Ahab committed crimes whose punishment was only delayed by the penitence imposed on him by the prophet Elijah, seeing that, in the end, the Lord had raised up King Jehu against his house. But Agobard kept for the last sentence of his declaration the most decisive precedent, that of Samson:

He loved a wife who did not love him, and who preferred to obey his enemies rather than the person who loved her. And because this righteous man believed in this unfaithful woman, he lost his sight and the rule over his people, and although later his former vigour was restored to him and he ended an ignominious life by a glorious death, which allowed him to achieve eternal life, he never recovered his authority.

And to conclude, after this transparent allusion: "Consequently, let our lord the former emperor deign to see to it piously that he does not lose the eternal Kingdom of Heaven, he who, having been abused by his wife, has lost his earthly kingdom!" . . . This kingdom "according to the will and the judgment of God" had thenceforth passed, as the emperor himself had hoped, into the hands "not of some enemy but of a cherished son"; it remained for him only "to examine his conscience and to humble himself under God's powerful hand by doing penance". Let each man accept the Divine judgment and let the whole earth, as the prophet (Habakkuk 2:20) said, be silent in the face of the Lord!

CHAPTER FIVE

Louis the Pious' restoration and the last years of his reign

Disagreement among the victors

The call for the blind submission of everyone with which Agobard's declaration concluded did not mean that it was not necessary, immediately after the coup d'état, to employ a less hasty procedure. But here the trouble began. Because the mutual agreement of the three brothers and their joint understanding with the church authorities, easy to establish where it concerned the overturning of the rule of Bernard and Judith, who were held to be responsible for all the evils, turned out to be precarious as soon as it was a question of consolidating the results achieved. Of a return pure and simple to the regime planned in 817 for the event of Louis the Pious' death, there could be no question: neither Pepin of Aquitaine nor Louis of Bavaria were prepared to accept this. Having been rewarded by their father when Lothar had fallen into disgrace in 831, neither was now prepared to yield precedence to their elder brother. Also, while the young Charles was excluded by his internment in the monastery of Prüm under the supervision of Louis of Bavaria, it was agreed that Louis of Bavaria's original portion should be supplemented by adding to it the territories at first reserved for Charles (Alemania, Alsace, Rhaetia) and besides them, the Main valley ('Austrasia'), Thuringia and Saxony, while Pepin in his turn was awarded at least a part of the territories between the Rivers Loire and Seine. Thus the Carolingian rulers reverted to the dismemberment of the Empire, which was precisely what they had prided themselves on wishing to avoid. A disappointing solution, against which protests arose at once among the clergy, and from which the pope seems to have sought to dissociate himself by deciding ostentatiously to return to Rome at once.

Furthermore, Pepin of Aquitaine and Louis of Bavaria immediately parted company with their elder brother by returning to their own kingdoms and by dating their charters not by the years of the reign of the new emperor, but by the years of their own reigns or by those of the former emperor as well, whose fate was left to Lothar's discretion.

The penitence of Soissons in 833

On this last point, the procedure to follow had been indicated in advance by Agobard in the declaration analyzed above: Louis the Pious should be induced to do penance and to examine his conscience until the end of his days in a monastery where he should ask God to forgive him his sins. In this way and in this way alone, public opinion, which was again very divided and which began to be profoundly troubled by the emperor's wretched fate, would be able to resign itself to the consequences of the coup d'état. It was necessary, in short, that Louis the Pious' withdrawal should appear as a voluntary abdication and the accession of Lothar as the normal result of this decision. Hence the odious pageant that was now staged by the usurper and his accomplices.

A general assembly which met on 1 October 833 at Compiègne was presented with the emperor's case, while he remained imprisoned forty kilometres away in the convent of St Médard at Soissons. During the prelates' discussions, the archbishop of Reims, Ebbo, in whose province Soissons was situated, personally led the examination of the crimes attributed to the accused, and he was entrusted to direct the ecclesiastical procedure which, on the religious plane, was to facilitate the dethroned emperor's access to redeeming penance. He carried this out with merciless vigour and bluntness, as is attested by the official transcript, which was drawn up in his name and that of his episcopal colleagues.

After a brief reminder of the role of first importance which fell to the Church, being the sovereign guardian of religion and morals, whose detractors should be chastised without fail, the authors of this document pointed out the disgrace of the evils brought about by the emperor's conduct. Instead of following the noble example given by his father, the illustrious Charles of pious memory, Louis "through his want of perspicacity and his negligence" had thrust the kingdom "into a condition of such ignominy and degradation that it had become to its friends cause for grief and to its enemies an object of derision". For having in this way failed in his duties as king, "angered God and scandalized the holy Church", and then finally "having driven the people subject to him to kill one another", he had been "suddenly deprived of the imperial power by a righteous judgment of God". But the bishops did not wish to leave him to his wretched fate without any support. "With the authorization of King Lothar" they had resolved to "warn him about his sins, in order to induce him to take a firm decision for his salvation". The dethroned emperor let himself be convinced easily: he asked to be reconciled with his son Lothar and to repent publicly.

Thus he was escorted into the basilica of St Médard at Soissons, in the presence of a large crowd of clerics and laymen, first among whom was Lothar himself. Louis threw himself on the ground before the high altar, confessed his faults humbly, begged the benefit of penance, solicited absolution from "those to whom God has given the power to bind and to loose". On their request he admitted, the transcript says, actually committing the sins which the prelates had charged him with and the detailed list of which he held in his hands. In its eight points he acknowledged himself to be:

(1) guilty of "sacrilege and homicide", for failing to live up to the obligations sworn before God towards his father and his people; of using violence toward his friends, of putting his nephew Bernard to death, of using religion for the purposes of his private vengeance;

(2) "an instigator of scandal, a disturber of the peace, a violator of oaths," as having contravened the decisions solemnly drawn up "for the maintenance of peace and unity" and having obliged his subjects to commit never-ending perjuries by requiring contradictory oaths of them;

(3) a violator of the precepts of the faith, for having, without good reason, convoked the army and the general assembly in the middle of Lent;

(4) a violator of divine and human laws, and again "a murderer," for having exercised reprisals against certain of his subjects who came in all humility to avert the dangers that threatened him;

(5) a perjurer, through the false oaths he had exacted on every occasion, and especially with the purpose of proving the innocence of Empress Judith;

(6) responsible for all the killings, rapine, conflagrations, all the usurpations of church property, under which the Christian people was languishing;

(7) also responsible for all the arbitrary partitions of the kingdom, in consequence of which he had forced the people to treat his sons as enemies, while he should have exerted himself to preserve concord between them in a fatherly manner;

(8) guilty, finally, of having, as the ultimate misery, incited his people to kill one another instead of leading them, as he should have done, towards well-being and peace.

This list by its very confusion betrayed efforts to arbitrarily increase the number of sins the emperor had to confess publicly. He handed the list of these back to the priests who had come to receive it and who placed it on the altar; he took off his sword-belt and his arms and placed them at the foot of the altar; he received from the bishops the habit of a penitent and was admitted by them to perpetual penance – the kind of penance from which, the transcript concludes, "one does not return to the secular life".

The emperor had thus voluntarily renounced – or so at least it could be claimed – the imperial dignity and the secular life. The ceremony had taken place, moreover, in conditions of publicity which guaranteed its validity; the detailed record of the proceedings made them credible and, as an additional precaution, each of the bishops present had been called on to annexe to it his personal affidavit. We have the one of Agobard, archbishop of Lyon, who emphasized, even more than the transcript itself, the voluntary character of the confession made by Louis and his desire for permanent retirement. In appearance, the situation thus created was clear: not only had Louis lost his power in fact on the 'Field of Lies'; he had now renounced it legally. By his voluntary withdrawal to the abbey of St Médard, where he was to continue to live in prayer, the imperial succession was open, and, by virtue of the charter of 817, the annulment of which had never been proclaimed, Lothar was his undisputed successor. Such at least is the way in which the situation was presented in the entourage of the eldest son of the dethroned emperor.

The restoration of Louis the Pious in 834

Unfortunately for Lothar and his friends, the actual situation was very different. From the start, Louis the Pious was not at all the willing penitent they had hoped for. At St Médard's of Soissons he had yielded only to force. Several of his partisans assert this explicitly, particularly the author of the so-called *Annals of Saint-Bertin*, who writes pointedly: "They ill-treated him until they had compelled him to put down his arms and change his robes, then they drove him from the church without allowing anyone to speak with him, apart from those who were delegated to do this". In other words they had locked up the unhappy ruler and had finally induced him to surrender only by wearing down his resistance. This is also the impression left by the official documents themselves if we look at them more closely. The ritual motions had been gone through, but it was so inaccurate to speak of a voluntary adhesion to these by the sinner that Lothar did not dare to leave his father in the monastery – or rather in the annexe of the monastery – where he had had him locked up under strict supervision, and after the ceremony at St Médard's, he took his father with him everywhere, out of fear that he would escape and return to secular life. The author of the so-called *Annals of Saint-Bertin*, whose information is usually correct, even states that during the first weeks of 834 Louis the Pious peremptorily withstood the unceasing onslaughts of those who "night and day", strove to persuade him to "leave the world voluntarily and withdraw to the monastery". For these suggestions did not correspond at all with his state of mind.

Now, little by little, the truth leaked out, and there was no lack of people ready to exploit it. Dissatisfied with having been used by their elder brother, Louis of Bavaria and Pepin of Aquitaine became restless; the former was more or less sincerely indignant about the ill-treatment inflicted on their father. A conversation which he had on this subject with Lothar at Mainz in December 833 only increased their antagonism. A reaction was making itself felt in favour of the dethroned emperor. Under the guise of avenging their father's honour and rescuing his person, Louis and Pepin soon agreed on a joint enterprise. Concerned for his safety, Lothar judged it prudent in February 834 to leave Aachen, which was too close to Louis of Bavaria's frontiers, and withdraw to Paris, and then to the monastery of Saint-Denis, taking his imperial prisoner with him. But fortune had changed sides. On 20 February, under the double attack of troops led from the east by Louis of Bavaria and those led from the south by Pepin, Lothar fled, without, this time, waiting to have himself followed by his father or without daring to take him along.

Delivered as if by magic, Louis the Pious immediately afterwards, on 1 March 834, obtained from the bishops, in the church of Saint-Denis, absolution of his sins and his return to the communion of the faithful. Immediately afterwards he was given back his royal robes and insignia and restored to the plenitude of his power. Only the chancery's use of a remarkable formula at the beginning of official acts – "Louis, by a return of divine clemency (*divina repropitiante clementia*) emperor Augustus" – was to remind his subjects of the tragic situation into which the loss of his authority had for several months plunged him. Greeted respectfully, at the assembly of Quierzy, which he passed on his way, not only by his two sons Pepin and Louis but by many of those who a few days earlier had left him to his sad fate, soon reunited with Empress Judith, herself rescued from the clutches of her jailers in Italy, Louis the Pious could once again go to celebrate feast of Easter with great pomp in his palace of Aachen on 5 April 834.

Only Lothar and his partisans, too much implicated to resign themselves to the inevitable, made a desperate effort to oppose a restoration of which they would be the first victims. A group of them, including Matfrid, the ex-count of Orléans, and Lambert, count of Nantes, succeeded in inflicting a bloody defeat on the imperial army on the borders of the march of Brittany, leaving the principal imperial commanders dead on the battlefield; another group, under the personal command of Lothar, made itself master of Chalon-sur-Saône, where it distinguished itself by massacres. But in August or the beginning of September the imperial army, commanded by Louis the Pious himself, arrived in full force near Blois and cut off the retreat of the troops that Lothar led along the Loire to meet those of Matfrid and Lambert; and suddenly realizing that the game was up, Lothar at last saw himself obliged to surrender. Throwing himself at his father's feet and imploring his forgiveness, we was forced to swear obedience to him once more, to promise to return to Italy, to agree to hold it, thenceforth, as a simple king, as his uncle Pepin had held it from Charlemagne, and finally not to leave it without explicit permission; and this time he actually did remain there without a break until the beginning of 839.

The reprisals

The situation nonetheless remained extremely confused. After so many contradictory events no one any longer knew exactly on which side justice was. But lately associate emperor by virtue of solemn charters, Lothar was now no more than a son in penitence, kept in semi-exile in Italy, without henceforth any title other than the royal one. On the other hand, forcibly reconciled with his father, he was evidently fundamentally hostile to him and not at all resigned to his fall from power. As for Louis the Pious, he was re-established on his throne; but could this restoration be lasting? Was it even valid?

The situation in any case created many problems, about which the learned Rhabanus Maurus, abbot of Fulda in Hesse, whose writings were accepted as authoritative throughout the Empire, thought he should write a short treatise addressed to the emperor himself. Strongly supported by quotations from the Bible and in the forbidding form of a theoretical treatise, he condemned in the name of religion the conduct of sons who fell short in the respect and obedience they owed to their parents or who thought they could seize the paternal inheritance without waiting for the normal occurrence of succession. He also condemned judgments delivered in a rash way, especially against repentant sinners, whose confession, he says, cannot in any event serve as the basis for an accusation, and often attests only to the purity of their consciences. He recalled moreover that the Lord is merciful towards those who repent. But lastly, citing the parable of the prodigal son, he exhorted Louis, by way of conclusion, to show indulgence to Lothar if, in spite of everything, Lothar should come to repent. Rhabanus thus provided the necessary appeasements to the restored emperor and to public opinion, and at the same time attempted to open the way for reconciliation.

But to dispel everyone's doubt, more was needed: grandiose expiatory ceremonies were organized in February 835 first at Thionville, where a general assembly had been convoked for the second day of that month, the day of the Purification of the Virgin, then in the cathedral of St Stephen of Metz (thirty kilometres from Thionville) for the Sunday of Quinquagesima, when, under the presidence of the bishop of that city, the arch-chaplain Drogo, half-brother of the emperor, a solemn mass was celebrated in the presence of forty-four bishops and a crowd of abbots and ecclesiastical dignitaries.

At Thionville the whole procedure of 833 was annulled and each bishop was required to sign a personal declaration repudiating the one he had signed at St Médard's in Soissons. At Metz, Ebbo, the archbishop of Reims, was moreover obliged to disavow publicly from the pulpit the measures taken on his responsibility a year and a half earlier. After this Louis was reconciled with the Church in great pomp in the cathedral and the imperial crown was replaced on his head. Finally, by way of concluding this remedial procedure, Ebbo, who had been, on the complaint of the emperor, referred on 4 March to an episcopal synod meeting at Thionville, was asked to resign his office of which, in a declaration signed by his own hand, he declared himself "unworthy because of his sins". Then in one of those equitable turn-abouts of worldly affairs, he was imprisoned in the vicinity of Lyon. The archbishop of this city, Agobard, and several other prelates, who had been most deeply implicated, having been summoned but not having appeared, were likewise condemned by default to lose their sees.

But these retaliatory measures only aggravated the general uneasiness without strengthening the personal position of the emperor. He had great difficulty in making his commands obeyed. Lothar obstinately evaded all requests for explanations and for rapprochement. In May 837, when his father had for a moment conceived the plan of going to Rome to settle the affairs of the Church there, we see Lothar hastily fortifying the Alpine passes in order to block his way. Several weeks afterwards, justifiably alarmed by the news that the Vikings had pillaged the island of Walcheren and the port of Duurstede in the Low Countries, Louis the Pious in vain requested the inhabitants of the menaced regions to co-operate for the defence of their lands: at the general assembly at Nijmegen he was powerless against their ill-will. How, in such conditions, could anyone any longer expect that the atmosphere of trust indispensable for governing in peace would be re-established?

The last testamentary dispositions and the death of Louis the Pious (837–840)

Henceforth, a single idea seemed to obsess the ageing emperor: to assure, whatever the price, the largest possible share of his inheritance for his youngest child, the son of Judith, who retained considerable influence over her husband. To attain this object he used every possible means, even at the risk of once again alienating his elder sons. In October 837, at a general assembly held at Aachen, he announced the attribution to this child of new territories, those granted him in 833, as the reader will recall, having fallen into the hands of Louis of Bavaria, to whom the emperor intended to show consideration temporarily, in the hope of procuring his support – for Louis of Bavaria had played an important part in manipulating public opinion in the emperor's favour just after the events in St Médard's at Soissons. Did not the emperor owe his deliverance to him? The territories assigned to Charles were all taken from the former share of Lothar who was now in disgrace: they formed an enormous conglomerate, comprising all the lands lying between the northern Frisian archipelago, the estuary of the Seine and the Meuse, and extending to the south as far as Paris, Étampes, Auxerre and Troyes.

But was Louis of Bavaria really prepared to guarantee this new division of territories? It hardly seems so, because as soon as the partition had been announced he entered into secret talks with his brother Lothar. Informed about this, the emperor had two violent meetings with Louis, in April and in June 838, after which Louis was ordered to evacuate instantly all the provinces of Germany (Alsace, the Main valley, Alemania, Rhaetia, Saxony, Thuringia, etc.) occupied after the events of 833, and to remain within his kingdom of Bavaria. From then on it was open war; Louis of Bavaria attacking Frankfurt in November 838, and his father retorting several weeks afterwards, at the beginning of 839, by coming with an army to drive him back into Bavaria.

To whom could the emperor now turn to guarantee Charles' future possessions? Pepin of Aquitaine, already for some time enfeebled by illness, died in December 838, leaving children who were still minors: an excellent opportunity to enlarge the share of Judith's son still further. But the most elementary prudence necessitated coming to an understanding about this with Lothar, the only surviving one of the emperor's two elder sons with whom communications had not been officially broken. An agreement was concluded in the spring of 839: Lothar having come to ask for forgiveness once more at the general assembly held at Worms on 30 May, a final partition of the whole imperial succession was effected to his advantage and that of Charles, only Bavaria being left to Louis, the rebel son. All the remaining territories were divided into two portions of apparently equal value between which, as the elder son, Lothar was requested to choose. By this choice his kingdom would comprise, besides Italy, more or less all the territory lying east of the Rhône, Saône and Meuse; that of Charles, the land lying to the west, supplemented by Provence and the counties of Geneva, Lyon, Chalon-sur-Saône and Toul, and this partition was to take effect on the very day of the emperor's death. The two brothers promised to help each other, but there was no longer any mention of the Empire: Lothar and Charles had been placed in a position of perfect equality.

After twenty-two years of conflicts in justification of which the unity of the Empire and of the Church had constantly been pleaded, the ancestral practice of division into portions arbitrarily carved out was resumed, without regard either for the higher interests of Christendom – which nonetheless, the attacks of Nordic pirates were beginning to imperil seriously – or for the maintenance of obligations assumed under oath. As an ultimate misfortune, the Empire sank into anarchy and civil war. No one any longer had confidence in the future; the holders of civil offices or ecclesiastical dignities risked being dispossessed at any moment. More than ever the quest for 'honours' proved disappointing. And how could anyone doubt the gravity of the affliction which consumed the Empire when he saw that the last months of Louis the Pious' troubled reign, after the summer of 839, were spent first, in putting down a revolt in Aquitaine, which was indignant about the shameful way in which it had been disposed of at the expense of Pepin's heirs, then in preparing a new campaign against Louis of Bavaria, still in rebellion. Only the illness and subsequent death of the emperor on 20 June 840 allowed this ungrateful son to escape the exemplary punishment which his father was preparing to inflict on him. The situation was decidedly very far from the ideal of peace and concord so conspicuously professed at the beginning of the reign.

BOOK THREE

THE DISMEMBERMENT OF THE EMPIRE

CHAPTER ONE

The partition and the policy of concord

Not only did it seem at the beginning of the summer of 840 that there was nothing left of the noble policy announced by Louis the Pious just after his accession, but everything seemed to indicate that the Empire founded by Charlemagne was about to disappear immediately. Nevertheless, the Carolingian Empire was to survive for many more years by adjusting to new circumstances and developing new features. One fact, however, was clear: the opportunity to merge the various territories under Frankish hegemony into a cohesive political body had passed. Louis the Pious left these territories divided, torn between several princes and with an unpredictable future.

Aquitaine, in which Charles Martel, Pepin the Short and Charlemagne had made so many efforts to subdue particularism, continued to resist obstinately all attempts at assimilation. It desired a king for itself, even if it had to be a Carolingian, and rose up almost unanimously in support of the young Pepin II, grandson of Louis the Pious, in order to avoid being included in the kingdom of Charles, that is to say, reduced to the state of an ordinary province. However, Charles – the future Charles the Bald – did not intend to let himself be dispossessed. At seventeen, he was full of enthusiasm; and he was urged on by his mother, the ambitious Judith, to make the most of the rights given him in the partition of Worms without surrendering any of them. For his part, Louis of Bavaria had not renounced any of the territories which, in the turmoil, he had either effectively occupied or planned to occupy; he was soon to be called Louis of Germany or the German, and this was indeed an epithet that corresponded to his aspirations. As for Lothar, finally settled in Italy, where he had for a number of years conducted himself as ruler, he retained the title of emperor and intended to exercise imperial power; he would attempt, at the least, to take back all the territories which his brothers were unable to defend. But in June 840 it was clear that he would have to reduce his claims a great deal if he wished to avoid turning his brothers against him once more.

The war of the three brothers and the oaths of Strasbourg

This fact was obvious to any impartial observer, but not to Lothar himself, obsessed as he was by disappointment about the opportunity missed in 833. He ignored the oaths taken at Worms a year earlier: once more we see him proclaiming the validity of the constitution of 817 and, through the imperial title which had then been awarded to him, claiming the whole paternal inheritance. Not only did he, as was natural, at the news of his father's death, make all haste to take possession of the territories which were his through the partition of Worms and particularly to occupy the palace of Ingelheim, where he was residing in August 840, but he announced his intention of exercising his authority in the territories occupied or claimed by his brothers.

On his arrival at Ingelheim he promulgated, in his capacity as 'August emperor', an act proudly dated in "the year I of his return to France (*Francia*) as successor of his father". In it he announced "in agreement with the advice of the bishops" the re-establishment in the see of Reims, "having lost it in the service of his cause", of Archbishop Ebbo, deposed in 835, as we have seen, by way of atonement for his role in the ceremony at St Médard's of Soissons. Now Reims, by virtue of the partition of Worms, was within Charles' territory; the ecclesiastical province of which it was the chief see itself also lay entirely within Charles' boundaries, and the twenty bishops consulted, whose 'consent' was registered in the charter, were all without exception strangers to this province.

This grave abuse of power, which conflicted with the rules of common law no less than with political conventions, was immediately followed by others, even more serious. After a skilful diplomatic preparation, Lothar at the beginning of October invaded the area between the Meuse and the Seine which had been awarded to Charles at the partition of Worms. The lay and ecclesiastical magnates, on whom he had exercised considerable pressure during the preceding weeks, threatening to deprive them of their offices and their 'honours', came to meet him: among them Hilduin, abbot of Saint-Denis, and Girard, count of Paris. On 10 October he was at the palace of Ver, near Senlis; soon after, he reached the Seine, then the Loire. Charles, already at grips with the Aquitanians, who refused to recognize him, was hardly in a position to retaliate. Lothar himself, threatened in the rear by Louis the German, did not wish to press his advantage further at that moment. Between him and Charles, who had encountered each other near Orléans, a truce was arranged in November, by the terms of which Lothar temporarily kept the territories that had come under his authority, that is to say the county between the Meuse and the Seine and some of the counties between the Rivers Seine and Loire. Charles agreed, until a final agreement was drawn up, to restrict himself to the provinces not occupied by his brother's armies.

Immediately afterwards, Lothar turned against Louis the German, who had for a very good reason never recognized the validity of the partition of Worms, which had been made largely at his expense because of his estrangement from his father. While Lothar appealed to the charter of 817 to claim the whole Empire, Louis the German held to the agreements concluded in 833, just after the deposition of Louis the Pious, which had reserved for him, besides Bavaria, most of the Germanic provinces (Saxony, Thuringia, the Main valley, Alsace, Alemania, Rhaetia, etc.). After Lothar's arrival north of the Alps Louis tried in vain to block his access to the regions of which he held himself to be the legitimate heir, but he was unable to prevent him occupying Alsace at once in July and August 840, nor from seizing Worms and Mainz. Only the immediate threat of an intervention by Lothar in Charles' kingdom had allowed Louis temporarily to escape the attack his older brother had prepared against the other eastern territories. But this was only a postponement. As soon as the truce was concluded with Charles, Lothar resumed the attack. In April 841 he crossed the Rhine above Worms and tried to repeat in the region of Mainz the strategy which had succeeded so well between the Meuse and the Loire. Deserted in his turn by a number of his vassals whom Lothar had been able to win over to his side by the same methods he had used in Charles' kingdom, Louis saw himself obliged to withdraw to Bavaria.

In France as well as in Germany Lothar's diplomacy employed

every means to detach vassals from his brothers by outbidding them and by thrusting himself upon them as the legitimate successor of Louis the Pious in the whole expanse of the Empire. But the risks they were both incurring made Louis the German and Charles draw instinctively closer to each other. Discussions were begun between them which quickly led to an alliance against the common enemy, whom their union had every chance of defeating. On both sides, indeed, Lothar was obliged to surrender territory. In the west, at the end of March 841, Charles had forced a passage over the Seine, south of which he had had to halt for a time; he was able to enter Paris again and to reach Troyes. In May he was at Châlons-sur-Marne. In the east, Louis, victorious on 13 May in the Riessgau, on the border of Bavaria, in his turn forced his way over the Rhine and hastened to meet his younger brother. Their encounter took place soon afterwards.

Between their two united armies and Lothar, who had just, in his turn, joined his nephew Pepin II of Aquitaine, Charles' rival south of the Loire, a clash was inevitable. The battle took place on 25 June at Fontenoy-en-Puisaye, near Auxerre, and after various changes of fortune finally turned to the advantage of Louis and Charles, without however the victors, who were themselves worn out, being able to pursue their fleeing brother. He did not consider himself defeated. From Aachen, then from Thionville, where he had withdrawn, he resumed his intrigues with his brothers' vassals and prepared, as a first measure, a new offensive against Charles. But this offensive, in September, ended in another defeat: repulsed on the Seine, Lothar could not prevent Charles from joining Louis again. On 14 February 842 these two brothers met each other again at Strasbourg and, fully realizing the necessity of a durable agreement against the common enemy, concluded between them a defensive alliance under circumstances of exceptional solemnity.

The oaths which Charles and Louis then exchanged – the famous 'oaths of Strasbourg' – are preserved for us by their cousin, the historian Nithard (the bastard son of one of Charlemagne's daughters, Bertha, and of the celebrated poet Angilbert), to whom we owe a very lively account – written before the summer of 844 – of the battles and negotiations fought out and pursued under his eyes between the successors of Louis the Pious. At Strasbourg, each of the two brothers swore publicly, Louis "in the romance language" (namely in French) in order to be understood by Charles' soldiers, and Charles in the German language, in order to be understood by Louis' soldiers, to aid his partner without fail and to act only in accord with him:

For the love of God, for the well-being of the Christian people and for our common well-being, insofar as God gives me the wisdom and power, I shall henceforth help my brother and aid him in all things as one should, according to equity, help one's brother, on condition that he will treat me likewise, and never shall I conclude with Lothar any arrangement which, by my intention, might be injurious to my brother.

After this, representatives from each of the armies swore likewise each in his own language – those of Louis in the German language, those of Charles in French – to see to the maintenance of these pledges:

... if Louis (or Charles) keeps the oath which he has made to his brother Charles (or Louis), and if Charles (or Louis) my lord, should, on his part, break his, I swear that, if I cannot deter him from this course of action, I shall never come to his aid against Louis (or Charles).

Thus, perhaps for the first time, the people not only officially witnessed in a language understood by all, but also were themselves associated in, the obligations entered into by their rulers. The alliance was concluded not only between Louis and Charles, but also between their subjects, whom in a preliminary harangue each of the two kings had informed of the content of the accord in order to make themselves better understood, having recourse once more to the French or German language, familiar to most of their listeners. This was an important novelty, which moreover resulted in the preservation of the original text of the oaths that were taken, which are precious evidence of the earliest forms of our present day French and German languages.

The treaty of Verdun

At Strasbourg, Louis the German and Charles had not only indicated their unshakeable determination to associate their destinies in order to protect themselves against Lothar's undertakings; it seems that they had realized the necessity of a lasting agreement which might revive among 'the Christian people' that 'concord', that 'unanimity', the need for which had so often in the past been stressed by the Church as well as by the emperors themselves. Before exchanging the oaths which we have just cited, the two kings had, in the preceding harangue, insisted precisely on the hope they cherished of working in this way toward the 'good of all' and toward the re-establishment of 'peace' by 'justice'. Just after the accord, their whole attitude seemed calculated to emphasize their desire to recreate unity: the historian Nithard, who accompanied them, describes their living together, under the same roof, in a close, brotherly intimacy, taking their meals together, sharing their cares and their pleasures. He shows us how this perfect 'concord' – the word flows very naturally from his pen – extended itself gradually from the kings themselves to their subjects, united in their games in what would later be called tournaments, in which all, "Saxons, Gascons, Austrasians, Bretons", mingled in a confident rivalry, forgot their diversities of origin and felt themselves again interdependent members of the same society: that of the great 'Christian people' of which Charlemagne and Louis the Pious had dreamed.

Lothar, who had dared meanwhile to venture as far as the Loire valley and the Maine, finally realised the futility of these temporary successes and hastily withdrew to the Rhine where, from the palace of Sinzig, some thirty-five kilometres downstream from Koblenz, he rejected the offers of negotiation made by his brothers. Reinforced by the arrival of detachments from Germany, they now decided to bring the matter to a conclusion. On 18 March they entered Koblenz, crossed the Moselle and took the route to Sinzig, whence Lothar withdrew on 19 March in the direction of Aachen, closely followed by their armies. From Aachen he escaped again, taking with him the imperial treasures and ornaments. He resumed his course, this time towards the south, as though by giving up the struggle he was at last also renouncing the attempt to enforce his rights to the Empire and was prepared to confine himself to Italy.

Louis and Charles, in any case, thought as much. From the palace of Aachen, of which they at once took possession, they surveyed the situation together with the prelates and clerics that were with them. Lothar's conduct was examined; an account was drawn up of his perjuries, his acts of violence; of the evils "which he had made the Church suffer by his greed"; and so the proof was given of "his incapacity for rule". The assembly was unanimous in holding his flight to be a result of the "will of God" who "by a just judgment" had driven him out "of combat, then out of his kingdom" as "chastisement for his heinous crimes" and had thus "turned the government of the Empire over to his brothers, better than he". Fortified by this statement, the prelates, faithful interpreters of the divine thoughts, after having assured themselves that Louis and Charles were ready to rule as good kings and "according to the will of God", invited them to take up the vacant inheritance and divide it between them.

Thus, once again, the kings turned to the rather too convenient procedure of a "judgement of God" which a clergy submissive to the masters of that moment was called on to interpret in the required manner. Of the regime established in 817 there was, of course, no longer any question: 'the kingdom', 'the Empire' remained, and no one thought of questioning the unity of the Christian people; but at the same time in the palace of Aachen, still full of memories of Charlemagne, and of which Nithard wrote, under the impression of these events, that "it was then the capital of France" (that is to say of the kingdom of the Franks), it was decided cold-bloodedly that, between the two kings who were held to be the victors, a new division in two equal parts was to be made, Lothar having to content himself with his kingdom of Italy. Passing at once from the intention to the act, a commission was nominated to decide upon frontiers which were not of great significance since they proved even more ephemeral than the preceding ones. Let it suffice to say that Louis' portion comprised the whole of the Germanic territories, including Frisia, and that of Charles all the territories lying to the west of the Meuse, plus Aquitaine and probably the ancient country of the Burgundians and Provence.

Lothar then made a last attempt at diplomacy to keep at least part of his share. Having fled not into Italy, as was believed and hoped, but to Lyon, where he had been able to re-constitute an army, he took up negotiations again with his brothers. Agreeing this time no longer to insist on his imperial title, or at least to demand nothing in return for renouncing it, he succeeded in having the principle of a territorial division into three parts recognized; and after the inevitable bargaining, the fundamentals of an agreement were arrived at in a meeting of the three princes in the vicinity of Mâcon on 15 June 842. Nevertheless, more than a year of bitter discussions and many conferences between their representatives were necessary to transform this agreement in principle into a final accord, which was eventually concluded at another meeting of the three princes at Verdun in August 843. This is the famous treaty of Verdun, which despite subsequent modifications, was long to remain the territorial charter of Europe.

The provisions of this treaty, whose text has unfortunately not survived, were as follows. The whole complex of territories composing the Empire was divided into three shares considered as equal. To Louis were reserved the Germanic territories and their dependencies north of the Alps and east of the Rhine, supplemented by the three counties of Speyer, Worms and Mainz, on the left bank of the river, as well as the whole of Alemania with Rhaetia (Grisons and Tyrol). Frisia, on the other hand, was not included. To Charles were reserved, going from north to south, the countries lying to the west of the Scheldt, then those to the west of a line joining the region south of Cambrai to that of Sedan, passing thereafter through the Argonne, the valley of the upper Marne, the plateau of Langres, the Saône (with a small enclave on the left bank, in order to include the whole county of Chalon), leaving the Lyonnais, Vivarais and Uzège to the east, and finally joining the Petit-Rhône south of Nîmes. The long stretch of territories lying between the German kingdom to the east and the French kingdom to the west was, with Italy, awarded to Lothar, whose kingdom thus extended from the north of Frisia to Campania. The palace of Aachen, the region of the Ardennes and the country between the Meuse and Rhine, cradle of the Carolingian family, were included in it. In this way, Lothar's titles were in the end to some extent honoured with preferential treatment, out of respect for his being the eldest son and implicitly, whether they wished it or not, because of the title of emperor which he continued to presume upon.

The shares were nonetheless carved out in such a way as to divide the inheritance of the dead emperor among the three brothers as reasonably as possible. Several considerations were taken into account. First, considerations of political and personal convenience: most of the Germanic countries reserved for Louis could no longer be separated from each other, nor could their allocation to Louis be seriously contested. The oaths of Strasbourg prove that their close linguistic relationship had already been accepted, and their subjection to Louis had been an established fact for a number of years at the time when the treaty was concluded. As for the kingdom of the West reserved for Charles, though its eastern frontiers might be disputable and Aquitaine might remain rebellious, it was beyond doubt that historically and linguistically it too formed a bloc which the events of the last years made it difficult to award to anyone other than Charles.

The most delicate task in the work of partition was to arrange a share for Lothar which, while including Italy, over which he had already ruled for a long time, would not exclude him from the 'Frankish kingdom', and particularly from the old provinces in which his brothers were to continue to exercise their power. Hence came the idea of carving up these provinces, together then called 'France' (*Francia*), into three sections: for Louis, the section beyond the Rhine, or eastern 'France' (*Francia orientalis*), of which the valley of the Main was the principal part, and which in a restricted sense was also called 'Austria' (*Austria*) or 'Austrasia' (*Austrasia*); for Charles, the area between the Meuse and Seine or 'western France' (*Francia occidentalis*), designated also by the name 'Neustria' (*Neustria*); for Lothar, the country between Meuse and Rhine which henceforth was to be 'middle France' (*Francia media*). In this way the three brothers could all call themselves 'kings of the Franks' (*reges Francorum*), and would each effectively rule over a fraction of this 'Frankish kingdom' (*regnum Francorum*) where ideal unity was no more destroyed by this new division than by all the previous partitions since the time of Clovis' sons.

One of the most difficult problems seems to have been that of the division of the vassals. Each new apportionment of territories as a matter of fact came up against the thorny problem of the transfer of obediences. Each king had his clientele of vassals who had taken the oath of fidelity to him personally and whom he was obliged to reward by the distribution of offices and 'honours', no one being allowed to hold 'benefices' in more than one kingdom, that is to say to recognize more than one king or the subjects of more than one king as lord. Also, the frequently changing attributions of territories each time invalidated gifts that had already been made, each new office-holder having to satisfy those who remained attached to him and to reward those who had left their former 'lord' to join him. The writings of the historians of this period, and those of Nithard in particular, and the letters that have come down to us from this troubled epoch, show how many complications these modifications of the political map created, and Nithard explicitly states that the problem of the lands to be distributed to the vassals weighed very heavily in the negotiations conducted after 842 between the three sons of Louis the Pious.

The complexity of the problems needing to be solved explains the apparent peculiarity of the territorial ordinance worked out at Verdun. It was necessary to reconcile too many divergent interests, to satisfy too many contradictory ambitions, especially those of Lothar, whose sincerity remained dubious and whose all-too-obvious desire was to give himself the means to resume the conquest of the Empire to the detriment of his two brothers.

Nevertheless, before separating, all three solemnly swore to remain peacefully in the territories which they had just agreed about, and their vassals confirmed this oath, whose text was then sent to the pope.

The policy of concord

This last detail is significant. In the confusion into which the Empire had sunk since 833, the Church alone seemed capable of preserving the unity of the 'Christian people', whose government Louis the Pious' sons had once more parceled out amongst themselves. But, in the absence of an emperor with authority over the whole of Christendom, the Church and its head became the trustees of the idea of which the emperor had up to then been the incarnation. Already in 806 when Charlemagne had decided upon the division of his kingdom among his sons, the Holy See had been officially informed about it and Pope Leo III had been called upon to place his signature underneath the documents, as though Charlemagne had realized in advance the important role the Church was to assume after his death in political affairs. It was the Church indeed which, in default of the secular power, drawn as it was into the whirlpool of civil conflicts, was now to take over the defense of Christendom directly and to occupy itself unceasingly with the restoration, at any cost, of that unity which was indispensable to the preservation of the cause on which its own future also depended.

Furthermore, it was not the papacy but the higher clergy and especially that of the kingdom of 'western France' – our present-day France – which in particular took over this role of defender of the political unity in order to safeguard Christian civilization. In November 843, while Charles waged war everywhere with unflagging energy in order to subject to his authority the provinces which the treaty of Verdun had awarded him while leaving him the task of conquering them, the Frankish episcopate, at a general assembly held at Coulaines, near Le Mans, presented the young king with the text of the deliberations which Charles, whether he wished to or not, agreed to publish at once; and this text is significant.

It opened with a reminder of the obstacles which had had to be surmounted in order to re-establish peace among the three sons of Louis the Pious and, thanks to the partitioning of the paternal kingdom, allow Church and people to breathe again after their cruel afflictions. But, the writer continued, the source of the trouble remained. It could be exorcised only by "unity in the obedience of God, in veneration of the holy Church, in fidelity to the king; in the will to strengthen and maintain the honour due to him, in peace, concord, and sincere friendship" – in other words by a unanimous desire to restore good will between all Christians within the Frankish kingdom. The decisions that followed were taken jointly and were formulated "with one voice"; all men, it was further observed, "constituting but one body in the one Church" and considering only the "common good".

Divided into six articles, these decisions aimed to fix the very conditions of the desired restoration by indicating to each his duty. Above all, everyone was exhorted "to honour" the churches and the clergy; secondly, "to honour" the king and to serve him uprightly. The king himself had "to honour" his subjects, that is to say, to treat them according to "reason and equity". Next, everyone had to help the king to keep this rule and see to it that no one put pressure on him in the name of private interests and, if the king should fail to live up to the above-mentioned rule, to turn him away from this faithfully, while treating him with the respect due to the "royal sublimity". Finally, it was the duty of everyone to try to bring back to respect for this "bond of charity" and this "pact of concord" by "admonishing in the spirit of Christian charity" anyone daring to violate it, and if this was not enough, to deal severely and strictly with him.

As we can see, all this implies putting into practice within only one of the three kingdoms that had emerged from the disruption of the Empire, but in a spirit that made them easily transferable to the whole, the general principles already formulated in the time of Charlemagne and maintained by his immediate successor during the first years of his reign. They could all be summed up in the notion of the close solidarity which ought to unite among themselves all those composing the 'Christian people'. Brothers in Christ, it is by the harmony of their goodwill that they create peace and concord, without which there can be no welfare in Christendom. For Christendom is like a single body, to whose life all its members contribute in close and harmonious co-operation.

Already Charlemagne had spoken of the "unanimity" that was indispensable amongst all his subjects; but he regarded himself as the absolute master of all decisions and as responsible to God alone for his initiatives. Since then the imperial power had experienced many vicissitudes, and the high moral authority which Charlemagne possessed had tended to pass imperceptibly from the king to the Church. In the course of the troubled years which the Empire had experienced since 829, the Church had not neglected to recall in more and more urgent terms that, if the kings were chosen by God to ensure the welfare of peoples, she herself had the task of ensuring the welfare of kings. This had already been stated by the Council of Paris which in 829, having been consulted about the misfortunes suffered by the Empire, had not hesitated to teach the emperor a lesson by submitting to him a small treatise written for his edification about the tasks and duties of kings. According to this tract, only those rulers deserved to retain their power who governed justly and who, through their justice, ensured the reign of God on earth through peace. Thus the bishops came to the following conclusion, in the request which they addressed to the emperor after the council: that it was their explicit mission, in virtue of the responsibilities they carried as sole qualified interpreters of the divine law, to guide the conduct of kings by their "warnings" and their "admonishments"; and they had not neglected to do this.

Since 829, this doctrine had become generally accepted. The principal drafter of the records of the Council of Paris, Jonas, bishop of Orléans, had taken it over almost literally and proclaimed it in a treatise on the duties of kings he composed shortly afterwards. Finally, the dramatic vicissitudes of the struggle conducted by Louis the Pious with his sons in 833 had familiarized his subjects with the idea that royal power was held by the incumbent, despite his sacred character, only on condition it was exercised in a normal manner.

In 843 at Coulaines the consequences of the doctrine were accepted: not only were Charles' subjects called on to guide their king by their 'warnings' and to protect him against the allurements to which he might yield through weakness or ignorance (Art. 5), but Charles pledged himself formally by Art. 3 to govern according to justice, which was the very condition of his authority: "We wish", he explicitly declared, that all our subjects should know for certain that henceforth we shall not deprive anyone, whatever his condition or dignity, of the honour to which he is entitled, that we shall not despoil him by caprice, nor under a perfidious influence, nor by an unjust cupidity, but that we shall use the means of justice, and conform ourselves to reason and equity. I guarantee to each man, with God's help, and whatever be his status or dignity, the maintenance of his law, such as his ancestors have preserved it in the time of our predecessors.

A great and disturbing novelty: not only is the authority of the king limited by the need to conform to the divine law, but it is, moreover, in this case subordinated to the carrying-out of the explicit promise which he is required to make to his subjects never to violate the rules of justice, the foundation of his power.

It was indeed not only the Empire that was in trouble. The principles on which it had been built had been vitiated one after another: after the break-up of unity, now even the concept of monarchy itself was undermined. It ceased inspiring everyone's unquestioning respect. But the Church was there to remind those persons, including kings, who might be tempted to forget that individual desires and ambitions should yield before the great law of unity and concord from which no Christian had the right to consider himself excluded, and that nothing was lost so long as this law was adhered to.

CHAPTER TWO

The regime of brotherly co-operation

Even though the political unity of the Empire had been sundered, the injury was perhaps not irreparable if, among the three kings who at Verdun had just partitioned between themselves the territories inherited from their father, a regime of brotherly solidarity could have been established. This was the object of the higher clergy's unceasing exertions for about a dozen years.

Lothar's claims and the conference of Yütz in 844

The main obstacle to agreement was Lothar, who was by no means resigned, notwithstanding the pledges he had given, to descend in rank and abdicate the rights upon which his father and especially his grandfather had presumed. He had been anointed emperor, and emperor he intended to remain. It was at Aachen, in the former palace of Charlemagne, that he installed himself immediately after the treaty of Verdun, and it was there that he seems to have wished to set up his principal residence. Italy became again for him what it had been for his father and grandfather: a simple dependence of his 'Frankish kingdom'; but this did not deter him from keeping a close watch, just as they had done, on the events taking place on the banks of the Tiber and, when necessary, intervening there as sovereign.

When, after the death of Gregory IV in January 844, the election of the new pope Sergius II gave rise to disputes, Lothar sent to Rome his young son Louis (the future Louis II), created 'king of the Lombards' for the occasion, with his uncle, Drogo, bishop of Metz, accompanied by an imposing army. The purpose of this mission was to hold an inquiry on the spot and to see to the maintenance of the imperial rights which had been defined in 824, by the intervention of Lothar himself, so as to subject the consecration of each new pope to the approval of the emperor and to the swearing of an oath of fidelity to his person. In 844 Lothar obviously intended, in his relations with the Holy See, to keep all the prerogatives he had held by virtue of the charter of 817. The new pope, because of the disputable nature of his election, was forced to yield. A council, in which participated, beside Drogo, twenty-two Italian bishops devoted to the son of Louis the Pious as well as a number of representatives of the Roman clergy, concluded that the electoral procedure had been valid; but Sergius was required, in recompense, to confirm the statute of 824 which placed the papacy under the permanent tutelage of the emperor.

It seemed then that the golden age of the victorious Empire was about to dawn anew. Not only did Sergius meekly agree to anoint Louis, the son of Lothar, as king of Italy at St Peter's, Rome, but he allowed to be extorted from him the conferment upon Bishop Drogo of Metz – who had shortly before been promoted to the archiepiscopal dignity – of the title of apostolic vicar "in all the provinces beyond the Alps", that is to say in all of Gaul and Germany. Kept in Italy himself, the pope declared in the bill of conferment, but anxious to ensure the welfare of the Christian people in other provinces, he was sending there in his stead "the archbishop of Metz, Drogo, son of the late glorious emperor Charles, whose skilful government had allowed the union of the empire of the Romans and that of the Franks into a single body." Taking into consideration indeed, he added, that Drogo was "the uncle of our most serene and most pious son, the great emperor Lothar, and of his most dear brothers, our sons the kings Louis and Charles, and that he is distinguished by his holiness and by the purity of his doctrine", he charged him to settle any difficulties that might arise on the far side of the Alps, and ordered all the bishops of the three Frankish kingdoms to obey him as they would obey himself. The powers delegated to him were very broad: in the whole area of the three kingdoms Drogo was to take the place of the pope in convoking and presiding over councils; he was to receive in the first instance the appeals to the court of Rome, all of this to be compatible with "the authority and dignity of our dearest spiritual son, the great emperor Lothar". An unheard-of privilege which, by the mediation of Drogo, whose episcopal see was within the kingdom of Lothar, permitted Lothar a right of inspection, even a right of supervision, over the entire Frankish church, and furnished him with a convenient means of interfering in the affairs of his two brothers.

On one point only were Lothar's plans foiled by the new pope's resistance. He had hoped to obtain at the same time from Sergius II the rehabilitation and the re-establishment in their sees of his devoted partisans Bartholomew, the ex-archbishop of Narbonne and Ebbo, the ex-archbishop of Reims, with whom he had remained in contact since 833. The plan was rather high-handed, since the two archbishoprics of Reims and Narbonne, and the whole ecclesiastical province of which Reims was the chief see, were actually within Charles' kingdom. The pope refused to accede to this request, but the move itself was significant: Lothar's acceptance of the provisions of the treaty of Verdun was evidently only temporary, and he seemed utterly resolved to extract every possible advantage from his imperial title. Obviously, if he were to continue to act in this manner, conflict was certain, since neither Louis nor Charles were inclined to allow the question of the re-establishment of an Empire, which they believed to be abolished forever, to be in any way re-opened to their disadvantage.

Fortunately, the Church was vigilant. In the very bull by which, yielding to pressure from Lothar, Drogo was made his vicar in Gaul and Germany, Pope Sergius II declared:

> It is not to be tolerated that the association of the three brothers united in the same faith in the Trinity should deviate from mutual charity and common equity. If one of them, preferring to follow the prince of discord, does not keep the general peace, it will be with justice and with the aid of God and in accordance with the canons, that we shall take care to chastise him to the best of our ability.

It is true that, in the words of the Sovereign Pontiff—the rest of the text proves it—this threat was aimed especially at Louis the German and Charles, Lothar hoping to assure for himself the guidance of the concert of kings desired by the church. But the principle was clearly formulated: the maintenance of brotherly co-operation between the three kings seemed to be the only means of re-establishing peace in Christendom, unsettled as it was by the fall of the imperial throne, and of averting the dangers that menaced it everywhere from without.

Whether or not the idea of further meetings between the signatories was foreseen in the treaty of Verdun, it is a fact that, on the request of the clergy, a first meeting between them occurred in October 844 at the palace of Yütz, near Thionville in Lothar's kingdom. The talks took place in a spirit of apparent cordiality. The prelates of the three kingdoms, gathered under the presidency of Archbishop Drogo, in whose diocese the meeting was held, submitted to the approval of the kings a programme in six articles, inspired by similar motives to the programme which, one year earlier at Coulaines, the bishops of western France had made Charles the Bald adopt. The general considerations that constituted its preamble were even partly identical to those that preceded the decisions of Coulaines. The kings were furthermore congratulated for having understood the necessity, in order to "avert the common peril and see to the welfare of all the people", of consulting the clergy, sole authorized interpreter of God's thoughts. Responding to their appeal, the prelates now told them in no uncertain terms what they had on their minds:

Let us declare to you, without wishing to offend you, most noble lords, that our holy Church, redeemed by the blood of Christ and restored at the cost of so much effort by your predecessors, has been lacerated, turned upside down and crushed by your conflicts. If you desire a prosperous reign here below and your salvation in the next world . . . , take care to preserve among you that charity of which the Apostle speaks, which derives from a pure heart, a good conscience and a sincere faith . . . , which excludes every obscure manoeuvre designed to injure and which, everywhere there is a need, provides help in the form of advice and prompt assistance, for it is written: 'The brother who is aided by his brother is like a fortress.' Instead of the discord spread around by the machinations of the devil among the people who have been entrusted to you, you should propagate peace, that peace which Christ going up to Heaven has left his faithful as the greatest of rewards, saying to them: 'I leave you peace, I give you my peace', because without it no one will see God.

After this exhortation to peace, the prelates called on the three kings to make amends for the evils caused by their discord by providing immediately, in the canonical manner, occupants to fill the vacancies in episcopal sees, or by restoring to their previous incumbents the bishoprics from which they had been unjustly expelled; by seeing to the nomination of monks as abbots in all abbeys; by returning to the churches the properties which had been taken from them; by removing the most scandalous abuses of power from which the monasteries of canons or nuns were suffering through the kings' fault; finally by reinforcing with the secular power the measures of discipline which the clergy thought it should agree to in order to ensure the well-being of the faithful; in short, they should render to the Church the honour that was due to her and help her to play once again fully and without hindrance the eminent role that fell to her. The prelates concluded with a summons to all, and to the three kings in particular, to do penance for their past mistakes, "an easy thing" they state, "if in the place of discord one were to plant charity", and if one listened to the voice of the Church, which was that of God Himself.

Yielding to these remonstrances, the kings pledged themselves to carry out the desired reforms between them, and to maintain henceforth "a regime of brotherly love and mutual charity"; and, putting theory into practice at once, they decided to send a joint delegation to notify Pepin II of Aquitaine, Lambart, count of Nantes, and Nominoé, 'duke of the Bretons', all in a state of rebellion, of their intention to take joint measures of coercion against them if they would not submit to Charles, their legitimate sovereign. In this manner it was thought that a kind of 'brotherly' condominium would be established which would permit the preservation of the Christian unity jeopardized by the partitions.

The Viking peril and the first conference of Meerssen (844-847)

The resolutions of Yütz aroused great hopes; but these were quickly deceived when, after the conference, each king, once he had returned to his own territories, thought only of his own interests. It is true that Lothar, in face of the distrust aroused in Charles' kingdom in the very bosom of the clergy by the institution of Drogo's vicarship, did not try to exploit the situation; but the joint action decided on against Pepin of Aquitaine, Lambert and Nominoé, was forgotten, and once more the relations between Lothar and his youngest brother became embittered to such a degree that, at the beginning of 846, Lothar requested from Pope Sergius II the immediate convocation of a council at Trier—in his own kingdom—to review the case of the ex-archbishop of Reims, Ebbo, which Charles and his bishops had judged to be so definitively settled that they had, in April 845, provided the see of Reims with a new incumbent in the person of a monk of Saint-Denis, Hincmar, who was destined to have a great future. The co-operation between Lothar and Louis in the same period was perhaps no less precarious, and if serious conflicts were avoided, it was doubtless the result of a desire for concord that grew out of the difficulties experienced by each of the kings within his own kingdom and the dangers of all kinds which they constantly had to ward off.

The danger from outside the frontiers was especially grave, above all the danger of the Vikings, which now took on such a threatening aspect that it alone should have prompted the kings to unite to handle it. In 841 a Danish band, going up the Seine, sacked and burned Rouen as well as all the monasteries in its vicinity, while in Zeeland Lothar thought himself obliged to abandon the island of Walcheren to the pirates. In 842, bursting into the mouth of the Canche, the Vikings went on to surprise and sack the port of Quentovic (near present-day Etaples), the Calais of that period, carrying off the population into captivity or massacring them. In 24 June 843, in the middle of the feast of St John the Baptist, sixty-seven of their ships dropped anchor at Nantes. Their crews dispersed through the city, broke into the cathedral during high mass, slew the bishop and his clergy while they were celebrating divine service, and set the building on fire. Then they looted and burned various parts of the town, devastated the monasteries of the region, occupied the island of Noirmoutier and finally ravaged the coast of Aquitaine. In 844 the Vikings sailed up the Garonne as far as the outskirts of Toulouse and plundered on both banks of the river.

The year 845 was a particularly miserable one. The three brothers each in turn received visits from these unwanted guests; but as always, Charles' kingdom had the privilege of receiving the hardest blows. In March, 120 Danish ships, under the command of the famous chief Ragnar—the Ragnar Lodbrok of Scandinavian legend—went up the Seine as far as Paris, where they landed on Easter Sunday. The city was sacked, as well as all the wealthy monasteries of the region. Charles was unable to repulse the invader. His troops, stationed at Saint-Denis, were overcome by panic, and he was forced to buy off the Danes with the heavy ransom of 7,000 pounds of silver. He could not, however, prevent the enemy from again devastating the Channel coasts on their return, nor could he stop the subsequent pillage of the coast of Aquitaine and the seizure of Saintes by other bands. That same year the pirates were active in the kingdoms of Lothar and Louis, who were equally powerless to avoid massacres and devastations: in the region of the Meuse and lower Rhine the population was decimated; on the Elbe, Hamburg was reduced to ashes.

The year 846 was hardly a better one for Lothar's kingdom. The

Netherlands were once more attacked and sacked by the pirates, who this time extended their ravages with impunity to the whole region, in which the great river port of Duurstede was an especial target.

At the other extremity of his kingdom, Lothar was obliged, at the same time, to deal with the Moslem peril, which seemed no less grave. This was the period when the emirs of Kairouan, who had succeeded in present-day Tunisia, under princes of the Aghlabid family, in making themselves independent of the caliph of Baghdad, gradually completed the conquest of Sicily, begun in 827. While looking for a foothold in southern Italy, their pirate bands began to harass' the coastal provinces of the western Mediterranean in Italy as well as in Provence. From 838 on these 'Saracen' pirates pillaged the Provençal coast; going up the Rhône in 842 to sack Arles; settling on the islands of Ponza, seawards of the Gulf of Gaeta, and Ischia, facing the Cape of Miseno; finally in August 846 they suddenly appeared at the mouth of the Tiber, sailed up the river and attempted to surprise Rome. The city itself escaped their attack; but on the right bank St Peter's, which was not then protected by any defenses, was sacked. Not only was the venerated basilica profaned but the Moslem pirates seized the ornaments and treasures that had accumulated there; they took with them even the stone of the altar under which the Prince of the Apostles lay. The church of St Paul 'outside the walls', on the opposite bank, was no more spared.

The news of this event caused agitation throughout Christendom. As Lothar himself stated soon after in a capitulary designed precisely to avoid the return of such catastrophes, "no doubt is possible: it is in punishment of sins" committed by Christians "that such a misfortune fell upon the Church; that the Roman Church itself which is the head of Christianity, has been delivered into the hands of the infidels; and finally that on all the frontiers of the kingdoms of Lothar and his brothers, the pagan peoples are victorious".

"On all the frontiers of the three kingdoms", Lothar said. And the fact is that just at that very moment in the course of the same month of August, Louis the German, at war on the frontier from the Baltic down to Bohemia and in Moravia with the pagan Slavs, suffered a crushing defeat in this area, which the semi-official author of the *Annals of Fulda*, however devoted he was to the Carolingian cause, was forced to admit openly.

In this triumph of barbarians who, as we have seen in the above-cited capitulary, were all designated by the common term 'pagans', and especially in the profanation of St Peter's at Rome, which aggrieved Christian consciences, everyone, just like Lothar and his counsellors, saw a solemn warning: "Consequently, it seems to us an urgent necessity", Lothar added, "to correct, with the assistance of divine mercy, everything that may have specially offended God". The most urgent task was to put into practice at last the policy of brotherly concord outlined at Yütz in 844. Under the influence of the dangers to which their dissension exposed all three of them, Lothar, Louis the German and Charles agreed to meet again on 28 February 847 at Meerssen, near Maastricht, in an attempt to unite at least against the enemies from without.

The deliberations were, it appears, rather arduous; they continued for fifteen days. In general, the matters discussed were the same as at Yütz, but the summary or agenda of the questions broached, which is all that has come down to us, clearly betrays a certain weariness: "Concerning the peace and concord", one reads at the beginning, "and the unanimity which the three brothers ought to maintain between them, and the bonds of charity, not feigned but genuine, that ought to unite them, so that no one can in future sow the seeds of discord among them" (Art. 1). In the face of the many dangers, the kings were called upon to "help one another, according to the possibilities of the moment" (Art. 2); they ought to inflict "joint retribution" against anyone, in whichever kingdom, who "dares by greed to violate the laws of peace" (Art. 3), which had already been decreed at Yütz against the rebels of Charles' kingdom. The honour due to churches, their rights, the respect for the legal status of each man, were once more recalled (Arts. 4 and 5).

The internal disorders were alluded to, not without discouragement: "Let the robberies and depredations which up to now have been committed as though in virtue of a lawful right, be utterly forbidden, and let no one henceforth be able to commit them and go unpunished" (Art. 6). To deal with this, it was laid down that *missi* would be instituted in the three kingdoms, in order to inquire about and to pronounce judgment on the cases reported, so that flight from one kingdom to another would no longer bring impunity to the culprits (Art. 7). An incident that had created much stir, that of the abduction of one of Lothar's daughters by a vassal of Charles named Gilbert at the beginning of the preceding year (it had been the cause of a heated conflict between Lothar and his youngest brother, in whose kingdom the two culprits had sought asylum) was doubtless the direct object of this measure. This article was followed by another, inspired by the same affair (Art. 8), in which it was stated that anyone who "henceforth dares to carry out an abduction", in any one of the three kingdoms should be "punished according to the law". Finally, after an article about the hereditary cession, to each king's legitimate sons, of the parts of the kingdoms which he wished to award them, three joint conciliatory moves were announced: vis-à-vis Pepin of Aquitaine, the Breton duke Nominoé, and the king of the Danes, Horic. The aim of the third was to obtain the cessation of the raids of which the three kingdoms were equally victims, and concerning which it was provided that, in case of the failure of their overture, the three kings would unite to face them.

Worthwhile decisions, in principle; but were the brothers actually resolved to carry them out as well? One is inclined to doubt it when one reads the text, fortunately preserved, of the public declarations made at the conclusion of the conference by each of the three kings.

Lothar, who spoke first in his capacity of the eldest of the brothers, restricted himself to announcing that they had all three agreed to allow co-operation, which is natural among brothers, to reign between them, and, in order to realize this, to promote as much as possible the mutual assistance necessary for the 'common advantage' – that is, whatever is in the interest of all.

Louis the German was somewhat less vague: he announced the sending of joint delegations to Pepin of Aquitaine, "to the Bretons" and "to the Northmen" to try to re-establish peace; Pepin was moreover to be summoned for the same purpose to a "plea" held by the three kings jointly; but concerning him, as well as concerning the Bretons and the Vikings, Louis said only that in the event of these overtures failing he and his brothers "would seek the advice" of their men about what to do next. He added moreover that Lothar would give "his men" the order to stop troubling Charles, and that they would all three in their respective kingdoms grant the justified claims of the Church.

All this nevertheless remained very vague. Once more they were content with promises, even conditional promises, without deciding anything concrete; and it could not have been forgotten that already at Yütz, three years earlier, overtures to Pepin and the Bretons had been announced without any practical result ever having been recorded—

perhaps even without anyone ever having translated the decision into action.

The last declaration, that of Charles, was not calculated to correct the impression of emptiness that those of his brothers had created, because Charles began by announcing the referral to a new conference, to start at Paris on the feast of St John the Baptist (24 June), of the decisions necessary to translate into practice the very general agreement that had just been reached. He exhorted his audience to keep the peace until that date and finished with some recommendations concerning the relations of lords and vassals as though, on the main subject, he had nothing more to say.

Thus, no more at Meerssen than at Yütz, did the policy of 'brotherly concord', of which so much had been expected, result in anything more than the mere enunciation of principles, whose implementation was postponed to a new conference. And the disappointment was such that the semi-official annalist of the Frankish kingdom of the west, Prudentius, the bishop of Troyes, careful as he was not to omit anything essential, and who almost always worked with the documents at hand, did not even mention the assembly of Meerssen; this was his way of concealing a failure.

The aggravation of the danger and the second conference of Meerssen (847–851)

24 June came and went without the conference announced for that date taking place. No one, except perhaps Charles, cared any more about it. The tripartite agreement for the security of the Frankish Empire and of Christendom, against which the barbarians were redoubling their attacks, was evidently a matter for high-flown words only. The three kings lacked the spirit of co-operation, that spirit of 'charity' and 'concord' of which they spoke so much, and a sincere reconciliation between them, without mental reservations, appeared unattainable. How could Charles in particular trust Lothar, whom he suspected of being behind all those who rebelled against him? The 'duke of the Bretons' Nominoé claimed to recognize no other ruler than the eldest son of Louis the Pious, and Pepin of Aquitaine knew he could count on

Lothar's support, overt or tacit. In February 848, when Lothar had gone to confer with Louis the German at Koblenz, rumour spread that he was trying to detach Louis from Charles in order, in connivance with him, to organize some treacherous move against Charles. Only the German king's loyalty caused this strategy to fail.

The outlook grew even gloomier. The destructive raids of the Vikings went on increasing. The joint overture provided for at the assembly of Meerssen had indeed been made to the Danish king Horic; but he seems to have had no real power over those of his countrymen who roamed the seas, and it is probable, moreover, that such an overture would not have impressed him anyway. In any case the result in practice was nil. In 847 the Vikings ravaged the coast of Aquitaine and laid siege to Bordeaux which, despite an unsuccessful attempt by Charles to rescue it, they succeeded in capturing at the beginning of 848. The city was sacked, and the pirates spread northwards to Melle, the seat of a mint, which doubtless excited their covetousness, and which they also sacked. Other pirates in 847 invaded the Low Countries; they occupied the great river port of Duurstede as well as the Betuwe, without Lothar being able to stop them. In 849 Vikings could still be found in Gascony and Périgord, from where they extended their raids to Limoges. In 850 the inhabitants of the northern provinces of Lothar and Charles once more saw 'a multitude' of their ships approach, which went up the Rhine, the Waal, the Scheldt and the Lys. Powerless to drive them back, Lothar was forced to concede the abandonment of Duurstede and "several counties" on the lower Rhine, to the leaders of the expedition.

Apparently spared by the Vikings during this period, Louis the German was obliged, in his turn, to hold his own against the Slavs all along his eastern frontiers. In 849, the Bohemians inflicted a heavy defeat on him which the semi-official annalist of Fulda tried to explain at length by pleading extenuating circumstances, without however concealing the magnitude of the disaster.

As for the Moslems, those terrible 'Saracens', whose menace lay heavy on all the coastal regions of the western Mediterranean, but especially on Lothar's kingdom, which lay close to their point of departure – Tunisia – and was more tempting also because of its wealth, they were kept in check only with great difficulty. In 847 they overran the province of Benevento and turned once more towards Rome without however pressing on to the gates of the city in that same year. As a matter of fact, the painful experience of the previous summer had borne fruit: Lothar had organized a collection in the whole extent of his kingdom for the erection of a "strong wall around the church of St Peter". The new pope Leo IV, who had succeeded Sergius II at the beginning of 847, busied himself actively with its construction, and the high ramparts which he raised soon made the suburb on whose fringe stood the venerated basilica a kind of small fortified city – the 'Leonine city' – capable of withstanding the invader. At the same time Lothar had ordered the mustering of a powerful army composed of Italians, Franks, Burgundians and Provençals, at the head of which he placed his son Louis, king of Italy. It was given the task of keeping the Moslems out of Rome and central Italy. The pope himself, the doge of Venice, and the duke of Benevento were invited to participate in this general mobilization of Christian forces against the infidel, and in fact Rome seemed protected for the time being. But in 849 the Saracens sacked the port of Luna, near La Spezia, in North Italy; then, extending their ravages along the whole length of the coast, they pressed on to Provence. In 850 they reached the port of Arles for the second time without encountering the least resistance anywhere.

In addition to these dangers from the outside, internal difficulties arose for each of the three kings which immobilized them at the moment when they needed all their forces to withstand the external enemies. Charles' kingdom presented a picture of the most lamentable confusion. In June 845 Charles had been compelled to leave to his nephew Pepin the government of the greater part of Aquitaine in exchange for a promise of fidelity which, as could be expected, Pepin had no intention of keeping and which, moreover, was already broken scarcely a few months after it had been made. In 848 hostilities were resumed between uncle and nephew and they continued up to the day when, in September 852, Pepin, having been made prisoner by the duke of Gascony, was delivered by him to Charles, who got rid of him by shutting him up in the already too well-known monastery of St Médard at Soissons.

The Bretons were no less of a nuisance to the king of France. In November 845, Duke Nominoé inflicted a defeat on Charles in the marshes of Ballon, near Redon, that almost cost Charles his life and in which many of his men fell. The Breton raids spread as far as the outskirts of Bayeux in 847 and Angers in 849; they continued in 850, in connivance with Lambert, count of Nantes, who defected for the second time in a short space of time. They were scarcely interrupted by the sudden death on 7 March 851 of Nominoé, whose son, Érispoé, prepared to carry on the tradition.

Though the difficulties that confronted Louis the German in his kingdom are not completely known to us, we do know that Lothar was not, in his territories, in a much better position than his youngest brother. In 845 he had been compelled to use force to subdue the spirit of insubordination of the Provençals. In Italy his authority and that of his son Louis, whom in April 850 he had caused to be anointed in advance as emperor at Rome by Pope Leo IV, were so little respected that they were able to maintain order only with the greatest difficulty. A capitulary promulgated around the end of that same year 850 informs us that brigandage was occurring everywhere in complicity with the counts and royal officials; that for the rest, neither the powerful laymen, nor even the church dignitaries scrupled, in the course of their journeys, to plunder the people with whom they spent the night; and that the wealthiest landowners often acted in collusion with highway robbers, with whom they shared the booty. The same document gives us, moreover, a sombre glimpse of the state of abandonment and disrepair of the public buildings; the royal palaces were no longer maintained; the bridges, unrepaired, collapsed. The fact that the administrative machinery no longer functioned is telling enough.

In view of such a breakdown within the three kingdoms and in the presence of such dangers the kings could not remain insensitive to the appeals for concord which the clergy repeatedly addressed to them, which encouraged them to expect that a return to God would open the way to earthly welfare as well as heavenly salvation. In October 848, negotiations were resumed between the three brothers with a view to settling their latest differences amiably. In January 849 Lothar had agreed to go to Péronne to visit Charles, in the hope of re-establishing with him peaceful relations and a 'brotherly concord'. Between Louis the German and Charles, in the same period, it was all friendship and trust: in the course of a meeting they had around May, the two brothers publicly agreed to place their wives and children under the guardianship of whichever one was to survive the other. The following year, in June 850, Louis the German went to see Lothar at Cologne, then took him hunting for several days in Westphalia. Their relationship seemed so cordial, one annalist writes, that "many were amazed by it".

Thus little by little an atmosphere of mutual understanding came about amongst the three brothers. A new effort was made at the beginning of 851 to bring their points of view closer in a permanent way and to achieve by means of a concrete pact the so far theoretical plan of 'brotherly concord'. A new conference was held around May in the same palace of Meerssen where four years earlier they had tried in vain to translate into actions the noble resolutions taken at Yütz in 844.

After so many successive conferences, everyone at last seemed won over to the idea of an entente, and indeed a few days were enough to bring it about. It is true that the kings again restricted themselves, as was usual at this kind of meeting, to the formulation of some very general principles; but this time there was more clarity and ardour in them. The documents resulting from these deliberations reflect the unanimous will to be done with the dissensions that engendered only weakness and confusion. So at the very beginning they declared that the past would be forgotten and the reciprocal injuries would be forgiven: the memory "of all the evils, all the contrarieties" suffered, "of all the usurpations, machinations, manoeuvres or tricks" of which each had been more or less the victim, was to be, the kings solemnly declared, "abolished and rooted out of our hearts" along with every trace of "malice or rancour" (Art. 1). Among them would remain only feelings of "true charity", that excluded all "dissimulation", each of the kings henceforth forbidding himself to undertake anything in a neighbouring kingdom, either directly or by recourse to "cunning propaganda" (*per occultos susurrones*) or calumny (Art. 2). The three kings were furthermore officially placed on a footing of perfect equality: they dealt with each other as "peers", that is to say, equals (Arts. 2 and 3), and promised to help each other all circumstances; the document even added that, being good brothers, they would sincerely share their griefs and joys (Art. 3). This entente was intended to survive them and after their death to extend to their children (Art. 3). None of the three contracting parties would give asylum or protection to the rebellious subjects of the two others; each was even obliged to exert himself together with his brothers in chastising them (Art. 4). A similar arrangement was made concerning the delinquents who, to escape ecclesiastical penalties, fled from the kingdom where they belonged to seek refuge in one of the others (Art. 5). Finally to crown the edifice, the kings proclaimed their faith in the ideal of general concord which the clergy had not ceased preaching throughout the Empire since the death of Louis the Pious: concord not only between the kings but between the kings and their subjects, whom Lothar, Louis and Charles pledged themselves in concert to guarantee against every arbitrary act; concord of the subjects amongst themselves in order to undertake the common task of the restoration of the Church and the state; communion of all in God; joint action of all against those who, whatever their rank or station, ventured to disturb this regime of peace (Arts. 6, 7 and 8). For this task of moral restoration each of the three kings promised to "recognize, without delay or excuse, the points on which he had violated the commands of God", to correct his faults, and in "all sincerity" to devote his utmost efforts to the welfare of all (Art. 7).

The personal declarations which, one after the other, Lothar, Louis and Charles made at the conclusion of the conference in commenting on the decisions that had been jointly taken, confirm the impression of détente that is apparent in the text we have just examined. "By the grace of God", Lothar proclaimed, finally won over it seems by the general enthusiasm, "we are here united among ourselves and with our subjects because we have recognized that, within our kingdom as well as outside it in our frontier marches, this is a necessity!" – "As my brother has said to you", Louis the German continued, "there is an urgent necessity for us and for the Christian people, who have been entrusted to us by God, to live united and in concord: it is the will of God and it is natural to true brothers. And it is because up to now we have fallen short of this that so many things contrary to God and grave for us and for you have occurred." Then he rejoiced by way of conclusion in the "unanimity" at last restored. Charles, echoing this, also stressed the absolute necessity of the peace that had been found again. All three spoke of "the kingdom" and no longer only of their respective kingdoms. The consciousness of the fundamental unity of this kingdom, the *regnum Francorum*, which survived the partitioning, remained profoundly inscribed on their spirits and in their hearts. They attached themselves to it once more with all their strength as to a sheet anchor, without however pronouncing the words 'empire' or 'emperor' which would have revived the conflicts.

This renewed consciousness of the Carolingian unity proves at least that the idea out of which the Empire had been born was not dead: more forcefully proclaimed than ever in this brotherly concord, the need for unity was so clearly emphasized in turn by each of the three kings that one might say that the Empire had survived its own demise.

The last pacts and death of Lothar (851-855)

The pact of 851 gave the impression that a new era was about to begin. The semi-official annalist of Charles' kingdom, Prudentius, bishop of Troyes, who had not even mentioned in his book the first conference held at Meerssen, has, between the dry notices which constitute most of his story, by a remarkable exception, transcribed the whole of the text of the 851 resolutions, jointly drawn up, thus emphasizing the extraordinary importance he attached to them.

But this again was only an illusion. What gave it apparent substance was that for the first time since Louis the Pious' death – one could even say since 833 – Lothar, who had constantly behaved as an adversary of any agreement based on the principle of co-operation or of equality with his brothers, seemed finally won over to the idea of a pact that might be able to check the barbarian invaders and preserve Christendom from disaster. The imperial title, which his brothers did not now contest, without however accepting that it denoted any superiority whatever in political affairs, sufficed, with the possession of Aachen and supervision over the papacy, to gratify his self-esteem. The imperial anointing, which he had obtained in advance for his son Louis II at Rome in the previous April without arousing the least protest, had confirmed his impression that no one any longer sought to quarrel with him about this. With the years, moreover, his point of view tended to change. The muddle-headed ardour of his youth had gradually made way for a more realistic appraisal of the situation. In 851 he was a man of fifty-six or fifty-seven; he had three sons, and he was obliged to think about arranging an inheritance for them that would be safe from the covetousness of others. How could he achieve this while remaining on a warlike footing with his brothers? His conversion to the idea of concord now appeared to be indeed sincere.

But, by a sudden and surprising tergiversation, it was Louis the German, up to now the apostle of peace and ever ready to mediate between Lothar and Charles, who from now on exhibited the most reservations, and soon the most resistance. Was it because, sensing himself at first beset by other enemies than theirs, he experienced less need for co-operation than his brothers? We do not know; but the fact is that, as soon as the treaty of Meerssen was concluded, he seemed to start avoiding Lothar and Charles, and then to intrigue against them. In 852, while Lothar had gone to aid Charles against the Vikings, we see Louis appearing mysteriously at Cologne with "a few of the magnates" of his eldest brother; in 853 it was with Charles' subjects that he entered into conversations the object of which must have been closely connected with his intention to support the rebellious Aquitanians by sending them his own son, Louis the Younger. This happened around March 854.

However, between Lothar and Charles the desire to co-operate became daily stronger in the course of meetings whose object was no longer to formulate grandiose principles, but really to work together. The two kings met each other for this purpose at Saint-Quentin at the beginning of 852, at Valenciennes in November 853, and at Liège in February 854, and the atmosphere of these meetings was increasingly cordial. At Saint-Quentin, which was in Charles' kingdom, he lavished tokens of brotherly affection on his guest Lothar which Prudentius, the bishop of Troyes, mentions with pleasure in his *Annals*. Several months later they fought side by side along the Seine against the Vikings who, after pillaging Frisia and the Scheldt valley, had established their winter quarters on the isle of Jeufosse, not far from Vernon. They did not separate until the pirates themselves decided to withdraw at the beginning of 853 and, to show his gratitude, Charles, before his brother returned to his own kingdom, chose him to be the godfather of his youngest daughter, who had just been born.

In November, confidential conversations continued at Valenciennes, where the two brothers consulted together about the despatch of *missi*, charged with re-establishing order in their kingdoms. These *missi* were to act according to the same programme. They were to communicate to each other all information concerning delinquents fleeing from one kingdom to another and to deliver them to each other. Thus for the first time a plan for the co-ordination of measures drawn up in two of the kingdoms that had resulted from the dismemberment of the Empire was worked out, which however did not prevent the two brothers, before going their ways, from consulting together once more about the Vikings. Still a grave danger, these pirates had moved from the Seine basin to that of the Loire, where they reached Tours at the very moment when Lothar and Charles were conferring at Valenciennes.

The *missi* nominated at this last meeting were explicitly called upon to present their reports as soon as possible so that Lothar and Charles could take them into account in new conversations arranged between them for the beginning of 854. These occurred in February at Liège in the same spirit of complete co-operation. Louis the German, though invited to the meeting, had not come; his intentions at this moment were only too obvious: his son Louis the Younger was on his way to Aquitaine, where the rebels were impatiently awaiting him. In these circumstances Lothar and Charles could not but take note of his abstention and hostility, deplore them, and strengthen their own accord. The usual public declarations made at the conclusion of their talks were a more decisive affirmation than ever of their close co-operation: "We desire", Lothar declared, "to assure you of our unity; for the well-being of the holy Church of God, for our common good and for the undertaking of our common charges, we desire to remain indissolubly united in heart and in action, being one in Christ, and you all being one with us" (Art. 2). "Know ye", Charles repeated, "that we shall be united in adversity as much as in prosperity, and that if God comes to our aid nothing will be able to turn us away from the love which unites us in a brotherly way. Everywhere we have need of help or support, we plan to support and defend one another insofar as the Lord permits. We wish to lend aid one to another against every earthly enemy".

These declarations remind one of those of Meerssen, but with something more vigorous and categorical in them which is unfortunately explicable in terms of the fact that there were only two contracting parties, and that the pledges they took were, as they said, both for the common good and also against their absent brother, Louis the German, whose attitude Lothar and Charles one after the other denounced more or less openly. Lothar noted dryly: "This year we have on many occasions invited our dearest brother Louis to a conversation together . . . ; but up to now, notwithstanding our desire, he has been prevented from coming by various circumstances and has postponed his participation, and we did not want to wait any longer to unite ourselves together, my brother and I". Charles, more frankly, added: "We have postponed this union up to now because we hoped that our said brother (Louis) would come and find us to unite himself with us. But when, hindered by various causes, he neglected to come, my brother and I decided, on news of the disturbances which his son is trying to foment, to ally ourselves together". Doubtless, this alliance remained in principle open to Louis, but while indicating this, Charles did not hesitate to say explicitly that Lothar and he already held the German for an adversary, one of the "earthly enemies" to whom they had alluded above, much more than as a possible adherent to the pact concluded between them: "If our said brother still delays in doing what we expect and instruct him to do (that is to say, to join us) we are agreed to lend each other aid and support as necessary to ensure to ourselves the peaceful possession of the kingdom which we hold from God".

Moreover, before taking leave of each other, Lothar and Charles bound themselves by identically worded oaths which had the possibility of going to war against Louis and his sons as their sole explicit aim: "From this day, if our brother Louis violates the oath he has taken to us (at Meerssen) or if his sons attack part of the kingdom which you have received, I will give aid upon your request . . . ." There is no doubt at all: from the idea of a general concord they had imperceptibly returned to a treaty of defensive alliance of two brothers against the third, as twelve years earlier at Strasbourg. But the accord of Liège marked a real reversal of alliances: for Louis, the intimate and cherished ally of Charles in 842, was now substituted Lothar, his implacable adversary of twelve years before; and it was Louis, now, who was excluded from the 'brotherly' alliance concluded in the name of the peace recognized as necessary to the well-being of the Christian world.

The alliance of Lothar and Charles was however not restricted to the persons of the two contracting parties; it extended to their descendants, to whom it guaranteed the territorial integrity of their inheritance. Lothar, the one most immediately interested in obtaining assurances on this point, had them given him in a declaration by Charles: "If one of us two survives his partner, he shall take into his keeping and protection the children and the kingdom of the deceased to protect them with God's aid from the machinations of adversaries and to ensure (to the interested parties) their peaceful possession of it" (Art. 2). And in the oaths which they exchanged at the conclusion of their talks, each of the two parties renewed this pledge. This means that the idea of a single *regnum* was lost from view: the territorial statute worked out at Verdun in 843 was considered inviolable, at least as far as Lothar's and Charles' kingdoms were concerned; and the two kings agreed to defend the integrity of these at any price by means of their entente against their third brother and his sons, especially against Louis the Younger, then about to conquer Aquitaine.

The alliance concluded at Liège was adhered to. When Louis the

Younger, having entered Aquitaine suddenly, tried to seize it from Charles, Lothar went at once to remonstrate with the German, whom he met on the banks of the Rhine in the spring of 854. The first contact was ungracious. The two brothers, Prudentius wrote in his *Annals*, began to "tear each other apart hungrily"; then they explained themselves, and separated in an atmosphere of *détente*. Soon indeed through the mediation of Lothar, who had gone at once in June 854 to Attigny on the Aisne to inform Charles of the situation, negotiations were resumed between the three brothers with a view to the general re-establishment of peace by calling back Louis the Younger, whose campaign in Aquitaine had yielded no results. The retreat of Louis the Younger shortly afterwards brought Charles closer to Louis the German, even to the point of disturbing Lothar, who was then already ill and whose death seems to have been expected at any moment by his two brothers.

Lothar's end was in fact very near. He died on 29 September 855 at the monastery of Prüm, not without having made provision for the division of his inheritance among his three sons, but leaving behind a complicated situation, which would almost inevitably test the whole edifice so laboriously constructed by his brothers and himself at the price of so many years of painful negotiation.

CHAPTER THREE

The Church as the guardian of Christian unity

The bankruptcy of 'brotherly co-operation' (855-858)

Up to now it had been possible to delude oneself with the hope that the policy of brotherly concord would eventually ensure sufficient cohesion among all the parts of the former Carolingian Empire to preserve at least the essence of the 'Christian unity' brought about in the West by Charlemagne, which Louis the Pious had intended to make into a political reality. But what was to become of this hope in the face of the new complications brought about by Lothar's death?

He had divided the inheritance among his three legitimate sons as follows: to Louis, the eldest, the kingdom of Italy and the imperial crown, which had already been awarded to him in advance several years earlier; to Lothar II who was at that time at most eighteen, the northerly regions, from Frisia to the plateau of Langres and the region of Alsace, perhaps even as far as the Jura; to the youngest Charles, still a child, the remaining territory. This division substantially changed the political situation: with the eldest son, Louis – the Emperor Louis II – the imperial title was more or less relegated to Italy, that Lombard Italy which, since the time of Charlemagne himself, had never been regarded as anything more than a dependency of the Frankish kingdom. Aachen, for the first time, was the capital of a kingdom of secondary importance, that of Lothar II. Its nucleus was doubtless 'middle France' (*Francia media*), but it was so ill-defined geographically that its frontiers, especially on the southern side, often varied, and it was so inconsistent in every way that, for want of a better name, people were reduced to giving it the name of its king only: *Lotharii regnum, Lothariense regnum*, 'kingdom of Lothar', 'Lotharian king-dom', a name that in the middle of the tenth century was finally transformed into *Lotharingia*, of which the Germans were to make *Lothringen* and the French 'Lorraine'.

From now on, then, the former Carolingian Empire was a mosaic of five kingdoms, unequal and without cohesion, which the previous agreements, in spite of the solemn oaths which had accompanied them, could not protect for long against the risk of new modifications. The co-operation of Lothar's three sons at least would have been indispensable to avert the danger, but the two eldest, Louis II and Lothar II, both felt themselves wronged, and the lords of Provence supported the young Charles, whose interests his brothers would no doubt willingly have sacrificed. The discussions among the three brothers, who, by a coincidence of ill omen, bore the same name as the three rivals of Fontenoy, turned sour: in the course of the conversation which they had together in 856 at Orbe, south of the Lake of Neuchâtel, they narrowly escaped violence; peace was re-established among them only with great difficulty.

The entente painfully restored in 855 between Louis the German and Charles the Bald remained equally precarious. At the beginning of the summer of 856 a massive uprising had broken out in Charles' kingdom and jeopardized his position. The rebels offered the disputed throne to his brother, just as the Aquitanians had previously done in 854, though it is uncertain how far the insurgents were in connivance on this occasion with the king of Germany. Engaged at the time in fierce battles with the Bohemians, who inflicted heavy losses on him in August 856, Louis, already sorely tried by a campaign conducted the previous year against the Moravians, was at that moment incapable of responding to such an appeal; but is it certain that, under other circumstances, he would still have rejected it?

For several months, nevertheless, it remained possible to believe in the maintenance of concord, if not among all the kings, at least between Charles the Bald, Louis the German, and their nephew Lothar II. Assured, at his accession, of Louis the German's support, which he had gone to request at Frankfurt in the autumn of 855, Lothar II had thereafter paid him another visit in February 857 at Koblenz and then, several days later (1 March), at Saint-Quentin, he had informed his other uncle Charles of these talks. The public declarations made at the conclusion of this last interview by uncle and nephew exhibit the utmost trust, or were at least intended to give their assembled followers the illusion that nothing had yet happened that could undermine that trust. Charles began by recalling that he had personally, since his father's death, "always received the advice which he needed from his dear brother Louis" and that it was "thanks to his mediation that the unanimity that becomes brothers" had reigned between the regretted Lothar I and himself. He then recalled the agreement sealed at Liège in February 854 and the obligations that arose from it for him with regard to his nephew; as well as the difficulties of all kinds which had prevented him from taking up earlier with his "dearest nephew" the conversation they had just had in which the sympathy "they had at heart for one another" had become evident. Finally he alluded to the talk Lothar II had had a few days before at Koblenz with his "dearest brother Louis", from whom he had received the welcome he had hoped for, "which", he added, "pleased me very much". On the strength of this, Lothar II and he had, he declared, renewed the pact of Liège, guaranteed to respect each other's kingdom, and promised, with the consent of their vassals, to lend each other aid and assistance, according to need, in the future.

Lothar, in his turn, declared himself resolved to adhere to the promise given by his father at Liège. He added that, in accordance with the agreements of Valenciennes, the *missi* of the two kingdoms would exchange delinquents who had fled from one kingdom to the other; he promised to carry out the provisions of the treaty concluded in 851 at Meerssen by the three sons of Louis the Pious; and, lastly, he praised the "generosity" of his two uncles who, if we may believe him, had both facilitated his accession to the throne.

In appearance, then, the spirit of Meerssen survived. But suddenly, in the summer of 857, it was learned that Louis the German had met his other nephew, the Emperor Louis II, in July at Trent, and had concluded a pact with him. The semi-official annalist of Charles the Bald's kingdom, Prudentius, presents this pact as a retort to that of Lothar II and Charles the Bald at Saint-Quentin, and historians have made innumerable conjectures about the significance of such a move. It seems clear however that its object was to cut short the plans which Lothar II had been making since his father's death to take possession of the share of the lands reserved for his youngest brother Charles, whose precarious state of health (he was an epileptic) had tempted Lothar II to count on this inheritance for himself. At the stormy meeting at Orbe in the course of the summer of 856 this had been the object of contention, and the months that followed were to prove that Lothar II had not renounced the realization of plans which came into conflict, as one might well expect, with those cherished by his brother Louis II. It was thus obvious that the hymn to peace intoned by Charles the Bald at the conclusion of his meeting with his nephew Lothar and the demonstrations of affection which he showered on his "dearest brother" Louis the German no longer corresponded to reality.

For the rest, the king 'of France' was obliged to reckon with ever increasing internal difficulties, to which, as could be seen more and more clearly, the intrigues of his "dearest brother" of Germany were no stranger. We have already seen that it was to Louis the German that the rebels of his kingdom had instinctively turned in 856. The delay the German king made in replying to their appeal had in the event allowed Charles to restore order without too much difficulty. But the weakness of the king of France was only too obvious. At one and the same moment his kingdom was attacked by the Vikings, who in 856 and 857 carried out their ravages unchecked in the valley of the Loire, where they penetrated Tours, Blois, and Orléans; in the Seine valley, where Paris was taken and burned; and in Aquitaine, where the pirates had just pillaged Poitiers in 857.

That same year 857 confronted Charles with a new and serious uprising of Aquitaine in favour of Pepin II, who had escaped from the monastery where he had been imprisoned in 852. North of the Loire, some of the 'Franks' also revolted, and at first Louis the German seemed not to be implicated in this movement, which continued to spread. We are even surprised to see Charles speak, in a capitulary of 14 February 857, of measures drawn up against the rebels in concert with the person he continued to call his "dear brother", as well as with their three nephews, the sons of Lothar I. But the following year, as Charles courageously withstood a violent Viking offensive on the lower Seine and the desertions in his army multiplied, the diplomacy of the king of Germany took a disquieting turn. His semi-official annalist, Rodulf, the monk of Fulda, reports that in the spring of 858 he had successive and mysterious talks with his two nephews, Louis II and Lothar II. Lothar II, whom he awaited at the beginning of May at Koblenz, left him in the lurch, and went to meet the king of France, to whom, faithful to his promise, he brought military aid against the Vikings. It was at that moment that the German king finally showed his colours and invaded his brother's kingdom.

For Charles it was a tragic moment. Abandoned by a large part of his men, who had been won over in advance by the invaders and were ready to support their plans, and engaged in fierce battles against the Vikings, he seemed incapable of resisting the invasion. His nephew, Lothar II, who fought loyally at his siade on the Seine, was unable in his turn to prevent the king of Germany from breaking through the Lotharingian frontier. The way was open for Louis the German, who played a simple and unscrupolous game: he even dared to proclaim–the annalist of Fulda confirms this–that he came to deliver the 'Franks' of the western kingdom and the Aquitainians from the intolerable "tyranny" of a prince who could not even defend Christendom against the "pagans". Bitter irony from the mouth of a man who was prepared to stab his brother in the back at the very moment when Charles was spending all his energy in checking the pagans of the North. Louis nonetheless counted on overthrowing him and adding his kingdom to his own, which indicated to Lothar what awaited him in his turn.

Louis' march was rapid, his advance decisive. He completed the mobilization of his troops in mid-August at Worms. He crossed Lothar's kingdom, arrived on 1 September at Ponthion on the Ornain, in Charles' kingdom, where he received the oaths of fidelity of his brother's magnates, who had come to meet him in great numbers. Thence he went on to Châlons-sur-Marne; then via Sens towards Orléans to meet the Aquitainians, winning the support of vassals everywhere. Warned, Charles hastened to the scene, unable to finish his operations against the Vikings. On 10 November, the armies of the two brothers faced each other at Brienne, near the Aube. At the end of three days of fruitless negotiation, the battle was about to begin when, betrayed by some of his troops, who went over to the enemy, Charles judged it prudent to decamp and retreated precipitately to Burgundy.

Thereafter the issue seemed to be decided: the magnates deserted Charles in a body and rallied to Louis who at Troyes proceeded, in order to reward the deserters, to distribute an enormous number of counties, bishoprics, abbacies, offices and properties of every kind. At the palace of Attigny, where he went afterwards, he received, before the end of November, an important promise of adherence, that of Lothar II himself who, suddenly intimidated, and also believing Charles' cause to be lost, saw no other way to preserve his own monarchy than by an outright change of allegiance.

But would the Church allow such an outrageous spoliation? At this

moment when the very principles of order so arduously re-established
in Christendom were in this way assailed by the ambition of a prince
who had for such a long time posed as the defender of peace, the
prelates of the Gauls let their voice be heard with a boldness and an
authority that, at the moment when all seemed lost, once more averted
the danger and compelled the invader to retreat.

The intervention of Archbishop Hincmar and the Gallic prelates

Among the prelates of the western kingdom, the archbishop of Sens,
Wenilo, although an appointee of Charles the Bald, had been one of the
few to rally to the king of Germany. He had not even feared, at first, to
conduct a campaign for him. But he did not receive much response,
and on the whole the higher clergy was on its guard, so much so that in
the palace of Attigny Louis had been reduced to having mass
performed by the disloyal archbishop, who was there outside his
diocese. Summoned by Louis to Reims for a general assembly whose
opening had been fixed for 25 November, the prelates declined. At any
rate we still possess the refusal, tactful but firm, presented to the
usurper by the bishops of the two ecclesiastical provinces of Rouen
and Reims: a document of capital importance, whose author was the
archbishop of Reims, the Hincmar whose role we have already
mentioned. He was for a time to find himself the eloquent voice of the
Church.

The document, of ample size, is couched in the form of a letter to
King Louis in reply to the summons he had sent to the bishops. They
began by withdrawing behind the material impossibility in which they
found themselves of replying in so short a time and at a moment of
such confusion to the summons which Louis had sent them; they then
went straight to the problems posed by the letters of royal summons.
The meeting, it had been announced, had as its aim to consult about
"the restoration of the holy Church, and the welfare of the Christian
people". Now, in these matters, they pointed out, things would go
better "if you showed yourself to be amenable to our previous
observations", because "what we have written, reported, said and
done, has been dictated to us . . . by God". In particular they recalled to

Louis the suggestion they had made to him at five different points during a conference with Charles, at which the two kings, surrounded by their followers, had examined together the remedies to apply to the evils reported. It was high time for Louis finally to follow their advice, they wrote, and they did not hesitate to formulate this for him in writing.

He should look inward and, without listening to the words of flatterers, weigh in his conscience the value of the "excuses and reasons he could give for his coming into the kingdom". He should think of the reversals of fortune which are always possible: "Those who now smile at you when they obtain what they wish, will smile at others when you are on the point of death and they try to obtain from them what they first obtained from you; but they might also do this even during your lifetime". Following the example of those who "organized revolts against their father", there were now those who did so against their brother, under the pretence of the words 'peace', 'safety for the Church', 'welfare', and 'unity' of the "Christian" people; but "the poison lies hidden under the honey, and the words of the Psalmist have been fulfilled: 'They speak of peace to their neighbours and have malice in their hearts' (Psalms 27:3)."

The abominable evils the country suffers from the pagans, so the letter went on, "are still surpassed by those which, against all divine and human laws, Christians inflict on Christians, parents on parents, a Christian king on a Christian king, a brother on a brother". Take care, then, the bishops exclaimed, that your palace "which ought to be a sacred palace, is not a sacrilegious one", and if you have come, as you say, "to redress the evil which has been done, do not do worse still". And since you say that you are guided by "charity", "let charity move you to go and fight the pagans and . . . in this way deliver the Church as well as the kingdom". In a general way, since Louis claimed to wish to "restore the Church of God", the bishops called upon him rather to follow the example of his brother, "their lord", and not to treat the clergy in the manner of Charles Martel, who had been damned for having confiscated church properties. Finally, seeing that Louis paraded his desire "to seek after the good and the welfare of the Christian people", might he not "correct himself before wishing to correct others, for it is written: 'Doctor, cure thyself' (Luke 4:23)." The prelates also thought it necessary to remind him at great length of his duties as king.

"If God", they conceded, "should decide to commit to your hands the cause and the welfare of the Church and the kingdom, we shall exhort ourselves to behave under your rule in a way which seems to us to accord the best with the divine arrangements. Because God can draw felicitous consequences from an evil beginning, He for whom what appears impossible to men is possible." But such an adherence could not be thought of as long as there was no certainty that "our lord, your brother, has [effectively] withdrawn from this part of the kingdom" – and the expression "our lord", which returns here for the second time, emphasizes that the matter was in fact not settled in the eyes of the authors; nor would it be until all the bishops of Gaul had been able to deliberate about it among themselves. Because, the prelates observed, it was they who "with the consent and according to the wish of the people of the kingdom, have anointed our lord your brother as king with the holy chrism".

Consequently, Louis should reread the history of Saul in the second Book of Kings. "He will see there with what respect, even though the Lord had reproved him and rejected him, Saul was to the end treated by Samuel", from whom he had received the royal unction. This priest Samuel, "whose place in the Church" the bishops "however unworthy, held", had shown them the way. As for King Louis, let him remember the conduct of David who, although "chosen and anointed by the Lord to replace Saul", was opposed to anyone "laying a hand on the anointed of the Lord". David however was "neither of Saul's family nor even of his tribe". He "knew him to be rejected by the Lord, knew himself to be personally chosen by God, and had not given any guarantee to Saul", whereas Louis the German had taken on formal obligations towards Charles the Bald, his own brother. David "did not attempt by war or trickery to take away Saul's kingdom from him"; even though surrounded "by flatterers and partisans, he did not let himself be drawn by anyone into this path"; he braved "the persecutions and risks of death to which he was exposed from Saul's side". And, becoming ever bolder under cover of biblical allusions, the bishops ventured to add: "You know very well, moreover, the treatment David prescribed for the person who, to obtain his favour, had boasted of having done violence to the anointed of the Lord"; but "in case anyone should be ignorant of it, let us recall that he ordered him to be put to death". Because "whoever lays a hand on an anointed of the Lord, does so to Christ himself, Lord of all the anointed or 'christs', and perishes under the blows of the spiritual sword". "We say this", the bishops added, "not through a desire to oppose to your domination arguments which could seem misplaced, but to emphasize more clearly, as our ministry requires it, the respect which we give your brother".

The prelates recalled, in conclusion, that ecclesiastics did not give themselves to anyone who wished to take them; they were not free to "bind themselves in vassalage and take oaths, as laymen do"; "consecrated to God", they belonged only to God. "When the time and the place seemed right, they would act as they thought fit to conform themselves to the just decisions of the Lord". King Louis should in no case count on them "to unleash, to start or to foster conflicts, revolts or wars, they to whom the Lord had given the task of preaching and maintaining peace", and to carry on only one battle: the "battle against the vices". The king should "take no notice of suggestions made to him by disloyal men and persons of low birth (*fellones atque ignobiles*)" and, "if he was a Christian king and ... desired to rule according to God", he should conform himself strictly to the bishops' advice, because, as successors of the Apostles, they had received from Christ the government of "the Church, that is to say of His Kingdom". These proud declarations tended to make the Church the arbiter of the situation and the clergy the interpretor of the divine will and the real dispenser of royal power.

When one measures the distance traversed since the assemblies of Coulaines, Yütz and Meerssen it becomes evident that the Church was indeed not only the indispensable guide, whose task was, among other things, to watch over kings and to guide them in the way of salvation; it was she who, in the name of the Lord, made kings by pouring holy oil on their foreheads, thanks to which their authority ceased being at the mercy of human caprice and depended only on God. But to whom should the task fall of deciding, in case of dispute, whether a king remained qualified or not to exercise power? In the letter cited above which he wrote in the name of the bishops of his province and that of Rouen, Hincmar carefully avoided the problem; but in his eyes, the answer was clear: only the bishops who had anointed the king according to the divine will, were able, by this same will, to decide if there was sufficient reason for holding a king to be abandoned by God. And what Hincmar, in November 858, contented himself with implying, without saying it in so many words, Charles the Bald in person accepted and declared explicitly several months later in June 859 when he wrote, and had written in his name, that having been anointed in the church of Sainte-Croix at Orléans in 848 in due form, "he ought not to be supplanted or forced to abdicate the throne, without at least having been heard and judged by the bishops, by whose agency he had been anointed ... and by whose mediation God gave His judgments". Thus a theory of monarchy was arrived at which was far removed from what Charlemagne had professed; it was one that placed the monarchy in the Church's power.

The re-establishment of unity by the Church

The first result of the Gallic episcopate's resistance was to weaken the position of the invader and leave Charles the Bald time to recoup and muster a new army. Taking advantage of the fact that his brother, who had gone to Saint-Quentin to celebrate Christmas, had taken with him only a small part of his army, Charles attacked him by surprise on 15 January 859 and obliged him to withdraw hastily towards the east.

The reversal was as complete as it was sudden. Among those who had formerly rallied to the king of Germany, it was now a question of who was to display the most eagerness towards the legitimate king who, in his turn, proceeded to grant abbacies and counties to reward the zeal of his partisans. At the beginning of February Lothar II, whose kingdom had just been traversed again by the crestfallen Louis the German in order to get back to his own kingdom, hastily came to make honourable amends. The bishops remained the pivot of the situation. Collected in provincial synods, they were consulted by the king, who depended on them for support, and day by day the stature of the archbishop of Reims, Hincmar, increased: he was the heart and soul of the resistance to the invader.

In 859 he was fifty years old. Educated at the monastery of Saint-Denis under Abbot Hilduin, he had received a thorough theological training founded on exceptionally extensive reading which he, better than anyone else, knew how to make effective. Like most of his contemporaries he had learned the art of insinuating his ideas under cover of his references, which he multiplied to the point at times of overwhelming the reader; but, in contrast to his many emulators, whose writings are often no more than packages of quotations presented without skill, he knew how to introduce his citations with an incomparable mastery and to link them with such logic that he led those to whom he addressed himself relentlessly toward to the conclusion he had in view. His letter of November 858 to Louis the German in the name of the bishops of the two provinces of Reims and Rouen was but one example among many of the closeness of his reasoning and the originality of his thought which had no need to conceal itself behind quotations to make a better impression.

Taken to the court in 822 by his teacher Hilduin when Hilduin had been appointed arch-chaplain, he had followed Hilduin into disgrace in 830, but was soon recalled to the palace. He won the confidence of Louis the Pious, and then of Charles the Bald, to such a degree that he was chosen in 845, with the consent of Charles, as archbishop of Reims after Ebbo's dismissal. The experience of affairs he had acquired at court, the very circumstances in which he had been called to the archbishopric of Reims, and the way he tided over the difficulties there honourably, while Ebbo and his partisans continued to agitate desperately, finally and above all his temperament, which was that of a man of action rather than a contemplative – all this marked him out for a role of the first importance in the conflicts of the period. Passionate, with a clear and decisive mind, ever ready for battle, always prepared to draw from his armoury of knowledge the weapons necessary for the struggle, he was to be, during a quarter of a century, the thinking conscience of the Church of the Gauls, and if the ideal of a Christianity of the West unified against barbarianism survived somewhat longer and often succeeded in conquering the egoism of the kings, it was to a very large extent the archbishop of Reims who was responsible.

It was he, in any case, who at the beginning of the year 859 was the undisputed inspirer of the policy adopted by the prelates in order to effect the general reconciliation of the West. It is hardly possible to doubt that it was he who, at the first meeting of the bishops in a council at Metz, on 28 May, wrote down the record of the most urgent decisions that had to be made. The assembly, which was composed of numerous prelates belonging to the two kingdoms of Charles the Bald and Lothar, each of whom was consulted before the meeting and perhaps was present, concerned itself with the recent struggle between Louis the German and his brother, the king of France. It deplored the excesses of which on that occasion, the Church and Charles' kingdom had been the victims, and, resolved to protect Christendom against a return of such pernicious risks, decided to send to the king of Germany a delegation composed of the archbishops of Reims, Rouen, and Cologne, and six bishops: those of Coutances, Laon, Meaux, Auxerre, Châlons-sur-Marne and Metz. These delegates were to have full power to give Louis the German absolution on the following conditions: (1) He must recognize and admit the injuries which, at the instigation of evil counsellors, he had caused the churches to suffer. (2) He must promise to do penance and to make amends for the wrongs he had committed. (3) He must promise to conclude peace with his brother Charles and to live henceforth in good relations with Lothar, so long as they did likewise. (4) He must give surety "never again to renew such a schism in the holy Church and Christendom". (5) He must withdraw "his protection and his favours from the wicked men who had driven him to offend God so seriously", and, as he had pledged at Meerssen, he must make them appear at the next plea held by his brother Charles or his nephew Lothar, so that they might suffer, if there was occasion for it, the punishment they deserved. (6) Finally, he must grant his support to the Church, whose unity was unaffected by the partition into kingdoms, so that "in view of the dangers of the moment, she would be restored, the clergy would enjoy the privileges and the authority to which it had the right, and the people would live in justice and peace". On these conditions, and these conditions only, the delegates were authorized to give Louis the German absolution; they were charged, furthermore, to warn him that any relapse would expose him to the chastisement of God and of the Church.

Obviously, in the eyes of the prelates who espoused the cause of peace, the essential reproach expressed against Louis the German was to have destroyed the Christian order. Above all his sin was to have brought divisiveness and trouble into that 'one Church' which represented, in the confusion of the epoch and among the diversity of the kingdoms, the only permanent reality. And no one was surprised, it seems, by this transference of political facts onto a religious plane: a revealing sign of the evolution taking place in the minds of men, which tended, with the tacit or explicit consent of the kings themselves, to allow control of the former Carolingian Empire to pass from the princes to the clerics.

The conversation begun several days later – on 4 June – at Worms, between the delegates of the bishops and Louis the German, was, in this respect, particularly significant. We have the good fortune to possess a detailed account of it which may be accepted as more or less accurate. Louis began by asking Hincmar, who led the delegation, whether he, as well as those who accompanied him, were free of all personal resentment regarding him. Once assured on this point, he listened to the written instructions which they carried but declared that before answering them, he must consult his own bishops, of which he had but "two or three" with him. When the episcopal representatives pressed him to begin the conversation on the points laid down in their instructions, he replied once more "from the height of his throne" that he could not "enter into discussions about this letter before he had examined it with his bishops". No doubt this was a delaying tactic, but it was also a very clear recognition that the matter was, above all, within the competence of the Church.

The evolution we have just pointed out asserted itself even more conspicuously ten days later, on 14 June, at a second episcopal synod held at Savonnières, not far from Toul, with the participation of four archbishops, and twenty-three bishops from Charles the Bald's kingdom, three archbishops and seven bishops from Lothar's kingdom, on whose territory the new assembly took place, and of one archbishop and four bishops from the kingdom of Charles of Provence, and with three abbots, two of whom were from Charles the Bald's kingdom, in all forty-five prelates. At these deliberations the rulers of the three kingdoms mentioned were personally present. These forty-five prelates, as they themselves emphasized in the record of their meeting, belonged to twelve of the eighteen ecclesiastical provinces of ancient Gaul: a number that gave weight to their decisions. The goal they set themselves was to re-establish the fraternal concord between the kings Louis and Charles and thus to make an end to the 'schism' that rent the Church and divided 'the Christian people'. To the crumbling of the royal power they wished once more to oppose "the unity of the Church" (Art. 1). And from the second Article onwards they did not hesitate to specify their programme in these terms: "The bishops, as their ministry and the sacred authority with which they are invested require, should unite to guide and correct the kings, as well as the magnates of the various kingdoms and the people entrusted to them, by giving them the benefit of their advice". To achieve this, they should show themselves assiduous at synods, as the canons require, so that their decisions compel recognition from the kings, as had been the case in the past. Such at least was the proposition of the prelates who, after the conspicuous failure of the policy of direct *entente* and of conferences between the kings, now decided to take the guidance of the Christian world and the kings themselves personally in hand: a notion dear to Hincmar, whose role remained preponderant: he was to develop it until his death.

Louis the German presented a difficulty, however, for he was neither present nor represented at Savonnières. But the assembly pointed out with evident satisfaction (Art. 3) that, in any case, Charles the Bald and his two nephews Lothar and Charles of Provence had resolved to remain united and to cooperate in the task, taken up by the Church, of promoting the common welfare.

The reconciliation of Louis the German and his brother was the most important condition; but the failure of the negotiation of Worms had made that difficult. Lothar II, interested for the sake of his own safety in the re-establishment of peace between his two neighbours, seems to have made a great effort to end their hostility. A first meeting between them at Andernach, downstream of Koblenz, on an island in the Rhine, at the beginning of the summer of 859, was also a failure. The two kings distrusted each other to such an extent that they had themselves accompanied onto the island chosen for the conference by a strictly equal number of magnates on either side. The list of their names had been agreed to beforehand, and the main body of each of the two escorts remaining in surveillance on the river bank, ready to intervene, one on the left bank, in Lothar's kingdom, the other on the right bank, in the kingdom of Germany. After a long and fruitless discussion, bearing particularly on the restitution claimed by Louis of the properties seized by Charles the Bald from those who had betrayed him in 858, it became necessary to arrange a new meeting for 25 October near Basel, that is to say once more on the frontier of Germany and Lothar's kingdom. But Lothar was unable to be present on the date set, and one postponement led to another, so that it was only on 1 June 860 that a conference between the two hostile brothers could conveniently be held in Koblenz, in the presence of and with the assistance of their nephew Lothar. The three kings appeared there accompanied by a numerous following comprising mainly powerful laymen and particularly counts; but it was in the sacristy of a church, the church of St Castor, and manifestly under the influence of the prelates who were at their side – most important of whom was the aforementioned Hincmar – that the kings drew up, after five days of laborious discussion, an agreement which would, it was thought, end the era of their dissensions. On 5 June the kings were finally able to communicate this agreement to their subjects. Speaking for himself and for his brother, Charles the Bald recalled the efforts made by Lothar, under pressure from the bishops, to restore peace and re-establish between him and his brother "that charity and brotherly concord without which no Christian can achieve salvation". The original proposals of the king of Germany, he added, had not been acceptable, but the most recent ones had appeared possible: therefore Charles asked for their ratification of the text of the agreement which was about to be read to them.

This text, which has come down to us, comprises twelve articles, eight of which were literally copied from the pact concluded at Meerssen in 851. Of the four new articles, two aimed at giving the Church the required sureties; the two others constituted a compromise between the requests of Louis the German demanding the annulment of all the sanctions of a political or religious nature taken against those who had gone over to his side in 858, and the rigid maintenance of these sanctions desired by Charles the Bald: large measures of clemency were promised after an examination of each individual case. In other words, as far as possible, the events of the last few years were wiped out, so as to return to the rule of concord proclaimed in 851. What was new was that the power of mediation was transferred permanently from the kings to the bishops, who would thenceforth assist the kings in the exercise of their authority.

The subjects' approval of this agreement allowed the kings to proclaim the entente officially on 7 June. They took an oath to exert themselves with their whole will, and their whole energy, "for the protection of the Church and the welfare of the Christian people", and also to aid each other in the accomplishment of the common task. Louis and Charles' nephews were explicitly included in this promise of mutual aid. The assembly concluded with the solemn declarations of Louis and Charles concerning this aid, the first expressing himself in the German language, the second in the 'romance' language (that is to say in French), with a resumé in the German language, and with a declaration of adherence by Lothar in the German language. The declarations of Louis and Charles, identical in content, declare first that, having entrusted responsibility for the task of finding a basis for an agreement to "their bishops and their other subjects", they had approved the text which they–that is to say, primarily, the bishops–had submitted to them; in consequence, they were all resolved, brothers, uncles and nephews, to live henceforth in complete harmony; "they desired from now on to use among themselves only words that would please God and serve their common well-being as well as their honour"; those of them who infringed this rule were to be summoned "to explain themselves and to be punished in such a manner that no one else would be tempted to do anything like it"; they were resolved to guarantee to each "in their respective kingdoms, his law, his right and his safety, as in the time of their predecessors," on condition of reciprocity; finally, they forbade themselves to receive any disturber of the peace until he had been cleared of all blame, and to commit any acts of violence or pillage within any of the kingdoms.

To this declaration, Charles, expressing himself in the 'romance' language and "raising his voice" in order to be clearly heard by all, quickly added a comment: "for the love of God, he pardoned those who had betrayed him and gone over to his brother"; he declared himself ready to restore to them "their allodia (or freeholds) and the properties which they had received from their lords" on the two following conditions. (1) "That they pledged themselves to behave peacefully in his kingdom and to live there as Christians ought to live in a Christian country". (2) That his brother treat likewise those who had refused to desert in his favour. He even agreed to examine with indulgence the possibility of restoring to those of his subjects who "returned voluntarily to him" the properties and 'honours' they had held from him and which their betrayal had caused them to lose. Then he exhorted everyone to go home in peace.

The negotiations, the record, and the royal declarations, all indicate in what spirit and under what influence agreement had finally become attainable. It was the kings who spoke, but their very words reflected the thought of those who inspired them, the bishops, at whose head stood Hincmar. They had resolved to make up for the kings' lack of co-operation. At that time there was no longer any question of the Empire, but only of multiple kingdoms among which the prelates sought to maintain a close co-operation by recalling that they represented the parts, no longer of one and the same 'Frankish kingdom', but of one indivisible Church. Henceforth it was she and she alone who, in the name of religion and of the ideal of peace of which she was the guardian, sought to end the discord. The only community spoken of was the religious one; but it was this, in the long run, which made possible the preservation of the political community, whose potential survived, despite everything, among the scattered members of the 'Christian people' who had been but lately ruled by the emperor.

CHAPTER FOUR

The pope's opportunity: Nicholas I

The official declarations which the Church had dictated to the Carolingian kings at Koblenz in 860 could not conceal the veiled rivalries that
persisted among them and which risked plunging Christendom ultimately into the depths of anarchy. Doubtless, the principle of unity had
again been preserved; but could respect for this principle be imposed
for very long on princes whose only ambition was to extend their
power at the expense of their neighbours? On the lookout for any
opportunity that might offer itself to them of satisfying their lust for
power, without the least regard for the rights of their rivals nor for the
common well-being which was constantly mentioned, those rulers who
were the most disinterested in their words were in practice often the
most unscrupulous.

A spectacular affair, that of Lothar II's divorce, was to make
possible an accurate evaluation of the real sentiments of the principal
actors in the complicated game that was then being played, and at the
same time to present the supreme ruler of the Church with a unique
opportunity to pose as arbiter of the situation.

Lothar II's divorce

Married in 855, shortly after his accession, to a young lady of the
region of the Valais, Theutberga, sister of the abbot of Saint-Maurice,
Hubert, Lothar had not yet had children by her, while another woman,
Waldrada, his mistress, had already borne him at least one son. If as he
hoped, he succeeded in having his marriage, which had remained

childless, annulled by the Church, and his union with Waldrada consecrated as legitimate, he could ensure the continuance of his throne, which was threatened with being left heirless. He concentrated his efforts toward this double object, which was attainable only if the canonical nullity of his union with Theutberga was recognized.

By 857 his strategy was ready. The process began with incriminating confessions from Theutberga, who admitted having been violated before her marriage by her brother Abbot Hubert, whose reputation was such that the story did not seem improbable. She also admitted that she had afterwards enjoyed unnatural relations with him. Unworthy of sharing the bed of her husband, she asked to be allowed to withdraw to a monastery to do penance there. Lothar, for his part, claimed to have known nothing up to then about the scandal which was now of public notoriety, and consequently requested the annulment of his marriage, which he claimed had been vitiated from the start by a mistaken impression concerning Theutberga.

Announced by Lothar II in January 860 to a small group of his bishops gathered at the palace of Aachen under the presidency of his arch-chaplain Gunther, archbishop of Cologne, this strategy produced the desired effect: the obliging prelates recognized the substance of the alleged facts, thus allowing the proceedings to be continued. A month later, in the same place, a second episcopal synod, composed to give the illusion of impartiality and universality, was called upon to examine Theutberga's case. Three prelates from Lothar's kingdom sat in it, two from Charles the Bald's kingdom (the archbishop of Rouen and the bishop of Meaux), one from the kingdom of Charles of Provence (the bishop of Avignon): a scanty delegation which made it difficult to claim, what they hoped would be believed, namely that it represented all the Carolingian lands. This synod, nevertheless, did not hesitate to pronounce judgement on the so-called request of Theutberga who was, according to her apparent wish, admitted to the benefits of perpetual penance in a monastery.

The reaction of public opinion to the news of this sentence was not immediate. The talks of Koblenz, on which so many hopes rested, had not yet taken place, and perhaps it was feared that too precipitate an action would jeopardize their results. But in June, as soon as the agreement was concluded between Charles the Bald and Louis the German, thanks to the good offices of their nephew Lothar, the archbishop of Reims, Hincmar, who, notwithstanding the urgent entreaties made to him had refused to participate in the synod of Aachen, finally broke his silence and issued a long statement on the subject of the divorce. With a juridical rigour, but also with a harshness of tone that betrayed his passion in every line, the writer delivered a formal attack on the procedure which had been followed; on the sincerity of the confessions received; and on the conclusions which the participants had ventured to draw from them. He demanded the meeting of a new synod, truly representative of all Carolingian Europe, before which the case could be re-examined from beginning to end.

Politics were not alien to the intransigent attitude adopted by Hincmar. This is hard to doubt when one learns that, within a short space of time, Abbot Hubert and then his sister Queen Theutberga, fleeing from Lothar's kingdom, had found asylum without difficulty in that of Charles the Bald, to whom Hincmar remained fully loyal. How can one avoid thinking that, by impeding the divorce, the archbishop of Reims intended to work for his master, who was obviously interested in leaving open for Lothar the perspective of an inheritance without heirs? Lothar, in his turn, was not deceived, and as soon as Hubert's flight was known, turned to his other uncle, Louis the German, to whom he offered the future possession of Alsace in exchange for his support. The Carolingians thus found themselves once more divided into two hostile groups, just as before the accord of Koblenz, with the difference only that Lothar had passed from the side of the French king to that of the German king.

The antagonism of the two parties sharpened in 861, Charles the Bald openly violating the pact of Koblenz by receiving in his territory subjects of Louis the German and of Lothar who were on the loose. Some of these were distinguished men: Count Ernest (father-in-law of Carloman, the son of Lothar), and his three nephews, Abbot Waldo, Count Uto and Count Berengar, all in revolt against Louis; and Count Adalard, in revolt against Lothar. All were welcomed and given 'honours' and 'benefices' by the king of France, who soon shamelessly took the offensive by attacking, in the autumn of 861, the so-called kingdom of Provence. This had been given in 855 to the youngest of Lothar I's three sons, and Hincmar, who had shortly before been the eloquent defender of concord and sworn faith, claimed that its magnates had revolted and wished to be delivered at last from a prince "unsuitable for the royal dignity and for the very title of king". This was an unblushing violation of all previous agreements and, on top of that, an undisguised act of hostility toward Lothar II, who had for a long time been a self-confessed candidate for an inheritance which everyone in the West held to be virtually open.

No one was ignorant of the fact that the youngest son of Lothar I, Charles, was in so precarious a state of health that his two brothers and especially Lothar II, expected his death at any moment. Since 858, Lothar II had clarified his attitude by conceding to the young king a rectification of the frontier (he had made over to him the dioceses of Belley and Tarentaise) against the promise of receiving his whole inheritance in the event, which seemed infinitely probable considering his weakness and youth, of his death without leaving a legitimate son. Soon afterwards, Lothar also bought out his other brother Louis II, by the cession of several other territories (the dioceses of Geneva, Lausanne and Sion) taken from his own kingdom. The surprise attack on Provence by Charles the Bald was thus a direct attack against Lothar himself.

However, the attempt failed, and afterwards Hincmar even went so far as to assert that his lord had never had the least intention of conquest. But the alarm had been great and it hardly seemed possible any longer to hope that an entente could be established which might facilitate Lothar's success in his matrimonial projects. He was now obliged to try to force the decision without the agreement of the clergy of 'France'. A last rapprochement which he attempted with Charles the Bald in his own name and in that of Louis the German around the end of 861 having proved abortive, he resolved to have the case of Theutberga settled by the clergy of his kingdom alone.

Eight 'Lotharingian' bishops assembled at Aachen on 29 April 862 were thus called on to make a clear and final decision. To the documentation of the case had been added a justificatory memorandum in which the king did not hesitate to use the dynastic argument: Theutberga was not only an unworthy wife, whom nonetheless he might have kept in the interests of peace; by her barrenness she endangered the future of the kingdom. With a majority of six votes against two, the episcopal synod, recognizing once again the veracity of the accusations brought against the queen and reflecting moreover that "one could not forbid the king to take a wife in order to beget sons", declared itself in favour of the annulment of the marriage and granted Lothar permission to contract a new one at his pleasure. Desirous above all of keeping up appearances, Lothar, after this decision, made a double advance to the Sovereign Pontiff: one to solicit his approval, the other to beg him, in his own name as much as in that of his uncle Louis the German, to remind Charles the Bald to respect the pact of Koblenz. Then, without even waiting for the answer, the sense of which was not in doubt, he married his mistress in the summer or the beginning of the autumn of 862 and had her crowned with great pomp.

This was audacious, but to carry this solution through he needed to count at least on the firm support of the king of Germany. Now, although Louis shared with his nephew a common hostility to the king of France, he had no reason whatever to raise the mortgage that encumbered an inheritance on which he himself – the future was to prove it – might well have designs. He lacked, moreover, the necessary means for the pursuit of a policy which implied serious risks for him at a moment when his power was much shaken by a series of revolts which he had difficulty in suppressing, in particular the rebellion – of which we have already spoken – of Count Ernest and his accomplices in the spring of 861, and that of his son Carloman, whose resistance he had been able to break in the spring of 862 only at the price of ceding some of the territories occupied by the rebel between the Inn and the march of Carinthia. It could be expected that this ungrateful son would take up arms again before long. At the same time, on the eastern and northern frontiers of his kingdom, Louis the German was obliged to devote himself unceasingly to keeping in check as well as he could the pagan Slavs, the Danes, and the barbarians newly arrived on the border of his kingdom, namely the Hungarians, whose raids into Germanic lands began precisely in 862. In these circumstances, even if he had wanted to do so, he was not in a position to involve himself deeply in favour of his nephew Lothar.

However, it was to his advantage not to leave the field open to his brother, whose unsuccessful attempt on Provence was sufficient indication of his ambition. So "in veiled terms", Hincmar declared, Louis succeeded in convincing Charles the Bald of the necessity of a meeting, which by common consent took place at the beginning of November in Lothar's kingdom, at Savonnières, near Toul, where already in June 859 one of the great episcopal assemblies had taken place which had prepared the way for the agreement of Koblenz. Its aim was to establish the basis of a compromise that would permit the restoration of peace.

This time once more the negotiations, which were laborious, were entirely conducted by the bishops, and the role played among them by Hincmar seems to have been preponderant. Before agreeing to meet Lothar, Charles the Bald and his bishops, Hincmar above all, stated their conditions, which they had taken care to formulate in writing in a memorandum whose author, there is every reason to believe, was the archbishop of Reims. Charles the Bald, in whose name the statement was presented, implied, not without audacity, that he himself had always loyally observed the obligations accepted at Koblenz, and he called the world to witness the broken promise of his nephew Lothar. It had not been his responsibility to organize the regular talks provided for at Koblenz to settle matters of common interest, and it was because he was always prepared to co-operate that he had not hesitated to come to the present meeting.

Continuing to reverse the roles and wilfully forgetful of his own conduct, Charles the Bald in his turn accused his nephew of having violated the pact of Koblenz by giving asylum to Count Baldwin, the ravisher of his daughter Judith, who was known to be guilty and who had been excommunicated by the bishops of 'France'; he reproached him above all for having disregarded the advice of the bishops concerning his marriage and left that of the Sovereign Pontiff out of consideration. Consequently, while soliciting with suspect haste the co-operation of Louis the German—"whom he called his only and dearest brother"—in order to arrange a settlement upon which was to depend "their common well-being, the well-being and honour of their nephew and the safety of all their subjects", he required from Lothar, before any renewal of the conversations, the categorical promise of an unconditional submission to the united judgment of the bishops of France, Lorraine and Germany. For was it not in the first place a "matter affecting the whole of Christendom" and therefore surpassing the competence of the clergy of a single kingdom? Lacking which, Charles concluded, Lothar "might do what he liked", but do not count on me, he said, to "separate myself from God in exchange for your friendship, nor to assist whoever it may be to do evil, for it is written: 'If you aid the impious and bind yourself in friendship with those who hate Me, you expose yourself to the wrath of the Lord'."

In order to break the deadlock, Lothar declared that he was ready to explain and justify himself, and when the conversations were resumed they agreed not to refer the question of the divorce any longer to a council but to the pope himself. In consideration of this the entente between the three kings was officially re-established on 3 November 862, and each of them had a declaration drawn up for this occasion, Louis to congratulate himself for having served as 'mediator' between his brother and nephew, and thus restored the spirit of Meerssen and Koblenz; Charles to protest anew his constant faithfulness to the previous obligations and his firm intention to maintain with Lothar relations of friendship normal between uncle and nephew, provided that Lothar would really be amenable to this, as he had promised to be; Lothar, finally, to give thanks for the efficacious "goodness of heart" of his uncle Louis and to promise to conduct himself as a good nephew toward Charles in so far as Charles behaved as a good uncle towards him.

While everything was thus re-established as it had been, nevertheless the pact was encompassed with numerous reservations, and an incident occurred when the brothers separated which was very significant of this situation. As they were about to proceed, according to custom, to the public reading of the three above-mentioned royal declarations, after having made them known only to the two hundred counsellors filling the conference hall, Louis and Lothar opposed their further publication in order to avoid exposing in public the griefs and conflicts of a short time before; but, disregarding this, Charles (perhaps at the instigation of Hincmar) informed the assembled people of all the points on which Lothar had been compelled to yield to him. In doing this he destroyed the calming effect of the agreement which had been brought about with so much difficulty.

The verdict of Pope Nicholas I

Among the events we have just reviewed, one fact stands out clearly: it was now on the Church and the Church alone that the solution of the question of Lothar's divorce, which had gradually become the key to the politics of the West as a whole, depended. However, by agreeing to refer the matter to the Sovereign Pontiff no one, either on the side of the kings or on the side of the bishops, seems to have reflected on the incalculable consequences which this simple transfer of jurisdiction might entail for the future of Carolingian Europe. Having become the

arbitrator of the situation, would not the pope be tempted to take over, in
the political sphere, the place left vacant in the West by the absence of
an emperor? Clearly everything depended on his personality, and it soon
became evident that the new pope was not the man to neglect an
opportunity offered him for the assertion of his authority.

This pope, Nicholas I, who would indeed prove to be one of the
great popes of this period, had at first, curiously enough, passed for a
rather withdrawn priest. All we know is that his election had taken place
in 858 on the request of Louis II, or rather that it had been imposed on
the Roman clergy by Louis, who was counting on the new pope's
docility. Obliged to deal with the man Hincmar described disdainfully
as "the so-called emperor of Italy", he was believed prepared to agree
to all sorts of compromises – but it emerged that he was not only
difficult to manage but unyielding in essentials.

Nicholas I began by deciding on 23 November 862 that the question
of the divorce should once more be submitted to the scrutiny of a
council that was to be held at Metz, but in which the prelates of
Lothar's kingdom were to be assisted by eight other bishops, two of
whom were to be from the kingdom of Germany, two from that of
France, two from Provence, and two from Italy, the presidency going
by right to these last, in their capacity as papal legates. A complete
record of the proceedings and the verdict were to be sent to the pope
for approval or revision before the sentence could be considered final.
His legates, moreover, had been given precise instructions, to which
they were obliged to adhere.

Various events, one of the most important of which was the death of
Charles of Provence on 24 January 863 and the settlement of his
inheritance, delayed the meeting of the council until June 863. Lothar
took advantage of this delay to exert diplomatic pressure and weave
intrigues. Among other things, he contrived to have the letters and
instructions which the papal legates carried intercepted before they
could communicate them to those concerned, so that on the day fixed
only the bishops of Lothar's kingdom turned up. Thus the synod of
June 863 was once again composed solely of Lothar's creatures, while
the two legates, having been more or less bought over to his side, were
careful not to implement any of their instructions. Under these
conditions, the assembled prelates readily agreed to justify Lothar, to
approve his conduct, and to condemn Theutberga. They even went so
far as to admit the paradoxical thesis which Lothar had shortly before

taken into his head to present, according to which Waldrada had been his legitimate wife previous to his union with Theutberga, who, by the same token, could no longer claim any other title than that of concubine – a concubine whose reputation was shamelessly dragged through the mire.

This was a clever conjuring trick, but its only result was to set the pope against all those kings and bishops who had so audaciously made play with him. Gunther the archbishop of Cologne, and Theutgald, archbishop of Trier, who had managed it all, were summoned to Rome in person to present the pope with the conclusions arrived at by the synod. They were received there as they deserved. After having acquainted himself with the documents which the two archbishops carried, and having submitted the case to a synod meeting in the Lateran Palace, Nicholas, towards the end of October, annulled the verdict pronounced at Metz by the accomplices of this new 'brigandage of Ephesus', pronounced the deposition of Gunther and Teutgald, forbade them to exercise the priestly ministry, summoned the other bishops who had been in Metz, under pain of the same sanctions, to perform an act of contrition immediately, and finally without more ado stigmatized the "crime of King Lothar" if, the papal bull added, "it is possible really to call him king". A special letter addressed by the Sovereign Pontiff to this unworthy king stressed his feelings of sorrowful reprobation towards a prince who, "giving loose rein to his passions", wallowed – as the Psalmist says (39.3) – "in the grave of misery and the gutter of filth, taking with him into ruin the people whom he had been charged to govern".

The two deposed archbishops tried, it is true, to resist the pope. At the beginning of 864 they even incited the Emperor Louis II to attempt a coup in their favour. Threatened in his capital, Nicholas I faced this violence with an incomparable steadfastness of soul. Withdrawing into St Peter's, he remained there for two days and two nights to implore divine mercy, until Louis II yielded to his inflexible will. Gunther and Teutgald replied to the measures taken against them with a vehement letter of protest addressed to the pope, whom they in their turn did not scruple with incredible insolence to rake over the coals. Hurling back against the supreme head of the Church the accusation he had directed at the Fathers of the synod of Metz, they, also, labeled as "brigandage" the impudent partiality with which, according to them, the pope had examined their conduct, "all doors closed, before a motley crowd in which laymen mingled with priests". They reproached him vehemently for having judged and condemned them "without regard for the canonical procedure, without any accuser presenting himself, without calling witnesses, without discussion, without defense, without the slightest confession on their part, in the absence of the other metropolitans and their suffragans, in the absence of their brother bishops, without anyone's consent, by an act of pure arbitrariness and tyrannical fury". And, hesitating no longer to place themselves in a state of overt rebellion against the person whom, at the beginning of their letter, they had affected to treat with the respect due to his high dignity and his sacred character, they concluded with these defiant words:

Your accursed sentence, which lacks all paternal kindness and which is alien to every feeling of brotherly charity, this sentence which you have directed against us in violation of all justice, all reason and all canon law, we refuse to accept; and considering it as invalid, we, together with all our brothers, scorn it and reject it. As for you, who remain in communion with the condemned and the excommunicated, with all those who reject the holy faith, and who reserve your favours for them, we refuse to receive you in our communion. It suffices us to know ourselves to be in communion with, and in the brotherly society of, the whole Church, that Church which you in your arrogant vanity disdain, and of which you make yourself unworthy by your insane pride. In your rash flightiness you are yourself struck by anathema when you write, 'Whoever does not observe the apostolic precepts will be anathematized,' because you yourself do not cease violating these precepts, as well as the divine laws and the sacred canons . . . . And we, who have now experienced your deceit and your craftiness, far from feeling ourselves humiliated by you, protest with a pious zeal against your iniquity.

Finally, so that no one might be ignorant of it, these two rebel archbishops aggravated their situation by sending a copy of their statement to their episcopal colleagues in Lothar's kingdom, having it preceded by a letter of advice in which the Sovereign Pontiff was called "the lord Nicholas who is called pope, who pretends to be an apostle among the apostles and who poses as emperor of the world". They did not hesitate to speak of his "insanity" (*insania*). This violent language, this barrage of insults, was of no avail. Not only did Nicholas I not deviate from the line of conduct he had decided on, but the bishops of Lothar's kingdom and even Lothar himself made their submission in letters full of justifications, all vying with one another in apologizing for having allowed themselves to be implicated. The archbishop of Trier very quickly decided to accept the sentence of deposition that had been pronounced against him. Only Gunther persisted in his rebellion, although abandoned by Lothar, who provided for a successor to him in the see of Cologne.

Thus Nicholas I's steadfastness had overcome every obstacle, and he now felt himself sufficiently strong to convoke a general council at Rome for 1 November 864, to settle under his presidency all the undecided questions in the West as well as in the East, including, evidently, that of Lothar's divorce.

The pope as arbiter of the West

The Carolingian monarchs were disturbed at the news of this summons. They saw in the proposed council a threat to their political independence and, as if upon command, no bishop of Gaul or Germany presented himself on 1 November at Rome. But Nicholas did not allow himself to be discouraged; he postponed the opening date of the council to 19 May 865 and sent out new summonses. Still troubled, Louis the German and Charles, realizing the need to bring their policies into agreement before a final settlement was made, met each other for this purpose in the middle of February at Tusey, on the Meuse in Lothar's kingdom. The record of their meeting begins with a declaration of impartiality; the two kings, who did not have easy consciences, thought they should specify that the motive of their meeting was neither "the desire to deceive or condemn anyone, nor any sort of undue greed". Their intentions were pure; a single will inspired them, that of working for the common good. Then, after promising each other anew the mutual aid which – they recalled it themselves – the pact of Koblenz had made a strict obligation for them, they reached the matter in question, namely the case of their nephew Lothar. Lothar, they observed, "subject to the passions of youth" and too ready to listen to the "advice of the frivolous men" of his entourage, had by his conduct "thrown the Church into confusion, led the priests into dishonour, and communicated to the Christian people the contagion of his disease". Also, considering that "the Church which had been entrusted to them – to him as well as to them – formed one undivided kingdom" and that the various peoples they governed likewise formed one undivided kingdom, that of "Christianity", they had decided to give their nephew "frank and sincere advice" which, moreover, he had requested from them. The official record says no more; but Hincmar, who must have been present at the discussion, asserts that Lothar was explicitly called on by his two uncles to stop the scandal created by the question of his divorce, that is to say, to send away Waldrada and recall Theutberga.

Not for a moment was Lothar deceived about the real motive for the "advice" which was lavished on him. He saw in it manifest proof that his uncles, whose protestations of impartiality could deceive only naive men, were agreed like robbers at the fair to a partition of his kingdom, which his continued marriage to Theutberga would sooner or later cause to be without heirs. Perhaps they were even planning to seize it before then. Confronted with this threat, Lothar hesitated no longer: better to call on the conscience of the Sovereign Pontiff than to let himself be despoiled in this way by his uncles. He at once begged his brother Louis II to make an overture to Nicholas I in his favour. Thus the pope's hopes were fulfilled: Lothar himself was obliged to acknowledge his supreme authority.

The attitude of Louis the German and Charles the Bald was less clear. At Tusey they had not dared to exclude the possibility of a personal overture of Lothar to the Sovereign Pontiff, but on the explicit condition that, before this could take place, the question of the divorce would be considered as settled, and that there would be discussion at Rome only of "indulgence", that is to say, of religious reconciliation. Moreover they had agreed to refuse permission to their bishops to attend the general council convoked at Rome, as we have seen, for 19 May 865. They claimed that the time allowed was too short, the distance too great, the means of access too uncertain, and the moment ill-chosen because the increasing attacks of the Vikings made it necessary for everyone to remain at his post. This made the pope even more resolved to proceed with vigour. While declaring that he was not deceived by the reasons put forward to excuse the absence of the bishops at the council, he despatched to the kings as papal legate one of the most important figures of the curia, his *apocrisarius* and loyal counsellor the bishop of Orta, Arsenius, with the task of settling the undecided questions in his name.

Arsenius was instructed not to spare anyone's feelings, not even those of Hincmar, whose claims to rule the Church of the Gauls had finally exhausted the pope's patience. Had not the archbishop of Reims, in a simple synodal sentence, deprived of his see in 862 one of his suffragans, the bishop of Soissons, Rothad, and ordered his imprisonment in a monastery, without even waiting for the confirmation of the pope, to whom the condemned had appealed? Making a personal matter of it, Hincmar had for a long time obstinately refused, notwithstanding papal summonses, to let Rothad depart for Rome, from where, accompanied by Arsenius, he now returned, reinstated in his office by virtue of a papal sentence of January 865.

Arsenius brought with him a packet of letters in which the pope spoke in a clear and decisive manner to the kings as well as to the bishops, notifying them of his decisions in terms that left no room for reply. The legate went to each to deliver the letter intended for him: to Louis the German, whom he met at Frankfurt in June; to Lothar, who received him at Gondreville, near Toul, several days later; then to Charles the Bald in mid-July, at the palace of Attigny. The bishops received their messenger in the same places. Arsenius had been instructed to make known to all of them by his oral commentaries the imperative character of the papal statements. Lothar, in particular, was summoned to send Waldrada away and to take back Theutberga. Escorted from France to her husband by Arsenius himself in August, she was solemnly recognized anew as his legitimate wife in the presence of ten bishops and archbishops, the king's chaplain, and a numerous crowd that had come from the various kingdoms. Six counts and six lords offered themselves as surety under oath that she would thenceforth be treated with the respect due to a legitimate wife and queen, and Lothar was informed that any new lapse on his part would be followed by an immediate excommunication. Finally, for even greater surety, Arsenius had Waldrada turned over to him, and took her with him to Italy.

On this point the pope's will triumphed. It triumphed likewise in all the sectors of the political and religious life of Carolingian Europe in which Arsenius had received a mandate to intervene. Furthermore, the legate succeeded in re-establishing peaceful relations among all the Carolingian rulers. The matter of Theutberga having been settled according to their wishes, neither Charles the Bald nor Louis the German any longer had reason to keep their nephew in quarantine. As for Charles, he had consented to receive him at Attigny around August to renew with him the friendly relationship decided on at Koblenz. Charles the Louis thereafter met each other in Cologne to confirm their entente in the presence of the papal legate. The inheritance of

Provence had itself ceased to be the subject of contention. After the death of King Charles in January 863, Emperor Louis II, considering the treaty by which the deceased had recognized Lothar II as his heir to be invalid, had succeeded in stealing a march on Lothar by assuring himself of the loyalty of some of the magnates of Provence, and a transaction was finally arranged between the two rivals, in the form of a partition, that seems to have reserved Provence and the dioceses of Embrun, Gap, Grenoble, Moutiers and Belley to Louis II, and awarded the rest to Lothar. Thereafter relations between Louis II and his brother had remained so cordial that Lothar found, at every moment in the course of his contentions with the Holy See, that his most certain and efficacious support came from the king of Italy.

It must be added that at this moment, apparently, each of the kings faced such difficulties in his kingdom that none could concern himself with the general affairs of Carolingian Europe. In France the ravages of the Northmen had reached alarming proportions, and the need to look after the defense of the country, which had been put forward by the king in 864 and 865 to justify the abstention of his bishops from the councils at Rome, was unfortunately not a mere pretext. The Northmen were camped in the heart of the kingdom, on the outskirts of Paris, and carried their raids far into the country; they were no less enterprising in the Loire valley; and we know furthermore that the king was obliged to multiply his efforts to keep his subjects, including his own son Louis the Stammerer, obedient. The king of Germany also had to face revolts and betrayals by his sons and by several of his magnates. As for Lothar, the least we can say is that the events of the last years had been a rude test for his authority and prestige. The field was thus free for the papacy, which was the great victor of the moment, and which seemed to be in a position to dictate its will to the West.

CHAPTER FIVE

The notion of empire revived: Louis II

There was, however, a gloomy side to the picture. The "emperor of the world" which Nicholas I, according to the archbishops of Cologne and Trier, aimed to be, lacked the means to provide for his own safety. Even in Rome he had no protection against physical violence; the factions, who had not disarmed, could challenge his position at any moment. Even more than with the factions, he was obliged to reckon with danger from without, and above all with the Moslems, who continued to menace the capital of Christianity.

From the moment when, from Sicily, they had gained a foothold in the south of Italy, their advance there had been continuous. Taking advantage of the differences that set the small Lombard princes of Campania against one another, they had gradually shifted their first continental base from Bari up to the region of Benevento, and from there up to the Volturno; they had succeeded in capturing the fortresses which defended the upper course of this river; finally they had reached the valley of the Liri, whence they began to head for Latium.

Alone, the papacy was powerless to check them, and its material weakness was for long years to condemn it not only to moderate its political plans but to ensure for itself at any price, in the person of one of the Carolingian princes, the official defender which the safety of Christianity required. This is as much as saying that after having lived for a quarter of a century in the noble illusion of a fraternal concord of which the Church had been the living soul, the pope was forced to face harsh reality by the necessity of providing, by means of a temporal ruler, for the defense of the common patrimony of all the Christians of the West. Since the most pressing danger was the one that threatened the See of St Peter, it was in finding the prince best qualified for this task that the popes henceforth unceasingly exerted themselves.

Emperor Louis II and the defense of Italy

For Nicholas I there could be no doubt or hesitation. The obvious choice was Lothar II's eldest son, the same Louis II to whom the imperial title had been given and who had already been engaged for a number of years with the defense against the infidels in southern Italy.

Born around 822, he was then in the prime of life. 'king of the Lombards' since 844 and anointed emperor in 850, circumstances had made of him an essentially Italian ruler. From 850 to the day of his death in 875, he was not to leave Italy except on three occasions, and each time for a short period only: in 856 and 864, to confer with his brother Lothar II at Orbe, a few leagues from his northern frontier, and in 863 to go to Provence to receive the inheritance of his brother Charles. All the rest of his life he spent in Italy, where he resided by preference in the ancient capital of the Lombards, Pavia, when military necessities did not call him to the region of Benevento.

His position of Italian sovereign – of "emperor of Italy" as Hincmar said disdainfully – was nevertheless such that he frequently came into conflict with the papacy. Even though he visited Rome only rarely and briefly, he constantly exercised there, either in person or through his representatives, the prerogatives which he held by virtue of the Roman constitution of 824, so much so that from the time of Leo IV (847–855) complaints reached the Lateran of his interference in papal affairs, and the relations between the two powers sometimes even degenerated into violent clashes. On the death of Leo IV, in July 855, the Carolingian rigorously insisted on his right of supervision over the electoral operations which resulted in the designation of the new pope, Benedict III. The electors had neglected to request his consent beforehand, and he had demanded, before approving their choice, a repetition of the voting in the presence of two of his representatives. This in itself was the result of a compromise, for he had at first attempted to substitute for the elect a candidate of his own choice in the person of the son of Bishop Arsenius of Orta, the infamous Anastasius, whom, for good reason, Leo IV had anathematized.

Less than three years later – Benedict III having died in April 858 – Louis had come without delay to Rome to supervise the new election on the spot and in person, in order to ensure the success of his candidate who, this time, was none other than the deacon Nicholas, proclaimed pope under the name of Nicholas I. In these circumstances

Nicholas had at first been entirely on Louis' side. We see him the day after his consecration receiving Louis at his table, embracing him tenderly at the moment they were about to separate, even reserving for him the surprise, when the emperor was already upon his way back, of rejoining him at some distance from Rome, to share his meal and embrace him once more. We see him, too, carrying his kindness so far as to surround himself with several figures whose presence would be surprising if they had not been more or less imposed on him by his protector. Among them was this Anastasius, whom Louis II had thought of making pope in 855, and who because of his intelligence and exceptional culture, Nicholas had appointed his secretary. Among them, too, was Arsenius, bishop of Orta and father of Anastasius, whose adroit intervention in the affair of Lothar's divorce did not improve his evil reputation, and, finally, the bishop of Porto, Radoald, a notorious vacillator, who had let himself be bought by Lothar II in 863. When, somewhat later, Nicholas wished to rid himself of these men, some harsh conflicts resulted: for example, in 860 and 861, when Louis II supported the archbishop of Ravenna against the Holy See, and in 864, when, as we have seen, the emperor went so far as to use violence to try to influence the pope to yield before the two archbishops, Gunther and Theutgald, whom he had just deposed as a punishment for their scandalous conduct in the matter of the divorce.

In the affair of the archbishops, Nicholas had withstood the storm with dignity. But notwithstanding his energy and the lofty idea he had of his own authority, he could not allow himself to break with a prince so necessary to the defense of Italy. After all, since his accession, the courage and military talents of Louis had been unstintingly applied against the infidels, from whom at any moment a fatal attack could be expected. In 847 he had stopped them short a first time near Benevento. In 852, after having attempted unsuccessfully to seize Bari from them, he had again put them to flight close to Benevento. In 860, when he was in northern Italy, the infidels, returning to the attack, had imposed a tribute on the duke of Benevento, threatened Naples, and perhaps attempted a march in the direction of Latium, so that it became necessary to take measures against them by mobilizing the whole of Italy, from the Po plain down to the regions directly threatened. It was for this purpose that a capitulary was promulgated in 866 by Louis II calling up all the free men of the peninsula because of the danger. They were divided according to their personal resources into two categories: the less wealthy, who were to be mobilized on the spot or near their homes, to ensure the guarding of fortresses and coasts; and the rest who, intended for the mobile forces, were to hold themselves in readiness to depart, equipped with all that was necessary for one year's campaign. This exceptionally long mobilization – the normal length of campaigns among the Carolingians was three months – indicates the gravity of the situation.

Why did not the Sovereign Pontiff, in a better position than anyone else to realize this, feel bound at once to give his full support to the only possible defender? Called upon by Louis II to make a financial contribution to the undertaking by relinquishing the splendid offering which the newly-converted khan of the Bulgars, Boris, had just sent him, he found himself compelled to accede, with more or less good grace, to this request which, according to Hincmar, was equivalent to a command: he sent not the whole, but a part, of the gifts received, apologizing for not being able to give more generously.

The future of Western Christianity, whether one wished it or not, thus appeared more and more closely bound up with the military potentialities of the young Carolingian prince whom destiny had made emperor, and even the proud Nicholas I was, towards the end of his pontificate, sufficiently convinced to resign himself to this evident reality.

Pope Hadrian II: satellite of the emperor

Once Nicholas had disappeared from the scene, on 13 November 867, the political effacement of the papacy became increasingly pronounced, while the importance of the role played by Louis II, the Carolingian who was henceforth seen by all as the bulwark of Christian Europe against the infidels, grew.

Nicholas' successor, Hadrian II, chosen in the absence of Louis II, who was detained at that moment in southern Italy by the military situation, was a rather obscure Roman priest. Blind in one eye and lame, he was a man without great prestige, affable and obliging, but without personality and without character, always ready to show his gratitude and his good will to an emperor from whom he expected protection, and of whose merits he boasted. Here at last was a prince who did not waste his troops against Christians, Hadrian wrote at the beginning of 868 to Louis the German and Charles the Bald, but who used them all "for the defense of the Church, for our own safety, for the deliverance of the faithful"; a prince who protects our frontiers against the Saracens; who had not hesitated to leave his capital and sacrifice the "peaceful repose" which he enjoyed there to go and give them battle; taking every trouble without counting the cost, braving "heat and cold", always ready to "endure ills and dangers for Christ's sake", not retreating before anything in order "to ensure the welfare and peace" of the Christians. The whole attitude of Pope Hadrian on this point was so dominated by his obsession with the Saracen danger and the feeling that only Louis II could protect Christendom against them that on 20 February 868, receiving strange monks at his table at the Lateran, he called on them to pray for "his most Christian son the emperor Augustus Louis, so that God Almighty might give him victory over the Saracen nation" and thus grant through his mediation "perpetual peace" to the Christian world.

Already inclined to efface himself before the saviour whom in his eyes Louis II appeared to be, Hadrian found himself, furthermore, in a personal situation so delicate that he could not afford to do anything that might alienate Louis II's friendship. Having been a priest for more than twenty-five years at the time of his election to the papal throne, he had nevertheless been married before entering sacred orders. Now, his wife and daughter continued to live under his roof, even while he resided at the Lateran, and this cohabitation caused him some embarrassment. It became known that in March 868, in the middle of Lent, his daughter had let herself be taken from the Lateran by her suitor, a young man who answered to the name of Eleutherius, and who was none other than one of the sons of Arsenius, bishop of Orta, himself likewise married. This was rather a scandal; and one in which Louis II was requested to intervene in person, by the two families in this way disgraced, that of the pope and that of the bishop of Orta, in an attempt to reduce the repercussions.

Arsenius, the first to act, hastened to take refuge in Benevento, where the emperor was then staying. According to Hincmar, who did not feel any excess of kindness towards the former papal legate, this was to put his fortune in a safe place; but, he adds at once, "while Arsenius was in conversation with the demons, he departed from this world without having taken communion". The pope also referred the matter to Louis II by begging him to have the ravisher of his daughter tried before a court. Never perhaps had a pope been in a more false and, in a sense, ridiculous, situation. But the incident had an especially dramatic result: driven to worse excesses, again if we may believe Hincmar, by his own brother Anastasius (that other son of Bishop Arsenius who had almost been pope and who, after serving as secretary of Nicholas I, had just been promoted by Hadrian to the dignity of 'librarian of the Holy See'), Eleutherius ended by successively cutting the throats of the pope's wife and of his daughter. The emperor's representatives at Rome apprehended the madman, whom they caused to be executed; but, needless to say, this scandal contributed neither to raising the prestige of the papacy nor to increasing its authority.

Thus, within a few months of Nicholas I's death, the situation in the West seemed to have changed completely, to the advantage of the temporal power. The pope gave the impression of such pliability that people deluded themselves into thinking they could make him revoke the measures taken by his sterner predecessor. In particular, Archbishops Gunther and Theutgald intrigued with him to regain their episcopal sees of Cologne and Trier; Lothar II counted on the revision of the sentence that had separated him from Waldrada and compelled him to take back Theutberga; Theutberga herself earnestly requested permission to terminate her married life; and in each case the support of the all-powerful Louis II was gained. Hadrian, who had no wish to dissatisfy anyone, especially not the Emperor Louis II, resisted weakly, begging Lothar to have patience and to wait for the meeting of a new synod. To give him at least some satisfaction, Pope Hadrian agreed, in February 868, at the request of his "dearest son Louis, most clement emperor, whom one should believe in all things" – these are his very words – to relieve Waldrada of the excommunication pronounced against her by his predecessor.

Clearly, the pope did not dare refuse the emperor anything, and this is why Lothar, whose appetite was only whetted by the first concessions, and who was, besides, resolved to try everything at any price to attain his goal, did not hesitate in June 869 to go to Benevento, where he hoped to persuade his brother Louis II to intervene personally in his favour with the Sovereign Pontiff. Detained by the Saracen war, Louis arranged for Lothar to be accompanied by his wife, Empress Engelberga, as far as Monte Cassino where, obedient to the orders of the emperor, Hadrian had come to receive him, and the matter seemed well on the way to solution when Lothar suddenly succumbed to an attack of malaria which carried him off at Piacenza on 8 August 869 on the way back to his own country.

The papacy and the settlement of the Lotharingian succession, 869–870

The immediate effect of this unexpected death was to pose, sooner than anyone expected but in the circumstances hoped for by Charles the Bald and Louis the German, the problem of the Lotharingian inheritance, because Lothar had left no children except those from his union, considered illegitimate, with Waldrada. In another period, Louis II, the heir most closely related to the deceased, might have been able to use this excellent opportunity to reconstitute in his favour the kingdom of his father Lothar I, that is to say to reunite into a single kingdom the old Frankish lands of the Meuse and Rhine, with their capital at Aachen, and the Italy of the Lombard kings, over which he had already reigned for twenty-five years. His imperial title, to which his military successes and the services he had rendered to Christendom was slowly restoring some meaning, would no doubt have been brilliantly supported by this union. But the struggle against the Saracens in southern Italy made all intervention north of the Alps temporarily impossible for him. His uncle Louis the German was himself not then available, having fallen so seriously ill at Regensburg that the doctors despaired of saving him. This was an excellent windfall for Charles the Bald, who, after quickly negotiating with the magnates of his neighbour's kingdom, was at Metz on 5 September, and on 9 September had himself crowned king there.

Foreseeing this development, Pope Hadrian, ever the docile ally of Louis II, had, upon the news of Lothar's death, despatched letters to the counts, bishops and magnates of the king of France to request them to obstruct any attempt of this kind on the part of their ruler and to remind them of the indefeasible rights of Louis II to his brother's inheritance. He reminded them also that Charles had bound himself by oath at Liège in 854 to respect to the advantage of his nephews the independence of the kingdom that had fallen to Lothar I at the time of the partition of Verdun; he boasted once again of the admirable

devotion of Louis II to the cause of Christendom; exalted the merits
"of so great a prince, and of an emperor so pious"; threatened with
anathema and with deposition (for the bishops) anyone who did not
oppose himself to the perpretration of the crime which Charles was
probably contemplating. A private letter called upon Hincmar to use his
personal influence with the king to dissuade him from this course of
action. Finally, Charles himself was ordered to renounce his plan. The
bishops and magnates of the Lotharingian kingdom were furthermore
urged by the same messenger to rally, under pain of anathema, to the
legitimate heir, Emperor Louis, "king, lord and emperor of all Gaul".

By an irony of fate, Hadrian's letters were dated 5 September; that
is to say, on the very day that Charles the Bald entered Metz. It was
only after he had taken possession of a large part of Lothar II's
kingdom and, above all, after the ceremony at the palace of Aachen,
that the king of France received the pope's messengers, accompanied
by an ambassador of Louis II charged with supporting their overture.
But, noted Hincmar, who was in Lotharingia at the side of his king, and
from whom we know these details, Charles "took no notice" of all this;
he did not even trouble to reply, nor indeed did any of his bishops,
neither Hincmar himself, nor any of his magnates. The threatening
language of the pope ill concealed his real weakness, and no one was
deceived by it. As for the emperor whose cause Hadrian II defended so
ardently, he was too far away and too absorbed by the struggle against
the Moslems for this reminder of his rights to be capable of alarming
the king of France.

The only person with whom Charles the Bald was obliged to reckon
was Louis the German. Less dangerously ill than was at first thought,
he intended to have his share of the booty. Even before Lothar died, in
868, he had come to an agreement with Charles the Bald with a view to
the partition between them by equal lots of "all that God was to give
them of the kingdoms of their nephews". He did not fail to remind
Charles of this agreement in September 869. But when he learned that,
not content with installing himself in Lotharingian territory and there
promulgating charters dated "the year I of his reign as the successor of
King Lothar", Charles, having just become a widower (on 6 October),
had remarried with great pomp at Aachen on 22 January 870 a young
woman of the region, Richild, daughter of the Lotharingian Count
Bivin and niece of Queen Theutberga, in the hope of making himself
liked by his new subjects, he threatened his brother with taking up

arms if he refused to proceed immediately with the partition agreed on. Not without difficulty, the entente was finally established at Meerssen, where the two kings met each other on 8 August 870: Lothar's kingdom was cut in two, from north to south, by a rather complicated dividing line that left to Louis Aachen, Cologne, Trier, Thionville, Metz, Mainz, Alsace and the Jura region, and to Charles the western regions. This was a real dismemberment, in which there was not the slightest concern for the general interest, nor for equity.

The only voice still raised in favour of the right and principle which the two kings of France and Germany had agreed to trample underfoot so cynically, was that of the papacy. The partition of Meerssen was scarcely a fact when once again a deluge of papal letters descended on the West, but with no more effect than before, and, as in the previous year, with a delay in information and despatch which emphasized their ill-timed and ineffective character. Dated 27 June 870, they brought, with an awkward lack of timing, congratulations for his impartiality to Louis the German, and to Charles the Bald vehement reproaches and threats of anathema just as useless as those of 869. The bishops, the magnates and Hincmar personally, were called upon to intervene to save the rights of Louis II who was "at the price of hard fatigue" fighting the good fight "against the enemies of Christ and for the liberation of the people of God". But to Hadrian's eloquence, his supplications, and his threats, no one paid any more attention than before.

Hincmar, however, whom the pope ordered to excommunicate the king of France if he did not give up his conquest, this time took the trouble to reply. But what a reply! In a long memorandum, the fiery archbishop, pierced to the quick, put the Sovereign Pontiff in his place in unbelievably bold terms by informing him of the amazement aroused in Gaul by his remarks. There are even some people, he went so far as to tell him, who recall that the popes, at difficult moments when the Lombards threatened to attack Rome, had eagerly accepted the aid of Pepin and his descendants to rescue them; they point out also that, against the Northmen, the prayers of the successor of St Peter were entirely ineffective. Hincmar added that, "if we are to believe the wordly literature, the kingdoms of this world maintain themselves by war and expand by victory, and not by the force of excommunications"; that furthermore, "one cannot be at the same time king and bishop" and that "if church affairs are within the competence of popes, public affairs are within the competence of kings". The fact that such declarations could come from the pen of a bishop, and, what is more, from a Hincmar, says a great deal about the change that had come about in the minds of men.

The deliverance of Bari (871) and the revival of the notion of empire

Beside the weak pope, whose threats left the kings of France and Germany indifferent and who was scoffed at by the archbishop of Reims, the emperor, before whom Hadrian effaced himself, looked like a great personage. Certainly on the military level, he was indeed the untiring commander whose devotion to the Christian cause Hadrian enjoyed praising. From 866 to 871 he never left southern Italy and had only one thought: to make an end to the Moslem invasions. The operations, sometimes successful, at other times indecisive, which he personally directed, never leaving the theatre of war for any reason whatever, led him at last, at the beginning of February 871, to the result relentlessly pursued since 867: the capture of the great Saracen base of Bari, on the Adriatic, and the almost total liberation of the peninsula.

To achieve this, he had spared no effort; he had not even hesitated to enter into negotiations with the Byzantine emperor, in order to obtain, in 869 and 870, the co-operation of a Greek fleet which could make up for the absence, particularly awkward when attacking a port, of any warships of his own. But it would finally be he himself and his troops who won the day. The pride he felt because of this may have somewhat gone to his head, if we are to judge from a letter which, just after his victory, he apparently dared to send to the *basileus* of Constantinople.

From the very first words, he took issue with his colleague of the East by contrasting his own title with the one he gave the Byzantine emperor. "Louis, by the will of Divine Providence emperor Augustus of the Romans, to his dearest spiritual brother Basil, most glorious and most pious emperor of the New Rome". It was he who was the true emperor; he was such by the will of God, as the very protocol of his charters indicates. It had pleased the Almighty to give the imperial throne to the most worthy candidate, by virtue of the holy chrism which the pope, the new Samuel, had poured over his brow, while Basil belonged to a line of princes who had "not only left the city of Rome, seat of the empire, but deserted the Roman people and even the Roman language, to emigrate to another city, in the lands of another people, and to adopt another language". Over against Basil, who represented heterodoxy or rather "cacodoxy", he, Louis, represented orthodoxy. That he belonged to the Frankish race was not important. There had never been any lack of Roman emperors who had sprung from races other than the Roman: Spanish, Isaurians, Khazars, for example. Since then it had pleased God to call on the Franks because, to speak in the words of the Apostle, the Lord has decided "to graft new branches of a pure faith in the place of branches he had cut off because of heterodoxy". Let him then "who has ears, hear"!

Finally, scoffing at the foolish pretension of an emperor who had so little knowledge of the language of the Romans that he was unaware that it possessed the word *rex* (king) and did not know that this was the equivalent of the Greek *basileus*, he noted his correspondent's "stupidity" in claiming the seizure of Bari as evidence of the military virtues of "his Greeks", on the pretext that, in the siege of the city, the Franks had been no more than a handful of men, solely occupied in "watching and eating". "Your men" he replied,

were like grasshoppers at the beginning of the attack; but thereafter, suddenly sickened with cowardice . . . , it is a fact that, without looking back, without eating, without fighting, without trophies of victory, they suddenly vanished and fled to their homes, while, after having vainly waited for months for the coming of your fleet, our men, few as they were and although tired out by many hardships . . . , had so well attacked the innumerable host of Saracens who devastated Calabraia . . . that thereafter the capture of Bari was easy.

Having said this and aired some other complaints, Louis II requested the Byzantine emperor to send to southern Italy a fleet sufficient for cutting the Moslems off from their bases, notably from Sicily. Otherwise the Frankish victories would remain ineffective, while the co-operation of a Greek fleet would allow not only the whole peninsula to be liberated but perhaps also Sicily itself.

The tone of this letter is such that some have considered it to be a forgery. Nothing, however, seems to bear this out. It was drawn up in the same spirit and almost the same style as many other documents originating in this period in the papal curia. It is particularly similar to a letter sent off some six years earlier by Pope Nicholas I to the Byzantine emperor Michael III, who had also used the Latin language barbarously, and to whom the Sovereign Pontiff had replied that those who "ridiculed themselves by calling themselves emperors of Romans while being ignorant of the Roman language" were the true barbarians. This skirmish was surely not the result of chance, but a proof that, in both cases, the writer of the letter was the same man: to wit, the well-known Anastasius, protegé of Louis II, secretary of pope Nicholas I, librarian of his successor, always ready to serve the cause of his imperial patron. In the eyes of Westerners the ruler of Constantinople had gradually become 'the emperor of the Greeks' (*Graecorum imperator*) so that, more than ever, Louis II could easily persuade himself, as he declared or had declared in his name, that he was the true 'Roman emperor'.

On one point Basil, in a letter unfortunately lost but to which Louis II replied, had scored, when he emphasized that this Frankish prince who claimed to speak in the name of Frankish power "did not rule over all the Frankish land" (*in tota Francia*). Louis' reply on this point is singularly obscure and embarrassed: "We rule over the whole of the Frankish country because it can be said that we hold the territories belonging to those who are of the same flesh and blood as us", which means that, taking up again on his own responsibility the theory of the indivisibility of the Carolingian Empire which was believed to be dead, Louis was posing as the overlord of all the Frankish kingdoms, even of those held by his uncles Charles the Bald and Louis the German. He was evidently claiming that they owed him the same respect and the same submission as Louis the Pious in 817 had claimed his younger sons owed toward their elder brother, the father of Louis II. But the facts cruelly belied such a claim, because Louis II continued to be powerless north of the Alps, and he had been obliged to limit himself to theoretical protests against his uncles' occupation of the kingdom left vacant by the death of his brother Lothar II. It is worth noting that the semi-official historians of Charles the Bald and Louis the German – Hincmar in the *Annals of Saint-Bertin*, and Meginhard in the *Annals of Fulda* – could not spare one word to celebrate the capture of Bari, thus proving that the repercussions of this victory were not great outside Italy.

The fact nevertheless remains that, in the papal circles to which Anastasius, the presumed author of the document we have just analyzed, belonged, the notion of empire had suddenly tended to take on new life. The protection of the Church and of Christianity required an emperor, and this is why the Empire, which had been believed to be dead, was about to revive.

CHAPTER SIX

The papacy's appeal to Charles the Bald

The problem of the imperial succession and the role of the papacy, 871–875

Almost immediately after the fall of Bari, the problem of the succession to the Empire arose. Louis II was taken prisoner on 13 August 871 in the course of an insurrection at Benevento, but rumour spread that he was dead. Each party took up position.

Fate had decreed that Louis, like his two brothers, had no legitimate sons; one child only, a daughter, having been born from his marriage to Empress Engelberga, or at least then surviving. The only possible heirs were his two uncles, Charles the Bald and Louis the German, and, as one can imagine, they were both on the alert. The annalists show them to us getting ready to intervene at the first rumour of their nephew's death, Charles going to station himself at Besançon, close to the frontier, on the road leading to Italy; Louis, at once making an arrangement with his rebellious sons which left him a free hand.

But the news was untrue. Louis II was not only alive but on 17 September he regained his liberty and resumed his activities of shortly before. But from this moment on the problem of his succession remained of the first importance in all the preoccupations of the political world in the West, and by the same token, in every chancery there was discussion only about the imperial throne and its future occupant. Empress Engelberga, who seems to have been a diplomat of the highest order, had been entrusted by her husband in 869 with the task of negotiating with Pope Hadrian on behalf of Lothar II at the time of Lothar's visit to Italy. She now exerted herself with singular astuteness in tempting Charles the Bald and Louis the German in turn

with the bright prospect of the Italian inheritance. But at the same time
another negotiation was being conducted by the Roman curia which,
this time without the knowledge of Louis II, attempted to settle the
problem in its own way. Among the shouts and tumultuous protestations, the challenges and threats that up to then filled the correspondence between the king of France and the Sovereign Pontiff concerning a great many church affairs in which they violently opposed one
another, it is most surprising to find suddenly in a letter of 872 sent by
Hadrian to Charles the Bald a passage in which – after hyperbolical
compliments on the wisdom, piety, justice and devotion of the king of
France, to whom the pope impudently asserted he had always,
notwithstanding contrary appearances, given the most sincere
respect – occur sentences like these:

> We confide to you under the secret seal – and this should not be disclosed except to the
> trustworthy – that . . . if your Nobility survives our emperor, even though we were given
> heaps of gold, we would never accept, ask or receive of our own free will any other than
> yourself in this kingdom and in the Roman Empire . . . If you survive our emperor, it is you
> whom we wish for . . . as head, as king, as patrician, as emperor.

Thus, not only had the question of the imperial crown once more
become a problem in men's minds, but it began to be evident that, even
if the papacy was incapable of ruling the Christian world as Nicholas I
had hoped, it had at least an essential role to play in the choice of a new
emperor.

The situation seemed, in this respect, very different from what it had
been in the first half of the ninth century. It is true that Charlemagne
had gone in 800 to have himself crowned emperor at St Peter's by the
Sovereign Pontiff; but no one, at that moment, had thought that by
placing the diadem on his head to the acclamations of the crowd
gathered in the basilica, Leo III had been anything else than an
instrument of the policy pursued by the master of the Frankish
kingdom. It was from his father, thereafter, and not from the pope, and
at Aachen, that Louis the Pious had in 813 received the same imperial
diadem. The anointing which Pope Stephen IV had performed after
this at Reims in 816, on the occasion of a visit to Gaul, had been no
more than a religious ceremony of protocollary significance which did
not seem to anyone to constitute the start of a new era in the relations
of the spiritual and the temporal powers. It was likewise at Aachen and
by the agency of his father that Lothar I had been crowned emperor in

817; the coronation ceremony celebrated in 823 at St Peter's in Rome on the occasion of the visit made by the young man to the Sovereign Pontiff being once more only a protocollary manifestation without constitutional value. But things had changed since then. In his letter to Emperor Basil, Louis II wrote: "The Frankish princes, who at first bore the title of king, have carried that of emperor from the moment they were anointed with holy oil by the Roman Pontiff". He also pointed out that his uncles themselves gave him the title of emperor "in consideration not of his age, which was less than theirs, but of the anointing which, by the laying-on of hands by the Sovereign Pontiff and by his prayers, had promoted him divinely to this dignity". When he subsequently attributed to the papacy a role of the first order in what one might call the imperial investiture, he was emphasizing forcefully the change that had come about in the ideas of the period on this subject.

The fact is that when in 850 Lothar I decided, in the full sovereignty of his rights, to associate his son Louis in the government of the Empire, his first deed had been to send him to Rome, where Pope Leo IV had conferred on him in a coronation ceremony the insignia of his new dignity. But now it was believed or pretended that the coronation at Rome was the fundamental constituent act in the creation of an emperor and the Sovereign Pontiff could, in the eyes of the kings themselves, pose without contradiction as the dispenser of crowns. It was not long before the consequences of such a view of the situation made themselves felt.

Pope John VIII and the imperial coronation of Charles the Bald in 875

On 12 August 875 Louis died near Brescia, after having spared no effort in the fight against the Saracens, whose attacks had not been diminished as much as had been hoped by the capture of Bari. Pope Hadrian had preceded him in the grave by more than two and a half years and had been replaced on the throne of St Peter by an old man, John VIII, who for twenty years at least had performed the functions of archdeacon in Rome. He had acquired a long and broad experience there. Notwithstanding his age, moreover, he was possessed of extraordinary energy, as his first letters and acts immediately indicated. But, like his predecessors, he was obliged to reckon with the Saracen danger and his letters, of which a large number have come down to us, show him obsessed by a permanent anxiety to ensure the welfare of Rome and of Christianity by giving Louis II a successor capable of pursuing the struggle against the menacing infidels.

Even before Louis II had breathed his last a new and dangerous development occurred. Around the end of 874 or at the beginning of 875, while Louis II was in northern Italy, the Saracens disembarked on the coasts of Latium, occupied Terracina, thirty-eight kilometres south-west of Rome on the Appian Way, and sick as he was, the pope was obliged to advance in person against the invaders. He succeeded in seizing eighteen of their ships, in wresting from them six hundred prisoners and inflicting bloody losses on them. But he could not repeat this feat and desperately called for help, demanding the immediate dispatch of troops to guard the coasts and to ward off new attacks.

The death of Louis II in August 875 obliged Pope John VIII to see without delay to his replacement. In September, taking things up where Hadrian II had left them, he wrote to inform Charles the Bald that the situation had been discussed with the cardinals and "the Roman senate", that many had praised "his piety and his faith", and that, remembering the proofs which the king of France had given of this, "not only in his time, but in the time of Pope Nicholas of blessed memory, he himself hoped that His Excellency would be chosen, for the honour and the glory of the holy Roman Church". In other words, Charles the Bald was still his nominee for the throne.

Before proceeding to the imperial coronation, it seemed necessary to obtain for Charles another crown which, since Charlemagne, had in fact always been awarded to future emperors beforehand: the royal crown of Italy. Especially now that the emperor had become an Italian sovereign, no other procedure could be imagined. But, although Charles was at Rome the preferred candidate or rather the only candidate, this was by no means the case at Pavia, where the assembly of magnates, early in September 875, split into two factions, one declaring itself for Charles the Bald, the other for the eldest son of Louis the German, Carloman, whose candidacy Louis II's widow, the Empress Engelberga, supported by invoking what she claimed were her husband's last wishes.

The absence of a decisive majority among the electors at Pavia left the field free for the rivals, the advantage being bound to go, so it seemed, to the most determined of them. Neither Charles nor the pope wasted time. While three papal legates – the bishops of Velletri, Porto and Arezzo – left in all haste to ask the king of France to come and be crowned emperor at Rome, Charles, at the first news of the death of his nephew, convoked with the greatest urgency an assembly of magnates at Ponthion on the road leading towards Langres and Italy, took command of his army at Langres, crossed the Saône, traversed the frontier of his kingdom on 1 September, then via Saint-Maurice in the Valais and the Great Saint-Bernard Pass, descended into Lombardy. On 29 September he was at Pavia. He brushed aside a first detachment of troops which Louis the German had despatched south of the Alps to block his way under the orders of his youngest son Charles the Fat; he neutralized by diplomacy a larger army which the eldest son of Louis the German, Carloman, was bringing through the Brenner Pass; then, having received the assent of a number of the magnates of northern Italy, he made straight for Rome where the pope was impatiently awaiting his arrival. John VIII welcomed him at the top of the steps of St Peter on 17 December, and he was at last anointed, crowned and acclaimed emperor of the Romans in the basilica on Christmas Day with the same ceremonial which seventy-five years earlier to the day had been reserved for his grandfather.

The annalist of Fulda, whose account forcefully expresses the chagrin felt in the entourage of Louis the German and his son Carloman, presents the event as the result of an unrestrained campaign of corruption, in which the gold stolen by Charles the Bald in northern Italy had had the same effects on what he called "the Roman senate" as in the time of Jugurtha. But, in reality, it was the Sovereign Pontiff who had prepared everything, organized everything, and by a rapid decision, arranged this first and decisive success for Charles.

It was also John VIII's authority which shortly afterwards obtained for Charles that royal crown of Italy which, because of the lack of unanimity among the magnates of Italy, he had been obliged to forgo in order to gain time over his rivals, instead of receiving it first according to the traditional sequence of events. In February 876 a second meeting of the magnates of the kingdom was held at Pavia, where the new emperor had just arrived. Here he was finally elected king. The official record of the assembly, which was presided over by the archbishop of Milan, Ansbert, and in which twenty Italian bishops were present with ten counts, mostly from northern Italy, explicitly states that the election of Charles as "king of Italy" had been carried out at the instance of the pope who, "through the inspiration of the Holy Spirit, had elevated him to the imperial dignity", and that the electors had understood that they themselves would be working "for the profit of the entire holy Church of God and their own welfare". It was in this capacity that they all unanimously promised allegience and obedience to Charles. At the meeting which he himself presided over thereafter in the royal palace of Pavia, the new king asked each man above all "to honour and venerate the holy Roman Church, which is the head of all churches, and to undertake nothing against her rights and her power". He further asked everyone to exert himself, for the honour of John, Sovereign Pontiff and universal pope, to "receive with the greatest respect the decisions" which the Holy Father "took in the name of his apostolic ministry and to carry them out with the obedience they deserve"; and not to commit any depredations in the papal territories nor in the patrimonies of the Roman Church, if they did not wish to be struck by the triple royal ban. It was only after all this that a very short article recalled in two lines "the respect due to the honour of the emperor and the obligation to obey his orders" under penalty of prosecution.

Charles the Bald as emperor

Emperor of the Romans by virtue of the anointing which the Sovereign Pontiff had conferred on him through the inspiration of God, king of Italy thanks to the skilful diplomacy of John VIII and in circumstances which, all things considered, remained rather precarious, because the record indicated, as we have seen, only ten votes in his favour from lay magnates, would Charles be capable of living up to the hopes placed in him? And would the Empire, which had just recovered at St Peter's, Rome, the brilliance of its first Carolingian ruler, again become the 'Empire of the Franks' in the sense given to these words at the beginning of the century? The general state of affairs in the West in 876 made any illusions on these two points impossible.

Charles the Bald was certainly not a weak ruler. Pious, well educated, familiar with theological problems, in which he had a lively interest, he was at the same time a man of action, energetic and courageous. Since his adolescence he had handled difficulties of all kinds, even the most serious dangers and the most apparently desperate situations, with a great strength of soul and a remarkable spirit of initiative, never letting himself be overcome by adversity and always ready to respond without hesitation to the calls of destiny. His expedition to Italy had just demonstrated this once more. But the means of which he disposed were not equal to his boldness, and it would not be long before it was evident that he was incapable both of effectively protecting the Roman Church and Christianity and of imposing himself as the ruler of the West.

The promptness of his decisions had at first disconcerted his brother and nephews; but they quickly recovered. While Charles hastened towards Rome, Louis the German, accompanied by his son Louis the Younger, attacked France, where he overcame various difficulties and celebrated Christmas at the palace of Attigny on the Aisne. No doubt, on the whole, Charles' magnates remained loyal to Charles, so that Louis the German, perhaps already ill, found it impossible to follow up his initial success and was obliged to go back to his own kingdom in January; but the most elementary prudence urged Charles not to leave his subjects by themselves for too long a time. So, though he had only just been recognized as king of Italy, we see him returning as quickly as possible to his old kingdom, after delegating the government of the peninsula to Boso, count of Vienne (brother of his wife Richild), whom he had, for the occasion, invested with the dignity of duke.

Charles needed only to show himself in France for the calm, momentarily disturbed by the unsuccessful attempt of the king of Germany, to return everywhere. But although this first difficulty had been surmounted, it was necessary to overcome another: he had to have himself recognized as emperor by the whole of the Frankish world. A large council of Gallic bishops had been convoked for this purpose for the beginning of the summer of 876. It was held at Ponthion (close to the present Vitry-le-François) from 21 June to 16 July, under the presidency of the new emperor, assisted by the bishops of Arezzo and Toscanella, who had come to meet him in April in the capacity of papal legates. Because thenceforth the pope, with whom Charles had associated himself closely, was behind him or at his side in all his acts.

Fifty bishops from France and the former kingdom of Lothar sat in the council; but, throughout the twenty-six days that it lasted, every-thing took place as though the deliberations had been prepared at Rome and the decisions drawn up in agreement between the pope and the emperor. Not only did the papal legates play a preponderant role in the debates, but almost every session was dominated by the reading and examination of letters which the Sovereign Pontiff had sent to congratulate some or reprimand others, or to ask approval for some measure or other or dictate to each the line to follow. Supplementary letters and instructions even arrived in the course of the council, at the session of 10 July, brought by two new papal envoys, one of whom was the pope's own nephew, the bishop of Gabies, Leo, *apocrisarius* of the Holy See.

At the same time no effort was spared to make an impression on the audience and to persuade it that, with the proclamation of Charles as emperor, a new era had begun. At the opening session Charles arrived in Frankish costume, accompanied by the two legates; but from the second session onward all the documents relative to his election as king of Italy, as well as to his elevation as emperor, were read aloud, and the assembly was urged to give its approval. Thereafter, the atmosphere gradually changed. At the fifth session the letters of congratulation sent by the pope to the new emperor were read; then the next day the sumptuous gifts that the pope had sent him were presented, particularly the insignia of his imperial rule: a sceptre and a golden baton. Finally, at the closing session on 16 July, the emperor appeared clothed in imperial dress of Byzantine style. He was escorted by the papal legates, themselves wearing the ecclesiastical ornaments usual at Rome, and the religious ceremony that marked the conclusion of the council was accompanied by a pomp and splendour never before seen in Gaul.

But the council was above all designed to impose the authority of the new emperor firmly on the whole of the Frankish world. Louis the German had probably been invited to send his bishops, but he had restricted himself to sending the archbishop of Cologne, who was presented with a letter in which the pope vehemently reproached the clergy of Germany for having by its inertia allowed her king to invade France at the very moment when Charles the Bald had been summoned to Rome to receive the imperial crown which God himself had reserved for him. But the archbishop of Cologne, together with two German counts, had come, not to participate in the deliberations of the council, but to protest against the annexation of Louis II's lands by the king of France, whom Louis the German reminded of their previous agreements concerning the possible partition of the territories which the death of their nephews would leave vacant. But he could have spared himself the trouble, for the whole point of the council was to broaden the field of action reserved for the new emperor, and this was why, among the measures referred to its scrutiny, there were some which concerned far more than Gaul itself. Thus the pope did not hesitate to notify him officially of the condemnations pronounced on 19 April at Rome against Bishop Formosus of Porto, the *nomenclator* Gregory, and several of the most influential persons of the city, accused of wrongful dealings against the Church and the Holy See. The papal letter concerning this serious incident, dated 21 April and brought by a special courier to the session of 11 July, was even addressed "to all the bishops of Gaul and of Germany", as though they had all been gathered at Ponthion.

Another papal letter, similarly addressed to all the bishops of Gaul and Germany, but dated 2 January, and thus written when Charles was still at Rome after the imperial anointing, had been read aloud at the first session, when it produced a certain chill in many of those present. It announced the creation of an apostolic vicarship for the archbishop of Sens, Ansegisus, who received from the pope a permanent delegation of power to convoke in his stead and in his place in the whole extent of the Frankish lands any synods necessary to settle current church affairs, as well as to serve as the regular intermediary between his colleagues, of Germany as well as of Gaul, and the Holy See. This was, thirty years later and in an analogous plan, a repetition of the manoeuvre attempted a first time at the request of Lothar I, for Drogo of Metz. The idea was to arrange in this way for the emperor, by means of one of his prelates who appeared to have shown the most devotion to him in his elevation to the imperial dignity, a right of supervision over the entire Frankish Church, and through this to help to extend his authority gradually over all the territories once united under a single ruler. At least it was hoped that the spiritual and moral unity of the former Empire would be reconstituted around him.

The scheme, however, was not to have any more success now than in Lothar's time. Without venturing to oppose the papal decree openly, the bishops present at Ponthion restricted themselves to declaring three times that they were prepared to accept it "on condition that the rights attributed to each metropolitan by the sacred canons and the decretals of the popes were respected". This semblance of support was all that was forthcoming; no one, except the archbishop of Bordeaux, who aimed at obtaining by his compliance the favour of being transferred to Bourges, having consented to take the straightforward promise of obedience to Ansegisus which Charles demanded. But when Charles had the archbishop of Sens seated in a place of honour from the first session onwards, this roused the dissatisfaction of Hincmar, who at once delivered a solemn protest. Thus the same fate befell the vicariate of Ansegisus as had earlier befallen the vicariate of Drogo: the institution remained a dead letter.

As for Louis the German and his followers, it was indeed necessary, in order to win them over, to find other means than clevernesses of this kind or measures of intimidation such as the threatening letters addressed by John VIII to the episcopate and the counts of Germany. On 28 August an embassy consisting of representatives of Charles the Bald and two papal legates, whose assistance was clearly indispensable in all the political acts of the new emperor, left France for the neighbouring kingdom to find a basis of agreement with Louis, his sons, his bishops and his magnates. Perhaps this would have cleared the atmosphere if, just after their departure, it had not been learned that Louis had breathed his last on the very day that the ambassadors had started on their way.

With the foolish audacity that was characteristic of him, Charles the Bald now had only one thought: to take immediate advantage of the situation to make up for his awkward retreat of 870, and to re-install himself at Aachen, which his brother had at that time forced him to evacuate. Only a few days had passed after Louis the German's death when his emissaries were in 'Lorraine,' scarcely ahead of his own arrival with his troops. In the middle of September he entered Aachen, then Cologne, where he received the news that the Northmen were moving up the Seine with a hundred large ships. Without allowing this peril to distract him for a moment from his plan, he continued imperturbably on his way toward Mainz, doubtless intending to occupy the whole left bank of the Rhine. He hoped to catch his nephews unawares while they were busy making arrangements about their inheritance which still remained to be settled, although a theoretical division between them had been made by their father in 865. This was a mistake, for Louis the Younger, whose possessions were the first to be threatened and which in any case were the nearest since they comprised Saxony, Thuringia and 'eastern Francia', had immediately taken up position on the Rhine. After a vain effort at negotiation, he crossed the river at Andernach, some twenty kilometres downstream from Koblenz, and a fierce combat took place on 8 October near the town, which turned into a complete rout for Charles the Bald. This was a hard lesson for the emperor, who was forced to flee non-stop to Liège with the remnants of his army and to leave the field open for his nephew, who shortly afterward made a triumphal entry into Aachen. Morally and physically bruised, ill of a pleurisy that almost killed him, Charles finally realized, but too late, that the notion of an imperial restoration as complete as he had dreamed of in the excitement of his first successes, was henceforth unattainable, and that if he wished to achieve lasting results he would have to limit his ambitions.

Charles the Bald and the Moslem peril

John VIII must have been hardly less disappointed than Charles the Bald at this turn of events, for danger beset him from every side. The Saracens had reappeared after the death of Louis II and, most disturbing of all, had found more and more support among the petty Lombard princes of southern Italy, with the duke of Naples, and in Rome, even in the Lateran Palace, since, in the spring of 876, they had been able for a time to entertain connections with the group of malcontents to whom we have already alluded. Its leader was one of the highest officials of the curia, the *nomenclator* Gregory, who was even explicitly accused by the pope of having desired to deliver the city to the Moslems, in connivance with several other persons attached to the papal palace. Whether the accusation was justified or not, it was certain that the danger had again become serious and that John VIII experienced an increasing anguish because of it, as his correspondence proves. Count Boso, to whom Charles had entrusted the task of watching over Italy in his absence, acted only in his own interest. In vain did the pope urge him to send help in September 876. A few days later he let him know with terror that, according to reliable reports, a Saracen fleet of a hundred large ships was setting sail towards Rome: Boso remained deaf to his entreaties. Duke Lambert, re-established at

Spoleto on the request of the pope himself, and his brother Guy, who had been associated with him in power with the task, it seems, of helping him protect papal territory, had thought only of their personal interests. As for Charles the Bald, he stayed on and on in Gaul and, although lavish with comforting words, postponed his visit to Italy. On 15 November 876 John VIII communicated to him his impatience and disappointment: had not Charles been chosen to be the supporter and protector of the Holy See? The prelates of Gaul, even Empress Richild herself, were begged to use their influence on the emperor to hasten his departure for Rome.

The news of the disaster of Andernach, in October, did not prevent the pope from renewing his entreaties. In the spring of 877 Charles, who had then scarcely recovered from his pleurisy, received a visit from two papal legates who gave him an even more urgent letter of 10 February: the Saracens were roaming the countryside up to the environs of Rome; they were masters of the valley of the Anio, a few kilometres north of the city; the fate of Christendom was again at stake. "Perhaps you think that the injury to our Church is only slight?". Alas, this is by no means true, complained the pope, who claimed that he was on the point of succumbing. "Do not force me", he went on to say, to "turn to someone else", but send me without delay the aid I have waited for so long. To this letter the pope added, three days later, a postscript to remind his correspondent that the fact that he had kept the imperial throne for him at the expense of his competitors entailed special obligations. Charles could not use his other cares as a pretext to escape these obligations; his duty toward the imperilled Roman Church took precedence before all others, according to the pope. The danger was urgent. Under the concerted attacks of the Saracens and of the duke of Spoleto, the Roman Church was threatened with disaster. In April when, despite these desperate appeals, no help had arrived, the panic-stricken pope found himself begging the commander of a Byzantine fleet then cruising in Italian waters to assign at once ten large vessels for the protection of the coasts near Rome. This did not prevent him from returning to the subject with Charles the Bald in May in terms more categorical than ever. He reminded him in the first line of his letter that "the Divine Majesty had chosen him before all others to elevate him to the dignity of the Roman Empire and had desired to crown him with the diadem of the Augusti so that he might constantly protect the Church of

Christ . . . and defend her against the attacks of the pagans". Before the
spectacle of the devastations which spread further every day, and
threatening famine, would Charles not be moved at last? There was
time only for him to hasten to the scene. The pope and his clergy
prayed, he wrote, that the emperor's precarious health would not suffer
too much from the change of climate!

The assembly of Quierzy in 877

This was cruel irony, addressed to a prince of fifty-two who was sorely
tried by illness, and who could no longer afford without serious risk to
permit the Northmen to continue to occupy the valley of the Seine. But
several months would have been necessary to organize the military
operations against them which the situation required, and neither the
pope's impatience nor the exigences of the defense of Italy seemed to
permit this. So, at the beginning of April, yielding to the entreaties of
John VIII, Charles the Bald decided to brave difficulties once more and
take the road to the peninsula. At Compiègne, where he had gone to
celebrate Easter, he decided on 7 May to levy a special 'tribute' of five
thousand pounds of silver to buy the retreat of the Northmen; then,
realizing the gravity of the situation, he convoked his subjects to a
general assembly at Quierzy on 14 June in order to arrange with them
the continuance of the government during his absence.

He was obviously not without anxieties. The imperial coronation
had up to then scarcely brought him anything but an increase of tasks
and troubles, and the harsh lesson of Andernach was not forgotten.
The long journey that he was about to undertake for a second time; the
risk of new attacks, to which he knew his kingdom was exposed, from
his nephews as well as from the Northmen; the dangers he was about
to risk by venturing into that southern Italy where the Saracen peril
required his presence; and finally the qualified confidence which his
son Louis the Stammerer, to whom it was necessary to entrust the
regency, inspired in him, since he had previously already had to
complain about his betrayals – all this constituted for the emperor, ill
and worn out before his time, a mass of preoccupations of which the
measures he drew up at Quierzy clearly bear the mark. He hoped that
on this occasion everyone would shoulder his responsibilities by

participating in a formal consent to the decision that he was about to promulgate; a fortunate chance has preserved the text for us, at least partly, of the questionnaire which he submitted to the magnates gathered at Quierzy and of the answers he received from them.

On the majority of the points, question and answer are clear, and the emperor obtained from his vassals the assurances he expected: a promise to respect the properties of the Church and the personal foundations of the emperor (Arts. 1 and 2); consent to the appointment of certain persons to accompany him to Italy (Art. 3); confirmation of the oaths of allegiance and loyal collaboration taken by all in the course of the previous years (Art. 4); guarantee of the personal property of the emperor's wife and daughters (Arts. 5 and 6); consent in principle to the defensive measures which the emperor judged it wise to draw up in case of attack by his nephews against his army or his kingdom (Art. 7).

In agreement with his vassals, Charles also decreed precautionary measures to be taken in his absence concerning vacant offices and benefices (Art. 9): in the event of the death of an archbishop, until the emperor had been informed of his decease the nearest bishop was to have the supervision of his diocese together with the count of the city concerned; in the event of a bishop's death, the care of the diocese would be taken over by a 'visitor' nominated by the archbishop, according to the canonical rule, who was to be assisted, as in the preceding case, by the count in residence at the episcopal city, until the emperor could be notified of the decease; in the case of an abbot's death, the bishop and the count of the district would take over, under the same conditions, the temporary care of the monastery. The choice of the new official, in each case, thus remained subject to the customary rules, that is to say subject to the assent of the ruler.

For the comital offices the same rules applied: on the death of a count, the administration of his county was to be entrusted temporarily to a council consisting of high functionaries of the county and the bishopric, until the emperor was able to settle the matter. But a clause that reveals certain important changes of procedure completes this provision: the rights of the son of the count, if he left one, were explicitly safeguarded, as though, in normal times, he was expected to succeed to the office. If they were on the spot, but were minors, the eldest of them would be temporarily deputed with the office, under the supervision of a council; if the eldest son of the deceased was of age, but was away with Charles in Italy, some of his relatives or good friends would be added to the above-mentioned council to watch over his interests. The same rule applied to the benefices of vassals: whether these benefices were held of the emperor, of a bishop, an abbot, a count or of any lord whatsoever, the rights of the sons, if there were any, were likewise protected, and a definitive investiture similarly postponed. Finally it was stipulated that the properties of bishops, abbots and abbesses, as well as those of counts and royal vassals, of their wives and sons, if any of them died, should be placed under the safeguard of public authority; any seizure of these properties to invite the judicial sanctions prescribed by law.

By another article (Art. 10) Charles stipulated that, in the event of his own death during the Italian expedition, he would concede to those of his vassals who, renouncing the world, decided to consecrate the rest of their life to praying for the peace of his soul, the exceptional right of freely disposing of their 'honour' to the advantage of any of their sons or relatives capable of serving in their stead. This article, improvised for the occasion, says a great deal about the evolution that had taken place in the juridicial notions of the period.

The articles that follow are of less importance, but betray the emperor's anxieties. Charles advised his son and his vassals not to believe without verification any rumours that might be spread about concerning his death, but if these rumours proved true, to take steps to carry out his last wishes (Art. 11). He named the executors of his will (Art. 12); he made provision about his legacy in case another son should be born to him, and also in the event of one of his nephews appearing worthy of receiving a portion of the inheritance, which well indicates his uncertainty about the fate of his Empire (Art. 13).

Considering thereafter the possibility that he might return safe and sound from his expedition, he requested his son to be in readiness to set off to consecrate himself to the service of the Holy See in Italy, and to be crowned at Rome (Art. 14). He named the various bishops, abbots and counts who, in each area were to assist King Louis in the government (Art. 15); he advised Louis to have near him always, according to his own example, a group of trusted men to defend him against his enemies whenever necessary (Art. 16); and finally he arranged (Arts. 17–33) down to the last detail the administration of affairs during his absence, without forgetting either the upkeep of defenses against the Vikings, or that of the forests; and even going so far, before concluding this chapter of his injunctions, as to specify that an exact count should be kept of the heads of game killed in the hunt by his son (Art. 33).

This care to arrange everything in detail, to restrict as much as possible the room for caprice or even the initiative of individuals, leaves the painful impression of an anxious departure, darkened by cruel uncertainty about the future. The essence of all these provisions was summarized in four articles which were read to the assembled people on 16 June; then the order for departure was given. On 20 June the emperor was at Compiègne, and on 1 August the army crossed the Saône on its way to Italy.

Charles the Bald's death in 877

Meanwhile, the Sovereign Pontiff was busy consolidating Charles' authority in the peninsula. While pursuing active and delicate negotiations near Gaeta to stop the collusion of the duke of Naples and several other petty chiefs of Campania with the Saracens, he convoked a council at Ravenna at the request of the emperor himself. At first fixed for 24 June, the affairs of southern Italy forced him to postpone it until the beginning of August. Its aim was above all, to ensure for Charles extensive and explicit support among the Italian episopate. Before the hundred and thirty bishops who had responded to the papal summons, John VIII pronounced a hyperbolical eulogy of the Carolingian emperor. After it the assembly unanimously declared that it approved and confirmed the choice that had been made of Charles as emperor and anathematized anyone who obstructed this.

It was at Orbe, north of Lausanne, on the road leading through Saint-Maurice in the Valais and the Great Saint-Bernard Pass, that Charles learned of this encouraging vote, which had been motivated by the acknowledgement that the choice made of his person had been desired by God from all eternity or, to speak with the document itself, "inscribed by God into the order of the world". At the beginning of September, John VIII received Charles in person at Vercelli, as he entered the Lombard plain, and travelled with him thence to Pavia, where suddenly the disturbing news reached them of the arrival with all his troops of the eldest son of Louis the German, Carloman, fully decided this time to block the way for his uncle and to contend with him for the Lombard crown as well as the imperial diadem.

Since the death of their father, on 28 August of the previous year, the three sons of Louis the German, Carloman, Louis the Younger, and Charles the Fat, had in fact divided between themselves by amicable agreement the various territories that constituted the kingdom of Germany. The eldest, Carloman, had inherited Bavria with its dependencies of Bohemia, Moravia, Pannonia and Carinthia; the second, Louis the Younger, obtained 'eastern Francia' (the future Franconia), Thuringia, Saxony, Frisia and the larger part of Lorraine, annexed by their father; Charles the Fat, the youngest, received as his portion Alemania (the future Swabia), with Alsace and, doubtless, Rhaetia. Now, by virtue of this division, Carloman was indisputably, with his brother Charles the Fat, the ruler most directly interested in the events of Italy and the best situated to intervene there successfully. It will be however remembered that, on the death of Emperor Louis II, it was Carloman who had been considered by a substantial number of the magnates of Italy for the double royal and imperial succession which this death had vacated, and that he had already attempted in 875 to seize it by a sudden descent into Lombardy.

A fierce struggle seemed inevitable. Having probably marched via the Brenner Pass, Carloman rapidly advanced in the direction of Pavia. Charles the Bald, who counted on the arrival of important reinforcements from France, considered it wise to retreat south of the Po to Tortona, where the pope, still at his side, proceeded to the coronation of his wife Richild as empress. Then when the danger became too great, Charles caused the empress to be conveyed with his treasure over the Alps again by the nearest pass, that of Mont Cenis. Carloman continued his advance, and Charles the Bald's reinforcements did not arrive because a formidable revolt had just broken out in France, which was led by some of the magnates charged with the command of the reinforcements. The most prominent of these were Count Boso, the brother of Richild, Abbot Hugh, one of the most conspicuous members of the Welf family and cousin-german of the emperor, Bernard Plantevelue, count of Auvergne, and Bernard, marquis of Septimania. They were followed in revolt by a host of other counts and many bishops of the kingdom. Of those who stayed in France very few, according to Hincmar, had remained loyal to Charles.

Historians have tried hard to ascertain the causes of this revolt,

which surprised Charles the Bald at a decisive moment. There is one
that is indisputably more important than all the others, and this one is
of the utmost significance: it was the Empire and all that it caused in
terms of new burdens which was the origin of this sudden levy of
soldiers. Charles had left for Italy in 877 "against the wishes of his
men", the anonymous author of the *Annals* of St Vaast's at Arras
declared in so many words. A dissatisfaction so much more understand-
able since the French king's departure had been made possible only by
the payment to the Norse invaders of a tribute which had seemed an
intolerable burden on everyone. Was not Charles' absence in such
circumstances really desertion? Already in 875 Hincmar reproached
him for having "voluntarily abandoned his kingdom to go to Italy",
leaving his subjects exposed without defense to attack by enemies. He
claimed that he had heard people reproaching the king "for having left
the kingdom at the moment when, shaken within, it was surrounded
without by pagans, and for having deserted – this very term was
actually used – those whom the will of God had entrusted to his
government and protection. Finally, referring to these facts shortly
after 877 in a letter addressed to Louis the Stammerer, the archbishop
of Reims, who since the affair of Ansegisus' vicariate had gone over to
the opposition, specified his complaints by accusing Charles of having
left everything in jeopardy in the country "because his advisers did not
dare to say more and were not given the opportunity of saying what
they knew to be necessary and beneficial for the kingdom".

It is difficult to state more clearly that the adventurous policy of
Charles the Bald had ceased to be welcome to his men; hence the
explosion of dissatisfaction and the general revolt that suddenly
shattered the emperor's rule just as Carloman prepared to attack him.
The indispensable reinforcements and their leaders having passed to
the rebels, the emperor could do only one thing: return to France as
soon as possible to save his crown. But he was too late. Worn out by
adversity, shaking with fever, he had time only to cross the Pass of
Mont Cenis on a litter, to die miserably on 6 October 877 in an
unknown hamlet of the Maurienne region.

CHAPTER SEVEN

Charles the Fat

Pope John VIII in search of an emperor: the council of Troyes (878)

For the second time in two years the imperial throne was vacant. The pope, who had spared no trouble for Charles the Bald in the chimerical hope that the king of France would be in a position not only to pursue the same task of protection as had been inaugurated by Louis II, but also to reconstitute an imperial power strong enough to impose itself on the West, now had no choice of alternatives. Of the son of Charles, Louis the Stammerer, there could be, it seemed, no serious question; it was only with difficulty that he was to succeed, in France itself, in having himself recognized and obeyed. Moreover, Louis the German's eldest son, Carloman, had quickly made himself master of the situation in northern Italy. While John VIII returned to Rome in haste, Carloman installed himself at Pavia, where he received the oaths of loyalty of the magnates in the first half of October and wrote to the pope to prepare his impending imperial coronation. For John VIII there was no escape. All he could do was to make the best of his position by stating his conditions. But fate was against the Carolingians. Scarcely had the negotiations begun when Carloman fell gravely ill and also had to be taken home on a litter. His army was decimated by a fatal illness which an annalist calls 'Italian fever', and it became necessary to postpone the enterprise to a more propitious moment. Since Carloman's health steadily deteriorated, the very idea of conferring the supreme power on him soon had to be put aside.

More than ever, nevertheless, the pope felt the need of a protector; especially since, in addition to the Moslem danger to the capital, Lambert of Spoleto's exploits had become a menace. From the beginning of 787, John VIII struggled in vain against this duke's claim to lay down the law to him, and he protested vigorously against the shamelessness of Lambert's correspondence. In March the duke of Spoleto, flanked by the marquis of Tuscany, Adalbert, succeeded in penetrating into Rome, introduced there in his train the former conspirators of 876, and instituted a reign of terror. He tried to cut off the Sovereign Pontiff, shut up in St Peter's, from all communication with his men and his clergy; held him thus blockaded for thirty days in the basilica, and, during this period, assured himself of control of the city.

John VIII appealed to Carloman for help in vain. He was unaware of Carloman's illness, believing him to have simply retired into Alemania to settle the succession of Lorraine with his brothers. Then, despairing of being able to save the situation by his own means, he chose to enter Frankish territory and make a personal overture to the Carolingians in an effort to save Christendom from disaster. He dreamed of a great council in which Louis the German's three sons, Charles the Bald's son and the bishops of their four kingdoms, as well as those of Italy, collected under his presidency, should at last become aware of the danger and jointly arrange means to ward it off. After launching an anathema against Lambert of Spoleto and his accomplices, he left Rome, at the end of April 878, took to the sea, stopped at Genoa, and disembarked at Arles on 11 May. From there he had himself accompanied by Count Boso as far as Lyon, whence he pursued his journey northward.

Before leaving Rome, and then from Genoa, he had, in letters addressed to each of the Carolingian kings, exposed the gravity of the situation and requested them to seal amongst themselves an alliance which the common welfare made necessary. He had also announced the forthcoming holding of a council in which he hoped that a solution would at last be found, thanks to the goodwill of all, to the distressing problem of the Empire, the primary condition, in his eyes, for the welfare of the papacy and of the Church.

But a double and painful disillusionment awaited him on his arrival in France. There he learned successively of the illness of two of the four Carolingian kings whom he expected to gather around him: that of Carloman, whom he had planned to visit after the council, and that of Louis the Stammerer, who was kept at Tours by a sudden illness which for a moment threatened his life. All that the king of France could do, for the time being, was to facilitate the pope's journey to Troyes, where he ordered ten bishops to receive him and where the projected council was to be convoked for 1 August. As for Louis the Younger and Charles the Fat, they turned a deaf ear. Neither appears to have considered for a moment coming to Troyes, and the pope had to resign himself to planning to go to see them too after the council, which would now be no more than a council 'of the Gauls', the bishops of Germany being no more willing to appear there than their kings.

From one delay came another, and the council whose opening had at first been planned for 2 July, then for 1 August, began only on the 11th of that month, and even then the only Carolingian on whose presence John VIII had in the end counted, King Louis the Stammerer, arrived several days late, so that the effect hoped for by the pope was entirely absent: not a single ruler was there for the opening session, and the only bishops (the bishop of Porto excepted) present at the assembly were from Gaul. After the arrival of Louis the Stammerer, John VIII delivered a pathetic speech of which we have no more than two short fragments, to call his hearers without delay to the rescue of the "holy Roman Church" in peril. He returned several times to this theme in the course of the council. But what response could his words find with a king who was sick and without authority, and with a clergy whose state of mind Hincmar well represented when he advised the young king not to follow the example of his father in this respect? The council agreed, at the very best, to confirm the anathemas and excommunications pronounced by the Sovereign Pontiff against his adversaries at Rome, and particularly against Lambert of Spoleto and his lay and ecclesiastical accomplices. Then it drew up various detailed measures, and disbanded without doing any of the things the pope had expected of it. Between John VIII and the king of France there were only polite exchanges, and as soon as the council ended Louis hastened to have his guest escorted to Italy by Boso, who had gradually become the most prominent figure in his kingdom and one whose ambition incessantly grew.

As for John VIII, he had gained nothing but the bitterest disillusionment from his journey into Frankish territory. The experience of the council of Troyes had been enough for him; he no longer thought it useful to pursue his attempt further by paying to Carloman and his brothers the visits he had planned. At least he had obtained, before leaving France, the opening of direct negotiations between Louis the Stammerer and his cousin, Louis the Younger. The first fruit of this policy of rapprochement was the interview of Fouron, between Visé and Aachen, where in the context of the general policy of detente advocated by the pope, the two kings agreed on 1 November to a *modus vivendi* concerning various matters held in suspense: maintenance of the partition carried out between Louis the German and Charles the Bald at Meerssen in 870 of the territories belonging to the inheritance of Lothar II; temporary maintenance of the *status quo* in the territories of 'Provence' and 'Burgundy' belonging to the inheritance of Louis II; explicit reservation of the rights of each to Italy. They agreed furthermore to extend their conversations, at the beginning of the following February, to include Carloman and Charles the Fat, in an effort to realize among them all the general accord desired by the pope. Thus the pact of Fouron was, in their thinking, a prelude to the re-establishment of that Frankish unity of which, since the death of Louis the Pious, the Church had never despaired.

But the plenary conference of the Carolingian kings planned at Fouron could not take place. Already very ill for a long time, Carloman was struck by an attack of paralysis at the beginning of 879 and lost his power of speech. Hastening to his bedside, his brother Louis the Younger, who counted on his inheritance, exerted himself on the spot to obtain in advance the support of the Bavarian vassals. Louis the Stammerer, in his turn, had such a serious relapse of his malady at the beginning of the year that he was forced to leave the task of government to his young son Louis III, and died soon after on 10 April. In these circumstances, the planned conference had to be postponed indefinitely, and in this respect as well, John VIII's hopes were dashed.

The choice of Charles the Fat

On his return to Italy, the Sovereign Pontiff, who for a moment seems to have set his sights on Count Boso, whom Louis the Stammerer had given him as an escort for his return journey, had tried to convene a new council at Pavia in December, to take up once more the vital questions that had remained unsolved at Troyes. No one, it seems, answered his call; certainly not the archbishop of Milan nor, probably, his suffragans. It seemed as though the whole world was trying to form a void around the unfortunate pope. Little tempted to venture into the

Italian wasps' nest, Boso himself, having become the favourite son of John VIII since they had taken the road together from Arles to Troyes, then from Troyes to Pavia, had preferred to go back to Gaul to ensure for himself on the other side of the Alps advantages more substantial than the dazzling possibilities held out to him by the pope.

The political outlook was more discouraging than ever. In France, the premature death of Louis the Stammerer on 10 April 879 at the age of thirty-three, had been the signal for a new setback for the monarchy. For several months, extreme confusion reigned in the country; powerful men fought one another with the sole thought of arranging for themselves at the smallest cost the largest measure of independence and material advantage. With the eldest of the deceased's sons, Louis III, aged scarcely sixteen, whom Louis the Stammerer had, in the last months of his life, charged with the government, some hoped to associate his young brother, Carloman, his junior by two or three years. But, both were born of a first union that was held to be illegitimate, and consequently both were set aside by a turbulent group who wanted the king of 'eastern Francia', Louis the Younger as their ruler. It was thus only with difficulty that, after a threatened invasion of France by Louis the Younger, Louis III and Carloman were jointly crowned and anointed in haste at the end of the summer by the archbishop of Sens, Ansegisus, in the tiny monastery of Ferrières in Gâtinais. They had been finally accepted as kings, after their advisers had bought off the king of eastern Francia by ceding to him the part of Lorraine that had fallen to Charles the Bald in the partition of 870. But in fact Louis the Younger had withdrawn solely to have his hands free in Bavaria, where he was lying in wait for the inheritance of his brother Carloman, then dying and without any other child than a bastard, Arnulf, who was also waiting to make the most of his opportunities.

To whom, in such a contingency, could John VIII turn? For several months his correspondence betrayed his confusion. Up to June 879 he continued, at least for the sake of form, to write to Carloman and ask him for aid, although he had known for a number of weeks of his state of health. At the same time, around March, he still felt obliged to remind Boso of the secret conversations they had had at the Council of Troyes and of the obligations they had undertaken towards each other; and he asked him to make a final decision about his intentions. Then, without awaiting the answer, he wrote to Charles the Fat on 3 April to say that he counted on him and reserved for him the 'honours' which his devotion would bring him. He repeated this in June; but, as he was entrusting the bishop of Parma with a mission in Germany at this time, he advised him to check on the spot whether it was Carloman or Charles the Fat to whom he should address himself; while specifying that the Saracen peril obliged him to receive at the soonest possible moment the aid of "any king whatsoever". As a further precaution, he wrote at the same time to Louis the Younger to confide to him that the support of "his magnates" would be indispensable, that he awaited his arrival with impatience, and that he was ready to turn 'the Roman Empire' over to him.

Pope John VIII could not make up his mind between these various possible emperors-elect. On 6 May he declared that he dared not leave Rome because he expected the arrival of 'a king of the Franks' any day. Which one? He could not predict it with certainty; and, being distrustful, he warned the archbishop of Milan not to receive anyone as king without conferring with him first, "because the ordained emperor should first have been called and chosen" by the pope: a bold claim which proves how far, little by little, even in the gravest crises in which he struggled, John VIII had let himself be drawn. It was as if to say that the Sovereign Pontiff was no longer only the supreme dispenser of the imperial diadem but that he also had the exclusive right to dispose of the Lombard crown, on the pretext that the imperial dignity was its natural complement.

In the course of the summer of 879 the situation became clearer. Yielding to the entreaties of the pope, who had requested him to keep his promises or retire, Carloman withdrew in favour of his youngest brother, Charles the Fat, to whom he yielded his rights to Italy, while at the same time he allowed his other brother, Louis the Younger, to install himself in Bavaria. In October, Charles the Fat occupied northern Italy without even taking the time to notify the Sovereign Pontiff of his intentions, so that John VIII was taken by surprise at the news and reminded the king of Alemania to respect the proprieties. After all, perfectly logical with himself, John VIII evidently intended to subject the crowning of Charles as king of Italy to papal ratification. When he summoned Charles to Pavia for 1 November in order to deliberate about the affairs of the Church and the kingdom, John VIII demanded above all the despatch of an embassy to inform him, in the required manner of Charles' arrival. He still saw in him no more than a candidate. Charles the Fat nevertheless, in November and December, behaved as though he were the regular successor of the Lombard kings.

In January 880 the meeting desired by Charles the Fat took place at Ravenna. In the presence of the pope, the lay and ecclesiastical dignitaries officially took the oath of allegiance to the new king. However, from the very first, John VIII was forced to recognize that the king of Germany was not the kind of emperor he had hoped for. A letter he sent to him shortly afterwards gives painful evidence of this: the interview at Ravenna left John VIII with empty hands; he declared himself ready nevertheless, notwithstanding his disappointment, to "use all his efforts to further increase the honour and glory" of the new king of Italy if the king, on his part, would exert himself "with all his piety and in a spirit of devotion to realize what is necessary for the welfare and the glory of the Holy See"; but he required a preliminary assurance that, at the time of his coming to Rome, the future emperor would confirm "the pacts and privileges of the holy Roman Church" and break with the enemies of the papacy. Thus papal doctrine was finally specified. Forgetting perhaps rather precipitately that in this period the pope needed an emperor more than Charles the Fat desired the crown of the Augusti, John VIII laid down the principle – which was to last throughout the Middle Ages – that before coming to Rome to have himself anointed emperor by the pope, the king of Italy (later called the king of the Romans) must first confirm the privileges of the Roman Church and bind himself with formal pledges toward the Sovereign Pontiff.

Charles the Fat demonstrated clearly how much value he attached to such demands. After causing John VIII in October 879 the disagreeable surprise of arriving unexpectedly in Italy to take possession of the royal power, he caused him another no less disagreeable surprise by returning to Germany in April 880 without warning on the news of the death of his brother Carloman, who finally died on 22 March. John VIII could only send a trusted legate after him, his nephew and personal adviser Farulf, and inform him by letter, in pressing terms, of the urgent need for an expedition by him to Rome, where dangers were growing. Without putting himself out, Charles replied by assigning two protectors to the pope who – bitter irony – turned out to be . . . the new duke of Spoleto, Guy, son and accomplice of the only too well known Lambert, and his companion in robbery, the marquis of Tuscany, Adalbert: remarkable protectors! Though John VIII finally came to

terms with Adalbert, Guy, nick-named 'the Fury', remained an implacable enemy, who scoffed at the pope, and if we are to believe the pope,
behaved as a "thief and a robber". It was obviously impossible to rely
on such a figure to stem the Saracen advance!

Although the Moslem threat had somewhat abated, it still remained
formidable, and the renewed collusion of the Moslems with the civil
and religious authorities of southern Italy was again becoming dangerous. The bishops of Naples, Amalfi and Gaeta were themselves
involved. By means of large grants of money, which seriously impaired
his budget, the pope succeeded from time to time in arranging naval
support in various places which allowed him to postpone the fatal day
of reckoning; but this assistance remained precarious, and often the
donations represented an outright loss, the parties concerned merely
pocketing the money but making no effort to provide help. Sometimes
also John VIII obtained military aid from one or other of the Byzantine
squadrons, but this was still no more than an accidental means; and,
while the Saracen fleets cruised at sea off Ostia, the unfortunate pope
again trembled for the capital of Christianity.

He was obliged, however, to spend the whole year 880 waiting,
counting only on the Greek fleets to drive off or check the Saracens, to
the point, it seems, of arousing Charles the Fat's suspicions. Kept in his
kingdom by pressing affairs, the king of Germany displayed very little
eagerness to make the journey to Rome, notwithstanding repeated
letters in which the pope indicated to him an impatience which did not
however induce him to put aside his pretensions. For he repeated in
nearly all his letters that Charles should have himself preceded by an
ambassador with whom all questions concerning the rights and
privileges of the Roman Church should first be settled in an unambiguous manner, the imperial coronation being conditional on an agreement
on this point.

In November Charles at last returned to Italy, and in December,
taking the Via Emilia, he marched rapidly towards Rome, which he
entered in the first days of February 881 – even sooner than the pope
had expected, because, on 25 January, John VIII expressed his
"amazement" at the news that Charles the Fat was en route without
having sent ahead of him the embassy which the pope had repeatedly
requested. Legates were despatched to meet Charles with specific
instructions to inform him of the pope's irrevocable will not to confer
the imperial crown on him unless the prescribed agreement concerning

the rights and privileges of the Roman Church was concluded between
them before Charles crossed the frontiers of the Papal State. John VIII
was immovable on this point of principle, which in effect determined
the whole subsequent evolution of the imperial constitution; and it was
undoubtedly only after having given the Sovereign Pontiff the required
assurances that Charles was at last admitted to the honours of an
imperial coronation at St Peter's Rome in the first two weeks of
February 881 (perhaps on the 12th of that month).

The advantages which the pope was to derive from this event so
long and so impatiently awaited were however mediocre in the
extreme. Neither against the Saracens, nor against the duke of Spoleto,
nor indeed against anyone at all, did the new emperor undertake
anything, notwithstanding the desperate appeals the pope addressed to
him. Departing from Rome immediately after his coronation, Charles
never went to southern Italy and never even returned to the banks of
the Tiber. Only northern Italy had the privilege of his intermittent
presence. Although he promised to send help, he did not keep his word;
nor did he see John VIII again except during a council to which the
pope had summoned him at Ravenna in February 882. There, it is true,
he did make certain decisions of principle against the enemies of the
Holy See, notably against the duke of Spoleto, but thereafter he turned
away more and more from Italian affairs and left the pope to his
unhappy fate. Prey to the gravest difficulties, betrayed by all, without
sufficient means to prevent the Saracens, allied with Gaeta, from
completely occupying the valley of the Garigliano and resuming their
raids into Roman territory, John VIII was to die tragically on 15
December 882, poisoned, it was said, by one of his household
servants, then finished off by hammer-blows on the head.

The hope of a recovery

Outside Italy, the accession of Charles the Fat to the imperial throne
had seemed for a moment to warrant hope of a recovery. Fate soon
made him the heir of the whole of Germany. His elder brother
Carloman had died, as we have seen, at the beginning of 880, leaving a
bastard as sole descendant, Arnulf, who was for that reason excluded
from the succession. Charles's other brother, Louis the Younger, who

had inherited Carloman's German lands and occupied the whole of ancient Lotharingia, had fallen so seriously ill in the summer or autumn of 881 that he died on 20 January 882; he too – by an unkind fate – left no legitimate heir because of the premature deaths of his sons. Although the authority of Louis III and Carloman in the West Frankish kingdom had easily, at the beginning of 880, checked a new attempt at conquest planned by Louis the Younger, it still seemed very precarious. The question thus arose as to whether Charles the Fat, now in the prime of his life, for he was born in 839, would be capable of reconstituting around himself that imperial unity the memory of which had since his childhood obsessed the minds of men.

Recent events had once more revived the old notion of Frankish solidarity. In the south-east of Gaul a rival, foreign to the Carolingian family, had presented himself in the person of the same Boso, count of Vienne, brother-in-law of Charles the Bald, whose disturbing activities since 876 in the entourage of the kings of France and of the pope we have already mentioned. Briefly delegated in that year by his brother-in-law to the government of Italy, he had married the daughter of Emperor Louis II, Ermengarde, who seems to have brought him something of that spirit of intrigue that obsessed her mother, the turbulent Engelberga, and a superabundance of ambition which, however, he hardly needed. Since then, his rebellion at the time of Charles the Bald's second journey to Italy, his unreliable attitude in the reign of Louis the Stammerer, his secret talks with John VIII at the time of the Council of Troyes, his ambiguous role at the accession of Louis III and Carloman – all these had made his dishonesty more than evident. He pursued only selfish aims, influenced more and more by his wife who, according to Hincmar, was indignant at the thought that, as the daughter of an emperor and almost wedded herself to an emperor (for her father's diplomacy had for a moment destined her for the Byzantine emperor Basil I), she now had a mere count for a husband! But, on 25 July 879, in one of his charters, Boso proudly assumed this unusual title: "I, Boso, who am what I am by the grace of God", while the notary who drew up this document called himself, no less proudly, 'archchancellor', on the model of the heads of the great royal chanceries. As for the regnal year of the two princes then seated on the throne of France, Louis III and Carloman, which, according to custom, ought to have been indicated in the dating, it was passed over in silence. The intention not to consider himself a subject of the sons of

Louis the Stammerer was obvious. Boso may even at that moment have considered these young men unworthy of kingship. This was without doubt what, several weeks later, the six archbishops of Vienne, Lyon, Besançon, Tarentaise, Aix and Arles, and nineteen of their suffragans intended to say, when, meeting with a certain number of 'magnates' at Mantaille, near Vienne, on 15 October 879, they took it upon themselves to confer the royal dignity on Boso. They had elected him king at that juncture, they declared, because, the death of Louis the Stammerer having left the kingdom without a protector, God had inspired them to choose the man in whom both Charles the Bald and Louis the Stammerer had placed their confidence, and whom Pope John VIII, praising his merits in all directions, had personally chosen as protector when he returned to Rome.

Thus a new figure, stranger by birth to the Carolingian family, profiting by the troubles that had arisen in Gaul after the successive deaths of Charles the Bald and Louis the Stammerer, aspired to usurp the royal title and to set himself up as a rival to the legitimate descendants of Charlemagne and Louis the Pious! One can imagine the emotions aroused in the West by such news. All the Carolingians at once felt threatened by this usurpation, which attacked the very principle of their power, which was founded, as we may recall, on the exclusive right of their family to govern the Franks by virtue of the anointing conferred upon Pepin the Short and his sons by Stephen II. Talks were arranged between all of them, not excepting the sons of Louis the Stammerer, in whose favour Archbishop Hincmar of Reims intervened with Charles the Fat, and a meeting of the four Carolingians surviving at that time – Louis the Younger, Charles the Fat, Louis III and Carloman – was arranged at Gondreville on the Moselle in June 880. Charles the Fat went there; so did Louis III and Carloman. Louis the Younger, being ill, had himself represented. A joint plan of action was drawn up against Boso, as well as several other measures of general interest, notably a campaign against a bastard of Lothar II, Hugh, who had been trying for some time to rule independently in what used to be Lorraine. The expedition planned against Boso was undertaken in July, the troops of Louis the Younger co-operating at first in the southwest of Gaul, with the troops of Louis III and Carloman, which had been at their side in the campaign against Hugh of Lorraine; then those of Charles the Fat arrived from Italy to join them under the command of their king. Thus the usurpation of Boso had wrought this miracle: the uniting of all the Carolingian forces upon the same battlefield, and this miracle lasted for several months, until November, and revived the sentiment of solidarity between the various Frankish kingdoms, formerly connected by their subjection to a single ruler.

The fact that Boso was eventually able to maintain himself in the south-west of Gaul and set up for himself a small independent kingdom there – the so-called kingdom of Provence – after contending for the throne of France with its legitimate occupants, did not diminish the effect of this temporary co-operation of all the Carolingian forces uniting against the usurper. When Charles the Fat had himself crowned at Rome in February 881, a few weeks after participating in the siege of Vienne, on the Rhône, alongside the armies of his brother and those of his young cousins of France, he could believe with some justification that with him, this time, the former Frankish Empire was well on the way to restoration. Moreover, in the Frankish kingdom of the West, at this very moment, Hincmar's voice was raised anew to plead for a return to the ancestral tradition and the unity of the Christian West.

After a temporary eclipse in the later years of Charles the Bald's reign, the authority of the archbishop of Reims had again become great. His influence seems to have been decisive on Louis the Stammerer, and it was constantly exercised to re-establish harmony and co-operation among all the Carolingians. Once Louis the Stammerer was gone, Hincmar had not hesitated to enter into relations with Charles the Fat when Charles became head of the Carolingian family. Since Charles did not himself have any sons, Hincmar had written to ask him not only to take his two cousins Louis III and Carloman, into his protection, but to adopt the two orphans, assign tutors to them, and make provisions for their safety and for that of their kingdom; in short to take all necessary steps for the maintenance of their rule. Louis III and Carloman would thus be temporarily subordinated to the German king, but would later become the legitimate heirs of all the territories assembled under his and their own authority. This was a bold solution which in any event circumstances were to make impossible.

At the same time Hincmar exerted himself through his writings as well as his actions to revive the ancient ideal of Carolingian grandeur. Already in the last years of Charles the Bald's reign, he had composed, for the king's use, a small treatise concerning the rights and duties of the monarchy, such as they had traditionally been since the time of Charlemagne and Louis the Pious. He returned to the subject in 877 in a letter to Louis the Stammerer in which he attempted to draw lessons from the past that might be useful for the present. On 2 April 881, in drawing up the acts of an episcopal synod held under his presidency in the church of Sainte-Macre at Fismes, he presented Louis III–who was the son of Louis the Stammerer to whom the government of northern France had been given–with a long series of articles taken from old capitularies. For the sake of the young prince he recalled the glorious time when Charlemagne reigned over the Empire, surrounded by his councillors, of whom, according to Hincmar, he always had three near him, and with whom he carefully prepared all his decisions. Model yourself upon this illustrious example, Hincmar declared to Louis III, if you wish to revive in this kingdom the traditions of justice and the ancestral virtues which alone will allow it to be rescued from disorders and from destruction by the pagans. For too long, instead of defending themselves against the Northmen, people had been content to purchase their departure, involving thereby in the same ruin, because of the oppressive tribute that had to be paid, both the poor people and the churches that had once been wealthy. For too long, also, "this kingdom, but lately noble and large, has been divided within itself".

Lastly, in 882, after the death of Louis III, who died prematurely on 5 August of that year, Hincmar, himself close to death, addressed a final admonition to the youthful Carloman, who was thenceforth alone on the throne of France. He told him that Carolingian rule could only survive if the kings recaptured the essence of Frankish grandeur, and this was why in his *De ordine palatii* he did not hesitate to present the king and his subjects with a complete picture of the political and administrative organization of the Frankish Empire in the time of its founder. A strongly idealized picture, to be sure, whose object was less to analyze the workings of a regime that had vanished, than to point out the characteristics through which, in Hincmar's eyes, the ancient 'kingdom' had formerly succeeded in imposing itself in the respect of all "by its very grandeur and by its unity".

Unification around the emperor against the barbarians

These warnings were not superfluous at a moment when from all sides the mounting flood-tide of barbarians threatened to sweep away the

last defenses opposed to it by the Carolingians, who were the last hope
of the West. While in Italy the papacy was exerting itself in every way
to check the advance of the Moslems in the direction of Rome, the
Scandinavian pirates were penetrating further and further into Frankish territory. Becoming bolder every year, they set up their winter
quarters at Ghent, at the end of 879; at Courtrai, ten leagues further
south, in 880; at Condé-sur-l'Escaut in 882; at Amiens in 883; and in 885
they were at Paris. Likewise in the regions of the Meuse and Rhine,
they were overwintering at Nijmegen at the end of 880; at Elsloo, near
Maastricht, in 881; at Louvain in 884. From these bases, each time
further from their point of departure, they spread with growing
boldness over all the surrounding regions, sacking and burning
churches and abbeys, royal palaces and towns, everywhere sowing
terror and death, everywhere gathering booty and prisoners. At the end
of 881, Aachen suffered the same fate; the palace of Charlemagne was
destroyed and the famous imperial chapel served as a stable for the
barbarians' horses.

For they were no longer satisfied with going up the rivers and
streams with their ships; they now had a cavalry which they sent
across the countryside, which broke through the defences of towns and
operated by surprise in vast areas from which the population, seized
with panic, had fled, in the hope of escaping the slaughter. This was a
scene of horror, which drew a cry of distress from the usually
impassive annalist of St Vaast's at Arras:

> The Northmen do not cease capturing and killing the Christian people, destroying
> churches, demolishing fortifications, and burning towns. Everywhere, there are only
> corpses of priests, laymen, whether noble or not, women, young people, suckling babes.
> There is no road, there is no place, where the ground is not strewn with corpses. We live in
> distress and grief at the sight of this annihilation of the Christian people.

From time to time, a king or a commander had the courage to tackle
the enemy. Thus in February 880 Louis the Younger bravely attacked
the Vikings who were entrenched in Thiméon, north of Charleroi,
and inflicted heavy losses on them, until the moment he discovered
among the dead the corpse of his dearly-beloved son. And so again on 3
August 881 King Louis III, by a stroke of boldness, barred the retreat
of a Norse army which was returning from Beauvais, laden with booty,
and gave battle at Saucourt-en-Vimeu, near the mouth of the Somme.
For a moment his troops wavered, but he dismounted, calmly re-assem-
bled his men, gave them back their courage, and got the better of the

barbarians who thenceforth, the annalist says, "began to fear this young king" of twenty. However, alongside these impressive feats, there were many setbacks, many retreats. On 2 February 880 in Saxony a large German army was cut to pieces by the Vikings: two bishops, twelve counts, among whom the brother of the queen, eighteen direct vassals of Louis the Younger and all of their retinues were left on the battlefield; 'innumerable men', the annalist of Fulda asserts, were made prisoners. It was a disaster without precedent. But, usually, people did not even put up a fight: the terror the Northmen inspired was such that they preferred to negotiate at once and to buy their departure by paying a tribute, the amount of which was open to negotiation. This was a mediocre palliative, which did no more than delay the date or shift the problem elsewhere, since the Norse chief only retreated from one place to go and attack another.

Who was now to rescue Christendom from disaster? Louis the Younger, the victor of Thiméon, died in January 882; Louis III, the victor of Saucourt, in the following August. His brother Carloman was not lacking in courage, and he showed it in more than one battle – before Reims at the end of 882, at the mouth of the Somme several months later – but he was still almost a child at sixteen years of age. Charles the Fat alone remained, and all hope came to be fixed on him. In May or June 882, on his return to Italy, where he had received the imperial crown one year earlier, he decided to collect a large army against the Vikings: Franks, Alemans, Thuringians, Saxons even Lombards were mobilized; the emperor took command of the army and went in July to besiege the camp of the Norse chiefs on the Meuse, at Elsloo; but to everyone's keen disappointment he too allowed himself to be persuaded, after twelve days, to negotiate with the pirates: by the payment of a large 'tribute' he bought their retreat into Frisia, where Duke Godfrey was officially installed on the vain promise of his alliance and his conversion to Christianity. People continued nonetheless to hope in Charles the Fat; and the fact is that, while he did not intervene in person for more than a short time, after the affair of Elsloo, he delegated the fighting to a brilliant general, Count Henry, whose glorious victories were crowned, in 885, by a stroke of boldness: the murder of Duke Godfrey and of his retinue, who were attacked in the middle of the Frisian country by the Frankish warriors whom Henry himself had led into the enemy camp under the pretense of new negotiations.

Meanwhile, the situation in the western kingdom deteriorated.

Carloman too, after trying to resist, had been obliged at the beginning
of 884, on the advice of his magnates, to buy some months of peace by
paying a tribute to the Vikings then installed at Amiens. But he did
not long survive this agreement, and his accidental death on 12
December 884 at the age of eighteen left France kingless and exposed
to the attacks of an adversary who was awaiting a favourable opportunity to resume his advances. The country, moreover, was in a state of
disintegration and anarchy, as the capitularies of the years 883 and 884
show, and from then on there seemed no way of ending the armed
raids, the robberies and depredations, which the church leaders,
through the pen of Hincmar and other prelates, had already for some
time constantly denounced in their synods.

Now, the only survivor of Louis the Stammerer's progeny was a
posthumous son, Charles, who later was to be called 'the Simple' – born
from a second marriage, but still of such a tender age (his fifth birthday
was in September 884) and of a legitimacy so disputable (the first wife
of his father was still alive and their marriage had not been regularly
annulled) that no one seems to have seriously considered permitting his
ascent to the throne in such critical circumstances. The only possible
solution was an appeal to the emperor, the only Carolingian then
capable of reigning. As this solution carried general agreement, Charles
the Fat was invited to receive the oaths of allegiance of his new
subjects, who went hastily and in great numbers to Ponthion in June
885 for the ceremony.

Without any doubt this eagerness is explained by the confidence
placed at that moment in the person of an emperor whom we are too
accustomed to judge in the light of the disillusions of the months that
were to follow. At this juncture, people saw in Charles only a young
and enterprising prince, whom up to that moment Fortune had hardly
ceased to smile upon, and for whom she had arranged, without his
apparently seeking it very much, the most amazing success: the union
under his rule of all the territories formerly subject to a single ruler.
His name too, aroused the hope that the glorious traditions would
finally revive. And perhaps it was not coincidence that, around this
date, a monk of St Gall, Notker the Stammerer, after the visit of the
new ruler of the West to his monastery in December 883, took it into
his head to compose for the instruction of this distinguished guest, not
as Hincmar had done, a *De ordine palatii*, but a kind of edifying history
of the great emperor Charles, from whom he desired his namesake of

the end of the century to learn some useful lessons. However laughable may be, in more than one passage, this book of the good 'monk of St Gall' whose stories were for too long held by historians to be true, he is at least in his way a curious witness to the state of men's minds around 885 and, indirectly, of the hopes aroused in more than one circle by the return of another Charles to the throne of the West.

The collapse

These hopes were quickly deceived. No more in Frankish than in Italian territory did Charles the Fat accomplish any of the things that were expected of him. His first act on arriving in Gaul had been to raise an army against the Vikings and to have it march on Louvain, where the Vikings were stationed. But, because of illness, the normal leader of the expedition, one of the most powerful figures of Neustria, Hugh called 'the Abbot', could not take command of the army, and consequently defeat was total. The annalist of St Vaast's of Arras tells us that the Northmen greeted the Frankish soldiers with sarcastic words like these: "Why have you come? You shouldn't have bothered. We know who you are and what you want: you want us to return to your homes? All right: we shall not fail to do so!"

And as a matter of fact, some weeks later, in June 885, the Vikings departed in a southerly direction, marched on Rouen, and entered the city; then, joined by a fleet of 700 large ships, they went up the Seine and assembled in November under the walls of Paris in an army of some 40,000 men, the largest anyone had ever seen. Paris resisted heroically under the leadership of Count Odo and Bishop Gozlin. Notified of the siege, Charles the Fat, who was detained in Bavaria, hastily sent to the rescue of the city his best general, Count Henry, then in the full brilliance of his renown, after the slaughter of the Northmen in Frisia. But this time Henry was less fortunate. With a tired cavalry, sorely tried by the inclement weather, he could not overcome the Norse troops who, solidly entrenched before Paris, refused battle. At very best, around March 886, he managed to throw their camp into disarray and inflict some losses of men and horses on them, in order to open a way to the city, for which he had brought provisions. Thereafter he set off again to find reinforcements and to warn the emperor, who at that very moment was returning from Italy. In that troubled period the inconveniences of a monarchy whose territory was too large, and whose ruler was called everywhere at once by equally pressing, but often irreconcilable needs, began to become apparent.

From Metz, where he had held a general assembly in July 886, the emperor decided to march to the rescue of Paris. At the end of August his army was assembled at Quierzy on the Oise. But Count Henry, sent out as a scout, allowed himself be surprised by the enemy and fell before Paris on 28 August, so that, when the emperor finally arrived at the head of his troops, to camp on the hill of Montmartre in October, the game was already virtually lost, because of the lack of a general capable of leading the attack. In addition, news spread that the Norse chief Siegfried, who had left Paris in March, was arriving with reinforcements. So, after driving back the besiegers on the left bank and himself crossing the Seine, the emperor decided to negotiate without waiting any longer. In exchange for the payment of a 'tribute' of 700 pounds of silver and permission to spend the winter in Burgundy, the Vikings agreed to raise the siege, promising to return to their homeland in the following spring. Once this pact was concluded, the emperor returned to Germany more quickly than he had come: having left Paris at the earliest possible moment on 6 November, he was near Metz on the 12th and in Alsace a few days later.

Dangerously ill, carefully transported from Alsace to the shores of the Lake of Constance, there obliged to undergo in February 887 a serious operation on the head – doubtless a trepanning – this emperor of forty-seven was thereafter no more than a shadow of his former self, and his abrupt departure from Paris – this departure with which historians have always reproached him as though it were a desertion, almost as though it were a betrayal – may well have been caused by the breakdown of his health.

The misfortune which had dogged his brothers and had taken them both from this life before their time without leaving any children, now pursued him in his turn. No more than they did he have legitimate children. In 885 he had tried in vain to have recognized as his heir a bastard, Bernard, for whose declaration of legitimacy he had up to then unsuccessfully requested the pope. He was alone. He now experienced the neglect in which his brother Carloman had lived the last months of his life, when the whole world watched the advance of his illness and waited for his death. He distrusted his entourage. At the beginning of the summer of 887 he abruptly dismissed his chancellor and arch-chaplain, Liutward, in whom he had formerly placed his confidence, and at the same time he withdrew from Empress Richarde whom he suspected of entertaining sinful relations with Liutward. Dissatisfaction mounted against this sick and moody emperor.

In the autumn revolts broke out almost everywhere: in Franconia, Saxony, Thuringia, Bavaria, and Swabia. Arnulf, the bastard son of Carloman, with whom the ex-chancellor Liutward had sought contact, was urged by the rebels to join them. He was a young man of thirty-five to forty, who had acquired his experience in Carinthia and Pannonia, and also in the course of the struggle against the Vikings in 882. The rebels elected him king. At Tribur, or Trebur, a dozen or so kilometres south-east of Mainz, where he had convoked a general assembly in November, the emperor was forsaken by everyone. He had only one resort: to place himself at the mercy of the usurper, who agreed to leave him the use of some estates in Swabia. There he died, forgotten by all, on the following 13 January, at Neidingen, near the Black Forest.

CHAPTER EIGHT

The dissolution of the Carolingian Empire

With Charles the Fat, the Carolingian Empire may be considered to have ended. The imperial dream was still for a long time to continue to obsess men's minds, but the ideal to which the Empire of a Charlemagne and a Louis the Pious had corresponded and which after them the Church had vainly tried to realize, thenceforth no longer had any reality. The Carolingian Empire had been born of a progressive extension of the 'kingdom of the Franks' (*regnum Francorum*) that is to say of Frankish rule, as far as the frontiers of the Christian West, excepting Britain and Ireland. Now, in 887, Frankish unity was no more than a memory about to vanish, and the Carolingian family, whose victories had allowed the task begun under the Merovingians to be considerably extended, was itself becoming extinct.

The birth of new monarchies

Here the facts speak clearly. At the moment he left Gaul, after his short and unsuccessful intervention, Charles the Fat had voluntarily entrusted extensive powers to the valiant defender of Paris, Count Odo, son of the famous Robert the Strong, who had fallen gloriously in the battle of Brissarthe in 886 in the course of his struggle against the Vikings of the Loire; and since then, it was not only Charles the Fat, but also the 'Franks of the East', as they are called by the annalist of St Vaast's of Arras, who appear to have been unconcerned about the fate of Gaul. After Charles the Fat, their King Arnulf left them to grapple alone with the Vikings; and he allowed the archbishop of Reims,

Fulk, to put forward a competitor to Count Odo in the person of Guy, duke of Spoleto, whom one would not have expected to play such a role. Also, without saying a word, he let the two rivals be crowned king, Odo at Compiègne on 29 February 888, Guy at Langres, almost simultaneously. It was only when, as a result of the final failure of the duke of Spoleto, the archbishop of Reims, not wanting Odo at any price, pressed the king of Germany to intervene in France, that Arnulf at last decided, about the beginning of June, at the Diet of Frankfurt, to take some notice of what was happening between the Seine and the Loire. Odo was at that moment in the eyes of the continuator of the *Annals of Fulda* still no more than one of the many "kinglets" who, having usurped power in various parts of "Europe", were trying "to conduct themselves as kings". Several days later, however, on 24 June, Odo achieved a brilliant victory over the Vikings near Montfaucon in Argonne, and it was with the aureole of this success, which had profound reverberations, that he agreed to go to Worms in August to pay a visit to Carloman's son.

In these circumstances, Arnulf did not for a moment think of challenging Odo's right to the royal title which the Franks of the West had awarded him; he accepted their decision, just as the archbishop of Reims himself in the end declared his adhesion. The archbishop consoled himself with the thought that by the act of going to Worms Odo became the Carolingian's 'man' – which, of course, did not at all accord with reality. But it is a fact that, having been officially recognized as king by Arnulf, with whom he henceforth entertained normal diplomatic relations. Odo could congratulate himself on having overcome the most important obstacles that up to then had impeded the establishment of a non-Carolingian monarchy in France. More precisely, in place of the dynastic principle which had been temporarily set aside because of the circumstances, a new principle had been accepted, with which already the electors of Boso at Mantaille in 879 had tried to justify their choice: that the person chosen should be the candidate designated by God as the one best qualified to take on the defense of the realm.

In the south-west of Gaul, Boso died a year earlier than Charles the Fat, in January 887, and it seems clear that his kingdom had from then on temporarily reverted to the authority of the emperor. But not for very long. In January 888 a new figure appeared, Count Rudolf, of the powerful Welf family. Already in possession of a number of counties in 'Burgundy'–notably those of Geneva, Lausanne and Sion–he caused himself to be proclaimed and crowned king at Saint-Maurice in the Valais, from where he went on to extend his authority over a large part of Burgundy, for a time even over Lorraine and Alsace. Meanwhile, in the whole southern part of the former kingdom of Boso, Boso's young son, Louis of Provence (whose name indicated that he was related through his mother Ermengarde, daughter of Emperor Louis II, to the Carolingian family) had himself elected and crowned king at Valence in the last months of 890.

The report of this election states that, in view of the anarchy that reigned in the country and the constant attacks of the Vikings and Saracens to which it was exposed, the members of the assembly had adjudged it impossible to go on prolonging the vacancy of a throne that had remained unoccupied since the death of Emperor Charles and which no one seemed more worthy of occupying than Boso's son. His tender age would doubtless prevent him from personally resisting the barbarians, but with God's help he would accomplish his task with the advice and aid of the great laymen and prelates of the kingdom and with that of his mother. While proclaiming loudly that the young prince was "the grandson of the late Emperor Louis of glorious memory" and that "the mighty Emperor Charles" (Charles the Fat) had designated him for the monarchy–which seems a rather bold assertion–the clerical members of the assembly of Valence, in particular the archbishops of Lyon, Vienne, Arles, Embrun and their suffragans, fortified, as they said, by the approval of the Sovereign Pontiff, and certain of interpreting the Divine Will correctly, declared that they chose him because he seemed to them "the best qualified" to respond to the exigencies of the situation. It was thus once again the new principle formulated at Mantaille that gained their adherence, the dynastic argument being, in their eyes, an additional reason, but not in itself a sufficient one, for the election of their candidate. In this case the dynastic argument was actually invalid, since descent in the female line did not then entail any right to the royal succession.

In a similar move, Italy also detached itself at the beginning of 888. Two rivals contended for its crown: Marquis Berengar of Friuli and Duke Guy of Spoleto, the very person who, "consumed by the desire to rule", as a contemporary chronicler has it, was at that time also trying to seize the throne of France. Son and successor of Marquis Everard of Friuli, Berengar, like Louis of Provence, belonged to the

Carolingian family through his mother Gisela, the daughter of Louis the Pious and Empress Judith. But he was no more a Carolingian than Louis of Provence, and when they conferred the royal crown on him at Pavia the magnates of Lombardy were probably moved by the same concern as those of France and Provence: to choose the man who, through the military qualities which he had up to then demonstrated in his position of command, seemed the obvious person to protect northern Italy against the Slavs who threatened its eastern frontier. Others, in view of the Saracen raids, which continued to be a serious threat to the south, and particularly also for the position of the papacy, had looked in these same years to the duke of Spoleto who, having given up his previous erring ways, turned, after John VIII's death, into a zealous defender of the Papal State against the Moslems. He had even won renown by inflicting various defeats on them in the Garigliano valley. Now, cherished by John VIII's successor Stephen V, who called him his "adopted son", was he not, more than Berengar his arch-rival, the obvious candidate for the crown of Italy?

Arms were to decide the fate of these two rivals. In an encounter that took place in the Lombard plain on the banks of the Trebbia at the beginning of 889, Berengar was beaten, and this "judgment of God" settled the fate of Italy. A new diet held at Pavia in February agreed on the necessity of re-establishing order by conferring power on someone designated by God. Through this new king, the evils overwhelming the kingdom everywhere since the death of the "glorious Emperor Charles", would at last be exorcized; he would be "a king, a lord, a protector" to all; the Roman Church would find in him a vigilant defender. In short, just as at Mantaille, there was only one concern: to choose the prince by whom Italy would be best protected against all harm. Neither the unity of the former Empire nor the dynastic aspect was now alluded to, even in the slightest manner. The political landscape had changed.

The claims of Arnulf of Germany

This does not mean, however, that in 888 the whole Carolingian past died at a single stroke. Revolutions that suddenly annihilate all previous traditions are few in history, and it should not surprise us, consequently, that the ideal of Frankish unity, which was still bound up with respect for dynastic privilege, remained deep-rooted in the minds of men longer than seemed called for by the actual circumstances.

Sole representative of the Carolingian family in possession of a throne, notwithstanding the illegitimate birth which had caused him to be excluded from power for a number of years, Arnulf did not seem at all resigned to being a mere king of Germany in a Europe that was fragmented into small independent kingdoms of equal status. We have already cited the passage in which the continuator of the *Annals of Fulda* spoke in denigrating terms of the "kinglets" (*reguli*) who, in 888, claimed to act as kings. Here he clearly echoes the entourage of the king of Germany who, invested with the dignity of being a Carolingian and the successor of Charles the Fat, assumed a supercilious attitude toward the small fry of usurpers. To the Diet of Worms, held in the course of the summer of 888, Arnulf summoned the petty king of France, Odo. Placed under pressure and in order to avoid worse, as the French annalist of St Vaast's confesses, Odo at last went to this meeting, thereby giving everyone the impression of an at least implicit recognition of the superior authority of the Carolingian. On the German side too the "humility" of his attitude was stressed, and the archbishop of Reims, desiring to disparage Odo, even spoke of "homage".

In October of the same year, King Rudolf of Burgundy, whose attempts at expansion in Alsace had been checked by Arnulf's troops, decided to negotiate with him, and went to meet him at Regensburg in the hope of making an amicable arrangement; and this move has generally been considered very similar to that of Odo of France, though the sources do not insist on such an interpretation. In the following month Arnulf departed for Italy, where he intended to make his rights to the monarchy respected. Berengar of Friuli, whom Guy of Spoleto had at that moment not yet been able to conquer, hastened to meet him at Trent. He was received "with clemency" by the German king, who condescended "to renounce his intention of taking away part of his kingdom", as the continuator of the *Annals of Fulda* puts it, obviously inclined to give a flattering version of the facts to assuage his ruler's self-esteem. Likewise, in 890 Ermengarde, mother of the petty king Louis of Provence, thought herself obliged, before her son's coronation, to make sure of Arnulf's approval, and explicit mention was made of this in the official record of his election.

Obviously, then, the fact of being a Carolingian, even though a bastard one, brought Arnulf great prestige, and indeed an authority essentially superior to that of all his rivals. Would he be content to stop there? In 890, according to an annalist, Pope Stephen V, whose confidence in Guy of Spoleto had diminished a great deal, informed the German king that he would be pleased to see him "visit the resting-place of St Peter and resume the government of the Italian kingdom to save it from the wicked Christians and from the pagans that threatened it". But at that time other more urgent tasks kept Arnulf in Germany, where Northmen, Moravians, and the intrigues of a bastard of Charles the Fat, Bernard, gave him plenty to think about. He thus saw himself obliged to leave Italy to its fate for the time being, although he had been preparing to intervene there since 888. He had not therefore enforced his rights, for the moment at least, against Berengar of Friuli. But less patience would be forthcoming toward Guy of Spoleto, whose ambition knew no bounds. Had not this man, once he was king of Italy, made up his mind to claim the imperial crown, which Pope Stephen had then been obliged to confer on him in February 891? And on top of that, had he not taken it into his head to extract from Pope Formosus, in April 892, the same honour for his young son Lambert, already associated with him as king of Italy since 1 May 891?

If he were to let such events pass without protest, Arnulf ran the risk of seeing himself ousted for good from the Italy to which Pope Stephen had requested him to come. Accordingly, he hesitated no longer. From 893 on he aimed once more at the conquest of the peninsula and of the imperial crown. At the beginning of 894 he occupied Lombardy and tried with every possible means to go to Rome to be anointed emperor.

At that moment his position in the West seemed to be truly strong. In the midst of the general confusion he was somewhat naively imagined still to represent the tradition of his great Carolingian ancestors. In October 891 he covered himself in glory by inflicting, at the head of a Frankish army, a severe and bloody defeat on the Vikings near Louvain. In July 892, leading a powerful army of Franks, Alemans and Bavarians, he undertook a victorious expedition in Moravia; and at the beginning of 894 he enforced his recognition in northern Italy by the bravery and boldness he displayed in his attack on Bergamo, as well as by the exemplary chastisement he meted out to the defenders of the city for having dared to resist him.

At the assembly of Worms in June 894, when he had just returned from this last expedition, Arnulf acted as the arbiter of the West. Brought into disrepute by a series of defeats in the course of the struggle against the Vikings, and abandoned by some of his magnates, King Odo of France found himself opposed by a group of malcontents, at whose head still stood Archbishop Fulk of Reims, who favoured the posthumous son of Louis the Stammerer, the young Charles (whom we call Charles the Simple),˙now almost at the age of legal majority, which was fifteen years. Arnulf was requested to decide between the two kings, Odo, the first to be crowned, and Charles, who was a Carolingian. The archbishop of Reims apologized for not having consulted the German king before anointing the young prince, arguing that "it was not customary" when for a deceased king was substituted "a member of his family, to consult a higher king". He added that the young king was prepared to govern according to the advice of his powerful neighbour. Arnulf received his young cousin, who came to Worms to request his protection, condescendingly, and, according to a French annalist, "granted him the paternal kingdom". In the following year, when this solution had provoked serious troubles in France and Charles had proved incapable of governing, Arnulf summoned the two rivals to his court. He gave his confidence to Odo who, unlike his rival Charles, actually made the journey to Germany and appeared before Arnulf laden with gifts.

Several days earlier, at the beginning of May, in a general assembly held in the palace of Tribur near Mainz, the German king had appeared in all the brilliance of his glory, surrounded, as the official record says, "with an immense throng of bishops, abbots, counts, magnates, clerks and laymen". From the height of his throne, clothed in his finest attire, he had received from the hands of his bishops the record of the conciliar decisions in which they eulogized the "prince who the King of Kings had deigned to place above all the orders of the ecclesiastical sublimity and over all the dignities of secular power, enflaming his heart with the ardour of the Holy Spirit and with divine charity, so that he appeared to the whole world as chosen, not by men and for men, but by the Lord himself". The palace of Tribur had been, on that occasion, the scene of pompous ceremonies, clearly intended to heighten the prestige of the Carolingian king on the brink of decisive events.

The last attempt to revive the Carolingian Empire in 896

It was indeed immediately after the diet of Tribur that Arnulf started for Rome to receive the imperial crown there, and his entourage deluded itself with the idea that the Empire was about to be reborn out of its ashes. In February 896 he was solemnly received by the 'Roman senate' and the representatives of the wards of the Eternal City, carrying their banners and their crosses. Following the tradition, all had hastened to meet him as far as the Milvian Bridge, from where they accompanied him in procession to the basilica of St Peter.

Pope Formosus, who had been expecting his arrival for months, awaited him at the top of the steps. He led him inside, just as Leo III had done with Charlemagne years earlier. The surroundings were the same as at Christmas 800; the ceremony was copied from the one then carried out. Arnulf was crowned emperor "according to the usage of his ancestors". The long open parenthesis after the death of Charles the Fat was at last closed. History began anew . . . .

Or so, at least, it was thought. But only the appearances were the same. Arnulf had had to use force to make his way to Rome, then in the hands of another emperor, the young Lambert of Spoleto, who had been officially enthroned, as we have seen, in 892 by the same Pope Formosus from whose hands the German king had just received the crown. Lambert, who had succeeded his father in 894, was certainly no more than a child, under the tutelage of his mother Ageltrude; but he possessed the imperial title and, confronted by this rival, however weak, the Carolingian cut a poor figure. Two weeks after the ceremony in St Peter's Arnulf was obliged to go on campaign to try to reduce, in his retreat of Spoleto, the child in whose name his authority was disputed.

The task was beyond his physical means. Suddenly prostrated by a stroke, this unfortunate representative of an exhausted race had to be taken back to Germany at once and he never returned. He died there in an obscure manner in 899. This last revival of the Carolingian Empire was thus ephemeral, and the imperial title was from then on granted, after Lambert of Spoleto, only to two petty princes to whom it brought no increase of prestige whatsoever: Louis of Provence and Berengar of Friuli, belated survivors of a world that now had disappeared for good.

CHAPTER NINE

On the threshold of a new world

In reality, the Carolingian Empire was dead because the notions to which it had for a time corresponded had been profoundly transformed. Although the idea of a unified Western Christianity remained deep-rooted in the minds of men, it had now ceased to be linked with that of a strong central authority dictating its law to the whole 'Christian people' and giving this people a single direction. Incorporated one after another into the territorial complex that Charlemagne made into his Empire, the peoples thus brought together by the will of the conqueror and by him united in the consciousness of a common religious faith, tended from the middle of the ninth century, without ever losing the consciousness of their spiritual solidarity, nevertheless to develop in divergent ways according to their political interests and their own needs. Notwithstanding the continual attempts of the Church to preserve their union over against the pagans and infidels, who were steadily becoming everywhere more menacing, these peoples increasingly asserted their ethnic individuality. The fragmentation of this nascent Europe into a number of distinct units, the first contours of the medieval states, is one of the more striking aspects of the period after the death of Louis the Pious, whose history we have just traced.

The decline of kingship

This disintegration of a state that drew the essence of its strength and its cohesion from the authority of its ruler can be explained first of all by the gradual decline of kingship itself. While Charlemagne's authority was unquestioningly and absolutely accepted by all the inhabitants of the Empire, that of his last successors tended to be no more than conditional. The oath of allegiance that bound each subject personally to the ruler remained, but little by little the practice arose of holding it to be valid only in so far as the ruler, in his turn, remained faithful to the duties expected of him.

The origin of this vital reservation should be looked for in the events that marked the reign of Louis the Pious; but it was shortly after his death that it became as it were a constitutional rule. We have already stressed the decisive importance of the assembly of Coulaines in 843 in the kingdom of Charles the Bald and analyzed the article by which the king, promising his subjects "not to deprive anyone, whatever his status or office, of the honour to which he is entitled", pledged himself to use thenceforth "only the means of justice, by conforming himself to reason and equity", and "guaranteed to each the observance of his own law". To the obligation of the subject to the king now corresponded the obligation of the king toward the subject, which necessarily implied that the subject could withdraw from his obligation if the king were to renege on his. Eight years later at Meerssen, Lothar, Louis the German and Charles the Bald jointly made analogous promises: "Let our subjects", they declared, "whatever their status or rank, be utterly assured that we shall never again condemn them, nor deprive them of their honours, nor oppress them contrary to law, justice and equity, and that we shall undertake no undue intrigues against them.." So, they added, they will be for us "true assistants" and will bring us "in a sincere manner their advice and their aid . . . as, by law, each ought to do with regard to his king and his lord". The same assurances were repeated many a time in the course of the years that followed.

In 858 a further step was taken in the kingdom of Charles the Bald. Because defections in favour of his brother Louis the German were proliferating around him, Charles demanded a new oath of allegiance from his subjects; but immediately afterwards he himself was obliged, in return, to take an oath of which we still have the text:

I, too, inasfar as I can do so in a normal way, with the aid of the Lord, shall honour each one of you according to his status and his person; I shall watch over his welfare without fraud or deceit; I shall respect his own law and his right, and to the degree that he shall have need of it and requests it reasonably, I shall display clemency toward him, conducting myself in everything as a faithful king is obliged to do toward his subjects. In so far as God gives me the understanding and the power, I shall not deviate from this line of conduct to the advantage of anyone, neither by favour, nor by ill will, nor through the influence of unwarranted incitements; and if I should allow myself to be seduced away from this by weakness, I shall exert myself, as soon as I am aware of it, to redress on my own initiative the wrong committed.

The king's oath, in the case we have just cited, is even more detailed than the one he required of his subjects. For the rivalry was so great at that time between Louis the Pious' sons, and particularly between Charles the Bald and Louis the German, that, in order to keep their subjects, the kings found themselves obliged to give them ever plainer assurances, the magnates threatening every moment to go over to the other party if they did not obtain satisfaction, and even going so far, in Aquitaine, as to claim the right of coalition to induce their king to respect his obligations.

In 869, before receiving the throne of Lorraine, Charles the Bald had had to give his new subjects, in exchange for their allegiance, guarantees analogous to those recorded in the oath of 858, and his declaration was this time presented by the bishop of Metz, who presided over the ceremony, as the very condition of his election: "It is well", the prelate asserts, "and even absolutely necessary, that we hear from his lips the declaration which a people loyal and united in their will to serve him expects from this most Christian king . . . ." It was only after this royal declaration that the coronation took place.

From then on it became the rule that, at the moment of his election, each new king gave to his future subjects a formal guarantee of fair and strict justice, as well as of a vigorous protection against anyone attempting to injure their rights. The loyalty of the king's subjects was obtained at this price, which meant that officially royal authority was conditional on the king's respect for the provisions of the contract drawn up with those who agreed to recognize his rule. Such was the situation in 876, 877, 879, 882, 888, and upon the accessions of Charles the Bald in Italy, of Boso in Provence, of Louis the Stammerer, of Carloman, and of Odo of France.

The extension of vassalage

It can scarcely be doubted that this new aspect of the monarchy was directly related to the gradual spread of vassalitic usages which had begun already in the time of Charlemagne and had since then steadily gained ground everywhere. Already in the formula of the 'promise' made by Lothar, Louis the German and Charles the Bald in 851, at the second conference of Meerssen, the last phrase, which concerned the conditions on which the subjects were to aid their kings–"as by right each of them should do toward his king and his lord" (*et suo seniori*)–itself indicates the transition that was taking place, since the king was treated at the same time as king and as 'lord', in the full meaning that this term of lord then had. No less significant were the terms in which Charles the Bald, in the text of the oath cited above, pledged in 858 to behave toward his subjects "as a faithful king is obliged to do toward his subjects", or the almost identical ones by which he bound himself in 876 to the magnates of the Italian kingdom. In both cases the phrasing seems to bear a surprising resemblance to what we are able to find out, in the absence of any precise text, about the obligations then entered into between lords and vassals, and it is characteristic that, in the oath taken in 876 by the magnates of Italy in return for the royal promise, the word 'lord' again appears in full: "I promise that from this day I will be faithful, as long as I live, to my lord here present (*isti seniori meo*)."

But even more than the terms used, the actual relationship of the subjects and the king arrests our attention. From where if not from the practice of vassalage could the king and his subjects have taken the idea of the reciprocal obligation which henceforth bound them closely to one another and made the faithfulness of the one conditional upon the loyal attitude of the other? Only vassalage had from its beginning acknowledged the principle of a breach in case of the default of one or the other of the parties to the obligations accepted. That the Carolingian monarchy should have come to this indicates that a fundamental transformation of society itself had occurred.

In fact, vassalage eventually invaded the whole of society. Foreign rulers were requested by the Carolingian kings to make their submission by acknowledging themselves to be their vassals. The example of Tassilo of Bavaria being summoned by Pepin in 757 to "commend himself" into vassalage was thenceforth so widely imitated that the act of homage may be considered as the regular manner of submission usual in this kind of case. The poet Ermold the Black, a contemporary of Louis the Pious, writes of the Danish king Harald: "With joined

hands he surrendered himself as well as his kingdom to the Frankish
king, and the emperor received his hands into his own", which is
exactly the same rite as that of homage; and this practice seemed so
normal in the second half of the ninth century that the annalists usually
restricted themselves to alluding to it, without dwelling on it, by
speaking of the 'commendation' of such and such a ruler, that is to say
his entering into vassalage, as a normal token of his submission.

Likewise, in internal affairs the vassalitic vocabulary and the
practices it presupposed spread irresistibly. Paschasius Radbert, the
biographer of Abbot Wala of Corbie, in a passage written shortly after
851, makes Louis the Pious say to his rebellious sons in 833: "You are
my vassals (*mei vassali*) and you have sworn fidelity to me", which
indicates that in the view of Paschasius, who was as we know much
involved in secular life, vassalage was the usual manner of submission
in a society that already formed a long chain of lords and vassals linked
to each other by the bonds of fidelity. "Know ye", Charles the Bald
declared at the conclusion of the first meeting at Meerssen in 847, "that
we desire to assure our subjects that their rights will be respected and
that they will not be injured in any way; and, likewise, we request you
to ensure to your men the maintenance of their rights and not to injure
them in any way". This was repeated in 869 by the same king in the
following manner:

We shall preserve for our subjects their law and their justice, just as they have been
applied to their predecessors in the time of our predecessors; and we desire and command
that to the vassals of our bishops, abbots, abbesses, counts and vassals, their law and their
justice shall be applied by their respective lords just as these have been applied to their
predecessors by their lords in the time of their own predecessors.

Thus a whole hierarchy of lords and vassals had then established itself,
to converge, step by step, in each of the parts of the former Carolingian
Empire, on the king, who had now become the lord of the lords.

The relationship of the king with the higher clergy was also affected
by this transformation. Whether it was, originally, because of the
'benefices' attached to their offices – as is suggested by a passage in the
so-called *Annals of Saint-Bertin* for the year 837, where mention is
made of "bishops, abbots, counts and royal vassals, possessors of
benefices" in the territories granted to Charles the Bald, who came to
"commend themselves" to him – or simply via the spread of vassalitic
practices, it is a well-established fact that, in the second half of the

ninth century, the kings got into the habit of requiring from the bishops, as well as from the abbots, a 'commendation' (*commendatio*) into vassalage, as well as a 'profession' (*professio*) of fidelity. At the accession of Louis the Stammerer in 877, the bishops of his kingdom made to him, on the day of his coronation, the following two declarations in rapid succession:

(1) I commend to you myself and my church, so that you will maintain law and justice and will assure us protection, as a king should do with regard to a bishop and his church.

(2) I declare that from this day and from now on I shall be faithful to my lord and king here present (*isti seniori et regi meo*), Louis, son of Charles and Ermentrude, with all my understanding and my power, in the exercise of my office, and that I shall aid him with my support and my advice, in my fidelity and my priesthood, as a bishop should normally do with regard to his lord (*seniori suo*).

These two successive declarations, which supplement each other, indicate how great the confusion had become, since the first formula of 'commendation' was to the king as such, while that of 'fidelity' was to him in his double capacity of king and lord. Even more revealing of this confusion are the terms which seven years earlier the bishop of Laon had used in a declaration of fidelity to Charles the Bald, of which we have the text: "I shall be faithful and obedient to my lord the king Charles in the exercise of my ministry . . . as a vassal (*homo*) should be toward his lord (*suo seniori*) and a bishop toward his king." In vain had Archbishop Hincmar of Reims protested in 858 against this extension of the vassalitic system to the relations of the monarchy and the episcopate, recalling with his habitual vigour that "the bishops, consecrated to the Lord, do not belong to the category of men, such as laymen, who can be constrained to commend themselves to anyone into vassalage (*ut in vassalatico debeamus nos cuilibet commendare*) . . . or to take an oath, which is forbidden by the evangelical, apostolic and canonical authority". The whole of society, the Church not excepted, was carried along in the current of broad changes that were creating a new type of social organization.

The assimilation of public offices and benefices

Even more fraught with consequences was the tendency, discernible from the middle of the ninth century, to reckon all the 'honours' and all the offices of state among 'benefices'. In 877 we saw the bishops of France 'commending' to Louis the Stammerer their churches as well as themselves; and this was exactly what, from 858 on, had been most offensive to Hincmar. "The churches which have been entrusted to us by God," he declared, "are not benefices of such a kind (*talia beneficia*) . . . that the king can give them or take them away as he likes and without consulting anyone." With regard to abbeys, the practice had by then already become established of conferring them in exchange for an oath of vassalage. As for the comital offices, to which, as is well known, benefices had already for a long time been attached, their assimilation to benefices was inevitable. We have already cited a passage in the so-called *Annals of Saint-Bertin* in which, on the occasion of a new attribution of territories made to Charles the Bald by his father in 837, mention is made of counts who came 'to commend themselves' to him for the benefices which they held. In 841, if we are to believe an especially qualified witness, the historian Nithard, a first cousin of Charles the Bald, Duke Bernard of Septimania sent his son William to Charles the Bald with the order to "commend himself" to him if the king would agree "to give him the honours which he had up to then had in Burgundy", which doubtless meant confirming him in the possession of the offices which he had up to then held there. Forty years later an annalist wrote blandly about King Louis the Younger, son of Louis the German, that he assured himself of the fidelity of Hugh, the bastard son of King Lothar II of Lorraine, by "giving him abbeys and counties in benefice" (*ei abbatias et comitatus in beneficium dedit*). It is in any case a fact that every confiscation of the properties of a rebel who occupied a prominent position in one of the kingdoms, every redistribution of territories among the various kings, invariably entailed, whatever the reason was, a redistribution of offices and benefices in which the counties were included indiscriminately together with abbeys and all other categories of 'benefice' and 'honour'.

However, the terms 'benefice' and 'honour' also drew closer together in meaning. Already during the events of the year 839 Bishop Prudentius of Troyes had distinguished between the properties in full ownership (*proprietates*) that were allotted to Lothar and what he called his "beneficiary honours" (*beneficiarii honores*), that is to say, the offices which he held in benefice. Likewise Archbishop Hincmar of Reims, thirty years later, spoke of a Count Acfrid (*Acfridus*), as possessor of the abbey of St Hilary of Poitiers and, he said, a large number of "other honours held in benefice" (*honorabilia beneficia*). 'Honours' – which were primarily comital, abbatial and episcopal offices – were thus assimilated to 'benefices' whose holders enjoyed them in their capacity as vassals of the king. In this way they ceased being conscious of holding 'public' offices, and tended to think only of the profit and authority due to them. This being so, it is not surprising to see instances of multiple countships increase in number, sometimes even when these were quite far apart, nor to find the comital office, just like the benefice, tending to become hereditary.

At first there were in the eighth century, as we have seen, only a few isolated examples of this state of affairs. In the course of the ninth century these increased in number. Let it suffice here to mention the county of Autun, of which recent scholarship has established that it remained for four successive generations in the hands of the descendants of Count Theoderic, himself the father of Count William of Toulouse. The custom was so well-established in the second half of the ninth century that, on his departure for Italy in 877, Charles the Bald considered it normal that, in the counties as well as in the vassalitic benefices, sons should succeed their fathers. This does not mean, to be sure, that he gave up his right of nomination or even, in theory, his freedom of choice: for the famous capitulary which he then promulgated at Quierzy, far from being, as has long been thought, a constitutional charter of feudalism, on the contrary aims explicitly at safeguarding the sovereign's freedom of initiative, and not permitting any part of his authority to slip away. But although nothing had been changed in the existing rules for the nomination of counts, it is evident that henceforth the holders of the comital offices, just like the holders of benefices, which would soon be called fiefs, expected a hereditary transmission and considered their counties as their own. This explains their resistance to kings who wished to deprive them of their counties. In 864 Count Bernard Plantevelue of Autun, when he was recalled by Charles the Bald, refused with armed resistance to yield his office to the successor the king had given him in the person of Robert the Strong. In 867–868 the same thing happened at Bourges where Count Gerard, likewise recalled, opposed the new holder of his county, Acfrid, of whom he finally rid himself by assassination. Several years later, in Germany, King Louis the Younger awarded a county of the "eastern march" to a person outside the family of the previous holders; but the dispossessed family united against the intruder, ordered him to get out of "the county of their forefathers", and began a mortal struggle with him.

Thus, behind the Carolingian facade, a new world – which we call feudal – was taking shape, which would slowly obliterate the old one.

The vassalitic principle substituted for the monarchy

The kings themselves hastened this evolution daily by renouncing more and more of their authority to the advantage of the vassalitic system. In order to hold the accomplices of his rebellious son Carloman in check, Charles the Bald in 871 could think of nothing better than compelling them to enter into the vassalage of whichever of his own vassals they chose; and, when not all of them obeyed this command, a capitulary of 873 confiscated the properties of those who had not yet at that moment chosen a lord. In other words, lacking the power to ensure order through their own officials, the kings shifted the task to the vassalitic system, which however was, all things considered, no more than an institution of private law.

Likewise, they used the 'benefice' as a surer means to strengthen the bonds of fidelity than the use of their sovereign authority. To Duke Solomon of the Bretons, who in 863 agreed to recognize Frankish hegemony, Charles the Bald gave 'in benefice' (*in beneficium*) part of the county of Anjou and the abbey of St Aubin at Angers in exchange for his oath of fidelity and the homage which Solomon had decided to perform to him; he added to this in 867, under similar conditions, it seems, the county of Coutances. We have already seen Louis the Younger doing the same with regard to Hugh of Lorraine, the bastard son of Lothar II. To overpower his rebellious sons, even Louis the German knew no better means in 871 than to give them benefices, and the rebels did not submit before they were completely certain of not being defrauded. The ninth century had not yet closed, but here was, already, a completely feudal situation.

In these circumstances, the principles of government that had inspired Charlemagne were no more than a distant memory. The kingdoms that had emerged from the dismemberment of his Empire were ready for a new kind of future.

Conclusion

During the whole course of its history the Carolingian Empire had felt the effects of the confusion that had prevailed at its birth. Neither Charlemagne nor his advisers had been able to arrive at any clear conception of what their aims should be. As regards the Roman Empire, which the king of the Franks had at first thought to be continuing through his person, it had soon become obvious that its throne had not been vacant, as had been thought in 800, and that Rome and Italy had long ago ceased to be an essential part of it. Fortified by the new dignity with which he had been invested in the ancient capital of the Caesars, Charlemagne had nonetheless conducted himself as the sovereign ruler of the whole Christian West; but he had never clearly appreciated the implications of the situation that had thus been created, and everything points to the fact that he at first considered it to be temporary, and personally associated with him.

To state this is not to disparage his genius, but only to situate the man in the context of his time. Some have desired to make of him a clear-sighted statesman, to attribute to him the well-considered planning of all the large-scale developments that began in his time, while settling upon his successors the responsibility for the unfortunate results that these had in the end. This is an illusion. Charlemagne was carried along by events more than is commonly recognized. It is true, however, that his powerful personality and his infallible judgement of the possibilities inherent in a situation always guarded him against the temptations from which his successors had more trouble protecting themselves.

He took an opportunistic view of things, successive achievements coming about step by step as circumstances permitted. This explains why, having founded the Empire in 800, he had resigned himself in 806 to provide for its partition between his three then surviving sons, in order to spare the Christian West the risk of a war of succession. This does not mean that he failed to see the advantages which Christianity could derive from the altered situation almost immediately afterwards when, in rapid succession, two of his three heirs died. The whole of his realm and the imperial crown could then pass undivided to a prince of whom it could be hoped that, by continuing his father's policy, he would consolidate the results already attained and make the Empire a permanent institution.

The most important mistake of Louis the Pious and his advisers was their desire to effect this all at once. Disregarding the actual situation, and riding rough-shod over existing traditions and interests, they were obsessed by a single idea: to work out a system that would immediately succeed in cementing imperial unity for ever. Their plan was clear and logical, but it was feasible only if it were to be put into effect step by step. By trying to impose it all at once they courted disaster. The reign of this second emperor, which had begun under the motto of unity, soon led to the gravest disorders and caused only confusion in those who were baffled by the constant modifications of the shares awarded to the heirs to the throne, when at first the practice of partitioning had been ostentatiously repudiated.

The uncertainties at the beginning thus continued until 840 and resulted soon thereafter, in the treaty of Verdun, in a seemingly permanent dissolution. However, although destroyed on the territorial level, the Empire remained, on the spiritual and moral plane, a living reality. The personal authority of the rulers who presumed upon the imperial title now counted for less than the idea they incarnated: that of the unity of the Christian West. And this is why no one was surprised to see the Church taking over from the powerless Carolingians the direction of this ideal community consisting of peoples who had again become political strangers to one another but remained united in religion and civilization.

Naturally when this happened it became a different kind of Empire. While at the start religion had been as it were absorbed by the political authority, it now dominated the entire scene. The pope, whose role in the time of Charlemagne had been that of a mere agent, ended by being the supreme dispenser of the imperial crown, and the essential objective he had in mind for the person to whom he awarded it was the protection of the Holy See. The result of this inversion of roles was that contemporaries came to have less and less regard for a title that brought more cares than honour. Far from being the lord of the West, as the first holder of the imperial title had been, the ruler who bore it at the end of the ninth century was no more than an auxiliary of the Sovereign Pontiff for the defense of the faith. Even on this level, the deplorable failures of Charles the Bald, Charles the Fat, and Arnulf plunged the imperial office into further disrepute until a prince who was not of Carolingian descent, Otto of Germany, again thought to try his luck and soon founded, on the ruins of the Carolingian Empire, another that was to have a long and astonishing future.

Index

Aachen, 1, 60, 62, 96, 127, 160, 208, 220–221, 222, 229, 244, 249, 268, 288, 289, 302, 303, 324
  assemblies, 157, 161, 162, 165, 183, 191–192, 211
  councils or synods, 149, 186, 268, 269, 270
  mint, 127–128
abbacy, 9, 104, 106–108, 114, 120, 135, 153, 160, 186, 253, 258, 306, 343–346, 347
Abbasids, 62
Abd ar-Rahman I, emir of Cordoba, 8, 62, 63
Abd ar-Rahman II, emir of Cordoba, 182
Abuses of the age, treatise, 185
Acfrid, count, 345–346
advocate, 136
Adalard, abbot of Corbie, 173, 174, 182
Adalard, count, 269
Adalbert, marquis of Tuscany, 312, 317
Adalgisus, chamberlain, 48
Adalgisus, son of King Desiderius, 74, 75, 79
Admonitio generalis, 144, 147
Ad Novas, 75
adoptianism, 112, 149
advocate (*advocatus*), 136
aerarium publicum, 110
Ageltrude, wife of Guy II of Spoleto, 338
Aghlabids, 235
Agilolfings, 101
Agobard, archbishop of Lyon, 167, 173, 182, 194–195, 196–197, 200, 203–204, 210
Ahab, 201
Aistulf, king of the Lombards, 15, 17, 18, 19, 22, 23, 27, 28, 30, 32
Aix-en-Provence, archbishopric, 321
Aizo, 182
Alcuin, 58, 60, 61, 65, 86, 88, 91, 92, 93, 94, 110, 114, 115, 149, 153
Alemania, Alemans, 5, 8, 12–13, 34, 42, 44, 59, 97, 187, 193, 194, 203, 211, 217, 222, 309
Alexandria, patriarchate, 21
Alpaidis, 7
Alsace, 42, 187, 194, 203, 211, 217, 249, 269, 289, 333, 335, 309
Amalfi, 193
  bishop, 318
Amblère, battle, 7
Amiens, 324, 326
Ampurias, county, 64
Anastasius, librarian of the Holy See, 282, 283, 285, 292
Ancona, 32
Andernach, 262, 303
Angers, 7, 240
  abbey of St Aubin, 347
Angilbert, 87, 89, 159, 218
Angilram, bishop of Metz, 112, 152
Angrarians, 47, 50
Aniane, abbot, *see* Benedict of Aniane
Anio, 304
Anjou, county, 347

annual gifts (*annua dona*), 116, 125
anointing, 16, 17, 19, 20, 24, 28, 29, 38, 39, 80, 143, 164, 176, 230, 241, 256, 257, 258, 290, 294, 295, 297, 315, 317, 321, 337
Ansbert, archbishop of Milan, 297
Ansegisel, 6
Ansegisus, archbishop of Sens, 301–302, 315, 310
Antioch
  bishopric, 21
  council, 145
Apennines, 77
Aquitaine, 13, 33, 35, 42, 43, 100, 193, 215, 221, 222, 233, 234, 238–239, 252, 253
  duchy, 6, 7, 9, 12, 33, 36–37, 43, 100–101, 215, 217, 234, 239, 245, 246, 248, 252
  kingdom, 43, 65, 67, 68, 100–101, 108, 127, 158, 159, 165, 212, 222
archchaplain (*archicapellanus*), 112
Ardennes, 42, 222
Arezzo, bishop, 297, 299
Argonne, 222
Arians, 11
Arichis, duke of Benevento, 81, 82
Arles, 235, 240, 312
  council or synod, 150, 161
  archbishop, 321, 333
Armorica, *see* Brittany
army, 104, 114, 118–122, 135, 141–142, 283–284
Arn, bishop of Salzburg, 54
Arnulf, bishop of Metz, 6
Arnulf, king of Germany, later emperor, 315, 329, 331, 332, 335, 336, 337
Arsenius, bishop of Orta, 278–280, 282, 283, 285
assembly, general (*conventus generalis*), 105, 106, 108, 113–117, 119, 125, 166, 170–171
Astronomes, the, 191
Attigny
  palace, 14, 49, 248, 253, 254, 279, 299
  penitence, 172–174
Attila, 58

Audulf, seneschal, 65
Augsburg, 44, 194
Augustine, St, 24, 146, 147, 148, 196
Augustus, Augusti, 11, 89, 91, 95, 158, 208, 216, 285, 290, 304, 317
Austrasia, 6, 7, 12, 42, 119, 193, 203, 223
Autchar, duke, 8, 33
Autun, 8
  county, 166, 193, 346
Auxerre, 211
  bishop, 260
Avallon, county, 193, 166
Avars, 45, 46, 50, 57, 58–62, 85, 129
Avignon, 9
  bishop, 268

Baghdad, 62, 235
Bagnorea, 81
Baldwin, count, 272
Balearic Islands, 63, 69
Balkans, 10, 56
Ballon, 240
Baltic Sea, 47, 53
ban (*bannus*), royal, 121, 131, 298
  of the host (*heriban*), 121
baptism, 61
Barcelona, 63, 64, 109, 182, 183
barganaticum, 126
Bari, 281, 283, 290, 291, 295
Bartholomew, bishop of Narbonne, 231
Basel, 262
Basil I, Byzantine emperor, 290–292, 320
Basques, 63, 64, 99–100, 183; *see also* Gascons
Bavaria, 5, 12, 13, 14, 30, 34–35, 43–46, 53, 54, 57, 58, 59, 61, 309, 314, 315, 329
  kingdom, 101–102, 158, 165, 193, 194, 211
  law, 101, 103
Bayeux, 240
Beauvais, 324
Belley, diocese, 270, 280
Benedict, St, *see* Rule
Benedict of Aniane, 159, 160, 161, 172, 175

Benedict III, pope, 282
benefice (*beneficium*), 35, 120, 135, 140–
   141, 142, 183, 223, 269, 307, 345–346,
   347
Benevento
   duchy, 77, 81, 82, 239, 281, 285, 293
   duke, 33, 80, 102, 240, 283
Bera, count of Barcelona, 64
Berengar, count, 269
Berengar, marquis of Friuli, 333, 334,
   335, 338
Bergamo, 336
Bernard, bastard of Charles the Fat, 328,
   336
Bernard, king of Italy, 101, 108–109, 166,
   169–170, 171, 172, 173, 187
Bernard I, duke of Septimania, chamber-
   lain of Louis the Pious, 183, 187–
   190, 345
Bernard II, duke or marquis of Sep-
   timania, 309, 345
Bernard Plantevelue, count of Au-
   vergne, 309, 346
Bertha, daughter of Charlemagne, 159–
   160, 218
Berthada, wife of Pepin the Short, 19, 37,
   72
Besançon, 293
   archbishop, 321
Betuwe, 239
bishops, *see* episcopate
Bivin, count, 288
Blaye, 9
Blois, 208, 252
Bohemia, Bohemians or Czechs, 53, 57–
   58, 120, 166, 235, 250, 309
Bohemian Forest, 57
Bologna, 32
Bolzano, 44
Boniface, St, 9, 13, 14, 15, 16, 17, 19, 20,
   24, 37, 38, 39, 52
booty, 60, 69, 100, 129
Bordeaux, 89, 239
   archbishop, 302
Boris, khan of the Bulgars, 284
Boso, count of Vienne, 299, 303, 309,
   312, 313, 314, 315, 320–321

as king of Provence, 322, 332, 341
Boulogne-sur-mer, 68
Bourges, 37
   archbishop, 312
   county, 346
Brabant, 193
Brenner Pass, 297, 309
Brescia, 295
Brienne, 253
Brissarthe, battle, 331
Brittany, 64–67, 69, 99, 171, 240; *see also*
   Erispoë, Nominoë, Solomon
Bulgars, 183
Burchard, bishop of Wurzburg, 15, 16
Burgundy, Burgundians, 6, 7, 8, 9, 12, 42,
   193, 328, 333
   law, 103
buticularius, butler, 111
Byzantine Empire, 10, 11, 15, 30, 33, 34,
   75, 78, 85–86, 88, 92, 95–96, 102, 290,
   291–292
Byzantine fleet, 33, 290, 291, 304, 318
Byzantium, 'New Rome', Constan-
   tinople, 15, 18, 34, 86, 95, 96, 292
   patriarchate, 10, 11, 21, 92, 149

Calabria, 10, 291
Campania, 222, 281, 308
Canche, 234
canonical legislation, 38–39, 96, 144–145,
   149–151, 152, 162, 180, 185, 203, 231,
   276, 302
capitation or poll tax, 124
capitularies, 13, 96, 105, 106, 116, 148,
   153, 323
   de villis, 127
   of Quierzy, 305–308, 346
   of Saxony, 49
Capua, 81
Carcassonne, county, 166
Cardona, 63
Caribert, king of Aquitaine, 100
Carinthia, Carinthians, 53–54, 58, 166,
   309
Carloman, son of Charles Martel, 12–14,
   22, 23, 35, 36, 37, 141

Carloman, son of Charles the Bald, 347
Carloman, son of Lothar II, 269, 271
Carloman, son of Louis the German, 271, 296, 297, 308–310, 311, 312, 317
Carloman, son of Louis the Stammerer, 315, 320, 321, 322, 323, 325, 326, 341
Carloman, son of Pepin the Short, 19, 29, 41–43, 73, 74
Caroline books, 149
Cassiodorus, 24
Catalonia, 63, 64
Cathulf, 42, 144, 148
census, royal tax, 124
Cerdagne, 63, 182
Cesena, 31
Chalon-sur-Saône, 170, 208, 212, 222
council of, 150, 161
Châlons-sur-Marne, 218
bishop, 260
chamber, chamberlain, 110, 187–188
chancellor, chancery, 112, 128–129, 320
chapel, chaplains, 111–112, 182
Charlemagne, 16, 19, 41–154, 157, 158, 160, 224, 323, 349–350
Charles, king of Provence, 249, 250, 251, 269, 270, 280, 282
Charles, son of Charlemagne, 55, 57, 65, 97
Charles Martel, 7–12, 13, 39, 52, 62, 100, 101, 255
Charles II the Bald, 180, 187, 190, 192–193, 199, 201, 203, 211–212, 216–280, 285, 287–290, 293–310, 320, 322, 340–347
Charles the Fat, 297, 309, 313, 315–329, 331, 333, 351
Charles the Simple, 326, 337
Childeric III, 13–14, 16
Chlothar II, 6
Christian people, 1, 11, 88, 144, 154, 158–159, 219, 220, 224–227, 265, 339
Christopher, *primicerius* of the notaries, 71, 72
Chrodegang, bishop of Metz, 18
Church, 24, 143, 160, 163, 174, 195, 224–227, 231–232, 235, 243, 246, 253–265, 273, 277

reform, 13–15, 37–39, 150–151, 161–164, 182, 184–186, 203, 232, 292, 296, 298, 299, 304, 306, 317, 339, 350
Cisa Pass, 77
City of God, 146, 147
clergy, clerics, 111–112, 116, 120, 148, 151–154, 160, 162, 174, 181, 184–186; *see also* Church
Clovis, 5
Codex Carolinus, 15
Colmar, 198
Cologne, 7, 35, 241, 245, 277, 279, 289, 302
archbishop, 260, 277, 286, 300
Comacchio, 31, 73
comes palatii, count of the palace, 112–113, 133
Compiègne, 35, 171, 190, 204, 305, 308, 332
concord, (*concordia pacis*), 145–146, 172, 186, 205, 212, 219, 220, 224–227, 236, 238, 241–243, 244
Condé-sur-l'Escaut, 324
constable (*comes stabuli*), 111
Conrad, count, brother of Judith, 190, 192
Constance, Lake, 328
Constantine I the Great, Roman emperor, 20–22, 80
Constantine V, Byzantine emperor, 15, 18, 30, 34
Constantine VI, Byzantine emperor, 88, 93, 95
Corbie, 191; *see* also Adalard, Wala
Cordoba, emir, 62, 63
coronations, 16, 75, 91–93, 113, 157, 164, 210, 287, 294–295, 297, 309, 315, 316, 318–319, 322, 333, 334, 335, 336, 338
Corsica, 69, 77
Corteolona, 176
corvées, 123
Couesnon, 65
Coulaines, 224–225, 232, 257, 340
count, 103–105, 111, 112–113, 115, 130–131, 132, 133, 306–307
county, 104, 106, 130, 183, 258, 347
Courtrai, 324

Coutances, county, 347
  bishop, 260
Cremona, bishop, 169
cubicularii, grooms of the chamber, 111
cup-bearers (*pincernae*), 111

Dagobert I, king of the Franks, 5, 6, 12, 100
Dagobert III, 8
Dalmatia, 10
Danes, 51, 54, 55, 56, 67–69, 109, 234, 271
Danube, river, 11, 57, 58–60
David, king of Israel, 17, 24, 25, 32, 143, 144, 153–154, 161
  nickname of Charlemagne, 89
denarius, penny, 128
Desiderius, king of the Lombards, 32–34, 71–75
Deutz, 48
diocese, 38
Diocletian, 91
Dionysio-Hadriana, collection, 149
discipline, ecclesiastical, 13, 38–39, 66, 116, 149–151, 185, 232; *see also* Church, canonical legislation
Dokkum, 52
domains, *villae*, 124, 126–127
Donation of Constantine, 20–23, 80
donations to the Holy See, 20–23, 31, 32, 77–78, 82, 163, 164
Drava, river, 53, 54
Drogo, bishop of Metz, 172, 192, 309, 229–232, 233, 301
duke (*dux*), 103, 109
Duurstede, 210, 235, 239

Eastphalia, Eastphalians, 47, 48, 50
Ebbo, archbishop of Reims, 204–206, 210, 216, 231, 233, 259
Ebro, river, 62, 63, 64
echevins (*scabini*), 130–133
Eger, 57
Einhard, 143, 146
Elbe, river, 47, 51, 53–58, 67, 119, 234
elections

episcopal, 152
  papal, 94, 165, 179–180, 230, 274, 282
  royal, 16, 297–298, 321, 333, 341
Eleutherius, son of Bishop Arsenius, 285, 286
Elijah, prophet, 201
Elsloo, 324, 325
Embrun, diocese, 280, 333
Emilia, 81
Ems, river, 52
Engelberga, wife of Emperor Louis II, 286, 293, 296, 320
England, 17, 52, 65, 67
Enns, river, 53, 59
episcopate (bishoprics), 9, 14, 38–39, 105–106, 114–116, 120, 149–152, 162, 172, 184–186, 195–196, 204, 224–227, 231–233, 253–265, 270–272, 306–307, 313, 343–346; *see also* Church, vassalage
Epistola tractoria, 122
Eresburg, 47, 48
Eric, duke of Friuli, 61
Erispoë, duke of the Bretons, 241
Ermengarde, daughter of Emperor Louis II, 320, 333, 335
Ermentrude, 344
Ermold the Black, 182, 342
Ernest, count, 269, 271
Erzgebirge, 53, 57
Estinnes, council, 13
Étampes, 211
Eugenius II, pope, 178, 179
evectio, requisitioned transport, 122
Everard, marquis of Friuli, 333
exarch of Italy, 11, 75
exarchate of Ravenna, 15, 20, 23, 28, 30, 73, 77, 79, 81

Faenza, 33, 73
fairs, 126
falconers (*falconarii*), 113
family (*familia*), 139
Fano, river, 31
Farfa, monastery, 177
Farulf, legate of the pope, 317

Fastrada, wife of Charlemagne, 59
Ferrara, 32, 33, 73
Ferrières-en-Gâtinais, abbey, 315
'Field of Lies', 199, 206
Field of March or Field of May, 114, 125
Filioque, 153
fines, 50, 131–132, 135, 136
fisc, 110, 126, 127, 136
fiscal administration, 123–126
Fismes, church of St Macre, 323
Flanders, 193
Florence, 81
Fontenoy-en-Puisaye, battle, 218
Forlimpopoli, 31
Formosus, bishop of Porto, Italy, later
    pope, 301, 336, 338
formularies, 138
Fouron, meeting, 314
Francia, 97, 200, 216, 221, 223, 252, 272
    occidentalis, 223, 224, 252, 253 (later
        Franconia)
    Orientalis, 223, 303, 309, 329, 331
    media, 223, 249
Frankfurt, 46, 58, 211, 250, 279, 332
    councils, 112, 149
Freculf, bishop of Lisieux, 175
fredum, fine, 131–132, 136
Frisia, Frisians, 5, 7, 8, 38, 52–53, 68, 69,
    70, 102, 193, 211, 222, 245, 249, 325,
    309
    law, 103
Friuli, 59, 79, 109, 183
Fritzlar, 47
Fulk, archbishop of Reims, 332, 335, 337
Fulrad, abbot of St Denis, 15, 16, 31, 32,
    112
Fulrad, abbot of St Quentin, 119, 125
Fustel de Coulanges, 143

Gaeta, 235, 308, 319
Gailo, constable, 48
Galicia, 63
Gap, diocese, 280
Garigliano, river, 319, 334
Garonne, 8, 37, 234

Gascony, Gascons, 8, 36, 37, 42, 43, 63,
    97, 99–100, 109, 166, 239, 240
gau, see county
Gelasius, pope, 184
Gellona, monastery, 183
Geneva, 74
    county, 212, 333
    diocese, 270
    Lake, 192
Genoa, 312
Gerard, count of Bourges, 346
Gerold, count in Bavaria, 46, 61, 101
Gerona, 63, 64, 182, 109
Gerung, chief usher at Aachen, 176
Ghent, 68, 324
Gilbert, vassal of Charles the Bald, 236
Girard, count of Paris, 217
Gisela, daughter of Louis the Pious, 334
Gisela, daughter of Pepin the Short, 72
Godfrey, king of Denmark, 67, 68
Godfrey, Norse duke, 325
Gombald, monk, 191
Gondreville, 279, 321
Gozlin, bishop of Paris, 327
gratia Dei rex, 25, 230
Gregory, nomenclator, 301, 303
Gregory the Great, pope, 24, 197
Gregory II, pope, 9
Gregory III, pope, 10–12
Gregory of Nazianz, St, 195
Grenoble, diocese, 280
Grifo, son of Charles Martel, 12, 14, 35,
    36
Grimoald, son of Arichis, 81, 82
Grimoald I, son of Pepin the Elder, 6
Grimoald II, son of Pepin the Younger,
    6, 7
Grosseto, 181
Gubbio, 31, 73
Gunther, archbishop of Cologne, 268,
    275–277, 283, 286
Guntram, king of the Franks, 24
Guy, brother of Lambert I of Spoleto,
    304
Guy, count of the Breton march, 65–66
Guy III, called 'the Fury', duke of
    Spoleto, 317, 318, 332, 333, 334, 336

Hadrian I, pope, 44, 73, 84, 86, 149
Hadrian II, pope, 284–295
Haggai, 184
Hainault, 13, 193
Hamburg, 234
Harald, king of Denmark, 182, 342
Helisachar, chancellor of Louis the Pious, 160
Henry, count, 325, 327, 328
Herbert, brother of Bernard of Septimania, 190
hereditary benefices and public offices, 104, 306–307, 346–347
heribannus, ban of the host, 120, 135
herisliz, desertion, 121, 133
Herstal, 42
Hesse, 35, 47, 48
Hildebald, bishop of Cologne, 112, 152
Hildegarde, wife of Charlemagne, 46
Hilduin, abbot of St Denis, 191, 217, 258, 259
Hiltrude, mother of Tassilo, 35
Hincmar, archbishop of Reims, 233, 254–265, 268–273, 278, 279, 284, 285, 286, 288, 289–290, 292, 302, 310, 321, 322–323, 344, 345
homage, 140, 332, 335, 342, 343, 347
Homer, nickname of Angilbert, 160
honours (*honores*), 166, 193, 212, 217, 223, 227, 264, 269, 307, 340, 344–346
Horic, king of Denmark, 237, 239
Hubert, abbot of St Maurice in the Valais, 267, 268, 269
Huesca, 63, 64
Hugh, bastard son of Charlemagne, 172
Hugh, count of Tours, 181–183
Hugh of Lorraine, 321, 345, 347
Hugh the Abbot, 309, 327
Hunald, duke of Aquitaine, 12, 36, 43
Hungarians, 271
Huns, 58
huntsmen (*venatores*), 113

iconoclasm, 10, 15
Iesi, 31
Ille, 65

immunist, immunity, 123, 124, 134–137
Imola, 32
impiety, 148–149
Ingelheim, assembly, 45, 59, 116, 182, 216
Inn, river, 35, 271
Innichen, 54
Irene, empress of Byzantium, 93, 95
Ireland, Irishmen, 54, 66, 159, 331
Irmengarde or Ermengarde, wife of Louis the Pious, 164, 175
Irminsul, 47
Isaurians, 291
Ischia, 235
Isidore of Seville, 24, 185
Israel, 24, 143, 144, 153
Istria, 77, 78, 79, 120
Italy, 11–12, 15, 21, 30–34, 35, 44, 48, 69, 71–84, 97, 198, 208, 308, 309, 310, 318, 333
  kingdom, 102, 158, 169–170, 176, 187, 188, 189, 209, 212, 215, 221, 222, 223, 230, 240, 241, 249, 281–287, 290–292, 309, 311, 312, 320, 333–334, 335, 336
  southern Italy, 15, 33, 235, 281–284, 287, 290–291, 303, 305, 308, 319
Ithier, chaplain of Charlemagne, 77
Iuda, Kornelimünster, 160

Jehu, king, 201
Jerome, St, 195
Jerusalem, patriarch, 21, 91
Jesse, bishop of Amiens, 191
Jenfosse, 245
Jezebel, 201
John, silentiary, 18
John VIII, pope, 295–319
Jonas, bishop of Orléans, 226
Josiah, king, 144
Judith of Bavaria, wife of Louis the Pious, 175, 176, 180, 181, 187, 188, 189, 190, 191, 192, 199, 200, 201, 208, 211, 215, 334
Judith, daughter of Charles the Bald, 272
judgement of God, 147, 199, 201, 205, 220–221, 334
Jumièges, 45

Jura, 289
justice, 145, 146–147, 220, 260
  administration, 104–109, 113, 129–133,
    134, 146–147, 180, 227
Justinian, emperor, 10
Jutland, 51

Kairouan, emirs, 235
Khazars, 291
Koblenz, 48, 239, 250, 251
  pacts, 262–265, 267, 272, 277, 279
Kornelimünster, 160

Lahn, 48
Lambert, count of Nantes, 208, 233, 340–
  341
Lambert I, duke of Spoleto, 303, 304,
  311, 312, 313
Lambert II, duke of Spoleto, 336, 338
land tax, 124
Langres, 222, 249, 332
language
  German, 218–219, 263
  Latin, 291–292
  romance, 218–219, 263, 264
Languedoc, 8, 9, 42, 68, 159
Laodicea, council, 145
Laon, 190
  bishop, 260, 344
  county, 193
Lateran palace, 21, 72, 76, 86, 87, 177,
  275, 285, 303
Latium, 281, 283, 296
Lausanne
  county, 333
  diocese, 270
law, laws, 96
  feudal, 307
  of the Bavarians, 101, 103
  of the Burgundians, 103
  of the Frisians, 53, 103
  of the Lombards, 102, 103
  of the Saxons, 103
  personality of, 103, 129, 167–168, 179
  Ripuarian law, 103, 166

Roman, 102
  Salic law, 103, 167
Lechfeld, 44
Leo, bishop of Gabies, 300
Leo, nomenclator, 177
Leo I the Great, pope, 197
Leo III, pope, 86–94, 152, 153, 163, 224,
  294
Leo IV, pope, 240, 241, 282, 295
Leo III the Iconoclast, Byzantine em-
  peror, 10, 15
Leonine city, 240
leudes, retainers, 6
Liber pontificalis, 23
Liège, 42, 245, 303
  bishop, 149
  pact 245–248, 251, 287
Limoges, 239
Lingones, 53, 55–56
Lippe, river, 48
Liri, 281
Liudger, bishop, 52
Liutprand, king of the Lombards, 11, 15
Liutward, chancellor of Charles the Fat,
  329
Loire, river, 36, 203, 217, 245, 252, 280
Lorraine, Lotharii regnum, 249–250, 287,
  288, 302, 309, 315, 320, 321, 333, 341
Lothar I, emperor, 158, 165–167, 176–
  182, 187–202, 211–212, 215–248, 294,
  340, 342, 345
Lothar II, son of Lothar I, 249, 250,
  267–281, 283, 286–287, 292, 293, 345
Louis the German, king of Bavaria, 57,
  165–167, 187–212
  as king of Germany, 215–302, 342, 347
Louis the Pious, king of Aquitaine, 43,
  63, 65, 68, 80, 97, 100, 127, 215, 350
  as Emperor, 54, 56, 57, 101, 157–212,
  226, 259, 294, 342, 343, 350
Louis the Younger, son of Louis the
  German, 245, 246, 247, 248, 299, 302,
  303, 309, 313, 314, 315, 316, 319, 320,
  321, 324, 325, 346, 347
Louis II, king of Italy, later emperor,
  229–230, 240, 249, 250, 270, 274, 275,
  278, 280, 282–295, 301

Louis II the Stammerer, king of France, 280, 305, 311, 313, 314, 322, 341–344, 345
Louis III, king of France, son of Louis II, 314, 315, 320, 321, 322, 323, 324, 325
Louis, king of Provence, 333, 335, 338
Louvain, 324, 327, 336
Lügenfeld, 199
Luna, 240
Lupus, duke of Gascony, 43
Lyon, 27, 221, 212
   archbishopric, 321, 333
   council, 184
Lyonnais, 222
Lys, river, 239

machtiern, Breton chiefs, 66
Mâcon, 221
magnates, 14, 114, 133
Magra, 77
Main, river, 42, 203, 211, 217, 223
Mainz, 222, 289
   councils, 112, 150, 161, 184
mansionarii, 113
mansiones, lodging stations, 122
Mantaille, 321, 332, 333, 334
Mantua, 77, 81
marches, 48, 70, 109, 243
   Avar march, 109, 166
   Danish march, 67, 109
   of Brittany, 65–67, 109, 208
   of Carinthia or Eastern march, 271, 346
   of Friuli, of Istria, 109, 183
   of Spain, 63–64, 65, 109, 182–183, 193
   of Toulouse, 166
   Slav or Wendish march, 109, 166
markets, 126
Marne, river, 222
marshals (*mariscalci*), 111
Martin, St, 111
Massif Central, 42
Matfrid, count of Orléans, 181–183, 185, 189, 208
Maurienne, 27, 310

mayor of the palace (*major domus*), 6–16, 110
Meaux, bishop, 260, 268
Mecklenburg, 53
Meerssen
   first conference, 236–238, 342
   second conference, 242–243, 244, 247, 251, 257, 260, 263, 273, 340, 343
   third conference, 289, 314
Meginhard, monk of Fulda, 292
Melle, 239
Mentana, 90
Merovingians, 5–17, 24, 41, 42, 65, 100, 110, 126, 127, 128, 134, 331
metropolitans, 38–39
Metz, 209–210, 259–260, 274, 275, 287, 289, 328
   bishop, 260, 341
   council, 274–275
Meuse, river, 7, 211, 212, 217, 222, 234, 324
Michael I Rangabe, Byzantine emperor, 96
Michael III, Byzantine emperor, 291
Milan, archbishop, 149, 169, 316
Milvian Bridge, 338
missaticum, 106, 108
missi dominici, 105, 106–108, 122, 123, 130, 145, 146, 157, 162, 179, 236, 245, 251
monasteries, monks, 104, 120, 149, 153, 159, 161–162, 172, 253, 258, 345–346; *see also* abbacy
Monk of St Gall, *see* Notker the Stammerer
money, 127, 128
Monselice, 77
Mont-Cenis, pass, 27, 30, 74, 309, 310
Monte Cassino, monastery, 286
Montefeltro, 31, 73
Montfaucon in Argonne, 332
Montiers, *see* Tarentaise
Montmartre, 328
Moravia, Moravians, 250, 336, 309, 336
Moselle, river, 193
Moses, 86, 144
   the 'New Moses' Pepin the Short, 32

Moslems
of Spain, 8–9, 12, 17, 62–64, 67–70, 133
of Africa, Sicily and Italy, 12, 67–69,
235, 239–240, 281, 283, 287, 290–291,
295, 296, 303–305, 318, 319, 334
mundeburdium, protection, 139
Nantes, 234, 109
Naples, 283
duke, 303, 318
bishop, 318
Narbonnaise, *see* Septimania
Narbonne, 9, 63
archbishop, 231
Narni, 31
Navarre, 63, 64
Neidingen, 329
Neustria, 6, 7, 12, 42, 193, 223
Nevers, county, 166, 193
Nice, 69
Nicaea
council of, 145
creed, 153
Nicephorus I, Byzantine emperor, 95
Nicholas I, pope, 274–284, 291, 294
Nijmegen, 171, 191, 210, 324
Nîmes, 8, 222
Nithard, 190, 218, 220, 221, 223, 345
Noirmoutier, island, 172, 234
Nominoë, duke of the Bretons, 233, 237,
238, 240–241
Nordalbingia, Nordalbingians, 47, 50–
51, 55
notary (*notarius*), 112
Notker the Stammerer, monk of St Gall,
326–327
Noyon, 42
nuns, 161, 232

oath, oaths, 171, 172, 176, 195, 205, 206,
212, 224, 242–243, 250, 263
of a king to his subjects, 340, 341
of allegiance to king or emperor, 81,
96, 99, 104, 106, 117–118, 140, 178,
179–180, 192, 196, 200–201, 203, 230,
311, 317, 326, 340–341, 327

of fidelity to a lord, 35, 45, 49, 101,
139–140, 142, 197, 253, 257, 342, 344,
345, 347
of Liège, 247, 287
of Strasbourg, 218–219, 322, 347
to prove innocence, 90, 177
Ostia, 318
Otricoli, 73
Otto I of Germany, 351

Paderborn, 48, 49, 87, 191
pagus, *see* county
palace (*palatium*), 110, 185–186, 323
count, 112–113, 133
palatii, De ordine, 323
Pamplona, 8, 62, 63
Pannonia, 59–62, 85, 309, 329
papacy, 10–12, 15–16, 17–23, 24, 27–34,
37, 38, 39, 43–44, 60, 71–84, 97, 149,
152–153, 163–164, 176–180, 224, 230,
240, 267–280, 281–290, 295–296,
303–305, 311–317, 350–351
Papal State, 20–23, 27–34, 71–84, 86–94,
102, 108, 164, 177–180, 297–298, 319,
334
Paris, 189, 211, 218, 234, 238, 252, 280,
324, 327–328
council, 184–186, 226
Parma, 77
bishop, 317
partitions of the realm, 5–6, 12, 41–42,
54, 57–58, 96–98, 116, 165–167, 187,
192–193, 206, 211–212, 221–224,
249–250, 280, 288, 289, 309, 314, 315,
350
Paschal I, pope, 164, 176, 177, 178
Pepin, son of Charlemagne, king of Italy,
44, 60, 61, 80, 81, 97, 101
Pepin I, son of Louis the Pious, king of
Aquitaine, 158, 165–167, 183, 187–
212
Pepin II, king of Aquitaine, 215, 218, 233,
237, 238, 239, 240, 252
Périgord, 239
Péronne, 7, 241
Pesaro, 31

Peter, St, 13, 20, 21, 22, 28, 29–30, 38, 79,
    89, 90
Pföring, 44
Philip, usurper pope, 71
Piacenza, 237, 287
plea (*placitum*) or tribunal
    of the count, 130–132
    of the immunist, 134–135, 136–137
    of the king, 113, 133
    of the *missi*, 133
    of the vicar, 132
Plectrude, wife of Pepin the Younger, 7
Po, river, 74, 81
Poitiers, 252
    abbey of St Hilary, 346
    abbey of St Radegund, 190
    battle, 8–9
Porton, 100
pontaticum, 126
Ponthion, 19–22, 253, 297, 299–302, 326
Ponza, isle of, 235
Populonia, 81
Porto, Italy, bishop, 297, 313
portorium, tolls, 125
pound, unit of monetary value, 128
praefectus, governor, 46, 65, 101
praepositus regiae mensae, prefect of the
    royal table, 111
precarium verbo regis, 141
Provence, 12, 42, 97, 212, 235, 241, 250
    kingdom, 261, 269, 280, 282, 314, 322
Prudentius, bishop of Troyes, 238, 244,
    245, 248, 251, 345
Prüm, monastery, 203, 248
Pyrenees, 37, 62, 63

Quentovic, 234
Quierzy, 12, 31, 328
    assembly and capitulary, 208, 305–308,
    346
    'promises', 23, 31, 77

Raab, 59
'rachimburgs', 130

Radbod, duke of the Frisians, 7, 52
Radoald, bishop of Porto, Italy, 283
Ragenfred, mayor of the palace, 7
Ragnar, Danish chief, 234
Ratchis, king of the Lombards, 15
Ravenna, 11, 17, 18, 31, 34, 73, 308, 317,
    319
    archbishop, 79, 84, 283
    see also exarchate
Regensburg, 46, 59, 287, 335
Reggio, 77, 81
Reginhard, chamberlain, 170
regnum Francorum, 5, 7, 12, 223, 243,
    247, 264–265, 331
Reims, 163, 294, 325
    councils, 150, 161, 254
    county, 193, ecclesiastical province,
    216, 231, 233
    archbishop, 216, 231, 233, 254–257, 310
Remigius, bishop of Rouen, 33
Rennes, 109, 189
requisitions, 122–123, 135
res publica, 2, 102, 143
'Restitutions' to the Holy See, 20, 22, 23,
    31, 32, 71–84
Rhabanus Maurus, abbot of Fulda, 209
Rhaetia, 187, 193, 203, 217, 222, 309
Rhine, river, 222, 234, 239, 302, 303, 324
Rhône, river, 8, 212, 235
Richarde, wife of Charles the Fat, 329
Richild, wife of Charles the Bald, 288
Riesengebirge, 53
Riessgau, 218
Rimini, 31
ring of the Avars, 58, 60, 85
Robert the Strong, 331, 346
Rodulf, brother of Empress Judith, 190,
    192
Rodulf, monk, annalist of Fulda, 252,
    297, 325
Roland, count of the Breton march, 63,
    65
Romagna, 32
Rome, 1, 10, 11, 15, 17, 18, 21, 22, 28, 29,
    30, 44, 72, 75–76, 79, 84, 86, 87, 94,
    163, 178, 230, 235, 239–240, 275, 277,
    279, 281, 295, 296, 297, 299, 303, 304,

Rome (*continued*)
311, 312, 316, 317, 318, 319, 322, 338
churches and monasteries: St Erasmus, 87; St John of the Lateran, 76; St Lorenzo in Lucina, 87; St Paul outside the walls, 77, 235; St Peter's, 21, 60, 73, 77, 90, 91, 92, 176, 230, 235, 240, 275, 297, 312, 319, 338; Santa Maria Maggiore, 76
Leonine city, 240
Rome, duchy, 23, 31, 32, 73
Roncevaux, 63, 100, 119
Rothad, bishop of Soissons, 279
Rothfeld, 198, 199
rotaticum, 126
Rouen, 234, 327
archbishop, 260, 268
Rouergue, 63
Roussillon, 8, 9
Rudolf I, king of Burgundy, 332–333, 335
Ruhr, 48
Rule of St Benedict, 149, 153, 159, 161–162
Rusellae, 81

Saale, 53, 57
Sabinia, 31, 81
Saint-Bernard, pass, 74, 297
Saint-Denis, 234
monastery, 12, 19–20, 28, 29, 207, 258
Saint-Gall, 326
Saint-Maurice in the Valais, 19, 297, 308, 333
Saint-Omer, 190
Saint-Quentin, 245, 250, 251, 258
abbot, 119
Saint-Riquier, abbacy, 160
Saintes, 37, 234
Salerno, 81
Salzburg, 46, 54
Samson, judge of Israel, 201
Samuel, prophet, 24, 290
'New Samuel', Pope Hadrian II, 290
San Leo, 31
San Marino, 31
Saône, 8, 222, 212

Saragossa, 62, 64
Sardinia, 69
Saucourt-en-Vimeu, 324
Saul, king of Israel, 17, 24, 25, 256
Savonnières, synod, 261–262, 271
Saxons, Saxony, 57, 7, 8, 14, 35–36, 44, 47–51
capitulary, 49–50, 52, 54, 58, 60, 62, 67, 70, 78, 103, 193, 203, 309, 325, 329
Scheldt, river, 222, 239, 245
Sedan, 222
Seine, river, 203, 211, 217, 234, 245, 305
seneschal (*senescalcus*), 110–111
Senigallia, 31, 73
Sens, 253
archbishop, 301
Septimania, 36, 42, 64, 97, 183, 193
Sergius II, pope, 229–231, 233, 240
Sergius, *secundicerius*, 71, 72
Sicily, 10, 80, 96, 235, 281, 291
Siegfrid, Norse chief, 328
Sigolsheim, 198
Sinzig, 220
Sion
county, 333
diocese, 270
Slavs, 51, 53–58, 85, 235, 239, 271, 334
Soana, 81
Soissons, 16, 27, 39, 42
church of St Médard, 204–206, 207, 340
synod, 13, 38
Soloman, duke of the Bretons, 347
Solomon, king of Israel, 24
Somme, 324, 325
Sorbs, Sorabes, 48, 53, 56–57, 120
Spain, 44, 62–64, 119, 183, 193
Speyer, 222
spiritual and temporal powers, relations, 86–87, 148, 160, 174, 180, 184–185, 195–196, 224–227, 257, 289–290, 350
Spoleto, duke, duchy, 33, 76, 77, 79, 102, 338
Stephen II, pope, 17–23, 27–33, 168, 321
Stephen III, pope, 71–73, 179
Stephen IV, pope, 163–164, 294
Stephen V, pope, 334, 336

Strassfurt, 119
Sturm, abbot of Fulda, 44
Styria, 53
Suetonius, 143
Suleiman ibn al-Arabi, governor of Barcelona, 62
Süntelgebirge, 44, 48, 56
Susa, pass, 30
Swabia, 309, 329
Swanahilde, mother of Grifo, 35
Syburg, 48
Sylvester I, pope, 21–22

Tarentaise, diocese of, or of Montiers, 270, 280
  archbishop, 321
Tassilo, duke of Bavaria, 30, 35, 43–46, 54, 58, 59, 101, 116, 139, 140, 342
taxation, 123–146, 135, 136
  telonea, tolls, 125–126
Terracina, 296
Tertry, battle, 7
Theoderic IV, Merovingian king, 8, 9
Theoderic, French count, 49
Theoderic, count of Autun, 346
Theodo of Bavaria, 45
Theodore, *primicerius* of the notaries, 177
Theodosius I, emperor, 174
Theodulf, bishop of Orléans, 89, 169
Theophano, Byzantine chronicler, 95
Theutberga, wife of Lothar II, 267, 268, 269, 270, 274, 275, 279, 286
Theutgald, archbishop of Trier, 275–277, 283, 286
Thiméon, 324
Thionville, 171, 172, 209–210, 218, 289
Thuringia, 5, 12, 44, 48, 116, 193, 203, 211, 217, 309, 329
Tiber, river, 235
Tisza, 58, 60
tithe, 61, 124–125
Toledo, bishop of, 149
Tortona, 199, 309
Tortosa, 64
Toscanella, 81

  bishop, 299
Toul, 212
Toulouse, 8, 166, 184, 234
tournaments, 220
Tours, 8, 42, 245, 252, 312
  councils, synods, 150, 151, 161
treasury, 2, 110
Trebbia, 334
Trent, 44, 251, 335
Treviso, 79
Tribur, 329, 337
Trier, 45, 194, 233, 289
  bishopric, 286
Troyes, 211, 218, 253
  council, 312–313, 315, 320
Tuscany, 32, 81
Tuscia, Roman, 81
Tusey, 277, 278

Umana, 32
Umayyads of Cordoba, 62, 182
Umbria, 31, 73
Unity, Christian, and unity of the Empire, 165–167, 174, 176, 194, 196, 205, 212, 224–225, 233, 243, 249–265, 301, 314, 320, 331, 334, 350
Urbino, 31, 73
Urgel, 109
  county, 64
  bishop, 149
Uto, count, 269
Utrecht, 52
Uzège, 222

Valais, 267
Valence, 333
Valenciennes, 245, 251
Vannes, 109, 171
vassal, vassalage, 35, 45, 49, 61–62, 137–142, 197, 223, 238, 306–307, 341–347
  and the Church, 257, 343–344, 345
  vassi dominici, 141
Velletri, bishop, 297
Venice, 77, 78, 79
  doge, 240

Ver, near Senlis, 38, 217
Verdun, treaty, 221–224, 247, 350
Verona, 74, 81
vicar (*vicarius*), 105, 132
Vicenza, 81
Vich, 63
Vienne, 322
  archbishop, 321, 333
  archbishopric, 333
Vikings, 67–69, 70, 210, 234–235, 237, 239,
  245, 252–253, 278, 280, 289, 302, 305,
  307, 310, 324–325, 327, 331, 333,
  336–337
Vilaine, 65
villa, villicus, 126–127
Vincy or Vinchy, 7
Virgil, bishop of Salzburg, 54
Viscount, 105
Visigoths, 17, 36, 64
Viterbo, 73, 81
Vivarais, 222
Volturno, 281

Waal, 239
wacta, warda, 68
Waifar, duke of Aquitaine, 36–37, 100
Wala, monk, later abbot of Corbie, 173,
  174, 176, 178, 181, 182, 183, 184, 185,
  191, 192
Walcheren, 210, 234

Waldipert, 72
Waldo, abbot, 269
Waldrada, mistress of Lothar II, 267,
  268, 271, 275, 278, 279, 286
Warnow, 53
Welf family, 187, 309, 332
Wends, northern Slavs, 53, 54–58
Wenilo, archbishop of Sens, 254
Werden, 48–49
Weser, 47, 50, 52
Westphalia, Westphalians, 47–50, 241
Widukind, 48, 67
Wihmodia, 47, 50, 51
Willehad, missionary, 52
William, count of Toulouse, 183, 346
William of Septimania, son of Bernard I,
  345
Wiltzes, 53, 54, 56
Worms, 44, 65, 116, 187, 196, 211, 253,
  260–261, 332, 335, 337
  county, 222
  partition of, 211–212, 215–216

Yütz, conference, 231–233, 237–238, 242,
  257

Zacharias, pope, 15, 16
Zeeland, 234
Zuiderzee, 52